JOSE

IRISH FOREIGN POLICY
1922–1946

AENGUS NOLAN

MERCIER PRESS
WHAT YOU NEED TO READ

MERCIER PRESS
Cork
www. mercierpress. ie

Trade enquiries to CMD Distribution
55A Spruce Avenue, Stillorgan Industrial Park,
Blackrock, County Dublin

© Aengus Nolan, 2008

ISBN: 978 1 85635 580 3

10 9 8 7 6 5 4 3 2 1

A CIP record for this title is available from the British Library

Cover image sourced from the de Valera Papers, UCD Archives.

FOR MY PARENTS, AND FOR JOYCE

Mercier Press receives financial assistance from the Arts Council/
An Chomhairle Ealaíon

Printed and bound by J.H. Haynes & Co. Ltd, Sparkford

CONTENTS

LIST OF ABBREVIATIONS

AHI   American Heritage Institute, Laramie, Wyoming, US
CAB   Cabinet Minutes, Public Record Office, Kew, London
D/FA   Department of Foreign Affairs (General Registry files)
DGFP   Documents on German Foreign Policy (Her Majesty's Stationery Office publication)
DIFP   Documents on Irish Foreign Policy
DO   Dominions Office, Public Record Office, Kew, London
D/T   Department of the Taoiseach (S. files)
FDRL   Franklin D. Roosevelt Library, Hyde Park, New York, NY, US
FO   Foreign Office, Public Record Office, Kew, London
FRUS   Foreign Relations of the United States (US State Department publication)
NAI   National Archives of Ireland, Bishop St, Dublin, Ireland
NAUS   National Archives of the United States, Washington DC, US (sometimes referred to by its administrative body the NARA, the National Archives and Records Administration, which also has a depository at Suitland, Maryland, US)
OSS   Office of Strategic Services Files (later became the CIA)
PREM   Premier's Office Files, Public Record Office, Kew, London
PRO   Public Record Office, Kew, London
PRONI   Public Record Office of Northern Ireland, Balmoral Ave, Belfast
RG   Record Group
SDD   State Department Dispatches
UCD   Archives Department, University College, Dublin

INTRODUCTION

JOSEPH WALSHE'S INITIAL involvement in Irish foreign affairs happened somewhat by chance. While on holiday in France in 1919, he came upon Seán T. O'Kelly who was promoting the cause of the new Irish state at the Paris Peace Conference. The fledgling Department of Foreign Affairs was desperate for assistance in gathering and disseminating propaganda, and so O'Kelly made a speculative offer to Walshe to join the cause of Irish nation building. There was little financial reward for the position, but Walshe, who had recently graduated from university and had previously left the Jesuit order, may have been looking for a new vocation. Whatever his reasons for remaining on in Paris, he certainly did not foresee his chance appointment leading to a career at the centre of Irish foreign policy that would span over thirty years. Walshe's diplomatic apprenticeship in Paris was short-lived, and just over two years later another 'accident' of history was to catapult him from being a bit-part player in Irish foreign affairs to having a leading role. By then, the Irish civil war had started to divide Irish civil, political and administrative life, and thus prevented the existing head of the Department of Foreign Affairs, Robert Brennan, from remaining on in that position. As Brennan had chosen the anti-Treaty side, he somewhat casually suggested to Walshe, 'Joe ... I can't take it but why don't you?' After considerable deliberation, Walshe took a pro-Treaty stance and accepted the position. Walshe's relative inexperience notwithstanding, his being in the right place at the right time once again ensured his position at the heart of Irish foreign policy-making for decades to come.

Following his recall to Dublin, Walshe was appointed acting secretary to the department in 1922 under the pro-Treaty Cosgrave government. He accepted responsibility for building the underdeveloped Irish diplomatic service, which had been

further impaired by the Treaty split. The difficulty of his task was increased by the lack of support for the department within government and political circles, as many favoured asserting foreign policy through Commonwealth membership. However, he would prove to be a staunch defender of the department's independence, and never ceased in emphasising the value of the work performed by the diplomatic service. Walshe's appointment, therefore, came at a time when the Department of Foreign Affairs was in flux and impressionable to his influence. The longevity of his tenure meant he would have free rein to organise the department as he saw fit. He relished the opportunity of working on this 'blank canvas', and during his time at the helm he transformed External Affairs into an essential government department with a highly developed expertise in foreign-policy affairs.

Walshe coveted his central role in Irish foreign-policy formation, and in the area of Anglo-Irish relations, in particular, his knowledge of constitutional law was crucial. We shall see in some detail how his membership on the teams representing the Irish government at the Commonwealth conferences during the 1920s revealed the depth of his expertise. Using fora such as the League of Nations and Imperial Conferences, Walshe helped emphasise the independence of the Free State government within the bounds of the Anglo-Irish Treaty. The government had accepted that Ireland's future lay within the empire for the time being, but Walshe believed that by using the mechanisms of the Commonwealth, much progress could be made towards attaining greater freedom and autonomy. To assist these efforts he forged alliances with other dominions while remaining wary of Britain's representatives. Walshe's efforts did not go unnoticed, and he was often singled out for praise in the way the Free State represented itself at international conferences. While Walshe was amassing his diplomatic expertise on the international stage, the 1920s was also a time when he was forced to defend the department's position within the government hierarchy. He faced down a number of threats to the department's existence, and his battles with the Department of Finance demonstrate his absolute belief in the importance of the work done by his own department. Despite the odds, Walshe, where possible, expanded Ireland's representation abroad, and his correspondence and instructions to his staff prove useful in assessing policy formation during this

period. While the Free State may have been somewhat unskilled in terms of foreign-policy matters at the start of the decade, it was by no means inexperienced in such matters by the end of the 1920s. This was due in no small part to Walshe's dedication and professionalism as head of the Department of External Affairs.

While Walshe may have reflected on his first decade in office with some satisfaction, he was soon to face another major change that would launch a new set of challenges for him and External Affairs. The time when Cosgrave relinquished power to de Valera is a fascinating period in which to view Walshe. Following the defeat of Cumann na nGaedheal in 1932, many in the Irish civil service feared a purge by Fianna Fáil of those who had shown loyalty to the 1921 Anglo-Irish Treaty. Throughout the 1920s, Walshe had been strongly critical of de Valera. However, having reappraised himself of Fianna Fáil's ideological principles, he established a good working relationship with de Valera, and became his chief departmental foreign-policy adviser. It was a relationship that was to last for many years to come, and one which would have to endure the enormous strains that local and international events would bring. Many criticised what they saw as Walshe's lack of ideological uniformity by the seemingly easy way in which he transferred allegiance from Cosgrave to de Valera. However, the continuity he brought during the change of government was important to the state's continued ability to formulate and execute sound foreign policy. On coming to power, de Valera became President of the Executive Council and chose also the External Affairs portfolio. The extent of de Valera's responsibilities, coupled with his ailing eyesight, meant that Walshe was allowed considerable leeway in the everyday running of departmental affairs. Walshe recognised that de Valera's dual portfolio gave him unprecedented access to decision-making power within the government. Walshe was quick to assert his influence in this regard, and, therefore, under de Valera's stewardship, External Affairs firmly secured its place in Irish government hierarchy, to the extent that some within the civil service complained that Walshe had been allowed to accrue too much power.[1]

The degree of authority that Walshe possessed over the organisation of the department means that he alone must shoulder the burden of criticism for its failings. While it could have been considered one of his primary roles, we will see that the organisation

of the diplomatic corps was an area in which Walshe can be
adversely criticised. Throughout his tenure, his instructions to
diplomats were cryptic, and this lack of communication meant
their potential was very often under-utilised. Walshe was far more
interested in his own diplomatic endeavours, and reports from
the diplomatic corps were simply used to supplement his general
information. Any attempts to comment on policy decisions were
sharply rebuffed. As a result, Walshe came into conflict with a
number of his staff over the years, and his correspondence with
diplomats such as Timothy Smiddy, Seán Lester, John Dulanty
and Seán Murphy demonstrates the nature of his sometimes
brusque administrative style.

Despite his apparent failings in the eyes of some of his own
staff, Walshe, under de Valera's leadership, continued to excel in
the area of diplomatic negotiation. In 1938 following six years
of economic conflict, a new Anglo-Irish agreement was signed.
Walshe's contribution to the successful conclusion of these negotiations should not be underestimated. His tireless approaches to
British officials since the beginning of the conflict were pivotal
to the success of the Irish government in achieving a favourable
financial settlement – one that also included the return of the
Treaty ports that were to prove so contentious during the Second
World War. This episode, among others that we shall examine,
demonstrated Walshe's diplomatic proficiency, which was used to
good effect in the turbulent decades after the foundation of the
state. That his diplomatic skills had become finely honed would
prove important for the challenges that lay ahead as global events
turned towards the impending world war.

Of major interest to this study are Walshe's diplomatic endeavours throughout the Second World War. Walshe played a leading
role in the implementation of the Irish government's policy of
'neutrality'. At the end of the war, Ireland had suffered little of
the direct effects of the conflict, and Walshe's diplomatic finesse
was pivotal to that accomplishment. It is also clear that the sometimes aimless and often duplicitous nature of Ireland's policy
placed an enormous strain on Walshe. To illustrate this, Walshe's
wartime relationship with the diplomats stationed in Dublin
is examined in some detail. The diplomatic reports provide us
with a fascinating insight into this gripping and controversial era
in Irish history. In truth, Ireland ran a major risk of losing the

relative safety of neutrality by surreptitiously aiding the Allies. Walshe encountered difficulties with the German representative, Eduard Hempel, when the biased nature of Irish neutrality became apparent. At the same time, while the Allies appreciated Ireland's cooperation, they did not accept it as an excuse for exemption from full participation in the war. Thus, Walshe encountered hostility and diplomatic pressure from both sides. However, notwithstanding these difficulties, his relationship with the Dublin-based diplomatic corps always proved immensely beneficial to the maintenance of government policy. To view Walshe's everyday diplomatic activities in this way contributes greatly to our understanding of his management of foreign policy during the war.

At the end of the war, Walshe vacated his position at Iveagh House and moved to Rome to become Ireland's first ambassador to the Holy See. While he favoured the frequent transfer of diplomatic staff, he refused headquarters that same privilege by remaining on as secretary for twenty-four years. By doing so, he denied the department new and innovative staff with fresh ideas and the chance to re-evaluate the workings of the Irish diplomatic corps. However, despite his faults and failures, we can reflect that by the end of the war Walshe had succeeded in constructing, from a pitiful foundation, an efficient diplomatic service and a department with vast expertise in foreign-policy formation.

While his role in Irish foreign affairs from 1922 to 1946 has not previously received comprehensive attention, Walshe does feature in a number of important studies of Irish history. Dermot Keogh, in his *Ireland and Europe*, for example, has paid close attention to the subject, while his 'Profile of Joseph Walshe' introduces the diplomat as an historical entity in his own right. David Harkness, in *The Restless Dominion*, looks extensively at Walshe's role in Anglo-Irish dominion affairs during the 1920s. The following decade is examined by Deirdre McMahon in *Republicans and Imperialists*, which considers Walshe's role in the Anglo-Irish negotiations that proceeded throughout the 1930s. For the war years, Robert Fisk's *In Time of War* outlines Walshe's role in a number of crucial events, including the management of Ireland's wartime diplomatic relationships. John P. Duggan's *Neutral Ireland and the Third Reich* provides an insight into Walshe's dealing with German internees and the German representative,

Eduard Hempel, during the war. Other works, such as T. Ryle
Dwyer's *Strained Relations* and Tim Pat Coogan's *De Valera*, have
also provided valuable references. These studies, among others,
outline Walshe's historical importance and highlight the need for
further study of his contribution to Irish foreign policy.

Central to this chronicle of Walshe's diplomatic and administrative career is the departmental documentation. However,
this material is not without significant gaps and omissions. For
example, Dermot Keogh states that when Walshe was the Irish
ambassador to the Vatican he destroyed many official files, dating
as far back as the 1930s, which he deemed unfit for future scrutiny.
Considering Robert Fisk's claim that seventy tons of documentation were destroyed by the Irish authorities in 1945, it is certainly
likely that many documents relating to Walshe and his work have
been destroyed.[2] The opening of the state archives in 1991 provided invaluable material relating to the Department of Foreign
Affairs. Access to these documents has been greatly increased
with the publication of the Documents in Irish Foreign Policy
(DIFP) series, with the first five volumes tracing Irish foreign
policy from 1919 to 1939. Of primary interest are the secretary's
files, a sub-index of the files of the Department of Foreign Affairs.
This series, which forms the basis of a large part of this narrative,
contains many records created by the secretary of the department,
and were used by him in the execution of his responsibilities. Their
very existence as a separate entity from the main body of departmental files again highlights Walshe's tendency towards secrecy.
Deemed more important, these files were kept separate to ensure
greater confidentiality. Similarly, for many years the de Valera
papers were not in the care of the state but held privately. These
are now available for public viewing at UCD, and they greatly
contribute to our understanding of Joseph Walshe.[3] It is interesting to note that in the 1950s de Valera himself suggested putting
together an account of Ireland's involvement in the Second World
War based on departmental papers. Walshe was surprised at the
request and seemed to ridicule the idea, believing the many gaps
in the documentation would make the task impossible.

Apart from the problem of locating relevant documentation,
it has proved difficult to positively identify Walshe as the author
of many of the existing letters and memoranda. This is because a
great many of the existing documents are unsigned, thus making

Walshe's contribution difficult to define. The significant degree of autonomy that Walshe enjoyed in the management of External Affairs can further complicate any assessment of his influence. It is often the case that Walshe wrote memoranda or policy documents that possess the signature of the contemporary minister. In other instances Walshe drafted letters beginning with the phrase, 'I am directed by the Minister to inform you that ...' On a number of occasions it has been found that the minister involved may not have given such a directive. Thus, the available sources have to be treated with careful consideration, and circumspect speculation is sometimes required. Another limiting factor is that there were many meetings, conversations, decisions and instructions that Walshe never committed to the permanence of a memorandum. His *modus operandi* meant that most sensitive matters were dealt with by personal meetings or over the telephone. Many of his letters and memoranda begin with 'further to our recent conversation', or remark that 'I will speak to you about this matter personally'. It is important to point out, too, that Walshe's secrecy was not directed solely at future historians attempting to trace his role in Irish foreign policy. In this study we shall see the frustration of a number of Walshe's senior colleagues who also were not privy to the records of important meetings. Clearly, then, creating a profile of Joseph Walshe is a task not without its challenges.

To bolster the departmental documentation we can turn to government archives of countries that had substantial diplomatic communication with Ireland. A search of the archives in Britain and the United States proved useful in this regard. Many of the relevant archives of the US Department of State provided material from the margins in which Walshe operated, while the presidential libraries and personal papers of diplomats based in Ireland, such as David Gray, open up a new vista on Walshe's work. The British archives proved equally useful, with John Maffey's reports illuminating many of Walshe's opinions, of which there was little reference in the Irish archives. Walshe had many meetings with British officials and travelled to London on numerous occasions. The resulting documentation reveals Walshe as a tenacious and competent diplomat, unafraid to challenge British convictions. In some cases, accounts of diplomatic endeavours from the non-Irish side proves more revealing, and

possibly more honest, than reliance on Walshe's own version of events. On the German side, the documents relevant to Ireland during the Second World War contain a number of useful references to Walshe. It is most interesting to juxtapose memoranda by Walshe and Hempel on various subjects. More importantly, due to the partial nature of the documentation generally, these sources provide an important alternative viewpoint on Walshe's personality and contribution to Irish diplomacy.

Despite the aforementioned difficulties, we should not be discouraged from at least attempting the task of piecing together Walshe's diplomatic career. His role in Irish foreign-policy formation is too great to ignore. While the culture of secrecy, the reluctance to commit many details to written memoranda, and the destruction of many documents have vastly increased the difficulties in assessing Walshe's role, there is sufficient documentation of notable interest to allow us, at the very least, to begin this diplomatic portrait. While, in certain instances, Walshe would attach instructions for documents to be destroyed after they had been read, ironically, in the cases where these letters have survived, Walshe's frankness is a notable feature. This is demonstrated in a particular way on a few occasions when his correspondence was uncharacteristically candid. These letters, we shall see later, make for particularly interesting and sometimes shocking reading. Using a diverse range of sources, therefore, a detailed profile of Walshe throughout his tenure at the Department of External Affairs can be formed. While not always successful or without flaws, it is clear that over a long and distinguished career Walshe provided the advanced diplomatic skill necessary for sound foreign-policy construction. At the same time, he battled local forces for the provision of a well-run, financially secure diplomatic service. Walshe's position in Irish foreign-policy history is unique, and focusing on this individual not only illuminates a previously little-known diplomat and civil servant but serves also to provide an alternative perspective on Irish foreign policy as a whole. By looking at the career of the secretary of the Department of External Affairs we see much more than the results of diplomacy – we discover the reasoning and skill that helped to form it. Using Walshe as our guide, we are treated to an insider's view of the origins of, and rationale for, Irish foreign policy in this formative period of Irish history.

CHAPTER 1

WALSHE AND THE FIRST DECADE
OF EXTERNAL AFFAIRS
1922–1932

JOSEPH P. WALSHE was born in 1886 in Killenaule, County Tipperary. At seventeen he entered the Jesuit order as a novice. After two years he was sent to Holland where he lived with French Jesuits, a number of whom had been forced into exile due to anti-clerical laws.[1] While there, he studied philosophy and developed his linguistic skills before returning to Ireland in 1910 to take up a teaching post in Clongowes Wood Jesuit college. Citing medical reasons, he left the order around 1916, before studying for a Bachelor of Law degree at University College, Dublin.[2] Little is known of his attitude or activities during this period of great change, but few in Ireland at the time were unaffected by the Easter Rising and the events that followed. What Walshe did not realise was that he himself would soon play a pivotal role in the development of the new Irish state.

Walshe had continued his studies to postgraduate level by taking a Masters degree in French. When he finished his exams he went on holiday to France with his friend Seán Murphy. By chance, in Paris, they met Seán T. O'Kelly, who had known Walshe as a student.[3] It was a fateful meeting as both Walshe and Murphy were to become important members of the Irish diplomatic service. O'Kelly, who was in Paris to promote the cause of Irish freedom at the peace conference, invited Walshe to discuss the possibility of working for the Irish government. The offer came, however, with the warning that remuneration for his work would be meagre and his greatest reward would be the honour of serving his country. Having left the Jesuit order some years

previously, perhaps Walshe saw his service to the Irish state as his new vocation. Whatever the reason, he agreed to the conditions set out and began his career in the Irish foreign service.

At this time Irish foreign affairs had little organisational coherence. Sinn Féin had won an unprecedented number of seats in the 1918 general election. It had pledged not to take up its seats in Westminster, and set out to establish an alternative government in Ireland. The new Dáil Éireann met for the first time in January 1919, with the aim of establishing the instruments of government in Ireland. Included in this was the provision for a propaganda department.[4] When the Cabinet was formed it proposed that responsibility for foreign affairs should be held by a triumvirate of Éamon de Valera, Count George Noble Plunkett and Arthur Griffith. It was a flexible arrangement. The Cabinet was organised with a certain degree of collective responsibility, and the title of Minister for Foreign Affairs was a loose one, reflecting the transient nature of the government itself.

The main aim of the Department of Foreign Affairs[5] at this time was to help establish the legitimacy of the parallel government that Britain regarded as illegal. The task was beset with difficulties. Lawrence Ginnell, the first director of the Publicity Department, a branch of Foreign Affairs, was arrested and imprisoned in June 1919. He was replaced by Desmond FitzGerald, who himself was arrested by the British government in 1921. He in turn was succeeded by Robert Brennan and then Erskine Childers.[6] The rapid succession of personnel, as well as the dispersed nature of responsibility for 'foreign affairs', did nothing to lend stability or cohesion to the formation of this new department. Soon, however, there was to be another change in personnel, with the arrival of Walshe, and this time the new incumbent would not be so easily ousted.

From the outset, de Valera realised the importance of propaganda in the fight against Britain and was determined to keep in close personal contact with the department responsible for that task. He insisted that Foreign Affairs send him weekly reports on its work: 'It is the one [department] for which I feel the most immediate personal responsibility.'[7] When Robert Brennan was appointed Under-Secretary for Foreign Affairs, de Valera issued the following instructions:

> Your duties will be to establish a general secretariat, and to main-
> tain regular correspondence with our representatives and with our
> friends in foreign countries, and to supply them with pamphlets
> and statistics as a foundation for informative articles upon Ireland.
> These should be, as I pointed out, of a permanent rather than an
> ephemeral character.[8]

De Valera sought the establishment of a department that would
be well organised and professional in its approach to all matters of
foreign interest. He hoped for the creation of a diplomatic corps
that would closely monitor events in foreign states, and a competent policy unit to oversee the formulation of policy decisions.
Foreign Affairs would have to be ready to act if the indication was
that any of the countries attached to the British Empire were moving towards greater independence. Throughout his political career
de Valera consistently attached much importance to propaganda
and foreign affairs, and his instructions to Brennan are a useful
indication of the tasks and functions that faced Joseph Walshe.

The departmental records around this time demonstrate
an embryonic struggle for clarity on the question of authority
over departmental affairs and policy formation. Count George
Plunkett, Sinn Féin politician and minister with responsibility for
foreign affairs, had welcomed the addition of Robert Brennan as
administrative head of the department: 'I am glad to have B.B.'s
assistance, and he can more easily get at information for my
work.'[9] Brennan, however, was uneasy with Plunkett's authority
in the department. He wrote to de Valera, stating:

> I understood when taking office I would have nothing to do with
> him [Count Plunkett] as regards direction of the Department and
> that I was to regard myself as if I was head of the Department and
> responsible to you personally and directly.[10]

De Valera could not clarify the issue fully and told Brennan that
he was not sure whether Plunkett was 'the Minister for Foreign
Affairs', but described him as 'an Associate Minister at least'. This
was indicative of the turbulent times in which both politicians
and administrators found themselves as they struggled to put
together the machinery of government. Ever the diplomat, de
Valera asked Brennan to do Plunkett the courtesy of asking his
opinion now and then on important matters.[11] Brennan insisted

that there was nothing personal in his objections, but he wanted to avoid 'clogging machinery' by joint decision-making and continuous consultation in the department which, at that time, in his opinion, was 'not running too smoothly'. One of Brennan's primary tasks was to initiate the general organisation of the department, and the government awaited his recommendations on how he proposed to restructure that office. De Valera suggested three organisational divisions: a general correspondent responsible for day-to-day tasks, including servicing the needs of Irish representatives abroad; a legal attaché to deal with international law, official procedure and to draft official documents dealing with foreign countries and treaties; and a head of research to collate propaganda material.[12] Brennan's own role as head of that department would be to supervise and delegate the work of these organisational sections.

Robert Brennan set about using the resources at his disposal to create an efficient diplomatic service. From each of the representatives abroad he expected monthly reports commenting on their work and a general report on matters concerning conditions in their host country.[13] An important step for the department's independence was that he arranged for all correspondence relating to Foreign Affairs to be sent directly to the department and not through the President's Office, as had been the case in the past. In addition, all communication between the foreign representatives and the trade and publicity departments was to pass through Foreign Affairs. It was necessary that strict financial procedures were put in place, and representatives abroad were required to furnish quarterly estimates of expenditure as well as monthly balance sheets. At a propaganda level, the foreign representatives were free to use their insight and local knowledge to comment on Ireland's position in the international arena. However, in matters of policy the general directions clearly outlined that authorisation for all decisions should come from Dublin.[14] This was a policy that Walshe was to enforce for many years.

While Brennan was increasing the administrative responsibility of Foreign Affairs, Joseph Walshe was working in Paris under Seán T. O'Kelly, but there is little documentation relating to his time there. In one fragment, however, dated April 1921, O'Kelly wrote to Brennan and reported on Walshe's work:

I am keeping him on for some time longer, but will tell him to see you whenever he returns. Last week he attended, on my behalf, a meeting of the Council of the International Catholic Congress, and read a paper on the Irish cause.[15]

What is clear is that when he was called back to Dublin by George Gavan Duffy, O'Kelly was not happy to lose Walshe's services:

Unwilling as I am to lose the valued services of Mr Joseph Walsh[e], I realise the position you are placed in, and though owing to other circumstances his being taken away means serious personal inconvenience, I am satisfied to let him go.[16]

These records serve to highlight that, while Walshe was well regarded, he was relatively inexperienced for the promotion that he was soon to receive. Paris was an important post, but the brevity of his duration there meant that he had little time to experience, first hand, all the intricacies of the diplomatic profession. He was, perhaps, not sufficiently qualified to take over the running of the department, but as events changed in Ireland so too did the make-up of the Irish diplomatic service.

In December 1921, the Anglo-Irish Treaty was signed, thus formally ending the War of Independence against Britain. The Treaty was a compromise; it did not achieve a republic but did attain dominion status for twenty-six counties of Ireland. Michael Collins, who had been director of intelligence in the IRA's fight against Britain as well as Minister for Home Affairs in the first Dáil, argued that while the agreement was not ideal it did give Ireland 'the freedom to achieve freedom'. De Valera, however, disagreed with the settlement made by his envoys in London, and vowed to oppose it. Enmity and animosity arose between former friends and political colleagues who had previously been united in their desire to establish an independent state. In January 1922 the Treaty was ratified by the Dáil, and later that year a general election further endorsed that decision. The country remained divided, however, and those who opposed the Treaty took up arms against the government. Thus began the Irish civil war, which was to be a fateful event in the rise of Joseph Walshe as head of the Department of Foreign Affairs.

Robert Brennan proclaimed his loyalty to de Valera and the

anti-Treaty side and could, therefore, no longer work on behalf
of the Free State government. Following de Valera's withdrawal
from the Dáil and the government, he was replaced as Minister
for Foreign Affairs by George Gavan Duffy, who had previously
worked as a Dáil Éireann roving envoy. Gavan Duffy was an
enthusiastic supporter of the expansion of the department, and he
believed that Ireland's reputation and the work of Irish diplomats
over the previous three years had been nullified by the disunion
and violence of the civil war. It caused him 'great anxiety' to see
Ireland's image being tarnished in this way, and he endeavoured
to stress the importance of 'the far-reaching effects of the loss of
World opinion'.[17] Walshe, while in Paris, found it extremely difficult to know what course to take.[18] In the end, not convinced
by de Valera's revolutionary argument, he sided with the constitutional government's position, and returned to Ireland in 1922.
The former Irish diplomat, Con Cremin, recalls when Brennan,
knowing that his conscience would not allow him to continue
as Secretary to the Department of Foreign Affairs for the new
government, said to Walshe, 'Joe, they asked me if I would be
Secretary of the Department of Foreign Affairs. I can't take it but
why don't you?'[19] Brennan, therefore, recommended Walshe to
Gavan Duffy, who was particularly concerned about the quality
of candidates available for the Irish foreign service. He believed
that many of the existing representatives were not suitable for
their posts:

> Our representative in Berlin knows little German, our repre-
> sentative in Madrid is only learning Spanish, and our Rome
> representative does not know Italian.

This goes some way towards explaining Walshe's own rather
anomalous jump from assistant to O'Kelly in Paris to head of
the department. Walshe was well educated. He had a degree in
law, a Master of Arts in French, and his years as a Jesuit semi-
narian afforded him a philosophical and theological background.
As well as French, he also spoke Italian, German and Dutch.
Considering Gavan Duffy's emphasis on Irish foreign representatives having good linguistic skills, it seems that Walshe may have
been more suited to a post in either Rome or Berlin than returning to Dublin. While he may have passed the scrutiny of O'Kelly

in Paris, Walshe had done little to prove himself worthy of the position of secretary. However, expediency and perhaps desperation won out, and Walshe capitalised on Brennan's generous recommendation to Gavan Duffy. Walshe accepted the post and was appointed Acting Secretary to the Department of Foreign Affairs.[20] Thus began his long and illustrious career at the leading edge of Irish foreign-policy formation, one that would span over three decades.

By the time Walshe took over from Brennan, the department was far from fully established. On a basic but fundamental level many of the Irish representatives had only a limited knowledge of the language of the country in which they were stationed. Walshe could initialise training programmes so as to have suitable candidates in future years, but there were many positions that needed immediate occupancy, and suitable candidates were proving hard to find. His task was beset by difficulties caused by the civil war and the Treaty split, which had diminished the already inadequate resources of the foreign service. Walshe's responsibilities were initially very similar to those of Brennan; for the time being, propaganda was to remain the primary objective of the department. As Brennan had done before him, Walshe would soon have to learn to cope with a rapidly changing environment, as more disruption to the political leadership of Foreign Affairs was on the way. His work under the ministerial guidance of Gavan Duffy was to last but a short time before the latter resigned over his opposition to certain sections of the Constitution that suppressed the powers of the Supreme Court and allowed the government to detain republican prisoners without trial.[21] Before his departure, Gavan Duffy drafted a memorandum that was a comprehensive analysis of the organisation of the Department of Foreign Affairs. This document is important because it indicates the relative state of the department at this time, and some regarded it as a blueprint for the future development of Foreign Affairs.[22] Walshe was still coming to terms with the running of the department, and so found the document a useful starting point on which to base his own ideas. He welcomed the memorandum, but was not overly influenced by all of Gavan Duffy's ideas as to where Foreign Affairs should focus its efforts in order to improve the service of the department.

As we have seen, Walshe was appointed acting secretary at a

time of great instability, for the department, the government and
the country as a whole. This had greatly affected Gavan Duffy's
ability to act effectively, and he had encountered immense difficulties as minister, admitting that he had been unable to 'extend our
activities abroad, save in the direction of establishing useful relations
in quarters which were formerly reluctant to be connected with us'.
Thus, Foreign Affairs at that time was still focused on establishing
the most basic functions of a foreign-policy department:

> Laying the foundations for future developments; steps have been
> taken to organise the Offices at home and abroad and to sys-
> tematise their work, in order to equip them for the much more
> important functions that they must shortly undertake.[23]

Walshe agreed with Gavan Duffy's main aims and a large portion of his work centred on establishing the Irish Free State's
relations with foreign countries other than Britain. This was diplomatic strategy at its most basic level but was crucially important
nonetheless. In December 1921, for example, Walshe wrote to
Monsieur le Brocquy, the officer in charge of Belgium's consulate
in Dublin. He wished to thank the Belgian government for its
good wishes on Cosgrave's election as head of the Provisional
Government.[24] It was important to initiate contact with foreign
states, and Walshe highlighted the Irish government's intention
to establish closer relations with Belgium. In this way, Walshe
had begun his task of announcing to the world the new status of
the Irish Free State. At this point in time, it was among the most
important objectives that the government sought in relation to
the Department of Foreign Affairs.

   The Gavan Duffy memorandum outlined twenty principal
centres around the world where he felt the Irish government
should be represented. It stressed the importance of the propaganda role of the Department of Foreign Affairs, saying, '[w]e
can recover our prestige by active propaganda and publicity.'
For the structuring of the department headquarters itself Duffy
made a number of important suggestions. He proposed that
the department should be managed by a number of permanent
'Heads of Department', each with a specific sphere of expertise
on which they would advise the minister or any committee of foreign affairs. Among those suggested were a secretary for foreign

politics, a legal secretary, a secretary for publicity and a secretary for trade. To coordinate all of these there was to be a general secretary who would report directly to the minister.[25] This was similar to a recommendation made earlier by de Valera, but the suggestions themselves were never adopted by Walshe, who had his own ideas on how best to organise the department.

When Walshe became fully involved in the running of the department, which had by now changed its title from Foreign Affairs to External Affairs, much work needed to be done. The Treaty split diminished the size of the already small overseas staff of the department. In 1922 the following were listed as Irish foreign representatives: Seán T. O'Kelly, Paris; E. Bulfin, Argentina; Harry Boland, US; Count O'Byrne, Rome; D. Hales, Italy; Frank Egan, South America; Miss M. O'Brien, Madrid; John Chartres, Berlin; and Michael MacWhite, Geneva.[26] By March 1922 Boland and O'Kelly had been deleted from this list due to their hostile stance towards the government; this created great difficulties for Walshe. Where possible, he made progress on the administrative reorganisation of the department. When Desmond FitzGerald replaced Gavan Duffy as head of External Affairs, Walshe was fortunate to have as his new minister an enthusiastic advocate of the diplomatic service as well as an energetic administrator. Patrick Keatinge suggests that FitzGerald initiated one of the first periods of consistent and coherent building of the department out of what he terms an 'administrative vacuum'.[27] Under FitzGerald, Walshe continued to standardise the routine administrative work of head office. It was a decisive period in the department's development, as Walshe viewed the establishment of an efficient foreign service as crucial in proving the value of the department's work to the sceptics at the Department of Finance.

Chief among Walshe's worries at this time was the doubt over the department's survival as an independent administrative entity. Following the establishment of the Free State many believed there was little need for a separate government department to deal with foreign affairs. For example, in November 1923 a number of opinions hostile to the existence of a Department of Foreign Affairs were expressed in the Dáil:

We are concerned with no foreign affairs. We have no colonies and no interests to clash with any other nation ... The Ministry

of Foreign Affairs ought to be scrapped and let the Executive
Council deal with any foreign matters that have to be dealt with
... the Ministry of Foreign Affairs ... will be known as a Ministry
for finding a job for Somebody.[28]

Thus, Walshe and the department lived 'under the threat of absorption' with the most likely absorber being the President's Office.
This, according to Dermot Keogh, may have had a bearing on the
decision not to give Joseph Walshe the status of secretary until
1927. Walshe was desperately anxious to see his official title of 'acting secretary' changed to 'secretary' in an effort to denote his parity
with other heads of department.[29] It wouldn't change his duties
or responsibilities, but it would help to secure his position and
perhaps lessen the ignominy he faced in civil service circles. The
Ministers and Secretaries Act (1924) provided for the permanent
appointment of Walshe as secretary of the department, but that
option was not utilised by FitzGerald. Walshe saw this reluctance
as an indication of the strength of those who argued that the state
did not need a separate department to deal with foreign affairs.

Walshe regularly came into conflict with Finance, which kept a
close watch on the expenditure of External Affairs. In April 1922
the Accountant General of the Department of Finance wrote:

> I do not agree with ... [the] suggestion that the Foreign Office
> should have passed to it the total amount of the Foreign Affairs
> Vote at the beginning of each half year ... my past experience
> with Foreign Affairs has convinced me that as regards the han-
> dling of cash the Foreign Affairs office has a disinclination to keep
> accounts properly.[30]

Thus, External Affairs was deemed to be incapable of manag-
ing its own resources. Adding insult to injury, the accountant
general rather caustically added that he 'did not believe that the
different representatives abroad would readily take to this new
system, as it looks to be more complicated than it really is'. This
attitude greatly irritated Walshe, but the Finance offensive was
not to be easily quashed. In March 1923 he received a number of
new queries from Finance with regard to the upcoming External
Affairs estimate. It seemed to him that Finance was unwilling to
understand or acknowledge the basic need for a department to
deal with Irish foreign affairs. To him its objections seemed to

question 'whether Ireland should have foreign relations or not'.
He wrote that if this could not be agreed upon, then 'discussion
on minor points of External Affairs expenditure becomes futile,
as in that hypothesis you are bound to reject the estimate en bloc'.
Walshe was exasperated by the fundamental ignorance concerning External Affairs, and in reply to Finance wrote:

> I give the bare outline of the reasons why we should maintain
> foreign agents, basing my self on the assumption that we are going
> to act as a co-equal member of the British Commonwealth of
> Nations. The very simplicity of the reasons may shock but that also
> applies to your question.[31]

This was hardly the stinging reply that the comments from Finance
warranted, but Walshe, ever the diplomat, felt he needed to tread
carefully for the time being.

The greatest cause for concern came during the lead-up to the
Ministers and Secretaries Act of 1924. With such scarce resources
available to the government, there was substantial pressure to reorganise the central administration of the state. The Blythe Committee
was set up for the purpose of outlining areas where possible savings
could be made. Its specific aim was to make recommendations to
facilitate the effective reorganisation of all the government departments. Its conclusion, which stated that 'the general administrative
work of the country could effectively be done by nine Ministers',
was of obvious concern to Walshe, as External Affairs did not figure on the proposed list of departments.[32] The report went further
towards undermining Walshe's position by suggesting that the
work of External Affairs could be allocated to the President of the
Executive Council, although it did acknowledge the right to an
individual identity of the diminished departments. The secretary of
the Department of Finance, Joseph Brennan, took advantage of this
and argued strongly in support of such changes:

> The unnecessary multiplication of departments is an obvious source
> of waste. A small country should not need and indeed cannot sup-
> port the elaborate organisation of a great and wealthy country such
> as Great Britain … The question of incorporating External affairs
> with the staff of the Executive council and the President's Office
> and attaching the whole to the President might be considered. The
> abolition of a Publicity Branch seems called for.[33]

Ronan Fanning points out that among the suggested changes under the Ministers and Secretaries Act was the proposal to transfer some of the responsibilities of the Department of Finance to other departments. However, this was not mentioned by Brennan, and was of little comfort to Walshe, who now faced the possibility of absorption into the President's Office.

In the midst of these administrative and financial difficulties Walshe had little choice but to continue the department's foreign-policy development. Anglo-Irish and Commonwealth affairs were of primary importance, but the League of Nations was also prominent as part of the government's desire to affirm the Free State's independence and sense of nationhood. Walshe recognised that if External Affairs created a monopoly of expertise in foreign-policy matters, it would make the department's denigration less likely. All international avenues, therefore, were to be used to further the cause of the Free State. If that also served to demonstrate the value of the Department of External Affairs within government circles, then so much the better. On the government's League policy itself, David Harkness asserts that the Free State's desire to register the Anglo-Irish Treaty internationally was a primary consideration behind Ireland's application for membership of the League. It was hoped that this would guarantee against Britain recanting the fundamental ideas contained in the agreement. The move represented a clear indication that the Free State was willing to make its own decisions in relation to foreign policy.[34] Walshe facilitated that action by establishing a permanent delegation in Geneva, and Michael MacWhite was given full official status in 1923. Walshe was a strong advocate of this assertion of national consciousness within the boundaries of the Treaty, but he also welcomed it because it served to heighten the prominence and importance of his own responsibilities.

There are differing opinions as to the level of importance the Irish Free State attached to foreign policy within the League of Nations. Michael Kennedy suggests that there has been an over-concentration by historians on Free State foreign policy in relation to the Commonwealth. He claims that during the 1922 to 1932 period, the Cumann na nGaedheal government actively participated in the League, recognising it as 'a crucial listening post' due to Ireland's inability to support a comprehensive

diplomatic network.[35] He points to the registration of the Treaty as an example of the importance of the League to the government. However, in the early to mid-1920s, Walshe and External Affairs developed no coherent or coordinated League policy, and Kennedy admits that the Free State's League policy during this early period was only 'ticking over'. This was in large part due to Walshe's own belief that, while the League was certainly important, it was at the Commonwealth level that the Free State needed to focus the majority of its attention.

It is easy to understand why Walshe believed that the forum that would provide the government with its most important opportunities to redefine the emphasis and meaning of the Treaty was the Commonwealth. While Walshe can be criticised for not developing a coherent League policy, no such accusation can be levelled against him in relation to Commonwealth policy. The Imperial Conferences were marked by close teamwork within the Irish delegation, which was well prepared and which delivered a confident and unified message. In the build-up to the 1926 conference, the Cumann na nGaedheal government made clear its wish that dominion status would not remain a static entity, and it was the determination of the Irish delegates that ensured it would be a watershed in Irish constitutional history. Walshe's part in that event should not be underestimated. The Free State was represented by President Cosgrave, Kevin O'Higgins, Desmond FitzGerald, Diarmuid O'Hegarty and Joseph Walshe. The government accepted that Ireland's future lay within the Empire for the time being, but changes would have to be made, and that message was forcefully delivered at the conference. The strength of the Irish team was noted by the *Irish Times* correspondent, R.M. Smyllie, who claimed that the overall report of the conference was based on a submission by the Irish delegates. He also believed that the Free State had the only delegation that really knew its own mind from the start and had a fully documented case.[36] Smyllie also paid a special tribute to the secretariat, which consisted of Walshe and Diarmuid O'Hegarty. As we delve into the departmental documentation that relates to the conference we will see that Smyllie was correct in highlighting Walshe's contribution.

At this time, some in Ireland hoped that Irish foreign policy would turn from the Commonwealth and move more towards

France. One suggestion was that a Franco-Irish *entente* be established by taking advantage of the growing disparity and disagreement between Britain and France at that time. It was estimated that France was the strongest of the European continental powers, and for that reason 'they should be played up to in every possible way'.[37] Propaganda, both at home and abroad, would, however, have to play a major role because 'the people as a body do not grasp the need of linking with the Continent, they require to be educated up to it'. In preparation for the 1926 Imperial Conference, the Department of Defence suggested that it was highly desirable to establish a precedent where the Irish Free State would remain at peace while Britain was at war.[38] It is not clear to what extent these comments influenced the Irish delegation at the 1926 conference, but it is known that Walshe resisted less realistic proposals and ensured a more pragmatic approach to the fundamental foreign-policy issues at hand.

Walshe's preparation for the conference, in particular, was central to the successes achieved by the Irish Free State. This is evident in the departmental documentation. He submitted a detailed 'preliminary memorandum' to Desmond FitzGerald entitled 'Relations with Great Britain: Difficulties Summarised'. This document was one of a number that formed the basis of the Irish argument at the conference. Walshe outlined the importance of the dominions acting on their own behalf in the world arena. The appointment of consular representatives to dominions, for example, involved a procedure that was entirely carried out between the state wishing to send the representative and the British government. Walshe believed this situation to be entirely undesirable:

> The manner of appointing consuls confuses foreign governments concerning the real status of the Dominions. From beginning to end of the procedure the Foreign Governments deal with the British Government alone and they can form no other impression than that the British Government alone has the power to sanction the appointment of consuls within the territory of the Dominions.

Walshe also outlined the central objective for the future conduct of Irish Free State policy within the Commonwealth. He believed that

The right to advise the King in all matters internal and external and the complete recognition of his Kingship on both sides in the case of each individual Dominion seems to be the only logical road to equal status.

Clearly, Walshe was coming into his own, and his academic and legal background was allowing him to find his voice. His strategy seemed to be to focus on key points that were open to legal reinterpretation. In order to advance these changes, Walshe recognised the need for an alliance with the other dominions and was wary of the British, who would 'be ready with subtle proposals destined to emphasise the Federationist character of the Commonwealth'. He perceived that this conference was one in which momentous achievements for the dominions could be realised:

The stage of evolution at which the Dominions have arrived, the anxiety of the British to bring the Dominions more and more into their foreign policy, and the continued instability of Europe combine to make this Conference incomparably more important for the Dominions than any one that has preceded it.[39]

With this in mind, his advice at this stage was that there should be extensive preparation for the conference, and he recommended that FitzGerald should travel to Canada to meet the Prime Minister as part of a policy to form alliances with other change-seeking dominions.

Largely due to Walshe's foresight and preparation, the conference was indeed a success for the Irish Free State delegation. He was among the first to recognise the implications of what had been achieved:

The 1926 Imperial Conference began a new era in the history of the Saorstát and its sister states and the favourable results are due in no small measure to the work of the Irish Delegation. An Irish Republic could not achieve a position of freedom better calculated to promote in peace our prosperity and our national institutions.[40]

From the outset, Walshe recognised that the individual right of each of the Commonwealth dominions to make and sign treaties with foreign countries was of primary importance for the Irish

Free State, as it was deemed to be a hallmark of independent statehood. Again, the substance of the Irish position on this issue was prepared by Walshe, who asserted that in cases only where the dominions themselves had signed a treaty were they involved.[41] Walshe firstly sought general agreement on the principle that 'no Dominion can be bound in any way except by the signature of a plenipotentiary appointed on its own advice.' For him this was fundamental:

> In international treaties this title set out in full before, or in reference to, each of the national plenipotentiaries on whose advice of whose Government the King acts will remove all doubt about the equality of status of Commonwealth nations, both inter se and vis-à-vis non-Commonwealth states, and will at the same time indicate the bond upon which the real unity of the Commonwealth depends.[42]

In the aftermath of the conference, Walshe explained that before the 1926 Imperial Conference it had been the practice for plenipotentiaries, appointed on the advice of the British Government, to negotiate treaties on behalf of the Commonwealth as a whole, while holding unlimited powers. While the dominions were often asked later to concur in their work by ratifying the treaty, the Saorstát, simply in order to make its point, had usually failed to ratify, even though this made little difference in international law. Now, however, following the efforts of the Irish delegation, Walshe pointed out that 'no active obligations could be undertaken except on the advice of a plenipotentiary appointed by a Dominion, so the Saorstát need no longer make its gesture.'[43] The achievement of this particular objective was an extremely important one, even if Walshe was only one of a few who realised it at the time.

The success at the 1926 conference and the resulting boost for Walshe's confidence was duly noted by one United States official, Charles M. Hathaway, who was Consul-General to the US legation in Dublin at the time. His reports provide an alternative and interesting perspective on the development of the Department of External Affairs. Hathaway had already recorded the growing number of consul representatives in Ireland.[44] He had previously been aware of the department's subordination within

the government, but following the conference both Walshe and FitzGerald had now adopted 'a very definite intention no longer to tolerate the inferiority status of their Department to the other Government Departments which they have laboured under from the beginning'.[45] Walshe and his minister planned to make the issue a matter of vital importance, and demand equal recognition with other government departments, as well as insisting on a lessening of the Department of Finance's control over External Affairs. The record would show the important work that had been carried out by External Affairs over the previous number of years, and with this new-found confidence Walshe started to make demands to increase Ireland's representation abroad, hoping in particular to have a representative at the Vatican within two years.

Walshe also had plans to 'regularise' the status of the department's foreign representatives by seeking exequaturs (recognition by a foreign government of a consul or other agent) of the Free State's 'trade agents' based in New York, Paris and Brussels. Hathaway predicted a period of intensive lobbying by Walshe and FitzGerald:

> If the Department of External Affairs is successful in convincing the Executive Council of the importance of the status of the Irish Free State to the general welfare of the country, that is of the importance of the work of the Department of External Affairs, a larger appropriation will be sought and it is presumed that the Minister in Washington will be provided with more and better paid assistants.[46]

However, the American diplomat was not confident that Walshe and FitzGerald could succeed in their task, and he believed the department was still in some danger of absorption:

> Just what argument the Department of External Affairs will be able to offer in favour of maintaining a separate department as against the policy of the other Dominions of leaving external affairs in the Prime Minister's control, I do not know. Certainly the suggestion of such a consolidation has not been lacking in Dublin.

Hathaway's suspicions were accurate, and when the financial estimates for the coming year were published they proposed

a reduction of nearly £1,500 in the External Affairs annual budget. However, Walshe and FitzGerald remained optimistic for the future of the department. They focused on the results of the Imperial Conference, describing them as 'epoch-making psychologically', outlining, as an example, how the British monarch was now under the direction of the dominion ministers in certain matters.[47] Walshe believed the favourable publicity surrounding the contribution of the Irish delegation at the Imperial Conference was a major boost for the department.

The 1926 Imperial Conference marked a new beginning for Walshe and External Affairs. The general election held in June the following year saw Fianna Fáil become the largest opposition party in the Dáil. In Cosgrave's newly formed Cumann na nGaedheal government, FitzGerald was transferred from External Affairs and replaced by Kevin O'Higgins, who was also Vice-President and Minister for Justice. Walshe was at first somewhat ambivalent to the appointment of O'Higgins; he was unsure if this was a signal that the government wanted to incorporate External Affairs into another department, as was the case in other dominions. O'Higgins, who had taken a keen interest in foreign affairs, was considered to be the most powerful figure in the Cabinet. He had been the leading delegate at the previous Imperial Conference, and his appointment to External Affairs could also have been interpreted as a boost for the department. It was, however, to be another in a long list of short-lived ministerial appointments, as two months later O'Higgins was assassinated by renegade republicans.

While he had been minister for only a brief period, O'Higgins proved to be a strong advocate of the development of the Department of External Affairs. He argued for increased government support, and recognised the increasing volume of work the department had to deal with. This was especially true following the 1926 Imperial Conference, as he believed that every word issued by the British government had to be carefully studied for 'chicanery and bluff'. O'Higgins also recognised Walshe's difficulties as the unconfirmed head of the department, especially in relation to Finance:

> The Head of the Department has no official status. He is carefully informed of the fact – almost taunted with it – by the Department of Finance at the beginning of a large proportion of their letters

addressed to this Department. His inferior position does not help his relations with other Departments, with Foreign Representatives nor with our own staffs outside Ireland.[48]

He comprehended that without the 'remuneration and fixed status proportionate to his responsibilities' it was going to be very difficult for Walshe to carry out his official functions with foreign representatives. O'Higgins gave Walshe much-needed support and the fact that he was a senior member of government made it all the more important.

Perhaps inspired by this vote of confidence, Walshe went on the offensive when he penned a memorandum in which he argued for the continued development of the department:

> A properly established Dept. of External Affairs is just as important to the state as the Shannon scheme, the Currency Commission, the Creamery Amalgamation scheme or any of the other large constructive enterprises set on foot by the present Govt.

It was all a question of status, said Walshe, who believed that without a 'constant and visible improvement in status' all other enterprises would not account for the fulfilment of the aspirations of the Irish people. He believed that:

> Because the question of status is at the present moment of our history the only really disturbing factor in the situation it seems improvident and unwise to allow completely subsidiary questions of service reactions, and small state expenditure to stand in the way of the establishment of an efficient dept. whose duty it is to promote our status and to remove that disturbing factor.[49]

Walshe saw the withholding of funds from External Affairs as petty when compared with the question of Irish Free State status in the eyes of the international community. Repeatedly referring to the question of status and the removal of what he termed the 'disturbing factor', he said that, following a recent visit to the United States, he concluded with absolute certainty that External Affairs would need 'very considerable financial help in our reconstructive work if and only if the disturbing factor is rendered powerless to interfere with our economic progress'. He pointed out the difficulty of keeping up with the vast quantity of work

under the remit of the department given the resources available to it. While providing information and promoting Irish independence he saw the need for greater emphasis on the League of Nations through which Ireland's status could be enhanced. Walshe sought a more proactive approach from his serving diplomats, believing it was important to demonstrate independence of action to the Irish people in order to convince them of the 'possibilities of our position as a member of the British Commonwealth'. He reiterated that this work in promoting Irish self-confidence was impossible without a properly established department and stated that the very existence of a separate ministry meant that its work was as important as that of any other government department. In recognition of this, he argued that the principal officers of External Affairs should be treated equally within the civil service as a whole.

While emphasising the difficulties of External Affairs in general, the ostensible subject of this memorandum was the position of Seán Murphy, who was to be appointed assistant secretary to the department. Walshe was insistent that Murphy be rewarded adequately for the position, and was unhappy with some of the arguments put forward against the proposed increase in Murphy's salary, describing them as 'naive chicanery'. He listed Murphy's qualifications, the importance of his previous post in France, and the fact that he had already spent a great deal of his own money to carry out his duties. Walshe was annoyed by the reaction of others in the civil service to Murphy's proposed appointment 'at a proper scale'. He stated that he would give his job to anyone – assuming anyone would want it – who could prove that Murphy was not the most suitable person for the job. Concluding his offensive on the general attitude within the civil service towards External Affairs, which he saw as a primary force restricting the development of the department, Walshe described his department as a 'national necessity' and pleaded:

> Let us treat it as such and not as a sort of charitable object for donations. As Secretary I am convinced that we can do very little real work until our principal officers are graded and paid as if we were the largest Dept in the State.[50]

Clearly, Walshe had taken enough denigration over the years and

he was not now, following some of the greatest successes of the state in the international arena, going to bow down to what he saw as shortsighted questions over minor financial matters.

Walshe received strong support from the President of the Executive Council, William Cosgrave, who, as a temporary measure after the assassination of O'Higgins, held the post of Minister for External Affairs from July to October 1927. Cosgrave wrote to the Minister for Finance, Ernest Blythe, reminding him of the value of the work undertaken by Walshe and his department, which involved 'highly technical work of a nature in which ordinary precedents are of little value, and which requires specialised knowledge of very high order'. Cosgrave again referred to the department's work at the previous Imperial Conference in glowing terms:

> The valuable memoranda furnished by them for the information of the delegates, were a striking proof of the study, zeal and ability brought by these officers to bear on their very difficult task. As you are aware, these memoranda were of considerable value even to the Canadian delegates, in spite of the advantages enjoyed by the latter by reason of their long experience and numerous technical staff.[51]

Walshe's position as secretary had recently been made permanent, and Cosgrave agreed that Seán Murphy's position as assistant secretary should also be regularised. Walshe was due to leave for the League of Nations within a couple of days, and Cosgrave was adamant that Murphy's position should be settled before his departure. Cosgrave would tolerate no further procrastination and he twice warned Blythe to follow these instructions forthwith.

Towards the end of 1927 Patrick McGilligan was appointed Minister for External Affairs. Though he simultaneously held the position of Minister for Industry and Commerce, he proved a very forceful and energetic External Affairs minister. McGilligan, who had begun his career as a civil servant, was quick to recognise the value of the work that Walshe had undertaken in building the department from its foundations. Dermot Keogh points out that by 1929 Walshe, largely due to McGilligan's efforts, had received all he could hope for from Finance, including a new legal adviser (John Hearne), two newly recruited cadets, and three new ministers plenipotentiary and envoys extraordinary.[52] In early 1928

the Department of Finance wrote to McGilligan announcing its agreement to upgrade Walshe's salary in line with his position. Walshe's annual salary at the time was £760; this was to be upgraded to £1,000, rising to £1,200 after three years.[53] The question of pay scale was also crucial to Walshe's standing within the civil service as a whole.

In 1929 the staff of External Affairs was increased. One addition was Fred Boland, who would later become assistant secretary and would eventually take over from Walshe following the latter's departure for the Holy See. Boland had seen an advertisement for the post of 'cadet' in the Department of External Affairs. As the Free State was in its infancy, he had some reservations about applying for the position. He received differing advice: some said that as Ireland was still part of the Commonwealth, Britain would continue to represent Ireland, while others said that the Free State would insist on shaping its own external policy. Despite these conflicting views, they all recommended that Boland should talk to Walshe for an 'informed opinion' as to the prospects for the Department of External Affairs. He began in July 1929, but was not impressed either by the 'ludicrously small' salary or the offices that External Affairs shared with the Department of Agriculture:

> The entrance hall of the building was invariably cluttered up with bags of fertiliser, cans of veterinary medicines, sacks of seed potatoes and other aids to agricultural production.[54]

It depressed Boland to imagine what foreign dignitaries would think on visiting the department. Walshe, however, was later rescued from this humiliation when, in 1941, Lord Iveagh donated his town house for the use of the Department of External Affairs.

Under McGilligan's charge, therefore, Walshe experienced a period of growth in both departmental size and stature. It was also a time in which foreign policy seemed to turn its attention back to the League of Nations. Michael Kennedy, for example, has traced the beginnings of a concerted League policy to the appointment of McGilligan, arguing that the years 1928 to 1932 boasted a 'high profile well-structured League policy'.[55] This was in large part due to the work of Seán Lester, who had entered the department in 1923 and was made permanent delegate to the

League of Nations in 1929. Walshe, of course, occupies an important place in the formulation of League policy, and Kennedy
attributes periods of inaction to a lack of resources rather than
a lack of interest. He uses the example of the Irish campaign
that led to the election of the Free State to the League Council
in 1930, which involved Walshe and McGilligan coordinating
efforts to attract the votes of the League members. Walshe was
grateful for McGilligan's attempts to demonstrate that foreign
policy meant more than attendance at the Commonwealth, and
certainly believed that the League of Nations was an important
publicity centre for the development of the Irish Free State. This
was confirmed for him by Britain's reluctance to assist Canada in
its efforts to be elected to the League's Council:

> No instructions of any kind were proffered by the British on the
> best way of canvassing or of voting for Canada. This was in sharp-
> est contrast with the invariable action of the British when they
> desire to have anything done at the League, and Canada could not
> have failed to notice it, even if her attention had not been helped
> in that direction by the Irish Delegation.[56]

Canada acknowledged Ireland's assistance in the success of its
candidature, and Walshe, in turn, recognised the contribution
of Ireland's representative, Michael MacWhite. For Walshe, the
matter put an end to the pretence that Britain represented all
the states of the Commonwealth at the League, and he recommended increasing the Free State's representation to the League
in order to further emphasise the dominion's independence from
Britain.

Stephen Barcroft has dismissed the view of a concerted Free
State strategy at the League and suggests a more haphazard approach
by Walshe and External Affairs in relation to League policy:

> The term 'policy', as normally understood, suggests coherent lines
> of governmental action, responding to some expression of interest
> or concern on the part of the voting public and its representatives,
> and implemented with a degree of energy and consistency by the
> Department of External Affairs. Given the virtual non-existence
> of all three of these criteria it is probably more accurate to speak
> of Irish 'activity' rather than 'policy'.[57]

It is true that ministerial responsibilities left Patrick McGilligan and later Éamon de Valera with little time for League affairs. According to Barcroft, Seán Lester, who replaced MacWhite as Ireland's representative at Geneva, attributed a large degree of the government's negative approach to the League directly to Walshe. Lester said that Walshe was 'not interested' in the League, that the department was 'indifferent', and that instructions were infrequent and inadequate.[58] Lester, therefore, seems to have been given considerable scope to formulate policy with little ministerial or departmental guidance.

In his memoirs, Fred Boland says that, even by the time of his arrival at the department in 1929, Irish foreign policy operated within extremely narrow parameters. He adds that despite the fact that Cosgrave had registered the Treaty at the League of Nations and that Irish ministers attended its meetings and assemblies, their primary interest within the League lay with winning the widest possible recognition for Ireland as an independent state.[59] Thus, it was not interest in the activities of the League or its functions *per se* that prompted Irish participation. The Free State was first and foremost preoccupied with promoting the perceived independence of Ireland on the world stage. Boland believes that it was only natural that their objectives centred on Anglo-Irish relations and that the League should have been used in this way. Walshe's attitude certainly seems to have followed this line. Where it made sense, the League was used to highlight Irish autonomy and independence but when other more important matters at home were consuming his time, Walshe was happy to defer the Free State's response to the broader issues of the League to the local representative there.

The lack of focus on League affairs was, perhaps, also contributed to by inadequate resources. Despite their successes in improving the profile of the department, McGilligan and Walshe still faced difficulties in persuading the authorities to provide adequate funding for expansion of the diplomatic service. Before the 1929 estimates, the Department of Finance prepared a memorandum that summarised the amount of budgetary savings that each department was expected to make (*see* Table 1).

Table 1

Estimates 1929/30
Suggested Savings on Estimates as Presented by Departments[60]

Department	Net of Total Estimates	Suggested Economies	Estimated Reduction[61]
General (Items 1,[62] 2 & 3)		80,600	
Finance (Items 1 to 30)*	2,994,461	50,000	1.5%
Justice	1,693,372	56,300	4%
Education	3,699,625	56,030	1.5%
Agriculture	454,961	12,900	3%
Lands & Fisheries	721,386	68,100	9%
Industry & Commerce	169,821	4,350	2.5%
Posts & Telegraphs	2,383,820	101,500	5%
Defence	1,448,387	11,162	.75%
External Affairs	65,317	13,000	20%
TOTAL		453,942	

* *Includes Superannuations of £1,780,000 and Works and Building £758,666*

These figures clearly explain the siege mentality felt by Walshe. The amount of the suggested economies, excluding External Affairs, averages at around 3.5 per cent of the year's total estimates. External Affairs, however, already having by far the smallest yearly budget, was expected to make a massive 20 per cent reduction in its expenditure. This was in comparison to Finance's own meagre 1.5 per cent sacrifice.

The open criticism and lack of understanding for the work of External Affairs, in particular from the Department of Finance, may go some way towards explaining Walshe's reaction to any criticism from within the department. During 1929, the Irish High Commissioner to London, Professor Timothy A. Smiddy, wrote to McGilligan with regard to his status and duties. Smiddy, a noted economist, had been minister plenipotentiary in Washington between 1924 and 1929 before he took up his British posting. In his correspondence with the minister, Smiddy discussed the issue of direct communication between departments of the Saorstát and British government departments in London, arguing for the adoption of 'a proper international and constitutional method of communication between Governments'. The suggestion was a valid one. Because correspondence between the British and Irish

governments did not pass through him, he had on more than
one occasion found himself in the embarrassing position of not
being aware of what his own superiors had communicated to the
British government. Walshe, however, did not take kindly to this
interference, and greatly resented Smiddy's direct communication
with McGilligan. He informed the High Commissioner that the
minister wished all correspondence from representatives abroad
to be addressed to the secretary of the department. Walshe also
responded to the suggestion that the High Commissioner's office
be used as the conduit of communication between the British and
Irish governments. Smiddy had described this as the 'recognised
method of communication between independent States', and said
that this method possessed 'a distinct constitutional advantage
over the existing method of direct communication by means of
despatch'.[63] Walshe was opposed to the suggestion and believed
that direct communication between governments to be more
satisfactory than through an envoy, and pointed out that before
1927 all official communication passed through the office of the
Governor General, leading to an element of 'apparent subordination'.[64] Walshe's response culminated in a pointed reprimand to
Smiddy: 'You will be asked to intervene when the need arises', he
said, and added that the minister did not intend, for the moment
as least, to place the office of the High Commissioner in a similar
position to that of a legation.

The friction between Smiddy and Walshe did not end there.
They clashed also on the seemingly inconsequential issue of the
way in which correspondence between the High Commissioner's
office and the Department of External Affairs should be headed
and signed. Walshe wrote complaining that the secretary to
the High Commissioner, T.J. Kiernan, was signing letters as
'Secretary' rather than 'for the High Commissioner'.[65] Walshe
was beginning to lose patience, but Smiddy persisted and pointed
to procedure in headquarters, saying, 'the question of "description" is quite unimportant and is evidently regarded so by the
Department since so many different signatures appear on letters
from the head office, all of the signatories signing independently, without a description such as "for the Secretary".'[66] While
seeming a relatively trivial concern, the ensuing correspondence
reveals much about how Walshe regarded himself and his status
as secretary.

Kiernan continued to probe the issue, and questioned why the High Commissioner was restricted to communicating with the secretary of the Department of External Affairs and not with the minister, as had been the practice in the past:

> The High Commissioner here has always taken the line of deal-ing only with persons of ministerial rank in London, and it is anomalous if he is precluded from communicating with his own Minister or if he is restricted generally in the manner suggested in your two letters.

He also requested an explanation as to why a change in the sig-nature of the secretary of the High Commissioner's office had been suggested:

> The Secretary signs letters which are written under the direction of the High Commissioner, just as the Secretary of a Department in Dublin signs as directed by the Minister. The High Commissioner notices that letters from headquarters to him are signed by Mr Walshe without description, and he thinks it desirable, since the matter has been raised by you, to have a general arrangement adopted on some basis which can be clearly understood.[67]

Kiernan was comparing his position as secretary to the High Commissioner in London to the position of Walshe as secretary to the Minister for External Affairs. Walshe's reply is important as he asserted that his position was without equal and that he was second only to the Minister for External Affairs. Walshe reaffirmed that all correspondence for the minister had to pass through him because the secretary was responsible to the political head 'not only for the work of the Headquarters staff, but also for the work of the officers abroad'. He clearly states that the posi-tion of High Commissioner was subordinate to the position of departmental secretary:

> The offices abroad are regarded for all purposes as an integral part of the Department of External Affairs, the High Commissioner and the Envoys ranking in the administration with the Assistant Secretary and the Legal Adviser at Headquarters, and the Secretaries to the High Commissioner and to the Legations ranking with the Assistant Principals at home.[68]

The fact that Smiddy had regular meetings in London with persons of ministerial rank was not relevant, according to Walshe. Smiddy, however, took issue with this and argued that while envoys are abroad and hold High Commissioner or ministerial positions they rank senior to the secretary of the department.

Smiddy's claim that he was more senior than Walshe and that Kiernan was on a par with Walshe was untenable. Walshe was justifiably annoyed, but he could have been more compliant on the question of direct communication between governments. Smiddy was left nonplussed as he argued that legations were established for the purpose of diplomatic communication and to enable the government at home to be kept intimately informed of the views of ministers and politicians and other political issues in the foreign country:

> I do not feel that I should continue to see the Secretary of State for Dominion Affairs since I am powerless to discuss matters with him. He will, in any case, cease to trouble me, as the interviews can not but be one-sided, Mr Amery talking to me while I listen.[69]

Smiddy planned that he and Kiernan would visit head office in Dublin in order to discuss these and other matters. Even in this, Walshe infuriated Smiddy by insisting that Kiernan would not be needed for these discussions. Smiddy soon resigned his position as High Commissioner and left the service of the Department of External Affairs. While there is little evidence to suggest that Smiddy left the service, or was forced to leave, because of this incident, it is clear that Walshe would not have objected to his departure.

Later that year McGilligan announced in the Dáil that he planned to reorganise the Department of External Affairs as its work was growing in both 'volume and importance'. The US minister to Ireland, Fred Sterling, commented on the address by McGilligan that asserted that, due to the efforts of the Department of External Affairs, the Irish Free State had gained enormous prestige on the world stage. 'We speak clearly and audibly in the concert of the world ... we have assumed an irrevocable share in the burdens of international life', said McGilligan.[70] He also referred to the planned opening of legations in Berlin and Paris as well as the proposed establishment of a Consulate-General in New York. The creation of an Irish legation at the

Vatican was one of Walshe's primary aims, and in this speech the minister informed the Dáil of the reasons behind the decision to proceed with that plan. Ireland's history, he said, was greatly influenced by the Catholic faith, and the papacy was now 'an exceedingly important factor in the affairs of nations'. Ireland, therefore, 'should not be less eager than other nations to secure its good will and cooperation'. McGilligan may have been the mouthpiece for this statement, but clearly, as we shall see, Walshe had a great deal to do with the sentiment behind it.

Earlier that year Walshe had travelled to London to secure Foreign Office goodwill and assistance towards the proposed exchange of diplomatic representatives between the Irish Free State and the Vatican. He requested that Britain's representative there, Henry Chilton, should make arrangements with Vatican officials for the exchange, as well as for a visit by McGilligan to the Holy City. Chilton was aware of McGilligan's proposed visit and its objective, and had been instructed to give the Irish Free State minister every assistance. By this time the matter had taken on an internal political perspective, and Walshe explained to British officials that the Irish government wished to demonstrate publicly that the Vatican recognised the current government as the lawful government of the Free State. The urgency was prompted by moves by de Valera to incite public opinion against the government, and Walshe wrote to McGilligan urging him to pursue the matter with some urgency:

> If you consider that de Valera's statement on the absence of the right to govern in the majority, as such, is worth bothering about at all, it strikes me that the evil consequences can best be … [dealt with] by treating the Vatican appointment as a matter of extreme urgency. There is a particularly dangerous type of poison in the statement which is certain to produce its effects however slowly. An exchange of Legations with the Vatican involving the recognition of existing regime is the only effective antidote.[71]

The government was concerned that the republicans would 'poison the mind of the Vatican against the Free State Government' to the extent that Walshe feared that when McGilligan would bring up the question of the exchange of representatives he would be rebuffed by Vatican officials.[72] He also thought that the Vatican

may want to play a waiting game to see how political events unfolded in the Free State. This explains why British assistance was so important, and Walshe believed that the possibility of de Valera coming to power would ensure Britain's support.[73]

However, the difficulty with the request, explained the Foreign Office under-secretary, Hubert Montgomery, was that if its representative mentioned that the British government supported the appointment of a legate in Dublin, then he ran the risk of bringing up the issue of the appointment of a nuncio in London. Britain did not want to consider such a question at this time. Walshe explained that there could be no postponement of the proposal, and if the exchange could not take place in the very near future they should at the very least obtain the agreement in principle of the Vatican to the idea of mutual representation. He said that the appointment of a legate in Dublin was more important than the establishment of an Irish representative at the Vatican. This was contrary to the impression McGilligan had given to the Dominions Office, but Walshe assured the British officials that what he said now was the position of the Irish Free State government. Walshe saw significant advantages in having a papal legate based in Dublin, believing he would be able to exercise considerable influence over the Irish hierarchy, who had not been forthcoming in their condemnation of de Valera.[74] He rather cynically commented that the appointment of a legate and the consequent recognition of the government would lead the clergy to examine their conscience; that is, he said, if they had any left![75] It was eventually agreed that the British government would advise the Vatican that it had 'no objection' to the appointment of an Irish representative to the Holy See. Walshe was temporarily satisfied with this carefully constructed formula of words, but hoped that a more positive formula could later be found. In this, he was ultimately successful, and Chilton was duly instructed to convey to the Vatican that the British government was 'in favour' of the appointment of an Irish minister in Rome.[76]

Walshe's efforts had ensured that he was eventually granted his wish to have an Irish representative at the Holy See. However, there was some difficulty between the Irish Free State and the British government with regard to the form the letter of credence was to take. The Dominions Office assistant under-secretary, Harry Batterbee, eased matters when he advised full cooperation

and wrote to Hubert Montgomery stating that it would be unwise to cause difficulties over what he considered were small matters, as they were negotiating with the Irish Free State over matters of greater importance.[77] For Walshe, the creation of the Vatican post was an important step forward, and he wished to appoint Charles Bewley to the post as quickly as possible.[78] Walshe had shown great skill and determination in creating the position in the first instance but, as we shall see, his first choice of candidate for the post would prove somewhat less auspicious.

In his autobiography, Charles Bewley describes his induction to his new post under the guidance of Walshe. Bewley's account, it should be noted, was somewhat embittered by his subsequent dealings with Walshe and the department, which led to his unhappy departure from the service in 1939. Bewley states that his first instructions came from Walshe after they had departed for Rome. He was perplexed as to why McGilligan could not have given him these instructions before his departure from Dublin, but he supposed that 'Ministers sometimes shrink from formulating their policy even to themselves and leave the task of explaining it to others in the hands of their permanent officials, who have no responsibility except that of interpreting the desires of their superiors.'[79] Walshe told him that the basis for the Irish policy was to collaborate closely with the British. While on their way to Rome they stopped briefly in London, and Bewley describes a somewhat fawning Walshe introducing him to Sir Hubert Montgomery:

> 'Yes, thank you, Sir Hubert! And thanks for your kindness in receiving us, Sir Hubert!' In his gratitude for Sir Hubert's amiability he shifted perpetually from one foot to the other: I could not help thinking of an overgrown puppy frisking around its master.

Walshe reiterated to Bewley the importance of keeping in with the British, saying, 'Whenever I have difficulties of any kind, I only need to write them a couple of lines, and they give me their advice. I don't know what we'd do without them.' They travelled on to Rome, where Walshe brought Bewley to Henry Chilton, the British minister to the Holy See. Bewley had misgivings about this course as they had not yet visited any of the Irish clergy in Rome. He had been warned by a friend of his, Con Curran (a brother to

Michael Curran, who was at that time vice-rector of the Irish college in Rome), not to show preference towards the British. Walshe dismissed the warning, saying, 'Curran thinks he knows our job better than we do!', but when they called on the rector of the Irish college, Monsignor John Hagan, they were slighted:

> Once we were outside the door, Walshe said, 'Did you notice that he treated us as tourists – that he made no reference to my position or yours?'
> 'It would have been hard not to notice it,' I replied.
> 'Outrageous!' exclaimed Walshe.
> I assented, but in my inmost heart I could not help recognising that there was, given his political tenets, every justification for the Monsignor's attitude.[80]

Walshe left Rome and Bewley was determined to provide the best he could for the benefit of his country.

The Free State had been assured that a papal nuncio would be appointed within a matter of months. A number of difficulties arose, however, with the Vatican stating that the proposal was complicated by the fact that the See of Armagh was not in the Free State, and the idea of an apostolic delegate was mooted as a consolation.[81] Walshe became anxious at the Vatican's hesitation, but he worked closely with Bewley to ensure that a nuncio was appointed. Their efforts were successful, and Paschal Robinson was named as the nuncio to the Irish Free State. Walshe worked rapidly to secure acceptance for Robinson, and little was spared in preparing a suitable welcome for the Vatican's representative. Following his arrival in January 1930 Robinson settled down to his well-appointed residence in the Phoenix Park.

Walshe considered the establishment of official diplomatic relations with the Vatican a major success. At this point in time he continued his efforts to expand and develop the Irish foreign service, but he may have been persuaded by McGilligan to accept some compromises in order to secure the department's future. In March 1929 it was proposed in the Cabinet that the salaries of the Irish representatives abroad should be reduced by nearly 50 per cent.[82] In return, Walshe was to be given new, higher-status missions in Europe, such as Paris and Berlin, and a new post was to be created in the Department of External Affairs. In the meantime, Walshe maintained pressure on the British Foreign Office

to give priority to assisting the appointment of Irish Free State diplomatic representatives in Europe. In fact, Walshe became somewhat terse with his British counterparts any time progress on these matters seemed to stall. McGilligan, possibly having been prompted by Walshe, wrote to the Dominions Secretary, L.S. Amery, asking why the Dominions Office had not taken any steps to secure the agreement of the respective governments to the proposed appointment of Count O'Kelly as minister to Paris and Professor Daniel Binchey to Berlin.[83] Walshe also spoke to the Dominions Office assistant under-secretary, Harry Batterbee, about the delay in dealing with the same matter. He expressed the hope that, after the diplomatic formalities had been dealt with, the appointments could go ahead without any undue delay.[84]

The Department of External Affairs was given another chance to increase its diplomatic prestige at international level at the 1930 Imperial Conference. Walshe was again credited for the significant developments in Anglo-Irish relations that were to take place, and both he and External Affairs were ready to accept the greater responsibility the Irish Free State was to gain over its own affairs. The departmental documentation lists Walshe as an 'adviser' as well as the secretary to the Irish legation.[85] He was accompanied by the Free State team, which consisted of Diarmuid O'Hegarty, Seán Murphy and John J. Hearne, as well as McGilligan, Desmond FitzGerald, Paddy Hogan and John A. Costello, who officially headed the delegation. By this time, Walshe's experience and expertise had become indispensable to this area of foreign-policy formation and execution, and in advance of the conference he accompanied McGilligan on a visit to the South African premier, in search of a dominion ally.[86] His official role at the conference was to act as secretary and adviser, but to content himself with that role at this most important juncture would have gone against his instincts.

In a speech to the Dáil, McGilligan had outlined the objectives for the forthcoming conference. The remnants of imperial control would be removed and the 'last legal vestiges of the organisation now superseded swept away'. Increased sovereignty for the individual members of the Commonwealth would also be sought. Walshe, again focusing on areas of legal argument in which he thought the Free State could make some gains, asserted that the conclusions of the 1929 Imperial Conference meant it was inevitable that the last restrictions on the legislative assemblies of the Commonwealth countries would finally

be removed.[87] This, he believed, would give the associated states equality with Great Britain and legislative freedom. Both McGilligan and Walshe, therefore, had ambitious objectives for the conference, and when the time came the Irish Free State's role in the enactment of the Statute of Westminster was hugely significant. This statute did not grant all that the Irish Free State had wanted, but did, as Walshe had predicted, facilitate the means through which the Free State could now achieve many of those objectives. It was a watershed in Anglo-Irish relations and a major coup for the Irish government.

The Statute of Westminster laid down that, in future, legislation by the British parliament would apply to the dominions only at their request and with their consent. The dominions, therefore, were now given the power to legislate for themselves. These powers greatly worried Winston Churchill, who believed that the Irish Free State now had the power to dismantle the Treaty completely. Cosgrave reminded him that the Treaty had been formed by common agreement, and could only be changed by consent.[88] In this climate of change, however, Walshe also believed that the Irish Free State's constitutional status could also be contested, and his memoranda on the idea display his opportunistic legal acumen:

> The ideal democratic regime is that in which the headship is stable and at the same time completely obedient to the people's will as expressed through their Ministers. In the Saorstát Government we do not take the view that secession from the group of associated states is, in any way, affected by this understanding.[89]

Because a number of the symbols of subordination remained repulsive to the Free State government, it was felt that some changes in this regard would have to be made. It was argued that the use of the British seals made, or appeared to make, the British government, and not the dominion, responsible for any document issued by that dominion. The Free State was also concerned with the principle that its advice to the king had to travel through the channels of the British government. Thus, application for 'direct access' to the king was initiated by the Free State through its High Commissioner in London, John Dulanty.

The British were alarmed at this latest request, and Walshe, not content to deal with the matter through Dulanty, travelled to London to assess the situation. Harkness has described Walshe's

account of these negotiations as having 'delightful frankness' and illuminating many aspects of Anglo-Irish relations at that time. This memorandum typifies Walshe's personality and diplomatic style, which both frustrated and endeared him to his contemporaries:

> They let me open the discussion. I did so on the following lines, which I hope you will approve, notwithstanding the inaccuracies and exaggerations.[90]

To some, such as Bewley, Walshe may have appeared sycophantic around his British counterparts, but this was part of his particular diplomatic style. He was focused solely on results, and he understood the procedures and protocols that needed to be followed. The resolution of many Anglo-Irish issues during this period led to major advantages accruing to the Free State, and Walshe must be given credit for much of that. Walshe saw the Free State as being far more advanced, in terms of constitutional development at least, than any of the other dominions. He explained to his British counterparts that it would be a 'fundamental error' to compare the Irish Free State with the other dominions which, to Walshe's mind, were 'still evolving out of the colonial stage'. Clearly, Walshe had no inferiority complex around his British counterparts, and he showed some audacity in telling Batterbee and his colleagues that MacDonald and the Labour Party had the direct opposite policy to the Conservatives on dominion affairs:

> They had apparently decided that the monarchy was bound to disappear within a relatively short time and it was not their desire to add to the power and prestige of the King by allowing the Dominions to have direct relations with him.

Walshe delighted in the sensation such remarks caused and added the following comment in parentheses:

> This insinuation seemed to have powerfully worrying effect on Batterbee and Co., and he disappeared soon after to have half an hour's talk with Mr Thomas [Secretary for the Dominions].

Walshe, by his own account, adopted a somewhat superior attitude in his conversation with the British representatives. 'There must be no British control', he said, 'not even in the form of

control over documents relating to our external affairs ... there must be the completest freedom of access to the King. No British Minister should, in future, be used as the channel between our Government and the King.' Walshe continued in this manner, outlining to the British the only terms that would make it possible for a 'friendly understanding' to exist between the two countries. He successfully navigated through the bureaucracy of the British officials who eventually, after many interruptions and arguments, came back to basics and 'dropped all the talk about interpretation of texts of Imperial Conference reports, about the need of uniformity and all the usual dope with which they have been annoying and boring us for such a long time.'

Walshe's approach was direct, and he warned that the Irish Free State would have nothing to do with British seals of any kind, and that McGilligan would brook no further interference in the relations with the Free State government and the king:

> In fact I did my best to produce the impression that you and all your colleagues were in exceedingly bad temper owing to the attitude of intransigence and intolerance adopted by the British Government for the last twelve months.

Walshe's exaggeration of his government's position was a deft negotiating ploy. He used it to reach a compromise involving the granting of a new state seal depicting the Irish harp but which included the head of the British monarch. Omitted was the royal arms, a well-known and hated symbol of British rule in Ireland. Walshe outlined what he felt was the brilliance of Free State tactics: 'Our real coup de maître in this whole matter was getting Dulanty to approach the Palace. That convinced the British that we were ready to go any length.' Walshe was justifiably delighted with these developments. Apart from his self-admitted hyperbole, his part in these negotiations portrays his legal-constitutional skill. The agreement had involved a degree of compromise, but Walshe advised that 'to put the image of the existing monarch on an Irish Free State seal used only for confirming the King's signature is to my mind a safe and logical constitutional procedure.' He looked to the broader importance of the step, as well as the potential political advantage to be gained by McGilligan:

If legislation and a full explanation is necessary you will have an opportunity of making a first-class political and international statement. You will be able to say that you have eliminated the last shadow of control of the British Government over the Irish Free State – that there is now no flaw internally or externally in the independence of the Saorstát.

In this memorandum, which is extensively cited by David Harkness, Walshe clearly recognised the uniqueness of the position now held by the Irish Free State, which had developed far beyond any of the other dominions. It was indeed a momentous achievement:

We shall have advanced further than any Dominion, placed ourselves in a different and better category … We have broken the unity which they attached to the physical oneness of the seal, and I think that achievement worth while.

The Irish Free State had sought complete control over its external affairs, and to achieve this Walshe was ready and willing to argue the point as forcefully as was necessary. Harkness has described him as an 'extreme nationalist', and, indeed, an analysis of the documentation during this period supports that conclusion.[91] This was an important motivating factor for Walshe, but the added prestige that his own department would receive as a result of greater autonomy in international affairs was also important. Walshe felt he had suffered subjugation long enough, not only to Britain, but to other Free State departments such as Finance. To completely run Free State foreign affairs was a significant development for Walshe and the Department of External Affairs.

Irish foreign-policy development was to continue to flourish, and following the developments at the 1930 Imperial Conference the Free State government decided to increase its efforts to remove the system of appeal to the Judicial Committee of the Privy Council. Walshe was particularly irritated at some descriptions of the Privy Council, which compared it to an international court, 'as if it had been set by the members of the Commonwealth for the purpose of settling their inter se disputes'. He outlined the Free State's objections to the council by pointing out that it was 'purely an English court set up by English legislation. The judges are appointed by the English Cabinet (the occasional presence of Dominion judges does not change its essential composition). Its

purpose was to protect English interests in the Colonies, where
the machinery of justice was not considered to be equal to that of
Great Britain.'[92] He further described the system as 'undemocratic'
and a 'constitutional monstrosity' because the function of justice
could only belong to each individual state. Walshe, however, cautioned that the situation in relation to the Privy Council and
the Statute of Westminster was a complicated matter, and he
stressed that further developments could cause difficulties.[93] He
outlined to McGilligan one possible scenario in which a British
reservation or amendment to the statute could 'in substance be
equivalent to a declaration that the Treaty created a static situation determined by the then existing facts in Canada'. F.S.L.
Lyons notes that the 1921 Anglo-Irish Treaty had defined the
relationship of the Free State on the same basis as Canada, and
that because Canada did not have the right to abolish the process
of appeal to the Privy Council, it was assumed that the Free State
did not have this right either.[94] Walshe believed that after the passage of the Statute of Westminster with such a reservation, the
Free State would be in a weaker position in relation to advancing
its constitutional status: 'Our position with regard to the relief
brought by the Westminster Act may easily be called into doubt.
A skilful amendment could no doubt exclude us from its benefits.'[95] Walshe believed that if this were to be the case it would
be better if the Statute of Westminster, 'fast becoming a menace',
did not go through.

Intense diplomatic action was needed if the benefits of the
statute were to accrue to the Free State, and Walshe was on the
lookout for conspiracies by Britain. The Irish High Commissioner
in London, John Dulanty, had told him that the Secretary of
State for Dominions Affairs, J.H. Thomas, was in favour of personal talks in order to settle the matters in dispute instead of
sending official dispatches. 'Of course he was!' said Walshe, who
was suspicious of British duplicity. 'He could always deny what
he had said.'[96] Walshe's fears were based on substance. There
was much British apprehension over the extensive powers being
handed over to the dominion parliaments. Winston Churchill
believed it would be possible for the Dáil to repudiate the Treaty,
and to prevent this he sought the insertion of a restrictive clause.[97]
Despite the nervousness and the diplomatic posturing, the Statute
of Westminster was passed into law in December 1931 to the

broad satisfaction of Walshe and the government. Two months later, however, Fianna Fáil came to power, and while the Cosgrave government was unable to avail of the new constitutional changes, de Valera would exploit them to the full.

Another major event that the Cosgrave government would be unable to benefit from was the hosting of the Eucharistic Congress, which would be an international showpiece for Irish Catholicism. Walshe considered it an important event for the Free State to demonstrate its independence in the eyes of the world. Cosgrave had wished not only to demonstrate that the members of his government were devout followers of the Holy See, but also to discredit de Valera as being anti-clerical. Walshe, it has been said, was personally in charge of a 'dirty tricks' campaign against de Valera in which the Fianna Fáil leader was linked with a 'red scare' suggesting a link between the IRA and communism.[98] There was little evidence for the claims against de Valera, but the idea was promoted by Cumann na nGaedheal as part of its electoral strategy.[99] Walshe shared these concerns and warned of the very real danger of communism in Ireland. He had hoped that the papal nuncio, Paschal Robinson, could persuade the Irish bishops to condemn the IRA as a communist organisation. When Bewley told him that Robinson was unlikely to get involved, Walshe made a despairing gesture, 'as if the burden of responsibility which rested on his shoulders was too great to be borne'.[100] Fianna Fáil's links with gunmen and the anti-clerical communist 'Saor-Éire' was countered effectively by de Valera, who since coming into constitutional politics had gained considerable respectability among the Irish clergy and hierarchy.[101] Contrary to Walshe's view, it seems that de Valera's commitment to Catholic values was, by this time, well established.[102] Therefore, despite Cumann na nGaedheal's preparations and its 'red scare' campaign, when the time came to open the Congress it was de Valera who would welcome the Pope's legate to Ireland.

The stance the Church had taken with regard to Fianna Fáil had gravely disappointed Walshe, who had hoped that Paschal Robinson might be able to convince the Irish hierarchy to denounce de Valera. Writing on the moral fibre of the country, he said that the support of the Church for the state, so necessary in normal circumstances, was doubly so in Ireland where 'the beginnings of the State were surrounded with confusion and false theories by political

leaders of the de Valera type'.[103] Reacting, therefore, to statements issued by de Valera, and the position of the Church, Walshe drafted a treatise on the nature of the state. He began:

> The idea of the State as the supreme social organism of a people is found in some form at all times and in all places from the beginning of human history, and it is and always has been regarded as an essential element of the natural law which guides men towards the fullest development of their faculties.[104]

This is not startling in itself, but as Walshe continued his treatise on the state became more a defence of Cumann na nGaedheal's position in relation to the Treaty. 'The State is not a Republic, nor a Monarchy,' he explained. 'These are particular forms of Government which suppose the existence of the State.' The state itself was the 'permanent collective will' of the people and he insisted that this could not be changed by the type of government in place. There is no doubting that his comments were aimed at de Valera and his followers:

> Being essentially part of the law of nature we owe it obedience and service, and while we may strive to change its particular form we can only do so by means which do not involve the existence of the State itself. Once the State has been established every act which might eventually lead to its break up and to a state of chaos is a crime against the natural law. No person in the State can regard himself as freed from obedience to it ... Thus, leaders of political parties, ministers of the Churches, Editors of newspapers, have a very definite obligation to inculcate obedience to the State, and failure to do so becomes a positive act against the natural law.

Walshe's respect for the Church did not temper his criticism of its stance on certain issues. He believed the clergy should do everything in their power to emphasise the legitimacy of the government. Under the guise of a general principle, Walshe demonstrated his grievance against the pro-de Valera stance held by some among the Irish Catholic hierarchy:

> One may wonder, in passing, why such a definitely anti-state crime as the assassination of Kevin O'Higgins was allowed to pass

without a restatement of these elementary truths of ethics and christianity being heard from the teachers of the people.

Walshe went to some lengths to point out the role of the individual as significant only in representing the collective will of the people. Referring to the position held by the British monarch in Ireland, he said that the individual himself had no active part in the process of forming the collective will; that he was merely a constitutional instrument for the purpose of manifesting the people's will. Walshe's philosophical reasoning may have been flawed, but he was attempting to negate the effect of de Valera's attacks on the Cosgrave government by lessening the significance of the pledge it had taken to the British monarch in accepting the Oath of Allegiance. Walshe argued that while the king in Britain represented the will of the people there, the symbol of the king in Ireland represented the will of the people of the Saorstát. There was no significance to be attached to the king as an individual; it was purely a symbolic constitutional instrument:

> The Treaty Oath never at any time involved the English Crown. It is an oath to the King only in his capacity as representing the collective will of our people, and it is accordingly an oath to the people of the Saorstát in their ultimate collective capacity manifested through the state. That is the only basis of such an oath taken by intelligent human beings in any country. The oath of fealty to an individual as such finally disappeared with the last relics of feudalism.

Walshe argued that the Oath of Allegiance was a solemn oath to be taken seriously, as it was a pledge to the collective will of the people of the Irish Free State, and to subvert it was to supplant that inviolable collective will. Here he was criticising de Valera's repudiation of the oath as an 'empty formula', and he asked what loyalty could anyone expect from the people if a section of the 'constitutional' politicians took the oath with 'their tongues in their cheeks'. He also asked how the Church could stand idly by while this assault on the 'foundations of all ethics and religion' was taking place.

Concluding his treatise, Walshe re-emphasised the allegorical nature of the Crown, which was commonly shared by all the people of the Commonwealth. The Irish Free State was part of

what he described as a 'several monarchy', which meant that the Saorstát was just as much a monarchy as Great Britain:

> The nationality of the monarch, who is simply and solely, a constitutional convenience does not matter a pin's weight. The monarch is nothing more than a rubber stamp used by the ministers of the state concerned to express the will of the people of that state. His individual will has no place in the constitution of the state.

While some may view the document as being inappropriate from a civil servant, due to its clearly political overtones, it demonstrates how Walshe felt entirely justified in defending the constitutional gains he had worked so hard to achieve. While he strongly defended the position held by himself and the Cosgrave government, his diminishing of the importance of the Crown in the Irish Free State perhaps indicated the next phase of foreign-policy strategy. If the king or the Oath of Allegiance was important only as a constitutional mechanism, then there could be little ideological objection to its being removed. His forthright statements would possibly allow him little room for manoeuvre if Cumann na nGaedheal failed at the electoral polls. It is clear, therefore, that Walshe was not at this stage anticipating the eventuality of a de Valera-led government.

Despite the advances and achievements made by the Department of External Affairs throughout the 1920s, opposition to the continued development of the department remained. Once more, McGilligan was called upon to defend Walshe:

> As our Department costs less than any other Department of External Affairs in the world, I can only conclude that the authors of the attacks are opposed to the work done by the Department for the betterment of our external position and the recognition of our independence by the States of the world.[105]

He further regarded 'the constant fostering of our relations with the Dominions and other nations' as one of the most important functions of the state. However, his memorandum describing the 'insidious attacks' on the department illustrated the continued lack of appreciation for the work of External Affairs. Perhaps foreign affairs was too abstract to define tangible results and benefits, and Walshe certainly did not make the workings of the

department readily transparent.[106] His secretive style and belief in closed government may have propagated ignorant attitudes that hampered the development of the department.

McGilligan explained that in the desired expansion of the diplomatic network it was considered wiser to 'proceed slowly rather than to establish straight away a piece of cumbrous machinery many elements of which would have to be scrapped with increased experience and knowledge of our peculiar needs'.[107] He explained that the department's policy for future expansion was to 'go forward slowly and to build up by degrees a staff trained from the beginning in the department'. He summed up the department's work by highlighting, in particular, the advancement in expertise that had been required to handle the 'vast amount of extremely arduous and highly exacting technical work'.[108] In fact, McGilligan went as far as to state that External Affairs was responsible for the Free State's international existence.

Another document contained in the McGilligan papers, but probably written after McGilligan had handed over control of External Affairs to de Valera, describes how the responsibilities held by External Affairs at this time had expanded and developed. It gives us a clear idea of the level of authority that Walshe had established over the Irish foreign representatives:

> The Department is in the first instance the normal and, in practice, the only channel of communications between the Executive Council of the Free State and the Governments of Great Britain and the Dominions. It is the competent authority for all questions relating to inter Imperial relations, legal, political, and economic. The representation of the Free State at Imperial Congresses has in ever growing measure devolved in the head of this Department.

It is interesting to note that this document places a strong emphasis on the department's work at the League of Nations:

> It is pre-eminently in the sphere of the League that lies the active foreign policy of the Free State. In Commonwealth relations the policy of this Department has been definitely centrifugal ... As all the above-mentioned developments took place during the period of Mr Cosgrave's administration the policy of the Free State is certain to become even more centrifugal during that of Mr De Valera.[109]

The reference to de Valera is interesting, and indicates the con-
templative mood within the Department of External Affairs in
relation to changes that de Valera might bring.

Joseph Walshe had served the Cosgrave government in a
competent and professional manner over a ten-year period, and
his part in its successes should not be underestimated. From the
beginning of his tenure in Dublin he worked to convince the
government that a Department of External Affairs was essential
to the further development of the state. From a mere skeleton of
a diplomatic service he worked with meagre resources and against
unsympathetic attitudes to establish a professional department.
He developed a unique expertise in a number of foreign-policy
areas, and became invaluable to the Cumann na nGaedheal government. Walshe was an important part of the team that tended
to Irish foreign affairs during this period. According to David
Harkness, the closely knit group, united by its central objective,
led to the development of:

> a unique team of friends, contemporaries and colleagues who had
> been with the department since the foundation of the State. Real
> teamwork was natural between Costello, O'Hegarty, Walshe and
> Hearne, Murphy and Boland. They were all young men, mostly
> with legal training. Civil servants or politicians, they were of the
> same age and from the same class, and they were operating to build
> up a new State. Friends before, they were friends still. Together
> they understood the common aim just as they understood and
> anticipated one another.[110]

Walshe is further described as the 'theoretician of the team', for he
'had the time and leisure denied successively to Kevin O'Higgins,
and to McGilligan and Costello'. Thus, continuity, always important, especially in periods of great change, was provided by
Walshe. He transcended the succession of ministers and bridged
an important gap between politics and policy. He was allowed
the time to develop ideas and his experience of the British civil
service was invaluable in predicting which approaches would
work. Later, the British government's Committee of Operation
of Dominion Legislation (ODL) remarked that this 'strong team,
which was difficult to deter at the best of times … was to prove
irresistible'. Anglo-Irish affairs was one of Walshe's primary

interests and responsibilities, and his aptitude for constitutional law, coupled with his eagerness for negotiation, made him well suited for that role.

The Cosgrave administration was not to last long enough to reap the political benefits of the work that had been done over the previous decade. The Statute of Westminster and the Eucharistic Congress were developments that Walshe believed were historic and momentous. De Valera admitted the importance of these achievements and, despite commonly held fears, continuity rather than change was a dominant theme in de Valera's lengthy period in office. Considering his past criticism of de Valera, Walshe had much to fear from the transfer of power to Fianna Fáil. Indeed, such was his antipathy toward the incoming president, it would not have been surprising if Walshe had resigned his post. As we shall see, Walshe did not resign, but, on the contrary, quickly gained the confidence of the new incumbent, and used this alliance to further ingrain External Affairs within the Free State polity. In fact, Walshe's influence and authority in the area of foreign policy, especially with regard to Anglo-Irish affairs, was to have an important influence on de Valera's policy towards Britain and the Commonwealth. Walshe was an important ambassador for the de Valera administration in promoting continuity and rational decision-making. We have seen how he had been a principal figure in the formulation of Irish foreign policy during the Cosgrave period, and this was not to change in the years to come.

WALSHE AND THE DE VALERA ADMINISTRATION 1932–1939

FOLLOWING THE 1932 general election, Fianna Fáil, with the help of the Labour Party, formed its first government. The transfer of power to a group that ten years previously had challenged the very existence of the Free State was a momentous event in the development of Irish political democracy.[1] The arrival of de Valera led to much anxiety among senior members of the civil service, many of whom had acquired or retained their posts on the basis of their pro-Treaty stance. Joseph Walshe had sworn his allegiance to the pro-Treaty government.[2] Others, including Walshe's predecessor, Robert Brennan, who had left the service in 1922 due to the government's anti-Treaty affiliations, were now expected to return under the Fianna Fáil administration. In his autobiography, Leon Ó Broin, who had been a junior official in the early 1920s, recounted how de Valera, fearful that the civil service would refuse to cooperate with his government, identified key posts occupied by past pupils of Blackrock and Rockwell colleges on whom he could rely.[3] However, the change of administration did not prove as problematic as had been expected. De Valera, while wanting to repay some of his faithful colleagues, realised the value of the support of an experienced civil service.

As we have seen in the previous chapter, Walshe had not only supported the Cosgrave government but had, on a number of occasions, strongly castigated politicians of the 'de Valera type'. These statements were submitted as memoranda to various Cumann na nGaedheal ministers, and de Valera was not likely to have been aware of them. However, considering the vigour with

which Walshe had criticised de Valera it would not have been surprising if Walshe had resigned his post at this juncture. Yet, soon after meeting the new President, Walshe came to see the arrival of de Valera as a new opportunity for the development of the Department of External Affairs. Indeed, Walshe would be roundly criticised by some as a 'trimmer' for the opportunistic way in which he modified his political convictions. Dermot Keogh points out that Walshe did not make himself popular when he began to attend the same daily Mass as de Valera.[4] Others, however, would admire the way in which Walshe not only survived but embraced the change of government to become one of de Valera's most trusted advisers.

Initially, Walshe had good reason to fear de Valera's plans for the department. Throughout the 1920s Fianna Fáil had opposed the yearly estimates for External Affairs on the basis that the representatives abroad did not represent true Irish opinion.[5] Walshe would have been justified in thinking that a change in the upper echelons of the department was close at hand. The former Irish diplomat, Con Cremin, has described how the members of External Affairs awaited the results of Walshe's first meeting with de Valera: 'all five or six of the diplomats at head-quarters – sitting around a table awaiting Walshe's return … The secretary returned and told a somewhat bemused gathering that, 'He is charming, simply charming.'[6] In this way de Valera secured Walshe's support. Conor Cruise O'Brien explains that Walshe's survival was based on his success in conveying two messages to de Valera:

> The first was that Joe could furnish valuable service with remarkable efficiency. The second was that he was prepared to sacrifice his former associates in the service of his new master. Successful politicians value servants of that type, even though they may not particularly esteem them.[7]

Charles Bewley, the Irish minister to the Holy See, who was in Dublin at the time, remembers Walshe's assessment of the new incumbent. He asked Walshe what he thought of de Valera as Minister for External Affairs:

> 'Dev is far and away the best Minister we've ever had,' he answered. 'You'll be delighted with him when you meet him.'

Walshe's enthusiasm went much further, and by the time de Valera called his 'snap election' in 1933 he was telling Bewley, 'It's as good as certain that we'll have a bigger majority this time.' Walshe was obviously pleased that de Valera appeared willing to compromise on certain matters, and Bewley asked him if de Valera would proceed in making Ireland a republic:

> Walshe giggled, as was his habit when pleased with himself and the world. 'I think we've got him off the idea of a Republic.'[8]

Bewley's account of Walshe at this time is interesting as it shows that Walshe believed his role was not to stifle any nationalistic aim de Valera may have had but rather to channel his efforts towards pragmatic and achievable goals. Soon after his first meeting with the new Minister for External Affairs, Walshe wrote a lengthy letter to de Valera advising him on a number of External Affairs issues. The letter, while dealing with official business, was meant as a personal communication for de Valera. It tells much about Walshe's ideas on specific issues such as the Oath of Allegiance, as well as revealing his highly personal administrative style. Walshe told de Valera that the oath could be abolished, but reminded him that his mandate was twofold; not merely to remove the oath but 'to take steps to achieve the independence of the whole of Ireland'. He believed that it was 'all a question of method', and stressed the importance of not making partition permanent through rash political action:

> I am convinced that the latter and more important part of your mandate can be rendered impossible of achievement by the slightest imprudence with regard to the method of carrying out the first.[9]

Walshe saw weaknesses in the arguments for the removal of the Oath of Allegiance. The assertion that the oath was not contained in the Treaty was indefensible because of statements to the contrary made by Irish ministers in the Treaty debates. He believed that the hasty introduction of a bill in the Dáil to remove the oath would, therefore, be careless and destructive to broader Irish objectives. Walshe counselled de Valera to carefully consider his actions:

> For me the whole future of this country depends on how the first

step is taken. A Bill introduced on Tuesday may prove to be a gam-
bler's throw ... What can we lose by waiting for one month? Your
political opponents here and in G.B. want you to go fast?

Walshe concluded that any impulsive action could place the political gains of the past decade in jeopardy. His expectations were
realistic, and he recognised that Ireland's economic position in
relation to Britain was worthy of consideration in relation to foreign-policy matters. 'A boycott of our goods could be engineered',
he said, knowing that Ireland's dairy and other food products could
easily and quickly be substituted by other countries. He warned de
Valera of the political consequences of such a scenario:

> Large elements of the people at home would then begin to turn
> against the Govt. and say we had made a mess of things ... even
> the threat of a boycott of our goods ... would render the difficulties
> of [economic] reconstruction enormously greater.

Walshe, however, did not simply attempt to restrict de Valera's
political objectives. He put forward constructive proposals while
at the same time warning that hasty action, in order to command
greater popular support at home, could 'stultify' future constitutional development.

Walshe was keen to occupy centre stage in foreign-policy
formation within the Fianna Fáil government. It is not surprising,
therefore, that his proposals to de Valera involved himself as a
central figure. He suggested that the British government be
informed that the removal of the oath was imperative for the
building of friendly relations between the two countries. On the
diplomatic front, Walshe offered to do much of the groundwork:

> There need not be any visit of Ministers to London. That would
> cause trouble here. Let me have an attempt at [seeing] an insight
> into the possibilities. I can convey positive views through the heads
> of the [Dominions] office to their masters. I can tell them that the
> Oath must be removed, if necessary without British consent.

Walshe's suggestions contained sound diplomatic advice. With
this method, he would be able to determine de Valera's position
and the attitude of the British government, while at the same
time avoiding a major confrontation. Walshe suggested that the

issue be first dealt with by the diplomatic corps rather than rely-
ing solely on political means of communication.

Dermot Keogh has described this letter as a 'shrewd attempt
to wean de Valera away from the politics of confrontation'.[10]
Indeed, we will see that one of Walshe's major roles at this time
was to influence de Valera in particular directions and temper his
approach to certain aspects of foreign policy. However, the apparent speed with which Walshe altered his stance on a number of
issues following the election of de Valera may lead some to question the strength of his convictions. Forgotten now, it seems, were
his previous objections to de Valera's anti-clerical, pro-communist
leanings. If we are to explain, albeit not justify, Walshe's about-
face we should point out that Walshe's past remarks concerning
de Valera were made in a different political context. De Valera
was now the constitutionally elected leader of the people, and
Walshe discovered they held similar views on a number of issues.
De Valera, in turn, realised that he could utilise Walshe's expertise. Under de Valera's leadership, Walshe understood that his
influence over certain matters would grow but diminish in relation to others. Although de Valera may have been less concerned
with the day-to-day operations of External Affairs, he would
maintain absolute control over foreign-policy decision-making.
Walshe would continue to influence, guide and implement foreign policy, but ultimately de Valera would direct it.

Despite his initial misgivings, therefore, Walshe came to see
de Valera's arrival as an opportunity to increase the standing
and influence of External Affairs. De Valera considered foreign
affairs a crucial area of importance and wished to maintain a
high level of influence over policy. This was demonstrated by his
own appointment as Minister for External Affairs, a post he held
in conjunction with that of President of the Executive Council.
Ultimately, Walshe saw this as something of a coup. The new
president would also be his minister, and therefore the most powerful member of the Executive Council. Walshe was optimistic
that External Affairs would receive priority treatment, and if he
could persuade de Valera of the merits of expanding the department he could be sure that there would be little opposition to
such proposals in Cabinet.

It has already been pointed out that when Walshe first met de
Valera he found him to be 'charming'. Walshe was surprised, in

fact, to find they were in agreement on a large number of issues. De Valera's foremost aim was 'the unity of this nation'. Walshe did not disagree with this, but had firm ideas on how this objective should be attained, and consequently counselled for prudence and patience. Knowing that this was difficult, he tried to give de Valera some hope:

> I believe that you can achieve the unity of this country within seven years and that we can have our complete independence without calling this country by any particular constl. [constitutional] name. 'Ireland' will be our name, and our international position will let the world and the people at home know that we are independent.[11]

While Walshe's prescribed course was not fully accepted, he did manage to temper de Valera's approach to Anglo-Irish relations. The following years would show that, despite having initiated an 'economic war', de Valera would remain open to negotiating with Britain. In order to do this effectively, he relied on Walshe keeping up to date with British opinion. Walshe provided extensive and expert information on these constitutional issues, ably assisted by the department's legal adviser, John J. Hearne. However, de Valera was not easily swayed, and chose his own course of action. Dermot Keogh suggests that the lessons of the following six years in Anglo-Irish relations may have encouraged de Valera to see the wisdom of Walshe's advice after the event.[12] Walshe, who was not opposed to de Valera's objectives, displayed tact and dexterity in shaping the president's approach.

From the outset, Walshe had to adjust to fundamental differences between the Cumann na nGaedheal and Fianna Fáil governments. While Cosgrave had sought the development of the Irish Free State through the Commonwealth, de Valera was intent on advance through a revolutionary departure from it.[13] Fianna Fáil's 1932 election manifesto promised two main objectives: the removal of the Oath of Allegiance and the withholding of the land annuities payable to the British exchequer. On coming to power de Valera indicated that the land annuities would no longer be paid. He rejected that there was any 'formal and explicit undertaking' to continue the payments in the face of Dominions Office insistence that to retain the funds would be a violation of an international agreement between the British

government and the Irish Free State.[14] De Valera's action was part of his overall attitude of progressive constitutional development, where the independence of the Free State would be advanced. There followed a tense period in Anglo-Irish relations as the British retaliated by taxing imports of Irish cattle into the United Kingdom. As the economic war escalated, de Valera continued his reformation of the Treaty, concerning himself primarily with the oath, the office of the Governor General and the Privy Council appeal procedure. While it had been hoped to keep the constitutional issues separate from the economic relations with Britain, this proved impossible. Walshe's earlier warnings to de Valera regarding Ireland's precarious economic position were now seen to be highly accurate.

In April 1932 de Valera wrote to the Secretary of State for Dominion Affairs, J.H. Thomas, describing the oath 'an intolerable burden to the people of this State' and that 'they have declared in the most formal manner that they desire its instant removal'. He further stated that:

> To England this agreement gave peace and added prestige. In Ireland it raised brother's hand against brother, gave us ten years of blood and tears and besmirched the name of Ireland wherever a foul propaganda has been able to misrepresent us.[15]

He added that the Treaty had meant 'the consummation of the outrage of partition, and the alienation of the most sacred part of our national territory with all the cultural and material loss that this unnatural separation entails'. De Valera reiterated the objection to the continued payment of the land annuities, stating that his government was not aware of any undertaking or obligation to pay them. Contrary to Walshe's advice, these statements were not written in the language of conciliation.

In June 1932 Thomas and the Secretary for War, Lord Halisham, met de Valera in Dublin to discuss the possibility of arbitration over the land-annuities dispute. De Valera accepted the principle of adjudication, but was unable to agree to the restriction of the panel of jurors to Commonwealth citizens only. Meanwhile, the money collected by the Free State authorities was to be set aside in a 'suspense account' in anticipation of an agreement. These funds did not remain suspended for long, and were soon to make

their way into the Irish exchequer. However, the proposal did for a time help to keep the idea of an agreed solution open. While penal trade tariffs were implemented by both sides, de Valera demonstrated a willingness to avoid all-out hostility. Walshe's appeals to keep the channels of communication open were influential in persuading de Valera to adopt a more diplomatic approach than may have been previously considered.

Later that year, de Valera included Walshe among the Irish delegation to the Imperial Economic Conference in Canada. The latter part of 1932 was a period of great activity for all concerned. 'The Department was going mad!' wrote Boland, who, having been sent to Paris in January was subsequently sent to Ottawa due to a shortage of staff.[16] At the conference, Walshe acted as adviser and secretary to the delegation, which included the Vice-President, Seán T.O'Kelly, the Minister for Industry and Commerce, Seán Lemass, and the Minister for Agriculture, James Ryan. Walshe's expertise in Anglo-Irish constitutional issues and his experience of such conferences was widely recognised. It was important that de Valera's team perform well on its first major international outing since coming to power. There would be considerable interest in the Irish delegation, and Walshe would be instrumental in providing the expertise necessary for a competent contribution.

The correspondence between the conference delegation and departmental headquarters gives little indication as to Walshe's personal input or his attitude towards particular issues, except as part of the delegation as a whole. The nature of his role meant that Walshe was always fully informed. Responsible for communication with Dublin, he was privy to the correspondence between O'Kelly and de Valera.[17] To draw any major conclusions would be to read too much into the available documentation, especially as the conclusions of the Ottawa conference were few, and the scope and latitude of the Irish delegates had been considerably narrowed by de Valera, who always kept in mind the Treaty negotiations of 1921.[18] Walshe's inclusion in the delegation was an indication of the growing trust de Valera placed in him. Their relationship had been advanced in the preceding months with the successful hosting of the thirty-first International Eucharistic Congress in Dublin in the summer of 1932. De Valera took advantage of the extensive preparations made by the Cosgrave government for this celebration of Catholicism. That de Valera was ready to display

genuine devotion as well as performing the statesman's role was of considerable relief to Walshe.

The Eucharistic Congress, however, was not without its diplomatic and procedural worries for Walshe. The Irish representative to the Holy See, Charles Bewley, reported that the Vatican would expect some state decoration to be bestowed on the papal legate, Cardinal Lorenzo Lauri, at the Congress. Walshe replied that the Irish Free State did not have any such decoration or honour that it could bestow on the Pope's representative, and the state did not wish to establish one especially for the occasion. Some offence was taken by the Vatican, which gave Walshe cause for concern. Further procedural issues would also be encountered. Somewhat comically, when Lauri arrived in Dún Laoghaire he mistook de Valera and the government ministers for 'special branch' men, as they refused to wear the formal dress and top hats, opting instead for 'dark coats and soft hats'.[19] Overall, however, these incidents were considered minor, and the Congress itself was regarded as a success, much to the delight of Walshe.

This international event did not interrupt the pace of constitutional change de Valera wished to introduce, and, indeed, the Congress was almost marred by the government's policy towards the position of Governor General. There was considerable tension with Britain during this period, as de Valera wished to diminish the responsibilities of James McNeill, who held the office at that time.[20] Through Walshe, he advised the Governor General not to invite government members to any official functions. Throughout this process de Valera used Walshe as a conduit to convey to McNeill the gradual erosion of the powers of the Governor General's office. The use of Walshe for this purpose was itself a symbolic slight, and McNeill reacted strongly, claiming that 'de Valera's message conveyed verbally by a civil servant had suggested a profound ignorance of the duty the President had owed the people in connection with the Eucharistic Congress'.[21] As the crisis came to a head, de Valera asked Walshe to compile a report on the visits he had made to the Governor General. Walshe pieced much of this memorandum together from memory. Even though it was a recent event it is somewhat surprising that he did not possess all the correspondence:

The other note which I cannot find and probably have torn up,

was dated about a fortnight later as it was an invitation to go and
see him urgently.[22]

Walshe's casual reference to tearing up his notes following an
important meeting is alarming. In this case the letter in question
may not have thrown any light on the substantive issues involved
but it highlights Walshe's approach to such matters and illustrates
the difficulties in putting together a comprehensive commentary
on such events. Had de Valera not requested a written memorandum our understanding may have been greatly diminished.

In his memorandum, Walshe recounted that, within weeks of
coming to power, de Valera requested that he pay his first visit to
the Governor General. While there was no animosity towards
McNeill personally, Walshe stated that it would be better if the
Governor General's office did not issue invitations to de Valera
or any of his ministers to attend a state reception organised by
him to honour the Pope's legate at the Eucharistic Congress. The
Governor General initially appeared to accept the situation, but
there soon followed a number of incidents in which the Free
State ministers snubbed functions that were attended by McNeill.
One such incident occurred when, at a reception at the French
legation, Frank Aiken and Seán T. O'Kelly left the function on
the arrival of McNeill. The following day Walshe visited McNeill,
who did not appear to have noticed the affront. Later, however,
he complained to the President about the discourteous treatment
he was being subjected to.[23] As the Eucharistic Congress drew
near, he became more irate, and in a heated conversation with
Walshe said that he had the right to invite anyone he liked to
particular functions. Walshe recalled that, about two weeks before
the Congress, McNeill said that he was going to invite a number
of distinguished visitors to his residence, with or without the
approval of the government.

McNeill threatened to publish the correspondence between
himself and de Valera on the discourtesies shown by the Irish
government towards his office. Walshe predicted that the correspondence would never be published. He regarded the threat
as 'the purest bluff', and said that no Governor General 'with a
grain of sanity would so jeopardise the very foundations of his
office ... It would be exceedingly detrimental to the whole insti-
tution in the Commonwealth, and unless he gets quite out of

hand he has no intention of carrying out his threat.'[24] His assessment in this regard, however, was quite wrong, and within a week McNeill had taken the step Walshe had refused to contemplate. In an attempt to turn things in his favour, de Valera used the situation as a pretext to reform the position of the Governor General. A number of approaches were made to the king through Walshe and Dulanty, who explained that the publication of the correspondence had severely strained their relationship with the Governor General. De Valera was willing to accept the king's suggestion that McNeill be given the opportunity to resign.[25] It was also proposed that the Irish Free State government advise the king as to the choice of McNeill's successor, and that the investment procedure should exclude the Oath of Allegiance. Clearly, the suggestion indicated a radical altering of the position of the Governor General.

These actions by the Free State on the oath, the annuities and the Governor General were seen as a further attack on the Treaty, and Walshe was instrumental in tempering Britain's reaction. In late October 1932 he met with Dominions Office officials and outlined a number of proposals aimed at resolving their constitutional and economic differences. Walshe stated that, while the law was currently being enforced, the Oath of Allegiance and the Governor General were resented in Ireland, and that as long as they remained in place there was little chance of Anglo-Irish relations developing along friendly and cooperative lines.[26] The Irish Situation Committee (ISC), which had been established by the British to deal with Anglo-Irish matters, considered these questions following Walshe's submissions. J.H. Thomas reported on the negotiations, stating that Walshe had travelled to London to talk with the Dominions Office about a settlement. He cautiously noted that Walshe had come with de Valera's 'knowledge and approval' for the visit, but did not have his 'authority' for what might be said. Using this ambiguity, Walshe suggested to assistant under-secretary Harry Batterbee that an agreement might be reached along the following lines:

· a settlement of the financial dispute on a fifty-fifty basis;
· acceptance of the settlement 'as a friendly settlement as between two Members of the Commonwealth';
· an immediate trade agreement.[27]

Walshe insisted that this was not an official offer but indicated that if there was general acceptance to the idea he would return to London in a couple of days to see what further progress could be made. Batterbee outlined to Walshe the essential points that the British government would adhere to before making any settlement, including that acceptance of the 1921 Treaty and the subsequent financial settlement was crucial before any further developments could be made. If the Irish government agreed to these principles as well as undertaking not to proceed with the Oath Bill and not to abolish the office of the Governor General, then Britain would consider proceeding with negotiations with the objective of arriving at a 'friendly settlement'.

At this stage, therefore, the British were not willing to allow much in the way of concessions, and Walshe was under pressure to break the logjam. Batterbee described Walshe as being on the defensive:

> Sir Harry Batterbee explained … that in his interview with Mr Walshe, he had endeavoured to elicit Mr Walshe's views without giving any indication of the possible attitude of the United Kingdom Government, except to indicate those points which he knew they regarded as fundamental.[28]

Batterbee claimed that Walshe had succumbed to his questioning and revealed confidential information while revealing nothing of importance himself. While we must be somewhat sceptical about this one-sided version of events, it is clear that the meeting had, from an Irish point of view, given a bad impression. Walshe may have appeared overeager to find a solution. The Irish Situation Committee concluded that de Valera was now getting desperate, and that his offer of a 'friendly settlement as between two Members of the Commonwealth' was regarded as a great step forward, if only they could be sure that it was a genuine expression of his willingness to accept the Commonwealth. Walshe had indicated to Batterbee that de Valera was continually moving towards a settlement, and that if a generous offer were made he would be likely to accept the Commonwealth and the immutability of the Treaty. After consultations with de Valera, Walshe, eager to make a better impression, returned with two documents outlining further possible compromise. Walshe was clearly enthusiastic

about reaching agreement, but circumstance did not favour an early settlement. De Valera had used the Governor General controversy to further his reform of the Free State's constitutional relationship with Britain. The British, therefore, were distrustful of any proposed agreement, considering de Valera appeared to be unstoppable in his efforts to dismantle the Treaty.

The Irish Situation Committee carefully considered what Batterbee should say in reply to Walshe, who was on his way back to London. It was recommended that a strong position be adopted on the 1921 Anglo-Irish Agreement, and assurances sought from the Irish government that no change to the Treaty could be made without the agreement of the British government.[29] The British also insisted that the validity of their previous financial settlements should not be questioned. While recognising that the trade question was of crucial importance for the Free State, they attempted to use this as leverage on the question of the oath and the office of the Governor General. If consensus could be reached on these two points then, and only then, would the British government be willing to begin negotiations on a trade agreement with the Irish government. De Valera's assault on Anglo-Irish constitutional relations caused resentment in British circles, and this made Walshe's task of finding agreement extremely difficult. While the official position was that the Irish Free State should not question the previous financial settlements with the British government, the British did indicate that negotiations on this issue could take place as part of any future trade settlement. Walshe recognised that the constitutional issues took precedence over the financial dispute, and he may have wanted to focus on that area, as de Valera was insisting on progress on the oath and the Governor General.

A week later Walshe and the Irish High Commissioner in London, John Dulanty, met the king's private secretary, Lord Wigram. Dulanty opened by saying that de Valera was anxious to get an early settlement. Wigram replied that agreement could have been reached had de Valera put forward some suggestion for the taking of the oath, which was in accordance with the Treaty and the Constitution. De Valera had suggested that the Chief Justice should act temporarily in place of the Governor General, but Wigram said that this would only be acceptable if the Chief Justice took the necessary oath. This did not suit the Irish, but it

was thought the difficulty could be overcome if de Valera advised the king that the recommendation was being made on the advice of the Attorney General of the Irish Free State. The king, however, could not consent to anything that was in breach of the Treaty or Constitution of the Irish Free State. Wigram warned that if de Valera did put forward this recommendation it would have to be backed up by the signed opinion of the Attorney General, and added that 'if His Majesty were in any doubt the advice of the Attorney General of the United Kingdom would naturally have to be taken.'[30] If Walshe had been hopeful that a formula agreeable to all would be found at this meeting, then he was to be sorely disappointed.

Having reached this impasse, Walshe and Dulanty risked escalating tensions by pointing out that if de Valera's formal advice to the king was refused there would be a constitutional crisis in the Irish Free State, following which it would be difficult to keep the king's name. Wigram retorted that as de Valera was the king's Prime Minister in Ireland, it was up to him to prevent any such constitutional crisis from arising. He continued that it was unlikely that the British monarch would act in an unconstitutional manner 'in order to have Mr de Valera out of a difficulty which was of his own creation'. Walshe, according to Wigram, was much quieter and more thoughtful than on his previous visit, and Wigram somewhat naively believed that this was a sign that Walshe and Dulanty had understood the situation as he had explained it. However, what Walshe had really understood was that these talks were doomed to failure and a different diplomatic strategy would have to be adopted. Ultimately, as neither side moved close enough to agreement, the talks ended inconclusively.

Deirdre McMahon is critical of Walshe in these negotiations, asserting that he seriously and inaccurately underestimated the extent to which de Valera and the British officials found each other's terms acceptable. This demonstrated what she terms his 'besetting sin', which, according to McMahon, was 'a tendency to exaggerate'. Walshe's timing was bad and his statements to British officials describing 'the harmony, friendships and close co-operation which should exist between ... two co-equal members of the British Commonwealth' could only have been seen as hypocritical to the British, who felt under siege from what seemed an aggressive constitutional assault against the Treaty, especially in the light

of the renewed crisis over the position of Governor General.[31] McMahon's assessment that Walshe had exaggerated the closeness of the two sides is accurate. De Valera's election platform had been based on the removal of the oath and the retention of the land annuities. He was not going to risk an electoral backlash by compromising on these issues, especially as the idea of calling an election to gain an overall majority was already being seriously considered. The British, for their part, were not sure if de Valera was a permanent political entity, and hoped that he might soon be ousted by the Irish electorate. Furthermore, they did not want to destabilise the Empire by opening the floodgates of constitutional change, and so were equally uncompromising. Thus, Walshe was leading negotiations that may have already been doomed to failure. Yet he made the trip to London with de Valera's approval, and his visit was useful in finding out what could be obtained from the British in the event of more serious negotiations. Ironically, his exaggeration of the closeness of the two sides may have brought them a step closer. As always, he was a persuasive force in fostering the idea that agreement was possible. For now, however, the climate was not right for agreement, and Walshe would have to bide his time until the conditions allowed for more compromising attitudes to develop.

These failed negotiations were followed by a period of respite in the intense Anglo-Irish contacts, during which Walshe was able to rejuvenate some of his lost energy. The previous twelve months had brought many changes and challenges for him. Before 1932 had begun he would not have imagined himself traversing the political divide from Cosgrave to de Valera. However, when the time came he guided the new President's foreign policy in relation to Britain, and took part in many lengthy negotiations. Walshe took pride in the belief that he had channelled de Valera's aggressive intentions towards a more temperate approach. He also established a healthy relationship with de Valera, and had used the opportunity to usher in a new era for the Department of External Affairs. Walshe's initial scepticism concerning de Valera's political pedigree had been quelled. The new President had firmly established himself as a Catholic statesman, and in the following year would compound this with a visit to the Vatican. Joseph Walshe would have dearly loved to accompany de Valera on that visit, but around the middle of 1933 he was in poor health.

Throughout his life he worried about his health, as there was a history of tuberculosis in his family. The events of the previous year had taken their toll, and at the end of April 1933 he was hospitalised in Dublin. He decided to see a heart specialist in Germany, and was pleased to hear that de Valera approved of his proposed visit to a health spa in Baden, and thanked him for his kind enquiries. De Valera's planned visit to Rome was an occasion that would indeed pain Walshe to miss, but he predicted that it would be a great success. Eager to ensure that de Valera was on the right track, he told him that 'there are a few things in my mind about Rome which I should like to go over with you.'[32] Walshe was reluctant to let de Valera visit the Pope without first proffering some advice on the intricacies of Vatican politics.

A month later, Walshe replied to a letter he had received from de Valera, who had by then completed his trip. Writing from Cologne, Walshe said he believed that official visits of that nature by the Irish President were crucial to the development of Anglo-Irish relations:

> There is no doubt whatever that your reception in Rome and Paris in your full official ... capacity was an event of the very first importance in our relations with Great Britain. It has brought us a favourable – perhaps a pen-ultimate settlement – distinctly nearer.[33]

He saw this visit as a breakthrough in what he termed the 'paper wall' and considered it 'another big push forward of our first line of defence against English interference'. As a logical extension of this visit, he urged de Valera to consider making an excursion to the United States. De Valera was no stranger to America, but this would be his first visit as the officially recognised head of state. 'We must not hesitate', Walshe advised, 'to make every possible use of our present status to reach our goal', adding, 'even though that method may cause misunderstandings (which you can dissipate in one speech) amongst some of our people, especially in America.' Walshe was supremely confident in the Irish leader's powers of persuasion, and urged him to take every opportunity possible to legitimise the Irish problem by making official visits and addressing international conferences:

If I were at home, I would urge you very strongly to spend at least a week at the London Conference and to find an opportunity for making a speech there. It is a great chance to continue the policy of creating new and salient historical facts which is the only effective way of getting the ear of the world.

Walshe was clearly disappointed at having missed the 'wonderful days in Rome', and he anxiously awaited a full report from Seán Murphy, the Irish representative there.

Walshe's heart treatment in Germany was proceeding well, and he was confident that he would make a full recovery. De Valera wrote suggesting plenty of walking, and sent messages of encouragement to the absent secretary. Walshe greatly regretted leaving External Affairs for so long. His primary consideration was to recover fully so that he could resume his duties as quickly as possible. 'I wanted to try and get fundamentally cured', he said, 'in the only country where they appear to take risks with the heart for that end.'[34] He had considered staying at home where he would have been able to keep in touch with the office but he had found the doctors in Dublin had little to offer but 'amiable tack' and 'unsatisfactory advice'. He added that they charged considerably more than the most senior specialists in Germany, who gave much better value for money by looking after their patients from morning till night. While convalescing Walshe became somewhat lonely and felt isolated from his work. He was not married and his correspondence makes no mention of family. He was grateful, therefore, for the contact with de Valera, saying it was 'a source of the greatest encouragement' which had greatly helped him towards recovery. 'Isolation and serious heart trouble', he explained, 'had combined to bring about a state of depression which was a definite hindrance to my cure.' De Valera had anxiously sought from Walshe information regarding his proposed return to Dublin. This was probably a genuine desire on de Valera's part, but it served as a boost to Walshe, who felt he was needed back home. Walshe wrote that his doctor had advised that he would not be able to travel home until September, and he thought it wise to cure himself fully in order that he could devote his full energies to the resumption of his duties on his return.

Walshe's devotion to External Affairs is evident when he says, 'Work is the only thing that makes life worth living, and you

never feel that so much as when you are reduced to almost absolute passivity over a long period. I only wish I could go back now.' However, not wanting to miss an opportunity, he was adamant that his temporary stay in Germany could be of some use. He followed, as closely as he could, German politics and came to admire the energised society he found there. He was impressed by the apparent regeneration of Germany under Hitler, who had become Chancellor earlier that year. Unemployment numbers, for example, fell from 6 million in January 1933 to 3.7 million in September of that year.[35] In comparison with other economies, Germany's economic growth was not so spectacular, but the organisation and propaganda of National Socialism led many to believe Hitler was Germany's saviour. Walshe's convalescence had given him time to think, and he advised de Valera that he too should take a holiday, saying that 'the most fruitful ideas often come to one away from one's work and ordinary preoccupations.' He told de Valera of the atmosphere in Germany and of the 'great experiments' that were being carried out, 'the essentials of which we may well have to initiate in Ireland'. Indeed, Walshe went considerably further when he advised the following:

> It seems to me inevitable that if you are to get leisure to think for yourself and your Ministers, as well as time to work you will have to give Parlt. [parliament] a holiday for an indefinite period.[36]

In this regard Walshe's correspondence is somewhat shocking, and it is hard to know how seriously we should take his comments. Perhaps, by being on leave, he felt he had the freedom to explore idle musings, but it is interesting that he did not confine his comments to the idea of giving the Irish parliament an extended holiday for the purposes of political expediency. For example, he told de Valera that a more aggressive strategy would be needed to deal with the partition problem:

> It is also exceedingly likely that you will have to carry through a policy of political unification. I know how abhorrent anything in the nature of force is to you, but there is no reason why you should not succeed by other and better methods than those employed elsewhere.

He was not advocating physical force but he did seem to be suggesting that constitutional government could be discarded during a period of crisis:

> The position of our state is at least as parlous as that of other states in which the ordinary constitutional forms have been set aside for a time by the majority – as is absolutely within their rights.

Walshe continued his treatise to comment on the education system. Compared to Germany, Walshe thought the Irish system was 'deplorable', and he felt it militated against de Valera initiating radical social change throughout the country. 'How different it is here', he lamented, 'where there is at least one intelligent, well educated, and cultured person in the smallest community ready to form a link in a great national movement.' Walshe believed part of the problem lay with the teachers in Irish schools. He wondered how many of them would be willing to spend their spare time working for the benefit of the general interest. He suggested the idea of teachers being 'real state servants' so that they might be more inclined to turn their interests towards working for the people as a whole.

Walshe also addressed the question of the recently published German–Vatican Concordat of July 1933, which protected German Catholic property and educational institutions on the condition that Catholic priests in Germany would abstain from politics.[37] Walshe was grateful that the Irish Free State did not need to have a concordat with the Holy See, but did suggest that the German concordat could be used to push for changes in the relationship between the Irish Free State and the Vatican. Walshe was suspicious that the British government was given prior knowledge of Irish episcopal appointments. He greatly objected to this malfeasance, and said that the Irish government should be asked for its opinion on all appointments and should have the right to object to any unsuitable candidates. As with the teachers, Walshe stressed the importance of having 'distinguished and saintly' bishops in order to develop 'an educated and cultured people'. A 'cultured and devoted' priesthood would also be expected to contribute in great measure to this by devoting every spare minute to the 'social and educational service of the people' in order to rid society of the 'inertia' he believed to be prevalent in Ireland at the time.

Towards the end of this letter to de Valera, Walshe returned

to the role of Dáil Éireann and how it might be improved. He had seen reports of the Dáil debate on the Book of Estimates and was outraged at the opposition criticism. Walshe was probably referring to the debate on 11 July 1933 in which Desmond FitzGerald, the former Minister for External Affairs, made a number of critical remarks directed towards de Valera. FitzGerald had said that the Ottawa conference of the previous year and the current Anglo-Irish economic war were a disaster for Ireland. He criticised de Valera for bringing in outsiders to make a number of trips to the United States. According to FitzGerald, this indicated that the Minister for External Affairs was not satisfied with the officials in his department. He also accused Fianna Fáil of taking covert steps to get the party financed by the Russian Bolshevik government.[38] But the criticism that probably most irritated Walshe was the questioning of the Taoiseach's visit to Rome. FitzGerald asked if de Valera's visit and personal pilgrimage was paid for out of the External Affairs budget. Walshe did not disguise his anger:

> I was pained and disgusted at the speech made by a certain opposition deputy, and I wished I could have been a T.D. for a day in order to answer it and my answer would have been fundamental and annihilating, because I know, only too well, to what petty whims, and personal motives the major interests of the people have been so frequently subordinated by that particular deputy.[39]

Walshe's suggestions in relation to the Dáil became progressively more radical. He used the letter as an opportunity to voice his personal antagonism towards the shortcomings of the parliament, suggesting that deputies might be given a 'holiday'. While it was fashionable to do so in the 1930s, Walshe did not wish to express any hostility to parliamentary democracy as such; rather, it was the politics of the day that frustrated him greatly:

> Having read that speech I am still more convinced that Parliament must remain a useless institution so long as it is used by the opposition solely as an instrument for getting back to power.

This was one of Walshe's more revealing letters to de Valera during his tenure as secretary of External Affairs. His desire to communicate, coupled with his self-admitted isolation, had led

him to commit to paper much more than he would normally permit; he greatly missed his regular meetings and telephone conversations with de Valera. However, considering the ruthless and racist nature of Hitler's National Socialism he had, perhaps, a naive or ill-informed view of Germany at that time. This was, perhaps, worrying, as Walshe was one of the Free State's primary diplomats and foreign-policy advisers.

If we are to put into context some of the ideas and the sentiments expressed by Walshe in this letter we must read it as a private and personal communication to de Valera. Walshe felt free to express certain ideas to de Valera about his experiences in Germany. There was little indication at this stage of the lengths Hitler would go to in his quest to rejuvenate Germany – economically, politically and ethnically. Walshe may have been impressed by some aspects of German National Socialism, but he was no Nazi sympathiser. This was apparent when he sharply criticised Charles Bewley's ideological tendencies during the mid to late 1930s. Following his tenure at the Holy See, Bewley had been appointed the Free State's representative to Germany, where he remained until 1939. Bewley made little effort to hide his admiration for events in Germany:

> I needed no argument to convince me that National Socialism, whatever might be its defects, should be upheld by the Western Powers as the strongest, perhaps the only, force which could prevent the spread of the Communist Empire over half Europe.[40]

Bewley, who had written to Walshe concerning the anti-German views expressed in an *Irish Press* article, received a strong reprimand from Walshe, who by this time had gained a greater awareness of Hitler's Germany. He chastised the Irish minister in Berlin for the personal and subjective nature of the complaint, and he made it clear that Bewley's views were not supported in Iveagh House:

> It would be unfortunate if a paper which is known to have affiliations with a political party in power could give expression to no views about foreign countries which might be unpalatable to their rulers. Foreign countries like Germany which offend against the good feelings of other nations by their persecution of Christians and Jews and generally ignore the sentiments of nations other than their own cannot expect the world Press, even when it does

happen to represent the views of the Governments, to ignore its fundamental duty of formulating the view of the average man in the country concerned.[41]

Walshe's reprimand of Bewley could be regarded as hypocritical considering his earlier views on Hitler's Germany. While it is not clear when exactly Walshe revised his views on Germany, it was not unusual for him to reassess his views on certain matters based on new information or on a change in general opinion. To be fair to Walshe, his views had been based on events in the early 1930s when Hitler appeared to be transforming the German economy and channelling the energies of the German public towards the greater good. By 1937, however, Hitler's real intentions had become much more apparent, and Walshe's instructions to Bewley were aimed at aligning him to that revised view.

Bewley was highly critical of Walshe and his management of External Affairs. He alleged that he had often sought instructions from Walshe but had received none. In this case, however, Walshe was clear in his opinion towards Germany, and Bewley was left in no doubt as to his advised course of action:

> If official Germany continues to insult actively the most sacred beliefs of the people of this and other Christian countries of the world, there may easily be a movement here in favour of closing down our Mission in Berlin. No doubt, in conjunction with the other Representatives in Berlin you have from time to time informed the Foreign Minister how impossible it is to secure a better tone towards Germany in the Press or in public opinion so long as the German Government openly vilifies the tenets which are common to us all.

Bewley believed that Irish foreign policy showed too much deference or 'servility' towards Britain, and he advocated a more independent line. He criticised the duplicitous nature of de Valera's foreign policy which, in his view, emphasised Ireland's independent nature solely for domestic political consumption. He had previously received a rebuke from Walshe, who criticised his emphasis on Ireland's 'anti-English or non-English nature of our policy'. For Bewley, without this emphasis Ireland could just as well have been represented abroad by Britain.[42] Walshe, however, fundamentally disagreed with this logic:

The actions or views of newspapers or of the Government of this country should not be regarded as ipso facto wrong because they happen to be in conformity with opinion in the neighbouring country, and the Minister is still at a loss to understand how this frequent community of view in international matters between this country and Great Britain can in any way prevent our Ministers abroad from pursuing their task of obtaining the fullest recognition for Irish nationality.[43]

Bewley was unhappy with the vagueness and ambiguity of his instructions generally. He sought clarification regarding the arrival in Berlin of a new ambassador from the Soviet Union. Considering Ireland's anti-communist stance he asked Walshe for specific directions regarding his relations towards the new arrival. Bewley was told to 'do nothing which might give a reasonable ground for feeling offended to the Soviet Ambassador'. Bewley believed the ambiguity in these instructions gave External Affairs the opportunity to blame him if something went wrong:

The responsibility for deciding on the course to be taken was left to me, while the Department apparently reserved to itself the right to disavow later whatever decision I might make.[44]

Later, with world conflict apparently imminent, Bewley asked for instructions and again met with silence, believing that this was punishment for previous insubordination. On visits to Dublin he claims he was ignored by Walshe and de Valera, believing that they feared the questions he would ask. He was soon recalled to Dublin and offered a lower-ranking position. He refused and resigned, but not before writing a final memorandum on the state of the Department of External Affairs. He cited Seán Lester as saying 'Our Department has never even begun to function', and Bewley wholeheartedly agreed. The primary cause for what he termed the failure of Walshe and External Affairs to adopt an independent foreign policy was the servility and 'inferiority complex' towards Britain. 'So long as British institutions … are regarded as the only possible model for Irish Government Departments', he said, 'so long will it be impossible to expect an objective or independent view on international affairs.' He blamed lack of experience and a 'reluctance or incapacity to learn', and the unwillingness of headquarters to inform them:

In other states one of the first duties of the Ministries of Foreign Affairs is considered to be the instruction of their Ministers abroad as to the policy of their government, and in particular as to the answers to be given to particular enquiries about their policy. The officials of the Irish Department of External Affairs obviously do not consider such instruction as any part of their duties, and indeed resent any suggestion that their present practice could be improved in any respect, with the natural result that Irish Ministers abroad are never in a position to explain the attitude of the Irish Government on any subject to the Government to which they are accredited, and that the Government to which they are accredited assumes that the Irish Government has no policy except that of Great Britain.

His assessment of External Affairs and of Irish foreign policy generally is scathing both of Walshe and the government in equal measure. He believed his position as a foreign representative was made impossible by the fact that Irish foreign policy was impossible to determine and that this seemed to be perfectly acceptable in headquarters:

If in fact the Irish Government has no such policy, the officials of the Department cannot be blamed for not communicating it. If on the other hand an independent policy exists, it is difficult to see why it should be kept as a secret not only from foreign governments but from the representatives of the Irish Government itself?

Bewley was highly critical of de Valera's secretive nature. This, he felt, was why Ireland's foreign representatives did not receive instructions and why Ireland's foreign representatives were not shown each other's reports or given a chance to meet. In conversation with Walshe he said that the Swiss government held an annual conference of its foreign representatives and suggested that Iveagh House should do the same. It was a reasonable suggestion to which Walshe replied somewhat sardonically, 'If they were to meet, they would probably combine against Headquarters.'[45] Bewley saw the intended humour in the comment but felt that it also reflected the spirit, influenced by de Valera's secrecy, that animated the department.

Bewley would have been fascinated to learn of Walshe's ideas

as contained in his letters to de Valera in the early 1930s but, apart from his views on German politics, it is also interesting to note that Walshe, in his correspondence from Germany, seemed to pledge his support to de Valera in the upcoming election. In 1933 de Valera called a 'snap' general election in which he hoped to achieve an overall majority. Walshe hoped so too, as he had become optimistic at the regeneration in External Affairs facilitated by the enthusiasm of Éamon de Valera. He was determined that the stature of the Irish Free State President on the international stage would not be lost on those who had criticised the need for External Affairs. He urged de Valera to remain on as Minister for External Affairs, and emphasised that 'the same mind must directly control what are, really, only two facets – the external and the internal – of the same groups of activities of our State life.'[46] Thus, in a very short time Walshe had completely altered his view of de Valera, and hoped, following another election, that he would be able to continue to harness the president's enthusiasm in support of External Affairs.

Walshe's opportunism did not escape the notice of officials at de Valera's 'other' ministry. It was the opinion of Michael MacDunphy, assistant secretary at the Department of the President, that Walshe and his department had usurped too much power. In January 1935 MacDunphy wrote: 'There is a growing tendency particularly within the last few years, on the part of the Department of External Affairs to take on its own initiative, action which should, in my opinion, receive the prior imprimatur of the Executive Council.' MacDunphy went as far as to say that Walshe was subverting the course of ministerial decision-making:

> The view expressed by the Secretary [Walshe] of the Department in conversation is that as the President, in the present Government, is also Minister for External Affairs, any action taken by him in the latter capacity, must be regarded as done with the approval of the President, and therefore with the approval of the Executive Council.[47]

This was not the first attack on Walshe by MacDunphy, who in 1932 had written a number of memoranda on the powers and functions of the Department of the President. One of its principal functions was its duty as secretariat to the Executive Council:

In this capacity it is the medium through which matters are submitted to the Executive Council for consideration and through which
the Council's decisions are communicated to the Ministers concerned for such Departmental action as may be necessary.[48]

MacDunphy saw Walshe's actions as a circumvention of one of his
department's primary roles. He felt it created a precedent 'which
may prove very awkward later if and when the folio of Minister for
External Affairs is held by a Minister other than the President'.[49]
These views were supported by Maurice Moynihan, secretary to
the Department of the President, whose relationship with Walshe
was strained at times.[50] While the Department of the President
and the Department of External Affairs shared de Valera as minister, this certainly did not result in the cooperation or unity one
might have expected. In fact, Moynihan and Walshe had very little
contact. Moynihan believed that Walshe would have regarded him
as somewhat of a 'whippersnapper'. In truth, Walshe may have
been envious of Moynihan's close relationship with and proximity
to de Valera.[51] Moynihan did not generally comment on matters of
concern to Walshe. However, in March 1936 he submitted to the
Cabinet for discussion a memorandum simply entitled 'Foreign
Relations' and which sought to secure 'unified control of relations
with countries abroad'. This was in response to a memorandum
written by Walshe a week previously. A simultaneous analysis of
both documents gives a clear impression as to how Walshe saw
the continued role of the Department of External Affairs and the
perceptibly differing views of Moynihan.

Walshe had opened with an assertion of the exclusive rights
of his minister: 'The duty of framing and administering a policy
for this country in relation to other countries is essentially the
business of a Foreign Minister.' He argued for a 'single Minister',
and was at pains to emphasise the detrimental effect of dividing
the tasks of foreign affairs:

> Manifestly an external policy must be based upon an essential unity
> of purpose and must form a political whole. Its value will largely
> depend upon its homogeneous conception, and its success will
> depend upon the continuity and consistency of its application in a
> variety of complex situations and circumstances.[52]

Thus, with terms like 'single', 'unity', 'whole', 'homogeneous' and

'continuity and consistency', Walshe let it be known that he
would not easily relinquish any of the responsibilities of External
Affairs. He argued for External Affairs involvement in 'all inter-
State intercourse' and for the minister's 'knowledge and control
of every aspect of the external activities of the Government'. He
claimed it was essential that 'no official or semi-official discussions or correspondence should take place between officials or
Government Departments of Saorstát Éireann and the officials or
Government Departments of other countries without the knowledge and approval of the Minister for External Affairs.' Walshe's
emphatic defence of the responsibilities of External Affairs, while
outlined to ensure the 'unity and consistency of purpose' which
'the best interests of the country require', are reminiscent of the
mentality Walshe displayed in an earlier period of siege in which
the role of the department was far less certain.

Moynihan presented Walshe's draft memorandum to the
Cabinet and wrote his own memorandum on the subject. Where
it disagreed with Walshe's conclusions or observations, it was careful to mention de Valera's agreement. For example, while it was
agreed that it was essential for the Minister for External Affairs to
be aware of any correspondence affecting foreign relations, it was
also recognised, 'the President said', that 'for the sake of conve-
nience, certain defined classes of communications might be carried
on directly by Departments of State'.[53] Moynihan was clearly indicating that de Valera was siding with him. Such interventions by
Moynihan were rare, and he studiously avoided any involvement
in foreign-affairs matters.[54] The delineation of powers and responsibilities between the President's department and External Affairs,
however, was a matter in which Walshe could not be allowed a free
hand, and so, in this case, Moynihan conveyed his reservations concerning Walshe's memorandum. He commented in particular on
the necessity for certain matters to cross ministerial boundaries:

> If the Minister for External Affairs were in the full sense to direct
> and control the policy of the State in regard to, for example, trade
> or financial relations with other countries, he would, to some
> extent, be taking over functions of the Ministry for Industry and
> Commerce, the Minister for Finance or such other Minister as
> might be vested with the general functions relating to the par-
> ticular subject.

That absolutely all correspondence between government departments and external powers should go through External Affairs
was regarded as impractical. Moynihan further challenged the
idea that communication to and from the Irish diplomatic community abroad was the sole preserve of External Affairs:

> There was some discussion regarding the statement in the De-
> partment of External Affairs' memorandum that 'by a well-settled
> rule diplomatic and consular agents accredited to a State have
> access to the Government through him' (the foreign Minister)
> 'and through him only'. Ministers felt that it was often conven-
> ient for representatives of other countries to have direct access
> to a Minister other than the Minister for External Affairs, and
> moreover that it would be difficult where a Foreign representa-
> tive requested an interview, to refuse it on the ground that access
> should be through the Minister for External Affairs only.[55]

Thus, the views expressed by the External Affairs' secretary were
seen as impractical, and flexibility was called for. Walshe was
clearly not going to have it all his own way on this particular
issue, and the strength of Moynihan's reply seemed to end the
matter. Moynihan's explicit reference to the support of de Valera
made Walshe's efforts null and void. Losing this particular battle
may have injured Walshe's pride, but it was to have little significance otherwise. Since the arrival of de Valera, Walshe and
the department had grown in respectability and stature. External
Affairs had proved its worth and would continue to do so.

Walshe soon became centrally involved in another major
diplomatic initiative that resulted in a new agreement with the
British government. In mid-1936, however, any hope of agreement
between the two states seemed a long way off. Walshe's growing
impatience with the economic war that was so destructive of
Irish economic development prompted him to try and construct
a more amicable relationship between Dublin and London. To
this end he hosted a meeting with Harry Batterbee at his home
in Dublin in April 1936. His aim was to have a semi-informal
chat with the Dominions Office assistant under-secretary on
Anglo-Irish relations. Walshe repeatedly stressed the importance
of ministerial-level meetings, and said that the recent encounter
between Malcolm MacDonald and de Valera had been extremely

useful. Batterbee expressed the hope that there would be some form of political agreement between the two countries in the near future, and asserted that the new king, Edward VIII, was anxious for this to happen.[56] For Walshe, the key to the normalisation of Anglo-Irish relations was the partition question, and Batterbee seemed to recognise the validity of Walshe's argument:

> I had wondered sometimes whether it would help if a United Kingdom Minister were to make a statement to the effect that, while a United Kingdom Government would do all they could to prevent any attempt by the Irish Free State to coerce Ulster by force, on the other had it was a delusion to suppose that, if the time ever came when the Irish Free State succeeded in persuading Ulster to come into a United Ireland by acts of friendship and goodwill and Ulster was ever ready so to come in of her own free will, the United Kingdom Government would attempt to prevent such a reconciliation.[57]

Batterbee stated that the British had rejected the idea of a united Ireland on the grounds that the government did not wish to coerce the unionists. Walshe replied that the Irish government, for its part, had no intention of coercing the six counties into a settlement, and said that 'the idea of coercing Ulster did not exist except in the imagination of some Tory propagandists'. The British official then suggested to Walshe that the Irish government should attempt to develop more friendly relations with Northern Ireland. Walshe replied that the Northern government had made this difficult through their statements against the Catholic population and through the gerrymandering of constituencies against nationalists. He insisted that both the government and the people of Ireland firmly believed that the British government held the key to any settlement, and added that 'the fact that she exercised that power or did not appear to exercise it left our people the definite impression that she did not want the unity of Ireland to be established.' Walshe continued to push the point, and told Batterbee that some were of the view that Britain hoped to use Northern Ireland as a bridgehead for the reconquest of Ireland. Walshe, of course, did not believe this himself, but de Valera had indeed 'got it into his head ... rightly or wrongly' that Britain was determined to keep the North as a 'bridgehead' and would prevent a united Ireland 'at all costs'.

On the greater economic issues, Walshe raised the question of

the coal–cattle pact of the previous year, which had allowed for an increase of Irish cattle exports to Britain and British exports of coal to Ireland. He viewed it as a significant step forward in the economic dispute. As both sides agreed that the economic war should end, they decided not to waste time discussing this matter. However, Batterbee enquired into the possibility of calling a truce in constitutional matters for a period of five years. Walshe, linking the constitutional with the economic question, indicated that there would be a high price for Britain to pay before it would even be possible to contemplate such a truce:

> I personally thought that it would be useless to think of any truce of that nature before a friendly and generous offer of settlement of the economic struggle had come from them [the British] and before the abolition of the office of Governor General. It seemed also to me that a truce could not be arranged until the ports now held by the British had been transferred to us.[58]

Here Walshe made an important discovery. Batterbee said he was quite certain that there would be 'no difficulty about handing over the ports once some political settlement had been made'. When pressed further by Walshe on the matter he reiterated that 'he had no doubt whatever about the transfer following a political settlement'. In this way Walshe had unearthed a key factor in bringing about a political settlement.

De Valera was adamant that he was going to remove the Governor General's office, and Walshe thought that the British should accept that fact. Walshe gave the impression that he personally would have little objection to a truce but hinted that de Valera would be harder to appease, and expressed the fear that 'some step might be taken by Mr de Valera on the constitutional side which would precipitate a crisis and would bring to a full stop the forces which with time and patience might bring about a settlement.' Walshe hoped, however, that if agreement could be reached on the economic war, the Governor General and the attitude of the United Kingdom towards a united Ireland then de Valera could probably be counted on to agree to a 'gentlemen's agreement' to make no further constitutional changes for a five-year period. Batterbee was wise to Walshe's approaches, and did not jump to any premature conclusions:

As is usual in talks with him, Mr Walshe was discursive and dif-
fuse, and it was difficult to canalize the conversation. In talking to
him one has the feeling that with him the wish is often father to
the thought, but after all it is his job to build bridges, and he certainly left me with the impression that he genuinely believed that
Mr de Valera does not wish to be pushed any further by the Irish
Republican Army and that he would be glad to be furnished with
some good reason or excuse for leaving things as they are and not
moving further towards a republic.[59]

True to Walshe's nature, there was a large element of improvisa-
tion in his comments, and Batterbee was careful to take this into
account when considering what de Valera's real wishes might be.
   Later that year Malcolm MacDonald attempted to bring
British and Irish officials together for discussions in London.
MacDonald was disappointed, however, that Dulanty was the
only Irish official present, as he believed Walshe to be crucially
important to the negotiations.[60] Walshe was on leave in Austria,
where he was undergoing further treatment for his recurring chest
and heart problems. On his return journey he passed through
London and, despite Dulanty's protestations, he absolutely refused
to remain for any length of time to take part in discussions with
British officials. The Dominions Office permanent under-secretary,
Edward Harding was profoundly disappointed at having let the
opportunity for discussions slip, but it was clear that Walshe was
very apprehensive about stopping in London.[61] Having been away
from headquarters for some time, Walshe would not have wanted
to enter into discussions with the British before being briefed by
de Valera. Dulanty further told Harding that he had recently
seen two members of the Irish Cabinet and neither were aware
that any communications had passed between himself and de
Valera on the subject of the possibility of a general settlement.
This was a sign, said Dulanty, of the importance de Valera attached
to the secrecy of this issue. It was another reason why Walshe was
absolutely adamant that he could not stop in London. While
Walshe recognised the futility of acting independently of de Valera,
this did not mean that he was unwilling to become involved. As
we shall see, on his return to Dublin, Walshe would direct much
of his energies to promoting a resolution to these issues.
   Towards the end of 1936 the secretaries of the Departments

of Finance, Industry and Commerce, Agriculture, and External Affairs decided that the economic war had reached a critical stage for the Free State. Much like a démarche, McElliot, Leydon, Twomey and Walshe co-signed a memorandum voicing their concern over the current economic and political situation with Britain. The approaching termination of the coal–cattle pact was a crucial juncture, according to the civil servants, who urged that it was now opportune to strike a new deal with the British as they were showing concern over food supplies in the event of a war. They counted the cost of the economic war by demonstrating that over the previous five years the amount collected by Britain in special duties on Irish exports was now beginning to exceed the amount withheld by the Free State in annuities. With the termination of the coal–cattle pact, further advantage to Britain would accrue. Thus, on the grounds of economic necessity, it was time for the Free State to make peace with her powerful neighbour. Walshe and his colleagues concluded that 'If existing relations remained unchanged, Great Britain will have recovered from the Saorstát the full amount of the alleged default.'[62] The statement was, perhaps, a brave move by these civil servants, but in reality they felt obliged to act as it had become obvious that the Irish Free State was the loser in the economic war against the might of the British economy. Clearly, Walshe would be to the fore in developing any new proposals for agreement with Britain.

Soon after, events were to bring Anglo-Irish relations to a head. In November 1936 John Dulanty met British officials to forewarn them that the following day's newspapers would contain details of de Valera's plans with regard to the constitutional development of the Irish Free State. The British expressed their reservations about any further moves to remove the king from the Irish Constitution, and said it would be a pity if any steps were taken that would prevent or delay a united Ireland. Dulanty called their bluff by asking them to detail their plans for a united Ireland, of which there appeared to be none. Sir Horace Wilson, described by Walshe as one of British Prime Minister Stanley Baldwin's right-hand men, counselled for caution and suggested that 'even if the King did not participate at all in internal affairs something might be done provided there was not a complete eviction.'[63] Walshe treated the comments sceptically: 'I don't attach any importance to these statements made by Civil Servants

– but they will show you how far the B.[British] have been obliged to move towards us by the system of the 'fait accompli'. It was perhaps a somewhat curious phrase for him to use, being a civil servant himself! Dulanty indicated that while de Valera's ultimate objective was a united Ireland he understood that this could not be achieved overnight, and that he could continue with his constitutional changes regardless. The proposed new Constitution, therefore, would remove the king from the internal affairs of the Irish Free State, although the monarch would be retained for matters relating to external affairs. De Valera was due to speak to the Fianna Fáil party that evening, and it was feared that he might commit himself to proposals that would give the appearance of 'banging the door'. Walshe attempted to convince de Valera not to use language that could be construed as indicating that the king would be totally removed, or that a republic would be set up.[64] It was clear that de Valera's aim was radical constitutional reform, and Walshe's role was to limit the damage to Anglo-Irish relations as best he could.

At the end of November, Batterbee travelled to Dublin once again. In his memorandum he does not name the officials he met there, but considering their past dealings it is unthinkable that he did not meet Walshe. It is clear that Irish officials would have been fearful for Anglo-Irish relations at this time, and Batterbee's comments clearly indicate Walshe's own apprehensions:

> They feared that events may move so fast that Mr de Valera may be compelled to commit himself by some public statement regarding the position of the King, and that in present circumstances a supreme effort ought to be made, and at once, to reach the basis of a settlement.

The officials Batterbee met warned that the only circumstances under which de Valera would accept the retention of the king was the recognition of the principle of a united Ireland, and urged him to persuade Craigavon that this was an unprecedented opportunity to come to a settlement that would ensure that Ireland would remain within the Empire. From these discussions there emerged the basis of a possible Anglo-Irish settlement in which the king would retain his current position and Ireland would remain part of the British Empire. In return, Britain would take a significant

step towards encouraging a united Ireland by creating a joint body made up of representatives from both sides of the border to deal with matters of common importance. This 'parliament', which was to be formed on the basis of consent, would have limited powers at first, but given time and goodwill would grow as confidence was engendered. The proposals further suggested that

> All persons belonging to the Irish Free State and Northern Ireland to be 'Irish Citizens'. In Northern Ireland such persons to continue to be called 'British Subjects'. This was impossible in the Irish Free State at present but it was suggested that there would be no objection to some such phrase as 'Nationals of Ireland, British Commonwealth of Nations': I stressed 'Citizens of the Commonwealth'. The whole idea would be that there would be no compulsion on either side provided the position was accepted that both the Irish Free State and Northern Ireland were part of Ireland which was a part of the Commonwealth.[65]

Other details of the proposal included acceptance of the principle that Irish ministers to foreign countries were to continue to be appointed by the king. In return, a trade agreement, defence cooperation and the handing back of the Treaty ports, as well as a generous financial settlement, were important parts of this somewhat speculative proposal which, in the absence of sufficient documentation, seemed to lack official political backing. Apart from persuading their superiors to agree to the terms of agreement, this group of civil servants felt that neither of their governments would be prepared to make the first move. Thus, in the interests of both countries they felt obliged to maintain the momentum of cooperation. It was a policy that Walshe would have been supportive of. He had demonstrated no reservations previously about negotiating with Britain, and his participation in these discussions would have been crucial to their having any chance of success.

Within days of Batterbee's visit to Dublin, however, Britain was thrown into a constitutional crisis that would act as a spur to Anglo-Irish negotiations. On 11 December 1936 King Edward VIII, who had been appointed to the throne earlier in the year, abdicated in favour of his brother George [VI]. This was

precipitated by Edward's decision to marry an American divorcee named Wallis Simpson. The abdication crisis meant that each of the dominion governments had to take legislative action to recognise the succession of George as king, and the British were now in a quandary as to how to approach de Valera.[66] As one historian put it: 'Over the past four years de Valera had worked to eliminate all mention of the King from the internal affairs of the Free State, and since the abdication Bill demanded confirmation of the King's position, this went completely against de Valera's previous constitutional policy.'[67] The crisis had by now been in the public arena for over a week and in political circles for a number of weeks. Deirdre McMahon has pointed out that, due to there being no British representative in Dublin, communications during this frantic period were haphazard and somewhat comical. At one stage Walshe, who had travelled to London to consult with the Dominions Office, horrified officials there by discussing with de Valera over the telephone, through Irish, details of the crisis. Walshe calmed the officials' security worries by telling them that no one at the telephone exchange in Dublin could understand Irish.[68]

The Anglo-Irish aspect of this crisis began in earnest when Batterbee contacted Walshe and asked what answer should be given in the House of Commons in reply to questions concerning the Irish Free State's position on the matter. Walshe remained secretive about de Valera's plans and simply said, 'The Government of the Irish Free State are summoning Parliament to make provision for the situation which has arisen.' This was not sufficient to calm Batterbee, who suggested that the Attorney General give some answer to the effect that the Irish Free State needed time to look into the constitutional implications. Batterbee hoped that some temporary statement could be made, but Walshe offered little in the way of understanding. De Valera had very specific plans and Walshe could divulge nothing. Under instructions from de Valera he issued the following statement:

> We intend to make legislative and Constitutional provision to meet the situation. In order to do so we are going to amend the existing Constitution so that the law would exactly express the realities of the Constitutional position in regard to the functions exercised directly by the King. The precise manner in which this is to be done has not yet been determined upon.[69]

The statement understandably frightened the British official.
Having read between the lines, he expressed to Walshe the hope
that the Irish government would do nothing to alter relations
between Britain and Ireland or to affect the constitutional position of the king, adding that he thought to use the abdication
crisis for such a move would be 'deplorable'.

Walshe was not worried by being branded opportunistic, and
he was particularly fascinated by the constitutional precedents
caused by the abdication. 'Saorstát Éireann', he pointed out, would
for a brief period 'be a completely independent Monarchy'. He
expected, therefore, an appeal from Baldwin to allow them to say
or do something that would prevent this situation arising.
Following Batterbee's failure to gain any concession, MacDonald
phoned Walshe and sought further clarification as to what the
Irish government proposed to do. The British officials felt they
could not write an answer for Baldwin without more information,
as to do so would create further ambiguity and confusion in the
House of Commons, and it would take some time to research the
implications of any action taken by the Irish government. The Dáil
was due to sit in two days, but MacDonald suggested that it would
be of great benefit to them if it sat the following day instead, and
if it were further agreed that British and Irish legislation could be
passed simultaneously. In fact, reported Walshe, MacDonald was
of the opinion that many within the House of Commons felt that
any British legislation would have to be postponed so that it would
coincide with that of the Free State. This would put them in a
difficult position, and he sought some cooperation from Walshe.[70]
Walshe understood that to summon the Dáil for the following day
could cause huge difficulties. He did not know if de Valera would
be able, or willing, to do so, but said he agreed to convey the
request nevertheless. MacDonald then added that this proposed
temporary arrangement was 'completely without prejudice to your
desire to introduce legislation later on in connection with the new
Constitution. He had no quarrel with that.' Having contacted de
Valera, Walshe then informed Batterbee that it had been agreed
that they would try to convene the Dáil for the following day but
that there were no guarantees. In the meantime it was agreed that
Baldwin would issue the following holding statement:

I have received a message from Mr de Valera that the Government

of the Irish Free State are summoning their Parliament, if possible, for tomorrow to make provision for the situation which has arisen in the Irish Free State.[71]

Batterbee was somewhat relieved that there was a chance that the two parliaments would consider the abdication at the same time. To Walshe, he seemed less troubled by any amendments the Irish government had planned, and Walshe began to see the advantage of the situation:

> When I expressed the hope that the flood of cypher wires would soon cease between us to allow us to get back to our normal work, he said that he hoped it would soon start to flow again on a question which would be more agreeable for both sides. I do not attach any importance to this last remark, except in so far as it confirms the impression just noted.[72]

The following day Batterbee, still anxious to acquire forewarning of the proposed Irish legislation, tried a different approach. He telephoned Walshe that morning and asked him for information on Ireland's legislation, purely 'for his personal information'. Walshe was extremely sceptical and was somewhat insulted by the manner of the request. The only information he could share was the titles of two bills that de Valera was preparing to introduce that afternoon. Batterbee wanted to know what the terms of the bills were, but Walshe needed more time to consider what he could divulge. Later that morning the assistant secretary at the Dominions Office, C.W. Dixon – obviously on Batterbee's instructions – contacted Walshe again to see if any further information could be ascertained. Walshe said that to reveal the terms of the proposed legislation would cause 'difficulties' for both sides even if he divulged information on a 'purely private and personal' basis. Nevertheless, he told Dixon what Batterbee really wanted to know, which was that Irish legislators would make provision for the succession of the new king, but he warned that there could be no official statement on the basis of their discussion. Walshe was at pains to point out the private and personal nature of the conversation, and referred to difficulties that had arisen with Malcolm MacDonald's predecessor, J.H. Thomas. Walshe had been betrayed before and was anxious that this should not happen again:

I knew that Batterbee would appreciate exactly what the position
was and the difficulties which had arisen in Mr Thomas's time from
using purely private communications as if they had been officially
made. I told Dixon that I had no intention of casting aspersions on
anybody, but that it was essential for me to go to the furthest limit
in order to emphasise the character of this conversation.

Walshe is vague on the details of these past difficulties but his
message was clear enough. Dixon understood the situation and
promised to convey the message to Batterbee. Walshe, however,
remained distrustful and expected Batterbee to face considerable pressure to generate some official statement from their
communication:

> I felt quite sure from my conversation with Batterbee that he
> would try by some plausible means to convert our private and
> personal conversation (as he continually repeated) into an official
> communication if the terms of the Bills were given to him and he
> thought the matter sufficiently serious to warrant the initiation of
> propaganda against us through a statement for that purpose made
> in the course of the debate in the House of Commons today.[73]

Later that day de Valera used the opportunity of Edward VIII's
abdication to remove from the Free State Constitution all direct
references to the king and the Governor General. Reference to the
Crown was indirectly retained, or, in Nicholas Mansergh's words,
'it acknowledged the role of the Crown in the Commonwealth
without an explicit, or indeed implicit, recognition of Irish allegiance.'[74] The British did not seem unduly perturbed by the
changes made. The following week Walshe informed de Valera
that the British government was appreciative of the legislation
which had provided for Edward VIII's abdication and the succession of his brother, George VI.[75]

     In conversation with John Dulanty, Malcolm MacDonald
indicated that he felt there would be no difficulties with the Irish
legislation, but did suggest that their legal advisers should meet to
iron out some minor difficulties. The Dominions Secretary needed
clarification of certain points in order to be clear on certain matters when answering questions in the House of Commons. He
further indicated that he was now willing to turn to the question
of a financial and trade settlement. The ports were also mentioned,

and Dulanty, convinced that 'real business could be done in these matters', advocated acceptance of the proposed meeting between the legal advisers. Walshe, however, resisted the temptation to talk on these favourable terms, and objected to the idea on the grounds that agreeing to discussions of this nature could be seen as an acceptance to negotiate over the validity of the legislation. Walshe believed that there should be no outward indication that the Irish legislation was in any way the business of the British government.[76] Clearly, Walshe believed the Irish government had acquired the right to a degree of goodwill from the British, and he was determined to use it wisely.

Walshe's unwillingness to act was also assisted by de Valera's absence from the country. At this time de Valera was in Switzerland undergoing treatment for his deteriorating eyesight. Walshe did not wish to burden him but felt it necessary to write on important matters that needed a decision. The British continued to seek discussions on the new position of the king in the Irish Constitution, but Walshe could not decide on the matter without approval. Before his departure de Valera had been undecided, but Walshe believed that the British government's expressed desire for the talks probably indicated that there was something in the Irish legislation that it disagreed with or wanted to change. He suspected that the British wanted definite assurances regarding the prerogative of the king to declare war. Walshe felt that it was not a matter that civil servants could suitably deal with, and he felt that conversations of this sort could be used or deliberately misconstrued by British politicians. He himself could not take responsibility, such was the delicacy of the discussions:

> We should have to say that the King's functions are exclusively confined to those set out specifically in the Act. We could not, for instance, say that he was an executive organ here, least that expression be used by Mr MacDonald in the House of Commons.[77]

To Walshe's mind the suggestion reeked of interference in Irish affairs, and he believed that any information given to the British on the proposed new Constitution could be misinterpreted or put to use against the Irish government. He suggested, therefore, that such discussions were a risk from an Irish point of view, and that Dulanty should be instructed to discourage the idea. De Valera

could rest assured that in this area of policy, at least, no major developments would be initiated by Walshe in his absence.

By the time the abdication crisis first came to light, de Valera's plans for a new Constitution for the Irish Free State were already well under way. In 1937 these plans gathered momentum and the British government braced itself for more sweeping changes in the constitutional relationship with the Free State. By now, however, many of the more significant changes had already taken place, and the Constitution, which resisted the temptation to declare an Irish republic, was ushered in with little requirement for diplomatic preparation from Walshe and his team. While de Valera remained the overall architect of the document, Maurice Moynihan and the Department of External Affairs' legal adviser, John Hearne, were chosen as the primary draughtsmen of the new Constitution. The files dealing with the drafting of the Constitution are available in the de Valera papers, and allow the reader to trace the progression of the document through its many drafts.[78] Walshe's opinion on various matters was sought from time to time. He was among a select audience treated to a preview of the proposed Constitution, and may have offered some suggestions to de Valera or Hearne.[79]

Perhaps Walshe's most important contribution to the formulation of the Constitution came in April 1937 when he was sent to the Vatican in an effort to settle a disagreement with the Irish hierarchy over the proposed section on religion.[80] The Vatican had little desire to become involved, but Walshe was called upon to use his skills and expertise in Vatican politics to assist de Valera in dealing with this sensitive matter. On his return from Rome he wrote a lengthy memorandum on the events that had taken place. Armed with a copy of the proposed wording, he had persuaded the Vatican to declare that it neither approved nor disapproved of the wording: 'Ni approvo ni non disapprovo; tacermo.' It was a notable success for Walshe. 'Tacermo' – meaning 'we shall maintain silence' – was an indication of neutrality, and this, coupled with the Vatican's non-disapproval, allowed de Valera to gerrymander the Irish hierarchy's consent.[81] While he did not contribute greatly to the formulation of the Constitution, Walshe's diplomatic adroitness did contribute to its successful introduction.

The new Constitution was ratified by a plebiscite on 1 July 1937. Walshe was entrusted to travel to London to gauge the British reaction. Malcolm MacDonald had assured Dulanty that

the note they intended to present on the day would not cause the Irish government any difficulty. Walshe wanted greater assurances and sought a preview of Britain's proposed statement. With Anglo-Irish negotiations planned, he did not want any difficulties to arise between the two governments. His primary concern was that there should not be the slightest hint that the British government had any right to interfere in the Irish Constitution. MacDonald assured him in this regard but also agreed to show him their statement the evening before the Irish Constitution was formally adopted. Walshe was satisfied with the contents of the British statement, and felt confident that the planned trade and political negotiations could now take place without interruption. In the event, the British government responded to the introduction of the Irish Constitution as follows:

> His Majesty's Government ... are prepared to treat the new Constitution as not effecting the fundamental alteration in the position of the Irish Free State, in future to be described under the new constitution as 'Éire' or 'Ireland', as a member of the British Commonwealth of Nations.[82]

Following the completion of this phase of de Valera's constitutional reforms, Walshe could now redirect his attention to the realignment of Anglo-Irish relations.

In their most recent discussions, MacDonald had demonstrated a helpful disposition, which encouraged Walshe in the belief that this latest round of negotiations could be successful. His first task in these diplomatic manoeuvres was to ascertain Britain's minimum demands. From his own point of view Walshe believed that the introduction of the new Constitution had removed a major stumbling block. Having achieved this, he said, the confidence of the Irish people was boosted. 'We had now come out of the mountains into the plain', said Walshe, 'and the way towards a settlement had become much easier.' For Walshe, the Irish Constitution was a supreme expression of Irish nationhood, and no negotiation on amending it could be entered into. For a fair agreement to be reached he believed it was essential to have a Constitution that expressed the will of the Irish people.

In an effort to sound out Britain's feeling towards an agreement, Walshe had approached Edward Harding of the Dominions

Office to see what his thinking was on the issue of the land annuities as well as other matters. Following this meeting Walshe's initial assessment was that, while the British had decided not to force de Valera on the issue of the annuities, he believed that it would be exceedingly difficult to renege on accepting responsibility for payment of certain financial obligations. He estimated that approximately £700,000 would be required to pay pensions currently being paid in Ireland, £7 million to cover local loans, and a lump sum of £3 million to cover the cost of paying pensions to people who had left Ireland and were currently living throughout the world.[83] On these he felt there was little room for manoeuvre. On the issue of the Treaty ports, however, Walshe believed there was reason for optimism. These ports had been retained by Britain since the 1921 Treaty and were of crucial importance to both sides, especially since war with Germany was looming. It seems to have been generally recognised at this stage that Britain would return these ports, which had been used as naval bases. It was the least the Free State would accept. Harding indicated that what Britain was seeking was to gain rights to enter the ports in an emergency. Walshe, arguing on the basis of national sovereignty, said that this could not be granted, but pointed out that in a major conflict between Britain and Germany the risk of attack on Ireland was just as great considering that Ireland would be seen as an important source of food for Britain. Ireland would do everything in its power to defend itself, and Walshe plainly intimated that there would be little option but for the two countries to cooperate.

Walshe reported that one of the primary worries of the British army was its fear that Ireland would declare itself neutral in the event of a conflict. Walshe stressed that Ireland would not let its shores become a base for attack against Britain, and that the government would adopt a realistic approach when considering the defensive power of Irish forces. The British were given the impression that in the event of an attack on Ireland they would be called in to assist. They had heard public statements in favour of neutrality but it is interesting that Walshe clearly ruled neutrality out as a possible option at this stage. He wrote to de Valera saying, 'I remember only vaguely such statements', and he blamed de Valera's minority coalition partners in the Labour Party for the confusion. On the basis of these rumours, which were interfering with his discussions with the British, Walshe argued for the

tightening up of government communications, saying that statements on external affairs in particular should only be made by
the minister of the department, and that 'casual remarks made by
prominent public men on the Government side could easily give
rise to suspicions which render our relations with our principal
"external affair" more difficult.' Walshe's memory, however, was
either deficient or selective. De Valera had on a number of occasions hinted that neutrality was indeed an option. In a speech
in the Dáil in June 1936 de Valera stated that, while many of
the other smaller states were spending vast amounts to build up
their defences, Ireland wished to be neutral. It was an unequivocal
statement in which he also gave the assurance that:

> If we held the whole of our territory, there is no doubt whatever
> that our attitude would be … that we have no aggressive designs
> against any other people. We would strengthen ourselves so as to
> maintain our neutrality. We would strengthen ourselves so that
> we might resist any attempt to make use of our territory for attack
> upon any other nation.[84]

Later, during the Munich crisis, de Valera made it clear that he
did not favour war, and indicated that the Irish government would
make every effort not to become directly involved in any conflict. Walshe was obviously not in favour of a policy of neutrality,
believing that Ireland's proximity to Britain would rule it out. It
was a significant assertion on his part, as he was evidently out of
step with de Valera's thinking at that time.

The net result of Walshe's approaches to British government
officials during this difficult period was that he maintained diplomatic contact throughout, and was therefore well informed as to
their views. This would be important when substantive discussions
began. Agreement did not come until both sides were ready to
settle on matters of particular interest. De Valera had introduced
his Constitution, the Oath of Allegiance was gone, the Governor
General's office was converted to an Irish presidency, and many of
the vestiges of the British Crown had been removed. De Valera
had not cut the link with the Commonwealth, and was happy to
reap any resulting financial advantages. Britain, for its part, had no
wish to continue the feud with its nearest neighbour, especially
one that could be a close ally, providing food, labour, recruits and

tactical security in a conflict with Germany. Thus, the scene was set for a new Anglo-Irish agreement, and Joseph Walshe relished the prospect of those negotiations.

During the opening months of 1938 discussions were frenetic. In January Walshe went to London to conduct the negotiations with the British government. He remained enthusiastic throughout, and wrote to the Taoiseach encouraging him to remain optimistic. The issue of partition was one of the first to arise. While Walshe believed that a united Ireland was a long way off, he did report that Britain appeared to be moving in the direction of agreeing to a 'common organ' that would facilitate cooperation between Belfast and Dublin. It was not all that de Valera would have wanted, but Walshe saw it as the beginning of the process of unification. There was still a lot of work to be done in this regard, but Walshe nevertheless urged de Valera to remain optimistic. 'I have a very real hope', he said – perhaps somewhat over-optimistically – 'that the British will take some substantial step towards the desired goal.'[85]

It is unclear if Walshe's efforts on partition were at the behest of de Valera. In any event, three days later he had another meeting with the Dominions Office permanent under-secretary, Edward Harding, in which he again urged for real progress on partition, and threatened that unless serious advances were made on the issue de Valera would find it difficult to come to an agreement in relation to defence matters. It was a clear warning to Britain that Irish assistance in a conflict was not guaranteed. Walshe advocated cooperation with Britain and was convinced that a deal could be made. His intuition told him that any agreement without a defence arrangement would be of little use to Britain, and that an accord of some sort was vital to their aims:

> The British are hankering after an agreement because it is essential for them to close the ranks as far as the Commonwealth is concerned, and still more because they wanted to get the goodwill and if possible the co-operation of the United States in the difficulties which are now facing them.

Walshe appeared to have been willing to offer a defence pact if the right concessions were offered; or at least he was hoping to give the British that impression. He felt he had a superior

negotiating position, and communicated to Harding that unless concrete steps towards unification were made there was little chance of any settlement. Such warnings from Walshe appear to have been a negotiating ploy, for, despite his demands for progress on partition, he realised that Britain would be very slow to abandon the Northern unionists. This was a more realistic assessment from Walshe, who saw that this position could in itself have its own advantages:

> They have said very definitely that instead of concessions which they can make to us in relation to partition, and it is because these limits are somewhat narrow that they are ready to give us practically everything in all other matters in dispute.[86]

Despite their unwillingness to distress the unionists, Walshe believed that compromise could be reached and an administrative organ common to both North and South could still be attained.

The British sought a specific suggestion from de Valera with regard to such a joint North–South body. Walshe understood that Britain could not be seen to be promoting Irish unification. However, it is unusual that de Valera had to be persuaded to put forward constructive proposals, although Walshe did feel that no matter what suggestion was made Britain would agree to nothing more than some form of council of Ireland. This, in his view, could be regarded as 'a symbol that the process of unification has begun'. He informed the Taoiseach[87] that the time would soon arrive when a favourable compromise could be made:

> With regard to the method they appear to be ready, if the suggestion is made by you, or approved by you, to press its acceptance on Craigavon.

The British government's main difficulty was that the unionists had large support within the Conservative Party. Any hint of coercion would scuttle the deal. Considering this, Walshe's diplomatic strategy was to push as far as he could on partition but pull back if it meant losing all, and to use any British reluctance to push for gains in other areas:

> I shall continue by every means in my power to persuade Harding of the gravity of the situation and to try and inform you as nearly

as I can to what precise point you can push them without running the risk of getting nothing at all on partition or on the other matters being discussed.[88]

In the meantime Walshe would use any means at his disposal to maintain international diplomatic pressure on Britain. To this end he turned to the United States for assistance.

At the outset of the negotiations de Valera, on Walshe's advice, wrote to the US president, Franklin D. Roosevelt, saying that a great opportunity had arisen to settle the Anglo-Irish disagreement. If Britain put an end to partition, notable results would follow and the '[r]econciliation would affect every country where the two races dwell together, knitting their national strength and presenting to the world a great block of democratic peoples interested in the preservation of peace.'[89] The Taoiseach urged the US president to use his influence with Britain to convince them to work towards this settlement. Roosevelt was not anxious to become involved, and indicated that while he supported such a reconciliation he could do little to persuade Britain through diplomatic or official channels.[90] However, he did mention that Joseph Kennedy – who was soon to arrive in London to take up the position of ambassador – had been given instructions to convey to the British government that the US president would be very happy if such a reconciliation came about. Roosevelt was reluctant to become enmeshed in the Irish issue, and was still less enthusiastic about putting pressure on the British over partition. Walshe, however, would not stop at that. An appeal to the US Secretary of State, Cordell Hull, would be made through the Irish representative in Washington, Michael MacWhite, whose instructions were to keep up the momentum of pressure on Britain. Walshe believed that a word from him to the British ambassador in Washington would have more weight than any Irish propaganda. Throughout all this Walshe remained optimistic and indicated to de Valera his belief that he could secure 'all we desire in non-partition matters and enough in relation to that question to enable us to carry out what the British regard as the essentials for an agreement'.[91]

In order to achieve his aims, Walshe felt he could not be away from the negotiations, and remained in London. In early February 1938 he told de Valera that, while he was anxious to return to Dublin, he believed it wiser to remain until agreement was reached.

Perhaps by being away Walshe felt the need to closely document the proceedings. From a lengthy manuscript report to the Taoiseach we are able to trace the progression of the negotiations. Walshe had gleaned much information about Britain's position, and had modified his stance on the basis of how much he thought Britain was willing to concede. Walshe understood the complexities of these negotiations, and realised that the British government was restricted by the Northern Ireland government, which believed that the general bias of the proposed trade agreement was unfair because it allowed Irish goods 'to enjoy freedom of entry into the United Kingdom, while Éire is to be entitled to retain a protective tariff barrier against competition from United Kingdom industrial products'. This was seen to have a more cynical motive:

> In short, the proposed Agreement promises to place in the hands of the Government of Éire the means of bringing further economic pressure on Northern Ireland.[92]

Walshe encountered further difficulties when he met members of the British Committee of Imperial Defence who had made him uncomfortable by their clear reluctance to cooperate with the Irish government in facilitating the handing over of the ports. They were worried that Ireland would not have the expertise or manpower to adequately staff these outposts. Walshe urged de Valera to work to remove this distrust, which could colour British military advice in such a way as to maintain Ireland's dependence on the British army in the event of an emergency. To Walshe, however, this was not the only reason why the British might wish to keep Irish defensive capacity at a minimum, and he aired the following reservation to de Valera:

> There are, of course, other reasons why they would not desire an extensive development of our forces until they had got rid of their suspicions.[93]

Thus, while advocating greater openness, his own distrust was apparent. He told the Dominions Office assistant under-secretary, Harry Batterbee, that the atmosphere would have to be cleared before greater cooperation could ensue, and said the British 'would have to examine the foundations of their suspicions of us

with the same care as we examined the cause of our suspicions of them'. As an example, Walshe cited information he had received from a distant relative of his who happened to be a lecturer in the 'Staff college'. The attendance of Irish officers had demonstrated the mistrust, as the information given in lectures was modified to take into account the Irish presence. It appeared to Walshe, therefore, that there was a very marked hostility towards the idea of a settlement that would remove Britain's right to the Treaty ports in time of danger. This distrust would not be easy to overcome, as the 'informant', with whom Walshe had met intermittently since 1925, had not noticed any substantial change in attitude over the years.

In this memorandum Walshe reassured de Valera that partition was his primary concern in his talks with Dominions Office officials, but he was decidedly less optimistic than before. In reality, however, he was becoming less interested in partition as it seemed to be a diplomatic cul-de-sac. The message he received was that the British Prime Minister, Neville Chamberlain, could do 'nothing fundamental'. Walshe had little idea how to move forward from this impasse. His advice to Harding and Batterbee was somewhat unimaginative, and he simply emphasised the discrimination of the Ulster unionists towards the minority. He felt that the repetitive citation of facts and figures to prove that this was the case was the most effective strategy to follow. Walshe, at this stage, was clearly willing to diminish Irish demands on partition if substantial gains could be made in other areas.

Because of the difficulties over partition, Walshe believed that Britain was willing to confer considerable advantage in the area of trade. Citing a report by the secretary of the Department of Industry and Commerce, John Leydon, he said that the British were willing to 'go the whole hog in trade – or nearly so', and indicated that free entry for Irish agricultural produce to Britain was a distinct possibility. In return for this, the British wanted some measure of security in the oncoming war. They wanted an agreement, but the price was defence, and without it, Walshe assessed, Ireland would get nothing. It all depended on what de Valera was prepared to accept:

The millions will go up or down according to the extent to which you modify or accept the existing formula. If it remains as it is

or substantially so you will certainly get them down to your ten millions.

Walshe continued to become increasingly sceptical about attaining any fundamental development on the partition question, saying, 'We have no chance whatever in the existing circumstances of getting any form of Parliament for the whole of Ireland. Even a form of council plus a formal renunciation of the principle of partition will be hard enough to get.' Nonetheless, he strongly advocated agreement on the basis that Ireland would get a favourable financial settlement, even if it meant that Britain would secure a defence arrangement. He stated that Britain believed that an important first step in solving the partition question in the future would be for the two governments to form an agreement on defence matters. The suggestion was vague, but Walshe thought it a logical step, and he reminded de Valera that 'cooperation is a dynamic thing depending entirely on our will at any given moment. If we find that they are inclined to forget partition we shall have it in our power to show them by inaction or positive opposition that unity is our constant aim.' While not achieving all their aims, Walshe advocated agreement, reminding the Taoiseach that development was an evolutionary process:

> I should be ready to make real sacrifices to get rid of the Treaty. The sacrifice we are asked to make in defence is more apparent than real, because it is the only means of preventing the possible permanent loss of our independence in the almost certain crisis of a great war.

For Walshe, the first step was to get Britain out of the ports and establish a convincing military force. With this done, the Irish government would be in a much stronger position to begin a new phase of persuasion on the issue of Irish unity.

The timing of the negotiations was crucial. Walshe hoped that Britain's ongoing negotiations with the Italian government did not advance very far before the resumption of their talks with the Irish government. His assessment of the international climate was that any favourable developments for Britain on the world stage could affect possible concessions on partition. The more fearful Britain was for the future, the more it would be willing to pay for

a defence arrangement. However, he warned that there should be no delay in finalising an agreement even if all that was sought was not attained. Having travelled home for a brief period in March 1938 to receive instructions, Walshe returned to London and renewed his efforts to complete an agreement.

The US representative in Dublin, John Cudahy, commented on the ongoing negotiations in London. He had spoken with de Valera in mid-March, and at that time the Taoiseach indicated that the conference was doomed to complete failure. The following day, however, after hearing from Walshe, de Valera was far more hopeful for some resolution of the economic issues. Agreement on a defence arrangement was not ruled out but seemed unlikely. De Valera took a firm stance on neutrality, even at this early stage. He told Cudahy that British intransigence on partition would rule out an Anglo-Irish alliance in the coming war. Nevertheless, he also made clear that Irish interests lay firmly in the British sphere, and his statements more than hinted at what configuration Irish neutrality in a future war would take:

> In any defence arrangement … the position of Ireland would be one of neutrality with the understanding that Ireland would never take sides with any enemy of Great Britain. He said it was quite apparent that in external affairs Ireland must by the necessity of events take a course parallel to England … England acted as a shield against the continent threatened with war and he was convinced that the international political outlook of Ireland would more and more fuse with that of England.[94]

In the meantime, Walshe maintained close contact with Harding and Batterbee, who were increasingly pessimistic about any agreement being reached. Walshe allowed for a degree of bluff in their statements, but considered genuine their fears for the deteriorating situation in Europe. This would, he predicted, lessen the time and enthusiasm for dealing with Irish matters. Given the gravity of the situation, he advised that if a deal could be made the chance should be taken, as 'a postponement of the Agreement – if there is going to be one – would in the circumstances be giving hostages to fortune'. Walshe believed that if the Hitler threat became more real, the chances were that Chamberlain would have to give way to a younger and more energetic leader. Chamberlain had shown

himself amenable to compromise. Another leader might not be
so willing to see the Irish side, especially in a war situation. 'The
phantom of the reunification by force of these countries is never
wholly out of my mind', explained Walshe, who considered that
in a war situation, with a myriad of incalculable factors, British
fears would supersede Irish concerns, leading to a possible return
of that dreaded spectre.

Walshe did not wish to be alarmist but felt compelled to advise
the swift conclusion of an agreement with Britain at this 'very
critical hour of our history'.[95] De Valera hardly needed this warning. As far back as 1936 he had told Boland of his desire to see
the conclusion of an agreement with Britain as he was convinced
that Europe was on course for war.[96] However, for an agreement
to be reached compromise would be needed, and this meant that
Irish pressure on partition would have to wane. Walshe believed
that final discussions could soon take place and that agreement
could be reached forthwith. Walshe's advice was not ignored, and
the following month agreement was announced. On 25 April
1938 documents were signed by both sides in London. The Treaty
ports were returned to the Irish Free State. De Valera's government agreed to pay £10 million in settlement of the annuities,
and a commercial agreement reopened trade between Britain and
Ireland.

It has been pointed out that while, in retrospect, de Valera
regarded this treaty as one of his greatest achievements, at the
time he was less than enthusiastic.[97] As long as Ireland remained
divided his most coveted aim would remain unfulfilled. Britain
may have believed that Ireland would join it in the coming war,
but Ireland also had to make do with a less than ideal agreement.
Walshe had not succeeded in attaining a united Ireland, but his
participation and leadership in the negotiations had ensured success in many other areas. The Irish naval bases were returned to
Free State control, and de Valera's neutrality was now – largely
due to Walshe's efforts – a realistic possibility.

CHAPTER 3

WALSHE AND THE APPROACH OF WAR
1938–1939

DURING THE INTENSIVE months of negotiations in 1938 Walshe had expended considerable energy in bringing about an Anglo-Irish agreement. In the brief hiatus that followed, he took the opportunity to rejuvenate himself before international conflict became his all-consuming concern. He took time out with a friend to travel around north-eastern Africa, staying in Egypt and Sudan. Writing from Khartoum in May 1938 he told de Valera of his adventures travelling south, where the people get 'blacker and blacker'. He met the Governor General, who introduced him to government officials and the workings of British rule in the Sudan. Walshe was fascinated by the rule of order in the Anglo-Egyptian condominium, and thought that Britain's head representative there had done a splendid job:

> He is an idealist … and his very long experience in the Near East-Africa has not made him the narrow minded imperialist one expects to find in a post such as his. He can go where he likes here with a few unarmed policemen. The Festival of the Birthday of the Prophet is on at the moment and although there are tens of thousands of arabs in the adjoining cities … there isn't a trace of disorder.[1]

With the right type of government and an open-minded approach, Walshe believed Britain could remain there indefinitely. He mused over the changes to the region over past centuries, and its potential future:

> … but with the growing power especially cultural – of Arabia

which is only just across the Red Sea and is their religious home-
land, one wonders whether any white nations can hold out in these
regions for more than fifty years. While the people move slowly
they are accustomed to sudden and profound changes. We have
only to remember that this whole area was Christian long before
St. Patrick came to Ireland, and there isn't a trace left except a few
recently discovered ruins of churches of the 4th century.

Walshe mixed in government and social circles, and met a number of Irish or Britons of Irish extraction who praised the recent
Anglo-Irish Agreement. They were proud to declare their Irish
connections: 'They tell you of their Irish blood after about two
minutes', he explained, whereas in the past 'they waited about
four days'. Walshe revelled in their praise of recent political and
constitutional developments back home. Even the name Éire, he
said, denoted the individuality of Ireland, with its unique language, culture and people, and brought a sense of pride to Irish
people scattered throughout the world. Walshe saw a new dawn
for Ireland that would soon enable the country to increase its
standing in the international arena. As was his habit while on
holiday, Walshe let his imagination roam:

> Will you give a little thought to the question of a colony when you
> have leisure. It would be a splendid training ground for our people,
> and colonial budgets can be made to balance without subsidies
> from the home Government.

Walshe was wholly impressed by his experiences during his travels
to the extent he could contemplate an Irish colony in Africa. This
was an ironic, if not wholly contradictory idea, coming from Walshe,
who had spent so much time negotiating with Britain to remove the
colonial shackles from his own country. It seems that when Walshe
went on holiday, so too did his inhibitions to new and radical ideas.

From Sudan, Walshe travelled to Egypt where he wrote telling de Valera that he hoped the decision to call a general election
was the right one, and that he hoped Fianna Fáil would win the
overall majority it desired. 'We all want you to be in the position
of sitting back without ... worries and building up the country
according to the ideals you have inspired us with.' Walshe continued his observations of British foreign interests and talked to
a number of officials concerning the Palestinian question. One

official believed that Walshe had been sent on a 'voyage of explo-
ration' by the Irish government. Walshe did not dissuade him from
that view, saying that de Valera had encouraged him to travel and
send reports from wherever he went. The Irish government, he
said, realised the 'importance of Egypt as one of the chief sensitive areas in the world and were fully conscious of the difficulty of
the problems involved in the renaissance of the Jewish and Arab
peoples'. Walshe emphasised de Valera's global views to the official, who had expressed his admiration for the Taoiseach's work
at Geneva.

While in Egypt, Walshe met the permanent head of the Department of Foreign Affairs, and both agreed their respective countries
should establish diplomatic relations. The idea of Irish officers
training the Egyptian army was also mooted. Walshe was keen to
identify new areas of cooperation, and found Egyptian officials
receptive to the idea of establishing such links:

> They see the advantage of linking up with the individual associated
> states [of the Commonwealth] rather than with G.B. alone. Egypt
> could form the first unit of the new groups which would change
> the Commonwealth's character and give us an opportunity of slid-
> ing quietly out of the King['s] orbit.[2]

Walshe said he was in favour of remaining in the Commonwealth,
but believed that only if it developed into a more broadly based
organisation could it be successful. He was surprised to find
common agreement on the issue of allowing other monarchies or
republics join the Commonwealth. He also believed that if a
legation were set up in Cairo it would soon become extremely
influential there, and that this in turn would increase Ireland's
prestige in the eyes of Britain. This, however, could only be done
by a 'zealous worker', of which Walshe believed the Irish
diplomatic service had far too few. To him, it seemed that many
of the staff of the Irish legations were too relaxed in pursuit of
their objectives, thereby making them 'almost useless as
instruments in our fight for the recognition of our national
distinctiveness, or as factors in our relations with GB [Great
Britain]'. To remedy this, he suggested a period of six years of
study in order to gain a 'complete knowledge of Irish', which
might serve as a 'tonic for all of them as well as for the service at

home'. However, Walshe was not living in an ideal world, and the ideas he generated while on this trip reflect the relaxed nature of his sojourn. He was glad of the break from the day-to-day pressures of External Affairs. In June 1938 he returned to Dublin to take on the challenges of the oncoming international crisis.

At this time the British and French governments were continuing their efforts to appease Hitler. They had done little more than protest at the occupation by German troops of the Rhineland demilitarised zone. In March 1938 they had allowed the Anschluss, or unification, between Germany and Austria, while the Munich Agreement in September allowed the Sudetenland to be annexed by Hitler, who used the threat of war to achieve his aims.[3] Both Walshe and de Valera supported Chamberlain's policy of appeasement towards Hitler. Walshe was optimistic that war could be averted, despite the universal gloom concerning the European situation:

> I have not shared this pessimism because I could not imagine the British Government going back at this stage on the principles of determination merely because they don't like the methods by which Hitler means to realise them.

The diplomatic negotiations in Munich were closely followed by Dublin, and while de Valera was in Geneva Walshe kept him informed of the situation at regular intervals. Walshe described Britain's objections to Hitler's method of reclaiming the Sudeten areas of Czechoslovakia as 'a mere matter of punctilio'. He instructed Dulanty to convey the view in London that he thought it a mistake to risk war on this matter of small detail. At this stage Walshe clearly supported the policy of appeasement, and hoped Chamberlain would stick to that policy:

> One has a definite impression that the British Government are getting a little funky of the opposition which is growing in Great Britain against yielding to Hitler's demands. Otherwise I feel certain that Chamberlain would insist on the Czech Government accepting some compromise which allowed the partial occupation by the German troops.

Walshe saw the position of Czechoslovakia being weakened in European public opinion, and felt that this would help avert the

danger of war. He thought Britain should think twice about joining communist Russia:

> Moreover British Statesmen must be becoming daily more con-
> scious of the potential yields of joining with Russia to destroy
> the only barrier, undesirable though it may be, between Western
> Europe and Bolshevism.[4]

A few days later Walshe wrote again reporting on Chamberlain's
manoeuvres, describing them as a wonderful triumph. The British
Prime Minister had announced in the House of Commons that
agreement with Hitler could be reached very shortly. Walshe was
considerably impressed by Chamberlain's war-saving formula,
and enclosed a copy of the proposals that allowed for the return
of the Sudeten territories to Germany. He compared Germany's
claim to Sudetenland to the Irish partition question, suggesting to de Valera: 'You may someday wish to use it as a model.'[5]
The suggestion may not have been outlandish, as one historian
has suggested that de Valera had previously drawn a comparison
between Sudetenland and Northern Ireland and the partition
question.[6] The announcement of the agreement caused huge relief
around Europe. Walshe reported the same relief at home at what
he thought was 'the beginning of the end of the crisis'.[7]

Despite the hope that the crisis had passed, there was a certain
degree of military and defence cooperation between the British
and Irish governments already in progress at the time. The British
authorities sought collaboration with the Irish police in monitoring the movements of members of the IRA, while, later, External
Affairs requested British advice on the best means of defending the
Treaty ports. The British were equally anxious to fortify the ports,
and in September 1938 Walshe and the Irish High Commissioner
in London, John Dulanty, organised meetings between British and
Irish-army officials.[8] Cooperation then evolved to a higher level,
with more frequent talks between prominent officials. Walshe and
Dulanty were always closely involved, even if they left much of
the details to their military colleagues. These talks included the
possibility of the supply of information and advice on War Book
measures by Britain to Ireland, and it was also agreed that Irish
civilian experts in a wide range of fields would travel to London
to discuss various matters of common concern with the competent

British authorities.[9] Collaboration was extensive and involved all
levels of officials. However, despite this cooperation it became
increasingly clear that Britain and Ireland had different ideas on
where Ireland should stand in any possible future conflict.

For Walshe, American opinion towards any potential war
and towards Irish involvement in it was of crucial importance.
Protection from Germany and possibly Britain would be guaranteed, he thought, by the United States government, which, he
hoped, would realise the strength of Irish-American opinion. In
early 1939 Walshe assured the chargé d'affaires of the US legation
in Dublin, John MacVeagh, that Ireland would remain neutral in
the coming conflict. No official declaration of neutrality would
be made, he said, but the retention of the Irish representatives
in Berlin and Rome would be sufficient to demonstrate that
Ireland would not enter the conflict. MacVeagh suggested that
Ireland's Commonwealth membership and its strategic proximity
to Britain would make it an automatic target for any enemy of
Britain. Walshe rejected this argument and restated the position
that, while Ireland would continue to supply food to England,
joining with Britain would not be sanctioned by the Irish people
as this would be sure to cause a 'revolution' if forced upon them.[10]
Walshe had by now reviewed his earlier position on neutrality.
Having aligned himself with de Valera, he was ready to promote
the idea with as much passion as it required. He indicated that
neutrality should be maintained despite political pressure or offers
of compromise from any quarter. To MacVeagh, Walshe appeared
to be completely convinced that neutrality in a world at war was
both feasible to maintain and advantageous for Ireland. This air-
ing of the principle of Irish neutrality was a useful exercise for
Walshe, who at this early stage was interested in gaining a flavour
of international reaction to the Irish policy.

Later that same month Walshe was put under further pressure
from the US representative. MacVeagh 'informally' delivered a copy
of Roosevelt's message to Hitler of 15 April 1939, and indicated
that a message from the Irish government welcoming the statement
was being sought as a 'constructive move in the promotion of
world peace'. This would be of assistance, continued MacVeagh,
in generating opposition towards aggression and war. Ireland was
clearly being asked on which side it stood, as MacVeagh explained
that such messages of support had been received from all over

the world, including countries from the Near East, the American continent and from Europe. Walshe tried to buy time to consider the request, and he told MacVeagh that he would instruct the Irish representative in Washington, Robert Brennan, to find out exactly which European countries had sent such messages and what the contents of those replies were. 'I should then be able to convey the desire of the State Department to my Minister with the relevant information', replied Walshe, somewhat impertinently. Walshe was dubious about MacVeagh's account that they had already received widespread support for the note. Walshe's suspicions proved correct, and Robert Brennan replied the following day, outlining that in fact 'very few' European countries had yet sent replies, although those that had been sent were supportive of the President's move. Walshe's stalling tactics were crucial and he fully realised the importance of the American request. There had been rumours that German diplomats were looking for the names of the European states referred to with a view to asking them whether they felt threatened by Germany. Walshe believed that if this question were put to the Irish government, an answer which did not offend Germany would have to be given. This left him in a difficult position. They could not afford to affront the US President, but if unqualified approval were given to Roosevelt's statement, it might imply that Ireland was accepting the US President's assertion that Germany had aggressive designs towards Ireland.

Walshe was not impressed by certain attitudes displayed by the Americans, which suggested that they did not regard the Irish Free State as an independent entity. They had been ungenerous in their stance towards clearing up a mistake that had described 'Great Britain and Ireland' as a single entity. Perhaps unwisely, Walshe allowed his pique to affect his judgement, and he was not inclined to be helpful towards the Americans at this stage:

> For these reasons one feels very reluctant to come to their aid in order to restore life to the President's damp squib. In any case, there would be no harm in waiting to see what response the appeal for replies is going to meet with in Europe ... Perhaps you could find a moment to tell me on the 'phone what your wishes are on the matter.[11]

While we are not privy to the conversation that may have taken place

between them, Walshe's advice to de Valera to wait and see, while somewhat predictable, was prudent in the circumstances. Walshe also drafted a possible reply to Roosevelt in case it was needed:

> Great sacrifices are required from the rulers of all nations to avert the danger of a new holocaust of the Youth of the world. I urge upon you to make a new appeal to the great Powers calling upon them to make the sacrifices necessary to build a new order based upon justice and upon respect for the freedom and integrity of all small nations.

This was a carefully worded statement which said very little except that Ireland did not wish to see a war occur. Walshe was searching for that space in which enough ambiguity existed to enable him not to offend anyone. The real lesson for Walshe, however, was that, contrary to what he previously believed, it was now evident that the US government could not be depended upon to ward off British insistence that Ireland join the conflict.

Walshe did not allow his relations with the Dublin-based US officials to deteriorate because of the incident. That same month Harry Balch, a junior official at the US legation in Dublin, wrote to the State Department to express his appreciation for his recent promotion. Balch's age, maturity and world view may have helped him to empathise with Walshe, who he described as an 'old bachelor'. Concerning de Valera's planned trip to the US later that year, he wrote: 'If plans materialize the Taoiseach (pronounced approximately TEASHOP), Mr DeValera, and a party will leave for the United States about the end of this month.' It was predicted that it would be de Valera's aim, while in the US, to make progress on partition. Walshe, who was to accompany the Taoiseach on the journey, was held in high esteem by this American official:

> Mr Walshe actually runs the Department of External Affairs. He is an awfully fine fellow. Do not fail to cultivate him. He is very able. You can talk to him without feeling that you must hold back some things unsaid. If there are any doubtful points raised by any of our good Irish American citizens in the United States on the Irish problem in Ireland which are bothering you you can talk them over with Joe Walshe in full detail without any fear. He has one of those broad impartial minds which sees both sides to any question readily.[12]

Soon after, however, de Valera felt obliged to indefinitely postpone his proposed trip to the United States due to what he described as 'certain grave events'. He was referring to the recent decision by the British government to impose conscription on Northern Ireland, to which he vigorously objected on the grounds that it would coerce the nationalist community into fighting the war for Britain. It was now clear, however, that diplomatic events would require re-prioritisation over all other plans.

Had the visit gone ahead, the Taoiseach would have been expected to perform a number of official functions for the Irish-American community, visit a number of major cities and make an official visit to President Roosevelt. Walshe had welcomed the planned visit as he wanted the chance to foster better relations with the US administration. The trip was cancelled, therefore, with great reluctance, and an opportunity to smooth the path for Irish neutrality was perhaps lost. De Valera expressed his regret and indicated the importance he attached to the visit:

> I was to be accompanied by the Secretary of the Department of External Affairs, and other officials whose knowledge of America or whose experience of certain duties would enable the work which I had in mind to be done properly.[13]

Walshe, therefore, had been expected to play an important role in securing the objectives of that agenda.

The cancellation of the trip was a significant setback in External Affairs' wartime preparations. De Valera remained worried that the State Department did not understand the Irish situation. He expressed these fears to the US minister, John Cudahy:

> He told me very frankly that he did not repose great confidence in the American State Department, being under the impression that it was subject to a pro-Anglo tendency. His last words were a caution against divulging too minutely this discussion.[14]

Despite the mutual goodwill felt between the two countries, de Valera realised the strength of Anglo-American links, and had therefore felt it necessary that he and Walshe travel to the United States to put forward the case for Irish neutrality. It was important that the State Department be convinced of the justice of the

Irish position, and that Ireland would not be willingly used by Germany against Britain.

The cancellation of the trip placed heightened importance on Walshe's relationship with the US diplomats in Dublin. That relationship would soon be tested when Walshe spoke to Cudahy concerning the Military Training Bill proposed in the British parliament, which provided for the conscription of Irish residents in the United Kingdom. Walshe explained that the sovereignty of Ireland was well established and recognised by Great Britain, that the Irish Constitution had clearly defined the status of Irish citizenship, and that the current attempts by the British government to conscript Irish citizens temporarily resident in Britain had no authorisation in international law. Constitutional law was Walshe's speciality, and Cudahy listened with interest to the secretary's arguments concerning the nature of the proposed bill:

> The weakness of the British position, Mr Walshe holds, is its effort to include in the Military Training Bill Irishmen on the ground that they are British subjects. If the language of the proposed measure were based upon residence as such and did not confuse the question of nationality, Ireland could not plausibly object.[15]

Thus, Walshe outlined that his objection was based on the fact that Irish residents in Britain were being singled out for conscription. He was, however, unsuccessful in his bid for support on this issue, and the US government maintained pressure on Ireland to declare its intentions with a pro-Allied slant. Cudahy told de Valera that Ireland and the US were in an analogous position with regard to the forthcoming war. Both, he said, 'were determined to preserve neutrality, yet neither could be indifferent to the fate of democratic political institutions'. However, the level of resolve to maintain neutrality and the degree of concern for the fate of democracy may not have proved as similar as Cudahy had thought. The distance from the area of conflict was a significant factor in determining the varying degrees of concern for pragmatic self-preservation versus principled consideration for European democracy.

According to Cudahy, de Valera admitted that 'in a general European war ... Ireland could not stay out, but must inevitably be drawn in on the side of Great Britain and France.' From this,

Cudahy concluded that Ireland was 'theoretically' on the side of the Allies but that 'geography' rather than 'ideology' had dictated the need for neutrality. De Valera recognised that modern technology in communications and transportation meant it would be very difficult to keep Ireland isolated from conflict. This realism led Cudahy to believe that neutrality was only being used to provide time to prepare its defences:

> The two islands were now one, strategically, and in any war of proportions, it was an ignorant viewpoint which thought that Ireland could witness with indifference a conquered England. Certainly Ireland's turn would be next.[16]

Walshe may have agreed with the sentiment of the Taoiseach's comments, but he would have been unwilling to admit it to the American diplomat. It was too early to use up Ireland's bargaining power without first having received corresponding advantage. The US position was of crucial importance to the Irish government. If America entered the war, the pressure on Ireland to join also would be considerable. Ireland looked to the US government and people to safeguard her interests. The United States in turn was looking for certain assurances from the Irish government as concern for Britain's ability to defeat Hitler grew. But as the war loomed closer, the fear of the German army became all too real. War was a prospect, Walshe realised, that Ireland was far from ready to meet.

De Valera, having transferred Fred Boland to the Department of Industry and Commerce at the outbreak of the economic war, now redrafted him to External Affairs to assist Walshe with the implementation of neutrality. Boland was given particular charge of Axis affairs, while Walshe was responsible for the Allies.[17] This explains why the majority of the wartime documentation surrounding Walshe deals with John Maffey and David Gray. Boland was greatly appreciated by de Valera, who felt more at ease knowing that Walshe was not alone to face the wartime diplomatic challenge.

Germany's representative to Ireland, Eduard Hempel, had been appointed in 1937. He had never joined the Nazi Party and has been described as a diplomat of the old school.[18] As war approached, Walshe was reminded of Hempel's reasoned views

when he came into contact with the more pro-Nazi elements in the Dublin legation. In February 1939 he met the recently appointed first secretary to the German legation, Henning Thomsen, whose opening remarks to Walshe were decidedly undiplomatic. He complained to Walshe that the people at his previous post, Norway, were more to his liking than the Irish. This was because the Norwegians were a Protestant people while the Irish were Catholic and dominated by the clergy. Walshe was not impressed by this impudence. Thomsen then went on to complain that in a recent pastoral Bishop Browne of Galway had accused Germany of 'violence, lying, murder and condemning of other races and people'. Browne had no right to discuss Germany's affairs, he said, pointing out that it was Germany's aim to confine priests to their own sphere and prevent them from interfering in matters of the state. Thomsen also said that the Irish government would have to take responsibility for articles critical of Germany in the *Irish Press*, as it was controlled by Fianna Fáil. He pointed out that Germany could criticise Ireland on a number of issues, and cited the extreme poverty of many of its people and the absence of any organised effort to remedy this situation. Walshe was not gratified by these illustrations but was careful not to become incensed by the comments:

> I gave all the usual replies, and a little more, to this outburst, but I was careful to let him run his full length before replying, as it seemed to my mind important to get to know the type we have to deal with in Herr Thomsen.

Thomsen was, he thought, a complete contrast to Hempel, who would not have conducted himself in this fashion no matter what his views:

> The German Minister, who – although sometimes lacking in a sense of humour – never allows you to forget that he is a cultured gentleman. Herr Thomsen is insolent, bombastic, and apparently devoid of any sense of the real values of life. He is the first German I have met who seems to combine in himself all the worst ideas behind the Nazi regime.[19]

Walshe told Thomsen that the Nazi Party's Dublin organisation was a source of concern to the Irish government. The leader of

the section was a Dr Mahr, who was also employed by the state as director of the National Museum. It was an embarrassing position for the Irish government, but Thomsen politely indicated to Walshe that the matter was none of his affair. It was a stark reminder to Walshe that, as war approached, Nazi opinion would leave little room for civility, and while Hempel might have been somewhat sympathetic this attitude was clearly in the minority.

In August 1939 Walshe met Hempel to outline the Irish position in the oncoming war. He stated that it was Ireland's firm intention to remain neutral unless forced into a belligerent position by being bombed or attacked.[20] Outlining the unique basis of this policy, he emphasised that Irish neutrality could not 'have all the characters of those neutral States which have had a long existence as separate States'.[21] From the outset Walshe's task was a difficult one. He emphasised the country's dependence and connections with Britain and sought 'special consideration' for Ireland, which sought to maintain its traditionally close relationship with its nearest neighbour. At the same time he told Hempel that there could be no such reciprocal arrangement for German interests. Walshe further warned that the German legation in Dublin would not be permitted to help in the prosecution of the war, and he threatened the mutual withdrawal of legations if this was not adhered to. The language used was significantly more stern than that used by Walshe during his first wartime meetings with British officials.

According to Hempel's report of their conversation, Walshe felt an attack on Ireland was unlikely from either Germany or Britain as it would incite the wrath of Irish-American opinion and thereby incur the disfavour of the United States government. Walshe sought optimum lenience from the German minister, arguing that, while remaining neutral, Ireland's trade with Britain was of vital importance. Yet, while pleading for this special relationship, Walshe was extraordinarily pragmatic in realising the implications for Ireland of this projected course of destruction of Britain. In Hempel's account, Walshe 'repeated the suggestion that in the case of German acts of war against Britain involving Ireland, any suffering incurred should be kept to a minimum'.[22] Walshe sought a statement from the German government not only outlining Germany's non-aggressive attitude towards Ireland but also requesting a declaration of support for Irish nationalist aspirations. In some respects this request seems somewhat

ludicrous considering Hitler's track record on issues relating to national borders. At this early stage, however, Walshe felt that with fear and confusion prevalent, it was prudent to make certain requests and to construct certain ambiguities under the aegis of neutrality in the hope of being able to maintain an overt yet ambivalent bias towards both sides of the divide. It was, of course, just as easy for Germany to maintain a similar posture, and so the diplomatic positioning had begun in earnest.

When the German Foreign Minister, Joachim von Ribbentrop, replied to Hempel's telegram, he agreed that some statement of respect for Irish neutrality should be made, and added that some mention of German sympathy towards Irish national aspirations could be included. Hempel carried out these instructions two days later when, in the presence of Walshe, he outlined the German position to de Valera. The Taoiseach reiterated his desire to remain neutral and maintain friendly relations with Germany, but reminded Hempel that trade and political reasons necessitated that Ireland show 'a certain consideration' towards Britain.[23] Hempel believed that the Irish government would make 'a sincere effort' to remain neutral. De Valera wanted some public declaration outlining the friendly attitude of Germany towards Ireland, and Walshe drafted a proposed statement for Hempel's approval. Hempel sent the draft to headquarters, which replied suggesting the following amendment: 'But when our promise is referred to, the words "conditional on a corresponding attitude by Ireland" must be added'.[24] Thus, Ireland's neutrality was not envisaged as a token gesture, as seemed to be the case in the statement drafted by Walshe. Hempel was further ordered to keep a close eye on government officials, public comment and common rumour for any signs that may indicate anything less than committed neutrality. With this in mind, it was through his regular meetings with Walshe that Hempel attempted to gauge Ireland's attitude towards Germany throughout the war.

On 1 September 1939 Britain declared war on Germany following Hitler's invasion of Poland. For a period of five months after the invasion of Finland in November 1939 there was little other major land confrontation. It was a period in which Walshe and the Department of External Affairs closely monitored international events but made few diplomatic initiatives. Following his preparatory meetings with Hempel, Walshe was then sent to

London to explain the Irish case to the British.[25] Walshe described
his mission as seeking a 'frank talk' with Anthony Eden, Secretary
of State for Dominion Affairs. He insisted that while wanting
to uphold the essentials of neutrality, the Taoiseach also wished
for close cooperation between the two governments.[26] Here he
asked for 'flexibility' in relation to Ireland, and he urged Eden of
the 'necessity of helping us to be friendly' in the implementation
of Irish neutrality, meaning that steps should be taken immediately towards unifying Ireland. In these discussions Eden's people
raised a number of 'important politico-technical questions', and
Walshe's objective was to put him *au courant*. In one session Eden
was accompanied by Sir Edward Harding and Sir Eric Machtig.
Walshe's account of his handling of this negotiating imbalance
shows something of his resolute diplomatic style:

> Mr Eden asked me straight away whether I had any objection to
> the presence of the others. I had to say I was very pleased to have
> them there, but I made up my mind that there was going to be no
> progress until I met him alone again.[27]

No matter how Eden tried, Walshe was determined to negotiate
in secrecy and confidence. 'He mentioned South Africa again, but
I waited for our next private meeting to resume the discussion
on this matter.' In fact Walshe also instructed Dulanty, the Irish
High Commissioner in London, not to accompany him to their
next meeting in order that Eden might speak more frankly.

In his report to the Prime Minister, Eden commented on
Walshe's talks with the Admiralty, which had 'succeeded satis-
factorily' in his estimation. Eden thought it was impossible to
be sure as to what course things would take as they were dealing
with a highly volatile factor, the Irish temperament. He believed
Walshe to be of a somewhat temperamental nature, reporting
wide fluctuations in attitude and opinion. However, he acknowledged that the negotiations with Walshe had given him optimism
in the belief that British policy, given time and patience, was on
course. Their policy was to develop and nurture friendly relations
with Ireland with a view to acquiring some of the facilities they
needed. The Dominions Secretary, therefore, was in a confident
mood for future Anglo-Irish cooperation:

Walshe has been profuse in his assurances that for the first time in history Éire is truly pro-British in sentiment. This happy state of mind, he asserts, is to be found among Ministers and Government Officials no less among the people.[28]

Dulanty, however, quickly dampened the enthusiasm generated by Walshe by showing Eden an Irish newspaper which ardently avouched that Britain was the one true enemy.

According to de Valera's official biographers, Longford and O'Neill, the main aim of Walshe's visit was to seek official British recognition of Irish neutrality. While he did not succeed in this, his talks did lead to the decision to have a British diplomat appointed to Dublin.[29] Walshe had previously raised this issue and was glad of the opportunity to advise Harding on the type of diplomat that would do well in Dublin:

> Whilst in some ways the appointment of a Catholic would be of advantage, there was no real necessity for this. Neither was there any reason for the prospective High Commissioner to have an interest in racing or golf.[30]

Walshe suggested that the candidate should not associate solely, as other diplomats had done, with the Protestant Ascendancy to the exclusion of the political elite. It was important that Ireland had a well-qualified diplomat as it would help Walshe's understanding of the British point of view. Anthony Eden suggested John Maffey as a suitable and well-qualified candidate. Initially Walshe and de Valera were sceptical, but Eden was not in bargaining mood and pointed out to Walshe that the British government had responded to de Valera's request and so he expected negotiations on the matter to be settled post-haste.[31] Walshe flew home to discuss the matter with de Valera, and returned to London a few days later to conclude this round of the consultations.

Soon after, Sir John Maffey made a number of secret visits to de Valera in Dublin with a view to resolving the remaining difficulties over his appointment.[32] He arrived on 20 September 1939, and made contact with Walshe who brought him to de Valera to discuss the issue of what title he was to take. There were various reasons on both sides why the term 'minister' would cause difficulties. Maffey quickly learned the areas that would require a sensitive approach.

During a discussion on neutrality he ascertained from Walshe that to mention the issue of facilities at Berehaven would 'upset the applecart'. The British representative decided to take Walshe's advice, considering the progress that was being made in other areas. Walshe had given Maffey a clear understanding of the importance of the ports and Ireland's perceived independence of action and determination to stick with neutrality. 'Action at Berehaven would undoubtedly shake the President's position', said Maffey, who cautioned that 'If such action is vital we shall have to take it. But we must think twice and count the gain and the loss.'[33]

In conversation with Maffey, Walshe emphasised the assistance that the Irish government had already provided to Britain. He pointed in particular to the transmission by the Irish authorities of a message to the British Admiralty regarding a submarine that had been spotted off the Irish coast. It was arranged that any further sightings would also be forwarded by code. Maffey acknowledged this assistance but indicated that if the British Admiralty heard of any German submarine activity in Irish territorial waters they would move in and attack, and that the only thing the Irish authorities could do was to turn a 'blind eye'. Walshe seemed to accept this, said Maffey, 'if silence is acceptance'. Walshe discussed the question of British planes landing in Irish territory. De Valera, it seems, contemplated keeping the planes and crews and putting them to use in Irish service. Maffey, however, was hopeful that the Irish position could be changed, as Walshe had repeatedly indicated Ireland's desire to be cooperative. The Walshe–Maffey relationship was established in earnest, and all matters great and small could be discussed.

Walshe was engaged in the difficult task of parallel diplomacy, trying to satisfy two opposing sides at the same time. William Warnock of the Irish legation in Berlin wrote to Walshe concerning a meeting with Under-Secretary of State Woermann, who expressed his satisfaction that Ireland had decided to remain neutral. He also wished to thank the Irish government for its efforts in ensuring the safe passage of fifty German nationals who returned to Germany from Ireland.[34] The Germans, however, had a further request. Woermann told Warnock of the difficulties they had encountered in communicating with the German legation in Dublin, whose communications had previously passed through Britain. He requested that Warnock be allowed to forward

correspondence for the German legation in the Irish diplomatic mailbag as 'a special favour'. Boland replied to Warnock, saying that the request presented 'too many difficulties and objections to be capable of acceptance'.[35] This request represented only the beginning of the many problems faced by External Affairs in dealing with both Allied and Axis concerns. While it was neces-sary to be sensitive to both groups, the approach taken on this issue demonstrates the unwillingness to favour Germany if it came into conflict with the Allied view.

In November 1939 the United States representative in Dublin, John Cudahy, attended a fund-raising meeting for a local charity. He was alarmed when it became an occasion for 'violent I.R.A. agitation'.[36] When de Valera began his address he was heckled by a large section of the audience who wished to protest against the confinement of a number of IRA prisoners who were on hunger strike in Mountjoy prison. Following the release of a prisoner on hunger strike, others had decided to follow the same course, but de Valera was adamant that the authority of the government would not be undermined. Cudahy was worried that the 'martyr complex' in the Irish psyche would lead to a wave of sympathy for the hunger strikers and a possible reaction against the gov-ernment. De Valera confirmed his apprehension that the IRA may gain popular support from the crisis. He explained that the economic impact of the war had led to discontent and 'because Fianna Fáil had been in power now for nearly eight years ... there was always a tendency among the Irish people, in common with the rest of mankind, to believe improvement always came with a change of Government.' A few days previously, in conversa-tion with Walshe, the US minister was shown a patently more optimistic picture. Walshe told him that the government did not regard the IRA with apprehension, but Cudahy, not convinced, pointed to the allegations that Germany was now supporting the IRA. Again, Walshe attempted to assuage these worries and claimed that there was no evidence whatsoever to confirm these allegations. It was not long, however, before Walshe was forced to inform Cudahy that the government had decided to release three further hunger strikers. It was an obvious defeat for de Valera, but Walshe explained that this was preferred to enshrining the prisoners as national martyrs. He explained that the censored press had been allowed little coverage of the event

and that soon the issue would be forgotten. 'No publicity for heroism to feed upon, no heralding victory for the strikers, no Martyr Complex', explained Walshe, who thought that the prestige of the government might have suffered in the minds of a few die-hard extremists, but among the Irish people generally there was no harm done:

> It was a significant thing, Mr Walshe concluded, defensively, that a hunger striker never tried to strike again, and those who had starved themselves for weeks were too weakened and exhausted to cause trouble for a long time after their release. He said the 'Martyr Complex' in Irish politics was something to be avoided like the plague, and this the Government had in mind vividly when it decided to save the lives of the hunger strikers.[37]

Walshe again assured Cudahy that the government had not the 'slightest apprehension' concerning the IRA, but the American minister was not convinced by the explanation of de Valera's 'complete about face' on the issue of the hunger strikers.

In December 1939 Cudahy wrote again expressing his concern about the strength of the paramilitaries. A further fifty-three IRA prisoners were released on the basis of a High Court decision that ruled that the warrants that authorised their internment were invalid and unconstitutional, despite the provisions laid down in the Offences Against the State Act.[38] Walshe was extremely worried about the consequences of the ruling, and told Cudahy that the government was considering reconvening the Dáil to amend the Constitution. He did not share the same concerns as the High Court for the rights of the IRA prisoners who had been detained without charge for over two-and-a-half months:

> Mr Walshe said that the Government had to have the power to arrest and detain persons whom it had reason to believe were members of the I.R.A. and who were a menace to the safety of the State.[39]

The fact that the government had not sufficient evidence to bring many of the prisoners before a special court was a secondary matter. Individual liberties were not among Walshe's chief priorities:

> The interests of the State, he thought, in such cases should be

above the individual rights of the citizen and the basic law should be amended to permit the Government to make preventive arrests and detections when the safety of the State demanded it.

When questioned by Cudahy concerning the detention of 'Republican suspects' by the British authorities in Northern Ireland, Walshe thought this a totally different matter altogether, and endeavoured to explain:

> In the case of the Ulster authorities they were acting against a minority which was fighting for a just cause, the unity of their country. The Irish Government on the other hand was merely preventing a small and illegal organization from endangering the safety of the State.

Walshe told the US representative that the Irish government had appealed to Britain concerning the death sentences passed on two IRA men who were convicted of planting a bomb and executing an explosion in Coventry. The sentence of death was too severe, thought Walshe, who felt clemency should be granted on the basis that the bomb had exploded prematurely, that the injuries caused were not, therefore, intentional, and that it was the policy of the IRA not to take life but only to cause material damage. Walshe's nationalism led him to retain 'a certain admiration for the courage and stoicism displayed by the prisoners during the trial'.[40] Cudahy, however, was not satisfied by the contradictory nature of Walshe's replies:

> I find it difficult to reconcile this point of view that foreign governments may not place I.R.A. members in 'deterrent confinement' whereas the Irish Government maintains that it can arrest its own citizens on suspicion and hold them indefinitely without trial.

Walshe's inconsistencies failed to alleviate Cudahy's fears concerning the strength of the IRA. The State Department, which had not encouraged the decision to remain neutral, was now unconvinced that the Irish government could maintain that policy in the face of joint IRA–German collaboration.

At the end of October, after two months of war, Cudahy reported that it was now possible to appraise the Irish situation. He believed that Ireland would remain neutral for the duration

of the war. 'It is a real neutrality', he continued, 'even though benevolently disposed towards England.'[41] The American minister pointed out the importance of the Irish ports as naval bases but insisted that it would be a grave mistake for Britain to attempt to use force in order to gain access to them. The ports, he admitted, would remain an important question but this would not concern him personally. Not satisfied with his Irish mission, Cudahy soon left, seeking greater involvement in affairs in continental Europe.[42] His replacement, David Gray, arrived in Ireland as US minister to Éire in early 1940.

In a contemporary interview in the *Irish Independent*, Gray related the story of his appointment to Ireland as US minister. When he first met Cudahy in 1938 he remarked: 'You've got the only job that I would like myself: Minister to Ireland.'[43] Cudahy reported these sentiments to Roosevelt, and two years later Gray received the post he desired. Gray referred to Roosevelt as 'Dear Franklin' or 'My Dear Boss', and it was, perhaps, his familiarity and blood relationship with the Roosevelt family that made his reports to the US wartime President both open and frank.[44] While commenting on the situation in Ireland he would sometimes include the latest joke circulating Dublin. Gray's wife, Maude, was Eleanor Roosevelt's aunt but various accounts describe Eleanor and Maude as more like sisters. Gray, who was seventy years of age when he took up the post in Ireland, was considerably older than Roosevelt, and in terms of family hierarchy would have ranked more senior than the President. While Gray's opinions and attitudes towards the Irish situation would have naturally coincided with many at the State Department, his family connections may have influenced these US officials in their reports and instructions towards their new volunteer in Ireland.

Before Gray left Washington he had been advised that in the interests of economy it had been decided to combine the chancery of the United States' Dublin legation and their Consulate-General offices. Thus, it was planned that the lease to the legation, which was soon due to lapse, would not be renewed. While in London, Gray told newspaper correspondents about the plan, which caused considerable consternation among Irish officials. Soon after his arrival in Dublin, Gray learned from Walshe why the prospect of the United States vacating the premises caused so much alarm. It appears that since his appointment Maffey had been trying to find

a satisfactory residence with little success. Upon reading Gray's reported statement in London he immediately sought permission to take over the lease. This was far from satisfactory for Walshe and de Valera, who now found themselves in an awkward position:

> Now it appears that the last thing the present Government of Ireland or any future Government conceivable for the next decade wants is to have the British High Commissioner installed in the house formerly the seat of the Chief Secretary for Ireland under the old regime. They feel it would give color to the charge already made by the I.R.A. that Ireland is governed from Westminster. Furthermore, they would greatly prefer not to have to tell this to Sir John Maffey.[45]

It was therefore felt inopportune for the US Legation to vacate the premises at this time. In his subsequent conversations with Walshe and other officials, Gray learned something of the nature of the relationship between his predecessor, John Cudahy, and the Department of External Affairs. He found that the suggestion that the lease was not to be renewed caused some animation because when Cudahy had renewed the lease two years previously he had been told to set the amount of rent himself. Gray reported that while he was in Washington he had agreed with the original decision on economic grounds but that he now understood something of the nature of the Irish–American relationship, explaining that the American legation in Dublin had been accorded 'a very unusual position' by the Irish government. He found that John Cudahy had established a 'peculiar relation' with the government, and 'was received almost as an official adviser, that he was invited to express his views' by Irish officials. The fact that the Irish government had chosen to honour the special importance of the US representatives by housing them in 'one of their national monuments' would make the vacation of the current premises a diplomatic and economic error. And so, in his first diplomatic move, he urged the State Department to reconsider its plans to relocate.

Dublin was David Gray's first diplomatic post and, not having served any apprenticeship, his diplomatic skills were untried and untested. It is true that many US foreign diplomatic posts were awarded by political appointment.[46] However, Roosevelt may have had some initial reservations concerning the possible nepotic nature of appointing his uncle-in-law to Dublin. Secretary of

State Cordell Hull followed up some initial enquiries and assured the President that 'the nomination was in accordance with existing law'.[47] Gray himself was delighted with being appointed to his mission of choice, and wrote to Roosevelt:

I wish to congratulate you on your excellent appointment to Ireland.
Aff. [affectionately] the Appointee.[48]

Kees Van Hoek believes that Gray was a very suitable candidate for the Irish post, arguing that 'The American Minister knew Ireland more intimately than any other foreign diplomat before accreditation.' Gray had lived in west Cork between 1933 and 1934 for the purpose of writing a book on Ireland.[49] Raymond J. Raymond expands on this, pointing out that Gray visited Ireland three times between 1934 and 1939, and thus concludes that Gray's experience of Ireland did, in fact, make him the most knowledgeable American envoy ever sent to the Irish Free State.[50] Only time would tell, however, if Gray was, in fact, a suitable candidate for this sensitive Irish post.

When Germany invaded Poland on 1 September 1939 a declaration of Irish neutrality was affirmed by Dáil Éireann. Information surrounding the initial formulation of the policy of neutrality is lacking, and it remains unclear what preparations had been made for the implementation of that policy. In October 1939 Walshe wrote that 'in deciding neutrality Government were exercising sovereign right as were Governments of Canada or France when declaring war.'[51] Other reasons given included the explanation that no other policy was possible in the circumstances and that the whole country was in favour of neutrality. The expression of Irish sovereignty was cited on many occasions as the primary rationale for the policy. In December Ireland's High Commissioner to Canada, John Hearne, was informed that the maintenance of neutrality was 'vital' as it was 'the most important proof the people have had of the reality of our status'. Walshe, however, was able to offer Hearne little other information or advice on how best to establish Irish neutrality in the minds of those in his host country except to say in a cryptic telegram, 'agree that best line about neutrality say nothing about it and assume needs no apology from you'.[52] He believed that in speeches or any public comments Hearne should

focus on Ireland's historical past. Walshe outlined that Hearne, as was the case with his Irish counterparts around the world, would have to fend for himself as head office would not be in a position to send him any detailed material to explain the Irish policy. It was the aspiration of the Department of External Affairs to limit the negative effects on the country, but there appears to have been little planning into how the policy of neutrality was to be implemented. Walshe's role is of primary importance in an analysis of the idiosyncratic exposition of that policy. His primary task was to meet Allied and Axis diplomats stationed in Dublin and brief them on the Irish position. Memoranda of his meetings with Eduard Hempel, Sir John Maffey and David Gray, therefore, form the basis of this analysis of Walshe's role during Ireland's wartime emergencies.

CHAPTER 4

WALSHE AND THE ESTABLISHMENT OF SUSTAINABLE NEUTRALITY 1940[1]

TOWARDS THE END of 1940 Winston Churchill stated that Irish neutrality caused Britain 'a most heavy and grievous burden'. In reality, however, the implementation of this policy was a burden on de Valera and Walshe, the two main protagonists in the formulation and execution of Irish foreign policy. They shouldered the burden of devising and maintaining neutrality, particularly during 1940 as the 'phoney war' came to an end. With the recommencement of hostilities on the Continent, a period of frenzied activity occurred in Iveagh House as Joseph Walshe endeavoured to establish Irish neutrality in the international diplomatic landscape. To facilitate this, Walshe engaged in detailed discussions with all sides. He travelled to London on many occasions, but most of his contacts were in Dublin with John Maffey (the British 'representative'), David Gray (the US minister) and Eduard Hempel (the German minister). Walshe's and de Valera's anxieties not to incur the wrath of the Allies was reflected in their policy of cooperative neutrality. Notwithstanding covert assistance to the Allies, the Irish government did not desire to enter the war against Germany. This formed the basis of the triangle in which Walshe found himself. Balancing on a neutral tightrope with a gulf of Axis or Allied belligerency on either side was no small concern when falling one way or the other could have meant certain destruction.

It is clear that with the commencement of hostilities External Affairs was thrown into disarray. The pace of life speeded up dramatically in the department, and Boland was recalled from Industry and Commerce to assist Walshe. Boland states 'the

rhythm of life moved up very quickly because the essential thing
in time of war is to make sure that everyone who should know,
does know. So there was a tremendous amount of paper flying around.' In 1938 Walshe had doubted that de Valera would
seriously consider the policy of neutrality. He was not alone in
thinking that neutrality was not a feasible option as, according
to Boland, support for neutrality at the beginning of the war
was around 25 to 30 per cent, and even those who supported
the policy had serious doubts about the government's ability to
enforce it. The ramifications of such a policy had not been clearly
thought out and little consideration was given to the best means
available to implement it. Walshe's worries were added to by the
fact that the Irish military was in no position to defend neutrality
if called upon to do so. Much of the responsibility for the safety
of the country, therefore, was left to the diplomacy of Walshe and
the Department of External Affairs.

Throughout 1940 Walshe's attitude towards the war underwent
substantial adjustment. This would greatly influence his advice to
de Valera and would colour his diplomatic discussions. He initially
believed it likely that Germany would be victorious. The fall of
France in mid-June, in particular, encouraged Walshe to maintain
Ireland's favourable standing with Eduard Hempel. His assessment made covert collaboration with Britain unappealing, though
it continued nonetheless. From meetings held in London in late
April and early May 1940 Walshe reported 'a general desire to
see the end of Partition' among British officials.[2] This, he believed,
was inspired by their pessimistic estimation of their chances in the
war. At first Walshe presumed this presented an opportunity and
suggested Britain hand over Tyrone and Fermanagh to the Irish
government as a 'gesture' of goodwill. Walshe outlined this idea to
British officials, and may therefore have deluded the British government into believing de Valera might compromise on neutrality
if it meant significant progress on partition.

However, Walshe ultimately rejected any notion that Ireland
should trade its neutrality for a deal on partition. From his meetings in London in early May, he gained the impression that
Britain was desperate for support from any quarter. He informed
de Valera that the members of the British government were 'too
soft, too class-prejudiced (they are almost all of the wealthy Tory
family type) to be able to win a war against men of steel like

Hitler, Stalin and their followers.'[3] He queried Britain's strength at this stage, and when it was suggested to him that the war was being fought in the interest of 'all those in the world to whom freedom and democracy were precious' he rejected these ideological supplications.[4] Walshe, it seems, saw little reason to support continued Irish covert cooperation with Britain, and his views towards Russia are enlightening. When in conversation with Anthony Eden, the British Foreign Secretary, he stated:

> the establishment of close relations with Russia (however remote that might be) might make a very real change in the general Irish attitude towards the Allies. The leaders of Germany were indeed anti-Christian but a large section of the German people were good Catholics and good Protestants and might be trusted in the end to re-establish the prestige of Christianity in their own country, but Russia's atheism was aggressive and incurable.[5]

Thus, while Walshe may have shared the same world-view as Britain he was not, perhaps, opposed to all of Germany's war-time objectives. This has contributed to the general consensus that Walshe was pro-German. However, the evidence suggests that for every statement to Whitehall officials critical of Britain, Walshe had an equally argumentative message to present to the German side. Walshe's diplomatic memoranda must be read in this light.

Soon after Walshe's talks with Eden, de Valera publicly stated the Irish government's stance on the moral implications of the war. On 12 May 1940, in a speech to a Fianna Fáil convention in Galway, he referred to the German invasion of the Netherlands and Belgium. He stated: 'Today these two small nations are fighting for their lives, and I think it would be unworthy of this small nation if, on an occasion like this, I did not utter our protest against the cruel wrong which has been done to them.' De Valera also identified a close convergence of interests between Britain and Ireland:

> My one regret at a time like the present is that there is still a cause of difference between the two countries. I believe … that the destiny of the people of these two islands off the coast of Europe will be similar in many respects. I believe that we will have many interests in common in the future as in the past. I believe these common interests would beget good relations.[6]

Such comments undermined Walshe's attempted placation of Hempel, and soon afterwards the German Foreign Ministry instructed Hempel to protest against de Valera's remarks. Hempel had already aired his concerns to Walshe, who expressed his regret and added that the statement was a mistake and would not be repeated. De Valera's statement also served to strengthen British hopes that in appropriate circumstances Ireland would be willing to consider proposals to join the Allied war effort.

Walshe has been adversely criticised for his seemingly over-friendly attitude towards Germany, and de Valera's 'rare moral courage' in denouncing Hitler's invasion of Belgium and the Netherlands has been juxtaposed with Walshe's expression of admiration for German achievements.[7] However, de Valera's moral indignation might be construed as hypocritical. If he was serious about the convictions revealed in his speech in Galway, then he could have chosen to have this view officially conveyed to Hitler's Third Reich. Instead, he allowed his diplomatic corps continue their work of appeasement towards Hempel. Self-preservation was the guiding principle of de Valera's neutrality, and it was Walshe's task to carry out that policy. Walshe could not afford the luxury of such condemnations nor had he the authority to do so.

However, the image of Walshe restricting de Valera's desire to decide Irish wartime policy on the basis of moral principle is inaccurate. There was no such divergence. Under de Valera's direction, Walshe ultimately agreed that neutrality was the most appropriate policy for Ireland. It has been said, for example, that however much de Valera would regret a British defeat it would have been the height of irresponsibility for him to 'wantonly sacrifice the interests of his country to a futile purpose'.[8] It was part of Walshe's task to carry out this policy, and if using language soothing to the German psyche was necessary, then he felt justified in doing so. In this endeavour, Walshe was somewhat successful. Despite an obvious wave of anti-German hostility throughout Ireland, he attempted to convince Hempel that Britain was Ireland's 'traditional enemy'. While the German minister correctly divined de Valera's sympathies lay primarily with Britain, he believed that under the guidance of Walshe and Boland the possibility remained that the Taoiseach would come to realise the potential importance of German supremacy for Ireland.[9] This was an important achievement for Walshe, in particular when it came

to deciding the diplomatic path to be pursued with Britain and the United States.

David Gray's preliminary reports from Ireland to the State Department indicated that while Ireland remained neutral there was growing realism among government members of the danger of their position, and that they were responding by preparing public opinion for cooperation with the Allies.[10] 'At last this Government is waking up to its danger,', he reported, 'though doing nothing.'[11] Gray believed de Valera personally lacked the determination to remain neutral, and tried to persuade him there could be no 'sitting on the fence'. In the years to come, through meetings with Walshe and de Valera, Gray repeatedly sought to alter Ireland's stance in relation to the world conflict. He would alter his earlier statement that Irish policy was a 'beneficent neutrality', and later described it as self-serving and cowardly. His argument was strengthened by several failed German espionage attempts to establish contact with the IRA and foment nationalist hostility against Britain. These issues were of major concern for Walshe.[12] In the end, the Germans' activities proved relatively harmless, but their presence alone created difficulties in convincing some Allied representatives that Ireland was not a potential security threat.

Consequently, to placate Allied concerns arising from these German espionage incidents, Walshe adopted a cooperative attitude in talks with British officials. On 23 May 1940 he and Colonel Liam Archer of the Irish-army's military intelligence section, G2, opened secret talks with British officials in London. The British Admiralty and the Air Ministry wished to discuss the possibility of military cooperation between the British and Irish governments. Walshe outlined de Valera's stated position that, while the Irish government welcomed British military assistance in the event of an attack by Germany, there was no question of allowing British troops on Irish soil before an actual invasion attempt had taken place.[13] This caused problems for the British, who determined that any effective assistance would require troops to be mobilised before, or at the moment of, an Axis attack.

Other matters dealt with at this meeting included a number of proposals advantageous to the Allied war effort. Walshe readily agreed, for example, that immediate measures would be taken to ensure greater security, and that all ships in and approaching Irish ports would be searched for troops, munitions, refugees and

suspicious characters. Archer outlined specific details of measures that the Irish government was taking to prevent enemy landings at aerodromes and seaplane bases. In return, the British offered their expertise to aid Irish efforts to secure possible landing sites against German invasion. The minutes of the meeting concluded by listing the major points of agreement, which included 'detailed planning to ensure the closest of mutual co-operation'.[14] Thus, Walshe, despite personal misgivings about Britain's relative strength against Germany, committed the Irish government to a level of cooperation that was in clear breach of her superficially uncompromising neutrality. This was the beginning of an unprecedented level of cooperation between the two governments that was to last throughout the war.

The following morning another meeting was held. Walshe signified his general approval of the minutes of their previous meeting but, always prudent, reserved the right to make any necessary amendments to the record.[15] It was considered that any assistance for the Irish army could come most speedily from Northern Ireland, and they therefore agreed that any detailed planning should be carried out directly between the army officials in Northern Ireland and the Irish military authorities. It was arranged that Walshe and Archer would fly to Northern Ireland with Colonel Dudley Clarke, who had been given responsibility for Anglo-Irish defence preparations. From there they would travel to Dublin where further meetings could be organised.

Colonel Dudley Clarke first received instructions of his Irish visit with the caution, 'This is an awkward, tricky business – Neutrals!' He got some idea of the security involved when he was told to make himself look as little like a British officer as he possibly could. 'That's really important. Our friends over there have asked for it specially, and if a single inkling of your mission were to leak out the whole thing would be ruined – quite apart from the personal consequences to the people concerned.'[16] Clarke described how the security he experienced after his arrival in Dublin missed no small detail, and included a thorough check of his luggage for any items that could possibly raise suspicions regarding his real identity.

On the way to the first meeting, Clarke and his Irish chaperons stopped outside what he described as 'a yard which might have been an engineer's dump for the Public Works Department'.

The camouflage was comprehensive at all times. 'From it I was led through a doorway and down a flight of steps, and then for an appreciable distance along twisting underground corridors. We emerged at last into an opening which was guarded by an armed man, where I was asked to wait while my guide disappeared further into the depths.'[17] Introductions were passed over and the business proceeded quickly. Clarke felt that the meeting finished on a more cordial note than it had begun.

Another meeting was arranged for the following day, which, says Clarke, was well in keeping with the melodramatic atmosphere of the whole affair:

> At ten o'clock on the following morning, in accordance with his mysterious instructions, I was diligently examining antiques in a museum, when the courier appeared at my side. There were few visitors at that time of day, and after a brief conversation we slipped away into a sort of Curator's store. From it a staircase led down, and soon we were back again in underground corridors.[18]

Walshe was one of the cloaked chaperons who escorted Clarke to his meetings with Irish-army staff through underground corridors with secret entrances and covert conference rooms, and with army staff 'disguised' in civilian clothes. Joseph Carroll describes Walshe as revelling in this secretive atmosphere:

> The next morning Clarke was examining some curios in the National Museum as instructed, when Walshe suddenly appeared at his side and drew him into the curator's store and back into the twisting passages.[19]

Before the conclusion of the visit, Walshe took personal charge of Clarke's visit to the Phoenix Park, where they had a picnic on the hills overlooking Baldonnel military airfield for the purpose of seeking his advice on how best to defend them. It all came to an abrupt end, however, when, 'a solitary cyclist [or a possible double-agent] so alarmed Walshe that he snatched the field-glasses from Clarke's hands and rushed him back to the Shelbourne.'

Clarke failed to convince Irish officials to allow British troops into their jurisdiction before an invasion, but it was agreed that a mobile column across the border would wait for the signal to come down and help the Irish army against the Germans. The Irish officers drew up a list of the weapons and equipment they

needed. It was also agreed that a military attaché, disguised as a civilian, would be appointed to Dublin for liaison purposes. Carroll claims that in spite of the bizarre aspects of his visit, Clarke left feeling that satisfactory arrangements had been made for defence and coordination if the need arose. Walshe, for his part, kept Clarke's identity secret.

From this point on, the Irish government, and Walshe's department in particular, received increasing numbers of requests and queries from the British authorities. Contact was close, and in June 1940 the Dominions Office warned Walshe of an 'imminent' German invasion of Ireland in conjunction with the IRA.[20] To organise their planned cooperation, de Valera accepted the appointment of General Harrison as a liaison officer in the event of an Irish call for British assistance. De Valera pointed to the necessity for supplies of arms, to which Harrison replied that he felt it to be one of his primary functions to ensure that the Irish army would be well equipped, and promised to request increased munitions. The detailed questionnaires that followed are a further indication of the level this cooperation reached. Questions ranged from information sought on burial accommodation available in Irish cemeteries; information on signal communications in Ireland; detailed questions on military issues; specific information requested on the Shannon hydroelectric scheme; plans for the reporting of military casualties in civilian hospitals and arrangements for the billeting of British soldiers in Ireland. Later, Walshe wrote a memorandum clearly listing the help given by the Irish government to Britain. It included: geographical information about the twenty-six counties; the broadcasting of information relating to German planes and submarines; permission to use Irish airspace over specified areas; a constant stream of intelligence information; the re-routing of German and Italian official communications through Britain, and allowing the British legation to have two secret wireless sets while confiscating the wireless set in the possession of the German legation.[21] When the gardaí discovered plans for a German–IRA attack on Northern Ireland, the Irish authorities did not hesitate in passing this information on to MI5 in London.[22] Humanitarian aid was also given to Britain in some instances.[23] However, of paramount importance was the Irish government's agreement to release many of the Allied air crews forced to land on Irish soil. Under the rules

of neutrality, such crews should have been interned for the duration of the war. Walshe was prudent to document the details of Anglo-Irish cooperation, and over the following months he would be forced to recount them in order to defend the policy of neutrality.

Despite the high level of Anglo-Irish cooperation, Gray was rapidly losing his sympathy for the Irish position, and asked the government what they would do if submarine warfare forced Britain to cancel its generous allotments of coal, petrol and other supplies to Ireland. The Irish ports were Gray's main grievance. He believed Britain had a right to their use, having shown good faith in giving them up in the first place. At this time Gray did little to develop any relationship or understanding with the Irish government and officials, but became friendly with the outspoken pro-Allied and opposition politician, James Dillon, who nourished Gray's already obdurate opinions. Somewhat to Gray's surprise, Dillon said that de Valera had informed him confidentially of arrangements with Britain for immediate aid if an invasion attempt were launched against Ireland.[24] Gray was not content with these developments, however, and continued to believe that Irish neutrality was presenting significant advantage to Germany.

Soon, sections of British opinion would also downplay Irish military assistance. As the months wore on, Walshe came under relentless pressure in his attempts to satisfy the demands of both belligerents, while at the same time ensuring that Irish neutrality remained intact. In June 1940 he wrote of his concern that the other government departments did not fully appreciate the delicacy of the diplomatic circumstances the country now found itself in. The Department of Justice, for example, suggested that all aliens other than those from the United States and Britain should be required to report to the Irish police authorities on a daily basis. Walshe pointed out the obvious problems with this idea: 'from the general political point of view, taken in conjunction with other measures imposed upon us by the necessities of the situation, it might give Germany an excuse for putting us into the category of belligerents.'

Of some comfort to Walshe was the confidence he placed in Irish intelligence and the police authorities, who were well aware of the movements of German nationals in Ireland. However,

Walshe warned against needlessly aggravating Germany. He had heard that house raids on a number of German nationals had taken place, and it was imperative that the Department of External Affairs should be consulted at all times on such matters. While the authorities may have had legitimate reasons for such searches, he pointed out that these would probably prove to be 'a relatively minor consideration when viewed in the light of the perils of the moment'. His department had broader considerations to think of, and Walshe was apprehensive at what might happen if his guidance was not sought:

> Indeed, I have come to the conclusion that the present crisis imposes on all Departments the obligation to abstain from any action whatsoever relating to Germany or German nationals until the Minister for External Affairs has been consulted.[25]

He was, of course, right to propose that External Affairs should coordinate all actions that could affect Ireland's external position.

In the meantime, Walshe continued his consultations with Hempel, who insisted that the German government respected Irish neutrality, and hinted that the final outcome of the struggle would be significant for the fulfilment of Irish national aims. This was intended to animate Walshe's expectations that a victory for Germany would lead to a united Ireland. Walshe, for his part, was satisfied that Hempel had accepted his guarantees that Ireland would remain neutral, and believed the German promises would remain intact, at least in the short term:

> The German Minister was very friendly. He said he understood perfectly the difficulties of our position. I explained to him that the measures taken by you [de Valera] were essential for the establishment of the unity of the nation. You were desirous above all things to protect our people from the disastrous effects of the war being fought out in Ireland. You earnestly hoped that neither belligerent would violate our territory.[26]

Hempel's account of this conversation proves more substantial. The German minister also reported an amicable meeting, confirming that 'the conversation, in which Walshe expressed great admiration for the German achievements, went off in a very friendly way.'[27] Walshe aired the view that Britain was Ireland's

most likely invader, and further hoped Hitler's recent statement, in which he claimed he did not intend to destroy the British Empire, did not imply the abandonment of German support for Irish ambitions. Hempel did not accept Walshe's expressions of admiration for Germany's achievements as significant without first hearing the views of the Taoiseach. Surmising de Valera would wish to see him after Walshe had a chance to brief him on the conversation, he reserved the right to send a supplementary report. As predicted, de Valera promptly summoned Hempel. This meeting, held in the presence of Walshe but under the auspices of de Valera, had a distinctly different focus: 'De Valera listened to my statements with interest but obviously attached principal importance to assuring me of Éire's continued adherence to strict neutrality.'[28] Therefore, important differences existed between de Valera and Walshe in their approaches to Hempel. The dissimilarity between Walshe and de Valera's approaches is partly explained by the fact that since Walshe's first meeting with Hempel there had been significant proposals from the British that gave the Taoiseach good cause for adopting a more guarded approach towards the German minister.

Walshe's meetings with British officials in early May 1940, and his statements at that time on the possibility of compromise on the issue of neutrality in return for movement on partition, were significant in leading to discussions between Malcolm MacDonald and de Valera the following month. MacDonald, a former Dominions Secretary, was chosen to travel to Dublin with the intention of persuading de Valera to abandon neutrality. MacDonald initially suggested 'a Joint Defence Council, on which representatives of the North and of the South would sit and consult and take decisions together'.[29] The proposal was couched in vague but optimistic terms: 'It might be only a first step to be followed by others. If the habit of co-operation on matters of common concern were established, it would be difficult afterwards to break it down.' De Valera reacted to the idea by saying it would only serve to provoke Germany. He told MacDonald that the British government should announce an independent and united Ireland. Then, with the aid of British equipment, Ireland could defend herself against Germany. Later that month MacDonald returned to Dublin with a new dimension to his proposal, 'that there should be a declaration of a United Ireland in principle'.[30]

Again, de Valera rejected the offer, only to be faced with another version days later. This more definitive offer envisaged a British statement accepting the principle of a united Ireland. In return, Ireland was to enter the war on the Allied side.[31]

David Gray, who had anxiously encouraged some form of cooperation between Dublin and Belfast, was unaware of the proposal. When informed of it by Maffey, he suggested that Britain had approached the matter in the wrong way, arguing that 'there should have been gestures preliminary of good will from Ulster'. He continued: 'The move the British have taken in promising a complete and immediate ending of partition I am afraid now will look like a trap.'[32] Gray nevertheless believed the offer was genuine, and he hoped de Valera would accept it. He resisted offering any encouragement because he felt that if de Valera knew that the United States was aware of the offer, it might give the impression that the Americans were helping Britain to lure Ireland into this 'trap'. He was annoyed at the position adopted by de Valera, and mistakenly believed the isolating quality of neutrality would gradually make the Irish more congenial to Britain's demands.

Gray also believed that Germany had given certain guarantees regarding Irish neutrality, and his suspicions were confirmed by Seán T. O'Kelly, who said that Hempel had made a commitment that as long as Ireland remained neutral Germany would not attack. 'They don't believe him but they would like to', O'Kelly told Gray. James Dillon informed him of the growing feeling that Britain was sure to be defeated unless the United States entered the war, and it was not thought likely that Roosevelt would take that course. O'Kelly explained Irish reluctance to the unity offer, saying they had been given similar promises during the First World War. The British, therefore, 'without meaning to deceive would find that they could not implement their promises just as in '14 and again in '16'. Dillon said he agreed with the rejection of the offer, arguing that if de Valera 'tried to carry the country for abandoning neutrality on the strength of the present British promises he would be beaten'. Gray was influenced by Dillon, and he told Roosevelt that de Valera had good cause to be circumspect about the British offer: 'You cannot blame him for thinking that he will fare better if he doesn't dip in.'[33]

The documentation produced by the Department of External Affairs at this time demonstrates little enthusiasm for the British

proposal. The unity discussions were in themselves a breach of
neutrality, and a statement declaring strict adherence to that
policy was now being sought:

> It is not sufficient to say that we want a Parliament for the whole of
> Ireland which will include among its rights that of going into war.
> Such a statement only sows suspicion in the minds of the Germans
> and of our own people, and makes the latter believe that we might
> possibly accept entry into a war, which, so far, is none of our con-
> cern, as the price of our neutrality.[34]

The timing of the proposition, as Britain's chances of victory looked
bleak, was a crucial factor in Walshe's antipathy to the proposal.
This view can be seen in departmental memoranda, which pointed
out that Ireland's entry into the war was the sole reason for the
British proposals. During the 1938 Anglo-Irish negotiations, de
Valera offered Britain the opportunity of a defence agreement in
return for concessions on partition. Britain's desire to unearth that
offer in 1940, therefore, appeared purely opportunistic. Panic, in
Walshe's view, was the driving force of this proposal.

An unsigned analysis of the British initiative (which was
most probably written by Walshe for de Valera) summed up
these considerable doubts about British motivations on partition. It described the proposals as 'very vague and half-boiled'.
Walshe was suspicious that the proposed joint committee, in the
'absence of any previous guarantee of the status of the Union as
a whole', could be used by the British to establish 'a new state
which would be far less independent than Éire'.[35] Walshe's pessimism regarding Britain's chances in the war was implied in
his caution towards the plan, especially since it postponed any
significant developments in uniting Ireland until after the war.
The report recognised that 'the truly appalling situation in which
they now find themselves, fighting alone against the might of
Germany, would be quite a sufficient excuse before the world for
concentrating exclusively on the defence of these islands against
Germany.' John Maffey surmised that it was this assessment of
British hopes in the conflict that made the offer unacceptable.
The following year he mentioned his theory to Walshe, who
rejected the comment and argued that the refusal of the offer
was based on 'distrust of the proposals' which relied upon British

fulfilment of the deal after the war.[36] Maffey's intuition, however, was not unfounded.

Document after document emanating from External Affairs at this time repeated the same Irish apprehensions over the war situation. 'It does not seem that there is a single organised State left in Europe or Asia which is not ready to profit by what they regard to be the impending downfall of Britain.'[37] The conclusion reached was that 'Britain's final folly was committed during the weekend, when Churchill by his accusations and his support of de Gaulle, threw France into the Totalitarian bloc and made England's defeat inevitable.'[38] This was not an uncommon view. In May Belgium surrendered to German forces and French and British troops had to be evacuated from Dunkirk. In June Italy declared war on France and the German army moved into Paris and occupied France for the remainder of the war. July saw Britain's sinking of French warships anchored off Oran in north Africa, followed by the Vichy government breaking off diplomatic relations with Britain. The outlook for Britain was therefore gloomy, and Walshe's pessimism about the Allies would remain until the Battle of Britain (which reached a climax in mid-August) encouraged him to reappraise the situation.

The decision to reject the offer of unity was therefore based on a number of criteria. The proposal itself was vague and did not guarantee Irish unity. Walshe told Gray that he and de Valera construed the proposals as 'a trap to be followed by strong arm stuff'. Walshe's fatalistic reports on Britain's wartime chances were of primary importance. The departmental memoranda that confidently announced that Britain's defeat was 'inevitable' and that 'neither time nor gold can beat Germany' must have had a profound bearing on de Valera's decision.[39] While many believe de Valera's greatest political regret was not achieving a united Ireland, Frederick H. Boland, the assistant secretary in the Department of External Affairs, suspected de Valera was not quite so eager for such a resolution. In his memoirs Boland stated:

> Dev had a very supple mind … I could never find out exactly from him whether he really wanted the Six Counties in or not. My belief is, he didn't. He felt that we were not in a position to accept such a big Protestant adjunct to our population – especially, all of them hostile to Ireland.[40]

Perhaps Walshe's advice simply served to support de Valera's personal inclinations at that time.

Walshe further speculated that Britain's desire to enlist Ireland to the Allied side was devised to reduce the cost of the war to Britain. His notes on the matter displayed his underlying suspicions:

> It is natural that England should not cease ... to adhere to the policy of having a weak country on her western flank. Some day she might hope to take back the fortress, but she could never again hope to defeat an Ireland with a strong and prosperous population ... To all true Britishers it would constitute a weakening of Britain. That has been an elementary fact of British policy for centuries.[41]

Walshe alleged the British 'are now using against us all the tricks and wiles which they commonly use against small peoples', and he believed for a period that Britain was as great a threat to Irish security as Germany:

> In view of recent events it is safer for us to make the assumption that the further and extraordinary means of communication being requested of us by the British are intended, not to meet the eventuality of a German invasion, but to facilitate the British Army in its task of re-occupation.[42]

These statements seem extraordinary considering the ongoing cooperation between the two sides. However, part of the problem was Walshe's dissatisfaction with Britain's lack of appreciation for Irish assistance, which constituted a considerable risk for Irish neutrality and security if Germany discovered it. Walshe referred to the First World War, pointing out the advantages of the new Anglo-Irish relationship for Britain's war effort:

> In Great War British had 60,000 men keeping order here, now they have feeling of security about Ireland which would be complete if they gave us arms.[43]

He was also annoyed by the manner in which Britain made its demands and noted: '[the] British will argue we should loosen censorship to convert those who are against war. (For them to be pro-Irish is to be pro-German).' With some frustration Walshe proclaimed, 'we could not do more if we were in the War', and

the list of cooperative efforts was indeed extensive. To receive credit was important for Walshe, who saw his government risk its neutrality while at the same time fielding a barrage of criticism from the British press.

Walshe was under severe strain and he was burdened by outwardly proclaiming strict Irish neutrality while inwardly compromising that policy. Many of his ideas and attitudes towards Britain during these months were contradictory and are difficult to decipher. In his memoirs, Fred Boland explains that contradictions in Walshe's reasoning and statements were not uncommon:

> To say that [Walshe] had a mercurial temperament is an understatement. His views and moods were liable to change at such short notice that it was often a task to keep them in any sort of precise focus. Joe himself was conscious of his occasional inconsistencies, but he wasn't disconcerted by them; on the contrary, he tended as a rule simply to laugh them off as if they were inspired by no more than a spirit of mischief.[44]

It is not surprising, therefore, that Walshe appears contradictory in relation to Irish neutrality. Initially he was against it, but following instructions from de Valera he supported the idea. Notwithstanding his apparent firm belief they would lose the war, he authorised extensive cooperation with Britain. And yet despite this extremely close collaboration, he remained suspicious of British motives. While his assessment for a period was that Britain would probably lose the war, Walshe did not necessarily desire that outcome. Ireland could not resist an assault from Germany and so Walshe had to do his best to satisfy that quarter. At the same time, Britain or the United States could not be alienated. Walshe was therefore willing to continue covert assistance to Britain, but, where possible, within the remit of sustainable neutrality. For him, there was no inconsistency in pursuing that policy, albeit at times a less than coherent one.

Walshe's attitude in 1940 can be partially explained by his concern for Ireland's position at the end of the war. He believed even if Ireland and the other European neutrals were invaded by Germany then 'neutrality at least has given them a right to the sympathy and good will of all other peoples in their eventual effort to regain

their independence.'⁴⁵ On the other hand, if Britain won the war, Walshe believed Anglo-Irish relations would return to normal soon enough, though perhaps after 'a few years of unjustifyable [*sic*] resentment'. However, if Ireland joined with Britain, which then proceeded to lose the war, this would result in the 'complete loss of our independence'. These calculations are central to understanding Walshe's diplomatic strategy during this period.

Another reason why Walshe's confidence in neutrality prevailed was that he believed the United States would finally support the Irish government. The vast majority of the American people 'whose good will we retain while we remain neutral can be a powerful – even a determining – factor in the restoration of our independence should we lose it during the war as a result of defending our neutrality.' He argued that while the possibility of a German invasion of Ireland existed, it gave no excuse for the abandonment of neutrality. Rather, it made the maintenance of that policy all the more essential, for he believed that 'a neutral state has a better chance of resurrection in the final settlement.' His estimation of the strength of the Irish lobby in the US sustained his conviction that Ireland would not be invaded or attacked by the Axis powers on the grounds that it would alienate public opinion in America. He argued that 'she knows how grievous a moral loss she would suffer if she attacked Ireland.'⁴⁶ Indeed, at one stage Walshe envisaged the use of American public opinion against British, rather than German, advances:

> American public opinion seems to me to be the only effective weapon left to us against an early occupation by the British Army as soon as British intrigues prove unsuccessful. It will be necessary to repeat to the American people that Irish neutrality is so fundamental a part of the Irish national position that to fail to defend it against all comers would involve the loss of our independence.⁴⁷

Thus, Walshe felt neither Germany nor Britain would attack Ireland as they did not wish to incur US hostility. Later in the war, Walshe re-evaluated this assessment as he did many of his early assumptions.

During the initial phases of the war, Eduard Hempel agreed with Walshe that neutrality was the best policy for Ireland, but for different reasons: it met German interests best. He thought

that if Ireland were to join the war she would most likely enlist with the Allies. The German minister believed the Irish government was endeavouring to do everything possible to maintain strict neutrality and, in particular, he recognised that Walshe and Boland exerted a 'strong influence on De Valera in this direction'. Hempel was annoyed by the damaging effect of German espionage in Ireland. Therefore, he recommended the German government issue a statement indicating its intention to respect Irish neutrality, in order to restore de Valera's confidence and to 'strengthen his power of resistance to British threats and to facilitate a possible future rapprochement with the Axis Powers'.[48] His superiors attempted to clarify the position, and the German Foreign Minister, Joachim von Ribbentrop clearly instructed:

> In all conversations there please put most emphatically that in connection with Ireland we have exclusively the single interest that her neutrality be maintained. As long as Ireland conducts herself in a neutral fashion it can be counted on with absolute certainty that Germany will respect her neutrality unconditionally.[49]

Hempel quickly relayed this attitude to the Irish government. He had previously made assurances, but believed both Walshe and de Valera remained suspicious of German intentions. The German representative now intimated to Walshe that the highest authority had reaffirmed the tenet of his representations. Walshe recognised that Hempel 'could now speak quite definitely and reaffirm in the strongest way' the previously expressed attitude towards Irish neutrality. Hempel admitted that German espionage attempts were damaging. However, he reassured Walshe that regardless of any suspicions created in the past, 'he was now able to affirm without reservations (on account of the definiteness of his last instructions)' that Germany continued to respect Irish neutrality 'so long as we did not tolerate any violation of it by the other belligerent'.[50]

Nonetheless, German espionage agents continued to arrive, and the case of Hermann Goertz in particular, who had landed in Ireland in May 1940 and was not captured until November 1941, introduced strain and mistrust into the Walshe–Hempel relationship. Walshe repeatedly exploited the matter by using it to give his defence of Irish neutrality a more offensive aspect.

At a time when the country was under intense pressure to join the war, such German activities were unhelpful to Walshe, who had to counter British arguments that Germany was planning to invade Ireland. Privately, Walshe believed the assurances Hempel had given, but this was of little assistance to him in his dealings with the Allies, who cited these incidents as proof of concerted German activity in Ireland.[51]

Walshe was repeatedly told that the German government had issued strict orders that Ireland was not to be used as a starting point for enterprises of any kind against Britain.[52] In the light of the 'accidental' bombing by Germany of an Irish ship, the *Kerry Head*, in August 1940, Walshe was once more given grounds to question these assurances. Following protests, he was again assured that German aeroplanes had been given careful instructions not to violate Irish territorial waters and that investigations were being made into the bombing of the Irish cargo ship. Walshe was persuaded to leave Ireland's financial claims against Germany for the accidental bombing until after the war, as Hempel found the matter inconvenient to deal with due to the difficulties in communications. Following this meeting with Hempel, Walshe penned a 'most secret' memorandum entitled 'Have we a guarantee against invasion from the German Government?', in which he reviewed his previous conversations with Hempel when the German minister had stated that Irish neutrality would not be violated and that the exclusive objective of Germany's fight was Britain.[53] The tone of the document portrays a general belief in the assurances given by Hempel, who seemed genuinely annoyed that such half-hearted agents had given the British government further excuse for exerting pressure on de Valera to enter the war.

In his meetings with Walshe at this time, the British representative expressed his concern about the reported German espionage activities in Ireland. The British authorities, however, did not deem themselves exempt from carrying out such activities in their own interest. This was despite the fact that the authorities in London were well informed on a wide variety of matters by official Irish sources. Cooperation on the political level was high, but it did not match the level of interaction between the military authorities. However, when in July 1940 a man and a woman were apprehended and found to be on a military reconnaissance exercise for the British government, Walshe considered it a most

serious incident.[54] Following interrogation, it was revealed that the captured man was Major Edward Rees Byas of the British army in Northern Ireland, who was in the Irish Free State for a golfing holiday. He admitted that he had taken notes as he had been instructed to survey certain routes in Ireland. Walshe recommended Byas should be detained until the government decided what steps should be taken. The Secretary of State for Dominion Affairs wrote to Maffey saying that the instructions issued to Byas were 'given without our knowledge or consent', and that the military had been given orders that this was not to happen again. It was hoped that the Irish government would accept an apology and release Byas because the action had been taken in a genuine effort to prepare the British military to help the Irish government in case of an emergency.[55] This explanation was not acceptable to Walshe, who did his best to play up the incident and sought further guarantees from Maffey that Britain was not planning an invasion of Ireland.

From a diplomatic point of view, Walshe was both annoyed and worried by these events, but was eventually placated by Maffey, who expressed no prior knowledge of any espionage plan towards Ireland. Walshe stated: 'He seemed to be genuinely horrified at the espionage episode, and he did not express any desire for the early release of the officer concerned. It may be significant that Maffey asked me not to tell his military aides about this matter.' Walshe warned that suspicion of interference in Irish internal affairs would undo all their splendid work and in particular Maffey's establishment of 'relations between the two countries on a basis of real friendship and understanding':

> At this, Maffey turned to me quite earnestly and said that he was in a real difficulty about these 'agents'. He would be grateful to me if I instructed Dulanty to go to Caldecote and tell him not to send Tegart or any other 'agent' here in future, that they were doing nothing but harm, etc. He begged me not to mention his name in this connection as he felt his position would not allow him to object to such missions. I was naturally amazed at this sudden complete avowal of the truth. It quite clearly arose from his conviction, however belated, that a very grave error of judgement had been made.[56]

Walshe believed that Anglo-Irish cooperation was jeopardised by

such intrigues, but he accepted Maffey's latest assurances. Because of the close interaction between the two countries at that time, Walshe regarded such agents as a betrayal of trust. His close association with Maffey was significant in preventing such incidents from souring relations.

Walshe tried to use the British spying incidents as a means of gaining advantage for the state. He complained to Maffey that the Irish army's deficiency of arms was unfairly criticised in the British press. 'It has been the strongest argument in favour of our accepting the presence of the British Army', he said, arguing that this could be easily remedied if Britain provided Ireland with enough arms to defend itself.[57] Later, he met Maffey with regard to a condition attached to the proposed delivery of military equipment that allowed for British crews to come with the equipment. Walshe said this made it impossible to accept the delivery, and Maffey promised to make representations to the War Office to fulfil the order without restrictions. In addition, the ongoing British press campaign against Irish neutrality was also a strain on Walshe, who complained to Maffey about the 'serious misconstructions' in matters relating to Irish neutrality. He believed it extremely unjust that Ireland should covertly aid Britain's war effort and receive nothing but criticism from journalists, who were necessarily kept in the dark regarding Irish assistance. Maffey mentioned that David Gray had told him that the Irish government had 'some ridiculous idea that a part of [the US] Press was British-inspired because it took an anti-Irish line'. Walshe replied that Gray was wrong in thinking that he thought the press in the United States was British-inspired simply because it was anti-Irish: 'We knew it from the fact that the anti-Irish messages appearing in a section of the American Press came from London and we knew that all messages going out from London were censored by the Ministry of Information. Our opinion, therefore, was not formed on some pet conception of British perfidy, but on sound fact.'[58]

Walshe was further annoyed when members of the British government further added to the popular discontent towards Ireland with rash provocative statements. It was against this background that Walshe sought greater assurances for Irish neutrality and territorial sovereignty from the British government.

At the end of July 1940 Hempel sent a report on the Irish

154   JOSEPH WALSHE

situation to his ministry. Walshe had apparently suggested that
a degree of mutual benefit could be derived through cooperation between Irish and German elements in the United States.
There would be obstacles to this, however, as Hempel outlined:
'The difficulty is, as Walshe, too, pointed out, that if any German
participation became known outside, it could easily lead to an
undesirable effect in the opposite direction.'[59] Walshe's statement
had the advantage of appearing helpful without promising anything concrete on the grounds of neutrality. As Hempel noted, 'I
assume that the Irish Government because of well-justified anxiety about a possible unfavourable British reaction against Ireland
must also avoid the appearance of co-operation with us.' Hempel
also reported Walshe's hope that the unification of Ireland was
a possible outcome of a German victory. Such attributed statements to the secretary can be read in a number of ways. It may
have been a genuine aspiration of Walshe's to see the fulfilment
of Irish irredentist aims in the event of German dominance:
if Hitler was in control of Europe, and if Ireland remained on
favourable terms with Germany, then why not at least mention
this 'small request'? Walshe's articulation of such aspirations,
however, may again have been part of the approach to persuade
Hempel of the sincerity of his impartiality. To speak of such Irish
hopes in a postwar Europe dominated by Germany would surely
serve to convince Hempel that the Irish government had nothing to gain in the event of a British victory, and therefore Irish
neutrality would not be flouted in favour of Britain.

However, as we have seen in the previous chapter, Walshe can
rightly be accused of having a certain 'tenderness towards the
new masters of the continent'. Following his health-spa retreat
in Germany in 1933, he was impressed by the initial achievements of Hitler, and told de Valera of the dynamic atmosphere
in Germany and of the 'great experiments' that were being carried
out there.[60] We have also seen how his initial assumption that
Germany would win the war was to influence External Affairs
policy for a number of months during 1940. To infer that Walshe
was indeed pro-German is possible from limited analysis of some
of the documentation, including Hempel's memoranda in which
he reported Walshe's favourable comments. This, however, would
lead to a somewhat one-sided conclusion.

The extent of Irish cooperation with the Allies – sanctioned

and organised by Walshe – has previously been outlined. In his conversations with Hempel it cost nothing to be agreeable. This was also true in the case of his meetings with Maffey and Gray, and so we need to tread carefully when drawing conclusions from the official documentation. Diplomatic conversations by their nature are inclined to be obliquely ambiguous. Coupled with this is the circumspection required when reading any of the memoranda produced by diplomats, since diplomats are susceptible to portraying their input into any reported conversation as effective. We see this time and again when we compare Walshe's reports with those of his counterparts. However, in all this we must remember to look at the end results if we are to judge Walshe's relative success or failure in his task of maintaining Irish independence and neutrality. If it was Walshe's task to convince Hempel of the uncompromising strictness and sincerity of neutrality then it was an assignment in which he was both resourceful and relatively successful. In a report to the German Foreign Ministry at the end of July 1940 Hempel concluded: 'Basically I have always given expression to a friendly and understanding attitude on the part of Germany toward Ireland.'[61] While it may be true that the Third Reich may not yet have had any grand designs on Ireland at this time, it must be recognised that for the German minister to adopt such a helpful stance at this early stage of the war was an important achievement, and Walshe's diplomatic manoeuvres must be credited for that.

It would be logical to assume that we could turn to Walshe's instructions to his staff abroad to gain a better understanding of how Irish neutrality was being formulated at head office. Indeed, while this set of documentation is illuminating, it throws more light on the ambiguities of Walshe's diplomatic strategy and on the vagaries of his own personality than on the genesis of Irish neutrality. When instructing his staff at the Irish foreign missions during the war, Walshe was often laconic. He told Irish representatives what he felt they ought to know in order to carry out their duties, and believed the legation's primary function was to promote and justify Ireland's reasons for remaining neutral. Much was left to the initiative of the diplomats themselves, as Walshe often imagined that these reasons would be obvious:

> Supposed dangers of neutrality far less than dangers of any
> policy likely to lead to our involvement in war. Latter would

entail internal division and disaster and make us cockpit of final struggle.[62]

In response to rumours concerning the offer of unity in return for Ireland's entry into the war, Walshe neither confirmed nor denied that talks with Britain had taken place. At times, his reports were ambiguous, as when he implied that there had been no collaboration between the British and Irish governments:

> Reference to Ireland in Churchill's speech yesterday may have conveyed suggestion to some people that there is secret collaboration between the two Governments. All such suggestions should be met with the emphatic statement that neutrality is the fixed policy of the Government and the unanimous desire of the people and that the Government is resolved to maintain the country's neutrality in all circumstances.[63]

Walshe was more forthcoming in his correspondence with Robert Brennan, the Irish representative in Washington. He outlined that Irish neutrality was not open to offers, but his statement clearly hinted that some British proposition had been made:

> Government determined to maintain neutrality even in face of offers of concessions on Partition problem. Departure from neutrality would break the unprecedented national unity achieved on basis of that policy.[64]

To the Irish representatives abroad, these instructions must have seemed enigmatic. While the fear of destruction was both justifiable and plausible, the assertion that the Irish government would not countenance any offers of national unity in exchange for participation in the war against Germany, as it would jeopardise what was termed 'unprecedented national unity', must have caused some surprise. Walshe cited de Valera to corroborate the chosen policy, 'so long as both sides keep out, the Taoiseach is determined to maintain our neutrality at all costs.'[65]

On 15 July 1940 Walshe sent a circular to the heads of Irish legations abroad indicating Ireland's firm resolve to remain neutral. These instructions had been prompted by the Irish representative in Washington, Robert Brennan, who had written saying that press reports had claimed that a deal had been agreed

that if attacked by a third power, Ireland would align with Britain, which would send defensive forces.[66] The following day, another official instruction was sent to all legation heads, outlining that:

> Taoiseach's answer was that we wanted the whole of Ireland as an independent neutral united country whose Parliament could come to any decisions it liked about the defence of the country ... The Government believe that the only safeguard of our ultimate independence is to keep our neutrality, even if a German invasion were certain.[67]

Walshe wrote to Brennan explaining his attitude towards the British offer. He described simply and frankly the terms of the proposed agreement and the reasons behind the rejection of Britain's promise for a united Ireland. He explained that in return for the British offer of unity, Ireland was to enter the war at once, and his reply to Brennan, sent on 16 July 1940, indicates that a British invasion of Ireland was not completely ruled out:

> The Government believe that the only safeguard of our ultimate independence is to keep our neutrality, even if a German invasion were certain. A British invasion is still a possibility.[68]

However, views and opinions in External Affairs changed quickly during this period, and surprisingly, Walshe, on 21 July 1940, ruled out the possibility of either a German or British invasion of Ireland. Walshe told Brennan that public opinion in Ireland had accepted the probability of a British defeat but that relations with Britain had much improved over the previous months, with Churchill's speech regarded merely as 'another bad blunder'. In his advice to the High Commissioner for Ireland in Canada, John Hearne, Walshe said that neutrality was 'an essential expression of our national independence'.[69]

In must be recognised that the question of keeping his foreign representatives well informed was linked with the question of the security of their communications. At the beginning of the war, it had been decided that the Irish representatives at Paris, Rome, San Sebastian, Berlin and Geneva should send daily telegrams on the international situation in order 'to place the Government ... in possession of a general appreciation of the European situation'.[70] In an attempt to ensure secrecy, as well as saving time and

money, it was proposed that a list of twenty-four single passwords would refer to statements outlined on a key-list; for example, '1 Glan' would mean 'situation seen from here appears to be normal today.' Other messages would have to use the Irish code, but in 1940 there appears to have been considerable disorganisation surrounding this system of communication; for example, in July 1940 Walshe wrote to France instructing that Cremin be sent to Madrid to explain the personal code to Ireland's representative there, John Kearney. This caused huge logistical problems due to restrictions on travel and petrol rationing.[71] It was a matter of the greatest urgency for Walshe, as the absence of the codes made any but the most banal communications with the Madrid legation impossible.[72]

It is likely that both Britain and Germany had broken the code used by Walshe and External Affairs.[73] For a period at the beginning of the war, Walshe, perhaps naively, believed the code to be secure. In response to a query by the Irish legation in Madrid, Walshe replied: 'Personal code safe. Wire essential details immediately.'[74] The following month he wrote to Washington: 'We believe code absolutely safe.'[75] Later, however, he received a message, warning, 'have good authority that all messages are being decoded.'[76] This was confirmed by a number of sources. MacWhite in Rome informed Walshe that most of his colleagues at the Quirnal had their codes changed frequently, but that despite this they had very little confidence in them and special couriers were used for important dispatches.[77] MacWhite said that the Irish cypher itself was quite good but that coding and decoding messages took up a considerable amount of time. Communications were indeed difficult. In September 1940, following Walshe's suggestion that Cremin go to Paris to deal with Irish citizens there, Murphy replied that O'Kelly was already in Paris. Walshe, it seems, had not been aware of this fact.[78]

While Walshe may not have received any definite information that the Irish code had been broken, it would have been prudent to assume that it had. His statements of confidence in the Irish cypher may have given some of his foreign staff a false sense of security. Had they not used their own judgement on the matter, this could have led to serious consequences. Walshe, however, was not in the habit of sending sensitive information to his staff abroad. He could not risk conveying material that was important

for Irish security, but it also had a lot to do with his general propensity for secrecy. When it came to justifying Irish neutrality, however, there was no such fear. Such propaganda was free for all to hear. Overall then, the information transmitted was of a limited nature; sensitive material could not be sent, and the Irish foreign representatives would have to read between the lines.

Walshe sought information from his legation staff but did not readily accept their advice if it was offered. Some of the heads of the Irish missions, however, were to provide valuable knowledge and realistic recommendations that proved hard for him to ignore; for example, Walshe hoped that through Ireland's minister in the US, Robert Brennan, the British would be persuaded that anti-Irish propaganda in the United States, or any attempt to re-occupy Ireland, would in the end deprive them of what he termed their last remaining hope – the support of the United States.[79] He urged the Washington legation to use Irish influence to convince the US of the right of the Irish policy, and to generate pressure on Britain to desist its public attempt to coerce Éire into joining the war. His instructions to Washington were somewhat startling, and greatly overestimated the ability of the Irish representative in Washington to secure US support:

> Could you inspire all Irish papers to launch campaign against pro-British American journalists who are misleading American public about Ireland and preparing opinion for a British invasion of Ireland.[80]

Brennan, who was alive to the charged atmosphere, suggested a more realistic approach:

> Shall carry out instructions but please realise atmosphere: outside of a few informed Irish, everyone here from highest administration to man in the street considers that we are foolish not to invite British aid and that England shows great forbearance in not securing weak flank by reoccupation: all arguments to contrary such as you use received with shrug.[81]

Walshe, however, wanted Irish neutrality explained to the Americans in emphatic terms. He suggested to Brennan the following statement as the model upon which he should base his explanation of the Irish position. 'Neutrality is of the very essence

of Irish independence. It is based on the fundamental and universal will of our people', he said, 'so much so that no Government
could depart from it without at once being overthrown.' Walshe
claimed that neutrality was not a bargaining factor but rather 'the
fullest expression of our independence in time of war'. It would be
defended vigorously. The telegram is signed with the Department
of External Affairs' codename 'Estero' (meaning 'foreign'), but the
hand is decidedly Walshe:

> By her seven hundred years of resistance to the invasion of a Great
> Power, she has done more than any other nation to keep alive
> in the world the principles of liberty and justice on which the
> American Republic was founded. Her neutrality is a manifestation
> of her continued resolution to save the remnant of our race from
> destruction.[82]

The Irish diplomats abroad were Walshe's 'eyes and ears'. It was
their responsibility to report what he himself could not glean
from Dublin. The theory ran that, based on these reports, Walshe
could formulate well-informed opinions and policies. In practice,
however, Walshe had preconceived ideas that, on occasion, did not
coincide with the reports he received. As Secretary of External
Affairs, it was Walshe's prerogative to disagree with individual
diplomats based on an overall assessment of reports from his foreign corps or from alternative sources of information, such as
foreign diplomats based in Dublin. However, as he came into
conflict with a number of Irish diplomats serving abroad, it can be
seen that his judgement was sometimes questioned, and that de
Valera himself did not always depend solely on Walshe for advice
on foreign affairs.

Walshe wrote to Washington on 18 November 1940 emphasising that 'for Ireland choice is between neutrality and loss of
independence', meaning that Irish autonomy would again be
lost in an alliance with Britain.[83] Brennan replied that from his
experience this was a dangerous argument to use. The counter-
argument, he said, was that the United States would guarantee
the restoration of Irish independence. He felt Walshe did not
fully understand the difficulties in justifying the Irish policy:

> Best line, I find, is to point out that England's friends are doing

her ill-service in encouraging her in course, which, if pursued, will only increase her difficulties. Please remember cry is getting louder each day that American interests are vitally concerned and that defeat of England means disintegration of America and disaster for United States.[84]

Walshe replied, again defending his views and statements: 'You are of course quite right to adopt language to local needs.' He believed, however, that the Irish position was not as solitary as the Washington representative believed it was. Walshe was adamant there were many Americans who did not identify with Britain, and was somewhat naive in believing that Irish interests could come above the United States' fraternity with Britain:

> As there is a real possibility of British defeat there must be some Americans who see that and who do not accept such a complete identity of interests.[85]

A hard-working Brennan kept Walshe well informed about events in the United States. As Walshe's relationship with Gray turned sour it was crucial that Ireland had a competent diplomat in Washington.[86] Similarly, when Walshe became convinced of defeat for Britain following the fall of France, the diplomat *in situ*, Seán Murphy, disagreed. He was no supporter of Pétain and the collaborationist regime whose attitude was based on the assumption that Germany would win the war.[87] Murphy disagreed with Walshe's opinion at this time that the Axis powers would be likely victors. Walshe did not appreciate being contradicted, and he suggested to Murphy that he should seek the views of the nuncio in France and keep in line with that opinion:

> You should keep in close touch with Nuncio who is more likely to know real views of French Right than other diplomats. From all our sources of information, belief is general, even in countries friendly to England such as America and Portugal, that Britain has lost the war and at the very most could only achieve a stalemate which might leave her part of her Empire, but it is recognised everywhere that she has no hope of regaining her influence in Europe.[88]

Walshe was already aware that the Vatican had displayed support

for the Pétain regime. His advice, therefore, not only contradicted Murphy's assessment of the situation but precluded the diplomat from forming his own opinion. On the basis of the Vatican opinion, Walshe appeared to pledge his support for Pétain and further predicted Ireland's future as part of a bloc of 'Continental Catholic nations'.[89] Murphy would have to wait some time to reply with the frankness he desired.

In November Walshe wrote to Murphy chastising him for his lack of reporting on the French situation. Walshe sought weekly reports on the general situation, summaries of local press reports and a chronicle of the day-to-day diplomatic activity in France.[90] Murphy replied that there had been very little to report since his last communication, and his expressed indignation at Walshe's comments bordered on insubordination:

> I would have sent telegraphic reports of my impressions of the situation here were it not for the fact that I understood from your telegram 98 that you only wanted reports which could be supported by some authoritative source and that you were generally better informed on situation here from elsewhere than I could inform you, which is correct.[91]

Murphy was clearly irritated by what he saw as Walshe's preconceived ideas, and made little effort to disguise his resentment: 'I gather from your telegrams ... that you have formed a definite opinion on the situation with which the views expressed in my reports are not in harmony.'[92] Murphy dutifully ascertained the views of the nuncio and sent Walshe the following: 'He thinks public opinion in free zone has hardened against policy of collaboration.'[93] Murphy also reported that, while the nuncio believed that de Gaulle had little personal support, 'what he represents has considerable support in the occupied territory.' It was obvious that Walshe would soon be forced to adjust his views on Pétain. Murphy, however, had more to say on the subject. Using the opportunity of a friend who was travelling to London, Murphy sent to Walshe a frank and detailed letter on the French situation and their difference of opinion. He seemed appalled by what he saw as Walshe's unprofessional behaviour. He believed that Walshe should have read his reports as a diplomat's best efforts to assess a difficult and complex situation:

> I have always endeavoured to give you the facts of the situation as I see it objectively and without prejudice and it is consequently somewhat disheartening to receive telegrams … which seem to suggest I am drawing on my imagination. Whatever may be your other sources of information I think my reports are entitled to be taken on their face value until at least they are shown to be incorrect.[94]

Murphy described the disenchantment with the Pétain regime as the policy of collaboration failed to produce the desired effect from the Germans. He outlined for Walshe the changing view of those in the occupied zone towards the policy of collaboration, and the increasing support for the strategy professed by General de Gaulle. With what he felt was a logical exposition of his views Murphy waited for a response.

Walshe's tone was decidedly conciliatory: 'Your written report 3rd December received. Most interesting and useful.' The telegram to Murphy is signed 'Estero', as was the general practice. In this case, Walshe was particularly glad to use this Department of External Affairs generic signature. It allowed him to stress the plural nature of collective responsibility:

> No criticism intended in our telegrams 98 and 391. You have evidently misunderstood our desire to know Vatican attitude. It is of course of utmost importance for *us* to know Vatican views at all stages of situation especially owing to character of Pétain Government. [emphasis added][95]

As opinion in France was changing towards Pétain, so too was Walshe forced to adjust his stance, and his reply to Murphy has been described as an apology:[96]

> The questions in our tel. 391 were put for purpose of obtaining more detailed information on the matters treated by you and were not in any way intended as criticism of the objectivity of your reports. Questions may often be necessary in order to elucidate special points.

After trying to indicate that the whole incident was just a misunderstanding, he attempted to appease Murphy's sense of pride and diplomatic stature:

Chief thing to keep in mind is that very frequent reports from you
are an essential factor in our day to day judgement of a situation
which affects our vital interests of our own State.[97]

Following this tête-à-tête, however, Walshe did not refrain from
further criticising Murphy in his telegrams to Vichy, but in this
case his comments were directed more at the frequency rather
than the quality or content of Murphy's reports.

In January 1941 Murphy wrote in response to Walshe's directive for close cooperation with the nuncio, and cautioned against
following this method too closely:

I am in constant contact with the Nuncio. His views regarding
situation here may not necessarily be those of the Vatican. Further
views that Nuncio expressed to me may not be exactly those he
gives to the Vatican.[98]

Murphy was adamant that weekly reports were a waste of time,
and he defiantly told Walshe that he would send reports when
there were matters of sufficient interest to comment upon. He
also maintained his view that the majority of French people saw
their only salvation in a German defeat.[99]

It has been stated that Walshe was hampered by the lack of
foreign missions, difficulties in communications and, in certain
cases, inadequate reporting by the Irish representatives. In this case,
however, Walshe chose to ignore Murphy's assessment, which
could have had important consequences for Irish foreign policy.
Murphy's independent stance in challenging the perceived wisdom
of his superior must be considered a brave attempt to prevent what
he saw as the flawed basis for potential policy decisions. From
interviews with contemporaries involved in the department at the
time, such as Con Cremin and Frederick Boland, Dermot Keogh
maintains that Murphy's démarche was significant in alerting de
Valera to the fact that Walshe may have been erroneous in his
judgement.[100]

Apart from the difficulties with his own staff, Walshe's most
acrimonious relationship during the war years was with the US
representative to Ireland, David Gray. Parallel to his efforts to
convince Hempel that Éire would not compromise its neutrality
in favour of the Allies, Walshe tried to convince Gray that the

Irish government would not aid the Germans. Gray considered de Valera's recent refusal of the British offer of unity to be based on 'the very natural fear that England is going down and not wishing to be tied to the wrong horse'. However, he believed Walshe had gone one step further, that of not only fearing British defeat but 'going definitely pro-German. The Nuncio tells me so and I have noticed a change in his attitude to me.'[101] In August Gray arranged a meeting with the specific aim of 'discovering how far Mr Walshe was pro-German and how far pro-British'.[102] He told Roosevelt: 'I like Joe very much but he has the reputation of being a suspicion monger and to some extent a trouble maker as he gets excited. I felt it was a good idea to get on a sound basis with him so we could talk turkey to one another.'[103] Walshe did not impress the US minister with the view that it was a distinct possibility that Britain would lose the war. While the prospect that 'England might create a stalemate with the aid of the Dominions and the United States' was not ruled out, Walshe insisted Irish foreign policy could not be predicated on the assumption of a British victory. If this turned out to be the case, Walshe believed it would be in Germany's interest to create and maintain, but not occupy, a strong Ireland. To Gray, this was wishful thinking; Germany would surely occupy and exploit Ireland and develop the ports for its own use. Walshe further revealed:

> If Britain won which he did not think possible or fought a draw which was a possibility then he thought Ireland would go on as before and that within the framework of the Commonwealth of Nations was Ireland's best chance.[104]

Gray, surprised by this thesis, thought it naive to assume Germany would forego the opportunity of using Ireland to control Britain.[105] Walshe was informed that the attitude of the United States was pro-British, and they were fearful of a German victory. From the US perspective, therefore, Walshe's stance and that of the Irish government was regarded as 'a stab in the back' for Britain. Gray opined that Ireland genuinely feared Germany, but insisted on implicating Britain as a possible invader. Walshe had referred to the recent British offer of unity, claiming that following the breakdown in talks there was a real danger of a British invasion. Gray had received assurances from Maffey that this had

never been their intention, and he thought it unlikely as long as American opinion was against it.

Despite Gray's comments, Anglo-Irish relations at this time remained agreeable. The two governments were working together to procure arms for the Irish army, and Walshe assured Gray that as soon as any invasion of Ireland by Germany had begun, British aid would immediately be sought. He was anxious to point out that Ireland would not be a liability to Britain. Gray, who believed Walshe's opinions represented very closely the government's attitude, concluded:

> I think they are all beginning to believe that we only want to be helpful in the long view of things, that we are now pro-British because we fear the results of a German victory, that we believe a German victory would be as bad for them as for us, and that appeals to anti-British feeling discredit them with us and are stupid because they do no good and only make the settlement of partition more difficult.[106]

Gray sought from Walshe assurances that Ireland was 'benevolently neutral', to which Walshe replied there could be no doubt this was the case, but said as a matter of coincidence it happened to be of benefit to Germany also.[107]

Gray believed that this meeting with Walshe had helped create a better atmosphere. Walshe had expressed his gratitude for their frank exchange, and he pressed Gray for some action with regard to the strong anti-Irish criticism the Irish government was receiving in the US press.[108] There was little Gray could do but he promised to look into the matter, and advised the State Department that the situation in Ireland was 'delicate' and suggested that Walshe's request should be treated 'sympathetically'.[109] Walshe pointed out that he knew there could be no question of American newspapers taking orders from the Irish government or in any way changing their attitude towards the world situation:

> We only ask those of them who have shown themselves particularly hostile to Ireland … to remember that neutrality is of the very essence of Irish independence at this state of our history. And, if we do not act as certain American papers wish us to act, it is not through any sense of perversity or any failure to see where our

interests lie. It is simply because of our conviction, founded on a
profound knowledge of our own people, that the action in question would put an end for ever to the existence of an ordered Irish
State.[110]

Walshe again explained to Gray that, 'almost by a miracle of history', Irish neutrality suited both sides of the conflict, although
for very different reasons. He thus saw the US press campaign
against Ireland as unfair, but made it clear that it was the British
who were to blame for this:

> The extent to which we blame the British for matter appearing
> in American papers is limited by our precise knowledge as to the
> source and as to the failure of the Ministry of Information to keep
> a guiding hand on those journalists in London whose superficial
> knowledge of international affairs leads them into the grossest
> errors concerning this country.

Walshe later wrote to Gray enclosing representative anti-Irish
newspaper samples from July. His assessment of their possible
effect was perhaps over-exaggerated:

> You will see on reading them that the Government here had suf-
> ficient reason for being apprehensive about the situation. It was
> not precisely a coup they were afraid of, though it would have been
> unwise to exclude such a possibility altogether.[111]

The context in which such press criticism occurred was important
to Walshe, who referred to various statements in the House of
Commons that did not rule out the possibility of a British invasion. The attached cuttings from the English newspapers, Walshe
believed, 'must have represented the view of some officials at least
in the Ministry of Information' as they had not been removed
by the censor. His suspicions were founded on the hypothesis
that 'a campaign of that sort could not have continued without
at least the permissive will of that Department.' While official
British complicity in press criticism against Ireland may have
been designed to put pressure on Irish neutrality, it did not necessarily mean that Britain wished to invade Ireland. However,
Walshe had noticed a 'complete change of attitude' in the British
press over the previous twelve to fourteen days, and thought it no

mere coincidence that it coincided with a similar change in the hostile American press:

> We have concluded from other very concrete facts that the change coincided with a change in the policy of the British Government towards us.[112]

Walshe became suspicious of increasingly organised collaboration between the governments of Britain and the United States.

In a letter Gray submitted to the censor, he also enclosed a copy for Walshe. In it, he admitted that 'one reason why I could never be a professional diplomat is that every time I write something secret and confidential I feel that I ought to tell your Government about it.'[113] Walshe would have readily agreed with Gray's diminution of his own diplomatic skills. Gray reported he was struggling to get Walshe 'straightened out' on a number of issues. He recognised Walshe's pivotal role in influencing Irish government opinion. He described Walshe as 'de Valera's eyes', and thought it important he remain as open and friendly as possible. This was of particular importance as he believed Walshe was 'personally defeatist on the War and not a good influence, though personally a very nice fellow'. Gray expressed concern about the implications of Irish foreign policy for the Irish people and for Walshe:

> He is trying to frame a middle of the road policy for which I can't blame him, but it is helpful to point out to him that the Irish Government having condemned the invasion of Belgium, having jailed German agents and confiscated their money, having jailed the I.R.A. who have representatives in Berlin can only hope as individuals to be liquidated in a painless manner by the Gestapo when Hitler comes.[114]

Gray believed the British were sensible not to coerce the Irish on the ports issue, as he felt the time would come when wartime circumstances would force the Irish to accede to the demands:

> In various ways I have been letting Joe Walshe (External Affairs) get doses of American viewpoint. He gave me an opening by his complaints about American Correspondents suggesting that Éire was betraying her own interests in not throwing in with Britain. I

told him that he probably hadn't heard the half of it, that what was
to come would be worse than anything he had got thus far.[115]

Gray realised that Walshe was not in agreement with this viewpoint, but hoped that he would eventually come to realise the
gravity of the Irish situation.

At the end of August 1940 Gray wrote a general memorandum on the Irish political situation for the Secretary of State. He
expressed some caution regarding the nature of his information:

> I have referred repeatedly to 'internal political conditions' which
> made neutrality the only possible policy for Éire in the present cir-
> cumstances, conditions which would make it impossible even for a
> national government to take the country into the war on the side of
> Britain though I think most of the Government leaders believe that
> Irish interests would be best served by a British victory. In speaking
> of these internal political conditions I have been obliged in large
> measure to take them on the faith of the Premier, of various Cabinet
> Ministers, and of the leaders of the Constitutional Opposition.[116]

Though Walshe was not in agreement with Gray's viewpoint, the
US minister hoped he could bring Walshe around to his way of
thinking. Later, he became more doubtful that Walshe could be
convinced to join the Allied cause until a German invasion of
Ireland was imminent. He adjudged Walshe to be naive for not
fearing that threat sufficiently:

> We would be silly to wait till Hitler got the control of the British
> Empire before we began to defend ourselves. Britain is our first
> line of defense just as she is yours. But you have never believed me.
> Now you see what has happened. You can speculate as well as I can
> as to what is likely to be the next step.[117]

For Gray, fear was key in persuading Walshe that the Irish position was untenable. He asked Walshe, 'Has it ever occurred to
you that if you don't watch your step Éire might get left out of a
front seat in the reshuffle, if that should take place?' Walshe could
only reply, 'If there should be a great league of English speaking
nations we should want to be in it.' Walshe admitted that the
Irish government wished 'to stick close to the United States', and
added, 'What we really want is to have an embassy at Washington

and build an embassy building but we don't want to be turned down and so don't like to make enquiries there.' Gray, of course, was more than happy to make discreet enquiries but believed there would not be any definite answer until the outcome of the war looked more certain, adding somewhat humorously, 'You may be a German province and not have any diplomatic representation at all.'

Gray believed that Walshe based his wartime foreign policy on the presumption of a German victory. 'Joe has been very defeatist, if not pro-Germanna [sic]', he said, 'and I think has been figuring out an Irish regime based on a German control of Europe. He has certainly been considering it a possibility if not a probability.'[118] As the likelihood of US involvement in the war increased, Gray's views on the Irish situation underwent some alteration. He became increasingly concerned to secure Allied access to the Irish ports. It was, therefore, only a matter of time before open conflict and contention over this issue would materialise between Gray and the Irish government.

Disagreement arose between Walshe and Gray in November 1940 when the US minister wrote what he described as a 'rough memorandum' based on an after-lunch conversation with Walshe. Walshe was furious at Gray's report, and replied immediately:

> I feel at liberty to describe your memorandum as a little post-impressionist, if not verging on the futurist. Of course, I may be wrong and I may have imbibed over-freely of the excellent wines which you gave us at lunch. If that is so, I was, of course, capable of saying anything, even the exact contrary of what I would wish to say in my sober moments.[119]

That opening phrase sets the context for the conversation, which Walshe clearly viewed as unofficial. Gray had overstepped the mark by regarding it as something more than that:

> In any case, my dear David, I do not think that an after-lunch conversation of that casual character merited being immortalised in a memorandum, and if you don't mind, I should much prefer to see the memorandum destroyed than to attempt to make any serious effort to correct your impressions of what I said.

In his seven-page memorandum, Gray speculated that if the

United States entered the war, the use of the Irish ports would become of primary importance. The reply he attributed to Walshe seems somewhat out of character, although he had believed he was speaking in a purely personal and private capacity:

> Walshe then said that he had little doubt that if America entered the war, there would be any difficulty about arranging for the lease of ports and air facilities to the United States, whether or not Ireland became a belligerent.[120]

Gray went on to say that it was Walshe himself who had suggested this idea to him when he first arrived in Dublin. Walshe, according to Gray's account of the conversation, suggested that if the US and Ireland became involved in the war and eventually emerged victorious on the Allied side, then a very close relationship would develop between the two countries:

> He even suggested the possibility of a common citizenship, a close economic relation, and the use of Irish ports and facilities for the policing of the North Atlantic.

Walshe, who wished for the destruction of the memorandum, was challenged to respond by what he saw as the permanence of the document. His memory of the conversation was in direct opposition to Gray's, but he was careful in the manner of his contradiction:

> You make me say that I had little doubt that there would be no difficulty about the arranging for the lease of ports and air facilities to the United States should she become belligerent. I do not think I was anything like so definite, but in any case I can make myself clear now.[121]

If Walshe did say a number of things attributed to him by Gray, then it is clear they were uttered in a personal capacity. Walshe now felt that Gray's action of writing the memorandum lent permanence and an official nature to the exchange, which had been based on a private and personal conversation. Walshe resented being forced to reply to the memorandum in an official capacity, and believed Gray had not grasped the fundamentals of diplomacy as he knew it. Their relationship would never be the same, with Walshe becoming more reserved and extremely careful of

every word. He had clearly been shaken by the incident and would have shuddered at the thought of the contents coming into the public domain.

In this instance, Walshe's premonition regarding the permanence of such written documents coming back to haunt him was proven correct. Nearly two decades later, the contents of the memoranda were the cause of a flurry of speculation and press comment. 'Secret Pact Denied' was the main headline in the *Sunday Review* in June 1958, two years after Walshe's death. The report was based on Gray's memorandum, which had been released by the American State Department. It was reported that Ireland had been willing to hand over ports and airfields to the US if they needed them during the war.[122] Robert Brennan reacted strongly against the allegations, describing them as a 'libel on a man who cannot now defend himself'.[123] The Department of External Affairs recognised Walshe's explicit correction of the Gray memorandum, and pointed out that the reports, which were based on Gray's uncorrected memorandum, were themselves an inaccurate simplification of its contents.[124] While the following press reports were unambiguous in conveying the Irish government's denial of the reports, Walshe's fear of posthumous scrutiny had been realised.

During this time, Gray was involved in another misunderstanding with Walshe and Robert Brennan. In early November 1940 Brennan called on the US Under-Secretary for the State Department to outline the Irish position on neutrality. He reported to Dublin that all had gone well with the Under-Secretary, who appeared to understand that 'Ireland could have no other policy and that Ireland's peace was an asset to Britain.'[125] In conversation with Walshe, however, Gray related a different story significantly less favourable than that indicated by Brennan:

> Under Secretary reported as saying we were endangering our own position by holding back ports which were apparently essential for British success.[126]

Brennan insisted that his version was the correct account of the discussion, but was willing to see the Under-Secretary again to clear up the matter. From the archival evidence it would appear

that Gray, in his dealings with Walshe and the Irish government, was far more aggressive than his superiors instructed. Walshe reported that Gray had:

> … prefaced his statement by saying that Americans could be cruel if their interests were affected and Ireland should expect little or no sympathy if the British took the ports.[127]

Walshe backed Brennan's interpretation, and clearly believed that Gray had received no official instructions for these comments. According to Gray, US policy towards Ireland was uncompromising. While this may have been a true reflection of the State Department's frustration at Irish intransigence, Gray's method of communication was abrasive and certainly did nothing to improve Irish–US relations during this time.

As we have seen, Walshe was often accused of having strong pro-German sentiments. Gray certainly believed this, and his view was supported by others at different times. One of the correspondents used by the British Ministry for Information was the Anglo-Irish novelist, Elizabeth Bowen. Having met Walshe a couple of times, Bowen formed the following opinion:

> [He was] not popular and seemed to be out of contact with any of the other people I met. He struck me as having a good intellect (he is a 'spoilt' Jesuit) and he has a personality you could cut with a knife. His judgement might well be questionable. His person is uncouth and his past (apparently) sinister. I was frequently told he was a pro-German. It would have interested me to discover if this were really the case, and, if so, why.[128]

As we have already seen, Walshe had previously expressed admiration for German achievements. To put this into context, he expressed this view in a conversation with Germany's representative to Ireland, Eduard Hempel. Joseph Lee notes the irony of this tribute from the chief diplomat of a small neutral state to a belligerent country with a proven record of transgression against such states.[129] Walshe's ability for euphemism knew no bounds, and as the war raged on he enquired of Hempel that 'as things were now beginning to look really lively, I hoped that our country would not suffer any serious inconvenience.'[130] However, Walshe did not regard the German threat flippantly, and the ensuing diplomatic

encounters demonstrated the fearful respect with which he treated the Third Reich.

As 1940 entered its final months, the diplomatic pressures did not cease for Walshe. A bombing of a creamery at Campile, County Wexford in 1940 was believed to have been an 'accidental' attack by a German mission that mistook the area for an English target. Walshe was worried that this and other such incidents would furnish further opportunity for Britain to argue that Ireland should enter the war. Joseph Lee has pointed out that Walshe and Boland used censorship to play down the effect of these incidents, and that the protests that followed were couched in deferential terms.[131] According to Carolle Carter, the Irish minister in Berlin, William Warnock told Woermann that the Irish did not want to be difficult in protesting the sinking of the *Kerry Head*, but were concerned because the British used these incidents as evidence that Ireland could not defend her own neutrality.[132] This was Walshe's primary concern. He felt that a formal protest resulting in the admission of error and sympathy would sufficiently ease the situation, but he was conscious that such events would further strengthen Allied pressure for Irish entry into the war.

When Walshe was asked by Maffey whether he ever believed that Britain was planning a re-occupation of Ireland, Walshe replied that at one time he felt quite sure that it was going to take place, and claimed that anybody who had as much evidence as he had would have come to the same conclusion. Maffey, wanting to clear the air of suspicion, admitted to Walshe that there had been extensive discussions between the politicians and the army on the issue of the British troops entering Irish territory, and that the military had pressed very strongly to enter Ireland's territory at the moment of a German attack without an invitation from the Irish government. He assured Walshe, however, that 'the political considerations had prevailed and the Army had to acquiesce'.[133] Walshe asked if he could presume that the military had not altered its position on this issue and would continue to push the plan, but Maffey assured him that the political decision was final.

Meanwhile, Winston Churchill, in a statement to the House of Commons, strongly criticised the policy of the Irish government to remain neutral and deny use of the Treaty ports to

Britain. Churchill saw this as a grave injustice, describing it as a 'most heavy and grievous burden' on Britain's war effort. This attack and ensuing British press denigration of neutrality worried many Irish government officials. Hempel reported to his authorities that Walshe believed the latest attack was more a sign of British desperation than a reflection of any real intention to seize the Southern ports. He maintained that the lack of defences at the ports undermined their value to Britain. Walshe also thought that any such aggression by Britain was unlikely because this would have serious repercussions for Anglo-American relations. The US government, he stated, was strongly influenced by the Irish-American diaspora.[134]

Hempel, however, believed Britain would continue to pressurise Ireland in an effort to gain concessions. He therefore enquired of his superiors if de Valera should be informed of a possible German willingness to assist Ireland in the event of a British offensive. His superior, Ernst Freiherr von Weizsäcker, State Secretary of the German Foreign Ministry, replied there would be no objection to de Valera knowing that German assistance could be depended upon in this event. In light of this reply, Hempel made a number of attempts to sound out the Irish government's attitude to the idea of German aid but found little opportunity to speak with de Valera directly. He settled instead on the idea of approaching Walshe to discuss this delicate matter.

Walshe revealed he had encountered anxiety in some Irish quarters concerning the possibility that Germany might sacrifice Ireland to Britain as a token in any future peace settlement. Walshe intimated that he personally thought this hypothesis unlikely due to 'Ireland's strategic importance'. Hempel thought that, while the ports were of major strategic importance, Britain was unlikely to initiate an attack against Ireland unless as a preemptive move against German intervention in Ireland. Walshe, keen to impress on Hempel the importance of Ireland acting alone in the event of British aggression, admitted:

> Even the Irish Army evidently considers avoidance of any first move by Germany of such fundamental importance that, referring to the possibility of holding out in the beginning with its own resources, it apparently envisages coordination with the hoped for German assistance only after an English attack has taken place.[135]

Ribbentrop cabled Hempel and suggested that any potential shipment of arms could be construed in such a way as not to represent a technical breach of neutrality.[136] Hempel believed the moment had now come to give some indication of Germany's continued interest in Irish neutrality. Some hints could be given to help persuade the Irish government that Germany would be of vital assistance in restoring a united Ireland. However, within a couple of days he reported having spoken with Walshe, who now felt more definite than before that Britain would not attack Ireland. Walshe, citing detailed reasons for this belief, was preparing Hempel for an explicit rejection of the German proposals.[137] He previously indicated to Hempel that de Valera appreciated the offer but felt there was no way that the arms could be covertly shipped to Ireland:

> If the English were to learn of the shipment, they would seize with both hands the welcome opportunity to assert the existence of a German–Irish plot; and, what was particularly dangerous, this would gravely jeopardise the freedom of movement secured in consideration of Ireland's neutrality by the vigorous efforts of the Irish-American community in the United States. The Irish Government therefore had no other recourse at this time but to abandon acquisition of arms until a British attack, which was unlikely for the time being, had become a fact.[138]

In typical fashion, Walshe, while declining the opportunity of tangible cooperation, had nevertheless made it quite evident to Hempel that German assistance would be sought if a British invasion became a certainty.

At the close of 1940 Herbert Shaw visited Ireland on behalf of the British government, and reported to London.[139] Shaw was interested in meeting both de Valera and Walshe. Realising the command structure of Irish External Affairs, he became more interested in what Walshe had to say. He described Walshe as an interpreter of world affairs for the blind de Valera. 'Walshe is highly intelligent and well informed of European and world affairs', said Shaw. (This was a statement that one British official thought should be qualified. In the margin beside this comment on Walshe's intelligence is a handwritten note: 'Unfortunately small and narrow-minded.')[140] Shaw gave a brief history of

Walshe's career and background, mentioning his Jesuit training and his ambition to become Ireland's representative to the
Holy See. He described the External Affairs secretary as having 'a suspicious and somewhat scholastic mind'. Considering
the extent to which Shaw believed de Valera to be dependent on
Walshe, his assessment of the workings of Irish External Affairs
is interesting:

> I recalled the blind Polyphemus feeling the reassuring backs of his
> sheep, though all unconscious of the lithe and crafty Greeks who
> hung by the wool of their bellies. I do not think, however, that,
> even if Mr Walshe has been the source of many of Mr de Valera's
> doubts and suspicions, he is necessarily past praying for, especially
> in an undefeated England.[141]

Maffey, of course, had already realised the importance of Walshe
in dealing with de Valera. He had heard much rumour and
gossip about Walshe. In one report at the end of 1940 he commented on the views of an unnamed informant, whom Maffey
describes as a 'rebel' and a 'hundred per cent Irishman'. Maffey
stated that while the views expressed by his source were prejudiced, they nevertheless reflected a point of view that could not
be ignored. The informant's views, which describe de Valera as
egotistical and power-hungry, are clearly prejudiced, but provide
an interesting opinion as to the perceived operation of External
Affairs and of Walshe's relationship with the Taoiseach. Due
to the power of the Irish censorship, de Valera is described as
having dictatorial power, and that he was influenced only by a
small ruling elite:

> The difficulty of the situation is vastly increased by the fact that
> he is to all intents and purposes blind, and can read nothing. In
> the business of Government only two persons have unlimited and
> authoritative access to him; in other words 'have his ear'. The for-
> mation of his judgements and decisions, therefore, must be largely
> influenced by what these two men say or read to him – or omit
> to say or read – and the emphasis they choose to give to various
> words and sentences.

Walshe and Frank Aiken are the two men referred to. Aiken, the
Minister for the Coordination of Defence, was seen as having

more influence with de Valera than any other member of the Cabinet. Walshe was deemed to be positively pro-German:

> Joe Walshe is self made, with no really solid background. He is convinced that Germany will win, and he is most anxious that we shall continue to sit on the fence, while taking great care to do nothing to annoy Germany. He has developed in recent months from a timid neutral, to a positive pro-German. His department is now almost a branch of the German Legation, and is unique among the Government departments in that respect.[142]

Opinions as to Walshe's influence over de Valera vary greatly. David Gray, for example, once stated that he did not regard Walshe as being overly important as regards influencing de Valera. In this he was probably influenced by James Dillon, who said that Walshe was 'a very decent personality but completely under de Valera's thrall'.[143] Maffey, however, took a more pragmatic approach towards assessing Walshe. He realised that Walshe had considerable influence on de Valera but did not overestimate this power. He valued his meetings with Walshe as they reflected closely the thinking and mood of the Taoiseach:

> Mr de Valera is still in his nursing home but Walshe is in constant touch with him and no doubt reflects his views. Opinions here change readily enough and too much must not be put upon what Walshe says today.

Walshe told Maffey that he had concluded, following recent events over Irish territory, that Germany appeared to be changing its attitude towards Ireland. Maffey reported Walshe's change of allegiance with some sarcasm: 'The German Minister (hitherto proclaimed a model of good behaviour here) was beginning to change his tone and defend acts which previously he was wont to regret.' Walshe said that the new attitude appeared to be, 'to Hell with everybody. Those who don't like the New Order must stomach it.'[144] Maffey saw this as a 'symptom of a new trend', and thought that the Germans would add to its development by further infringements on Irish neutrality. He advised London that this was a significant development and one that they, along with the American government, should do everything they could to encourage in order to bring about a more pliable Irish govern-

ment. He advocated friendly persuasion, however, pointing out that the Irish psyche was not well disposed to coercion, especially from the British. Maffey had previously suggested to de Valera that Britain's Secretary of State for Dominion Affairs should visit Ireland to establish direct contact between both governments. De Valera had been less than enthusiastic about the idea. However, Walshe now approached Maffey to rekindle the suggestion, and this was seen as a positive indication that Dublin was moving in the right direction.

Throughout 1940 and during the following years of the war, Walshe remained in regular contact with Gray, Hempel and Maffey. His meetings with Hempel were crucial in maintaining good relations with Germany. The Allied diplomats were not happy with the position adopted by the Irish government, and for that reason Walshe was sometimes regarded as being pro-German in his outlook. For a period during 1940, Walshe believed the likelihood was that Germany would win the war. This belief influenced External Affairs policy to the extent that Britain's proposal for unity was rejected. Walshe was somewhat suspicious of British motives and plans with regard to Ireland. Despite this, however, he facilitated detailed and extensive cooperation with Britain, which clearly breached neutral theory. His conversations with Hempel were sometimes supportive, but this would never come to anything more than serving Walshe's desire to maintain the status quo with Germany. The policies pursued throughout the war revealed that while the Irish government actively supported Britain it would not countenance any active cooperation with Germany. Walshe did not deviate from such a policy, and was willing to aid the Allies as long as the sustainability of Irish neutrality was not seriously threatened.

WALSHE AND THE LIMITS
OF WARTIME DIPLOMACY
1941

FOR A LARGE part of the war, David Gray believed the German legation in Dublin was of crucial importance to the Axis war effort by providing information to Berlin and by supporting espionage activities in Ireland. This view was challenged by Walshe, who believed that Gray was exaggerating the size and influence of the legation:

> Actually it has not more than half a dozen men with two or three women typists. Its behaviour has been uniformly correct and the stories of its activities as a vast centre of espionage are without foundation.[1]

Gray's suspicions, however, were heightened by Germany's request for an increase in staff for its Dublin office late in 1940. Hempel called on Walshe, seeking an urgent meeting. The German Foreign Ministry had sent instructions that three additional officials had been appointed to augment Hempel's staff and were due to arrive before Christmas. The proposals caused instant consternation. The planned means of transportation – a Lufthansa civil plane direct from Germany – was at the centre of the Irish objection. Permission for a German aircraft to enter Irish territory would not have been viewed kindly by the British government. On 3 January 1941, Walshe told Hempel that the proposed increase in staff would cause undue 'political embarrassment', and added that he believed the proposal 'was the work of some official in Berlin who did not possess that keen appreciation

of the situation here which Herr Woermann and the other senior officials of the German Foreign Office had always shown.' Walshe refused Hempel's request that the issue be dealt with through the Dublin legation, and instructed Warnock to tell the German Foreign Office that the move was 'politically impossible'.

The following day Hempel met Walshe and again insisted that Germany had a 'technical right' to the increase of staff. Hempel made it clear that a refusal would be a 'serious matter', and he referred to the possibility of a breach in diplomatic relations. This was a difficult moment in the Walshe–Hempel relationship. Walshe argued that the Irish government was entitled to expect the German government to have due regard to Irish interests in this matter, but Hempel countered that the German request 'represented no more than the exercise of a right that which they undoubtedly possessed' and, therefore, 'there was no room for discussion'.[2] Walshe was keenly aware that acquiescence to the application would aid Allied propaganda attacks on Irish neutrality, but was also worried by the repeated references to 'serious consequences' in the event of permission being denied. He tried to get Hempel to detail the nature of this threat, but Hempel stated that this had been an expression of his personal view and that he had no official instructions on that matter. His tone, Walshe noted, was decidedly less menacing than in their previous meetings. Based on Walshe's estimation, therefore, that Germany would not press the matter, de Valera flatly told Hempel to get the request withdrawn as it would undoubtedly be refused.

Walshe's calculation was correct, but he was relieved nonetheless when Hempel arrived to say that, due to the views of the Taoiseach, the German government had decided to withdraw the request. However, the plan to increase the staff of the legation was not abandoned altogether, and Walshe reported a few days later that while they had recognised that the means of transporting the new staff had caused difficulties this did not preclude them from arranging travel to Ireland by some other means. The German Foreign Office, therefore, put forward the suggestion that the required officials be released from the American continent and travel to Ireland by the normal means. Walshe promised to consult de Valera on this suggestion, but would have preferred to see an immediate end to the issue. In this case there was little cause for a refusal, but in an effort to discourage any advancement in

this proposal Walshe suggested to Hempel that it might be wise to inform his superiors that 'the ordinary means of travelling to Ireland from the American Continent was by the Pan-American passenger line to Lisbon and thence to England by British plane.'[3] With little option, Walshe later clarified his position and told Hempel that the government had no objection to the arrival of the officials if they came by the ordinary means of transport. It was a difficult start to the year for Walshe. In this case the immediate crisis was faced down but he knew that it would be used as evidence of untoward German activity in Ireland.

David Gray's allegations that Ireland was being used as a spy centre served to remind Walshe that any unapproved activities by Germany could give the Allies further pretext to exert pressure on the Irish government. The vulnerability of Ireland's position was highlighted by this incident, and compelled Walshe to give serious consideration to planning in the event of Ireland becoming a country of occupation. Some historians have suggested that Irish foreign policy during the war was based on reaction to events as they arose. In this way the theory and practice of Irish neutrality evolved as the war progressed. Indeed, there seems to be little in the available archives to suggest that there was substantial inquiry or contemplation into the nature of neutrality itself. However, there were efforts to make some practical preparations in the event of war in Ireland. Before war began, de Valera suggested the setting up of a committee – which was to include Walshe and the heads of a number of other government departments – to consider what practical steps the government could take in the event of war. Its task was to draw up general proposals and to prepare an Emergency Book consisting of instructions to be carried out in the event of an invasion.[4] Throughout the war, therefore, Walshe was involved in extensive planning within his own department and with other government agencies to ensure that some measure of organisation was in place in the event of an invasion of Ireland.

In response to queries from Maurice Moynihan, secretary of the Department of the Taoiseach, Walshe outlined that one of the major priorities in the event of an attempted invasion of Ireland would be to maintain communications with the outside world. Thus, he advised that the provision to destroy the Athlone broadcasting station should be reversed so that the government

could protest the invasion to the world. The destruction of the station would be of little inconvenience to the invaders and a possible future liability to Ireland:

> The two likely invaders are in a position to provide themselves with a powerful station at any time after a successful invasion of this country. Whatever we destroy we have to re-make ourselves, and I understand that, if Athlone is destroyed, it would take us years to restore it.

In the event of an invasion, the Department of External Affairs would remain to face the enemy. Walshe readily volunteered himself and his primary staff for the task:

> No matter what decision is ultimately taken about the transfer of the central Government, the principal staff of this Department should remain in the capital in order to provide a channel for dealing with the invader when he arrives there and to do everything possible to lessen the harshness of the measures which he may wish to impose on the people.[5]

However, the following month, in another letter to Moynihan, Walshe saw no reason why External Affairs could not carry out its functions from a remote emergency headquarters:

> If the Central Government has to be transferred to a provincial centre, we would require to maintain, and transfer to the centre in question, the following minimum staff: One Secretary, one Assistant Secretary, one Legal Adviser, two Assistant Principal Officers, two Cadets, one Accountant, one Archivist, five Clerical Officers, three typists.[6]

Walshe may have been prepared for hypothetical danger but his representatives in mainland Europe had more palpable cause for concern.

In the event of an invasion, all Irish representatives abroad would protest to the government to which they were accredited. Walshe advised that according to international law no declaration of war against the invading country itself was needed. Resistance was sufficient, and, indeed, such a declaration would tend to obscure the defensive nature of the Irish government's position.[7] Walshe studied the question of what should be done with the

citizens of the invading country who were resident at the diplomatic mission in Dublin. He suggested that they should be
housed in a hotel to prevent any secret communication with their
home country, pending arrangements for their repatriation and
the return of their Irish counterparts. Walshe, always conscious
of the letter of international law, even in the height of extreme
crisis, saw difficulties with this proposal, pointing out that on
invasion the legation property of the intruding country would
'pass at once into the hands of the "neutral" power and, therefore, to search or occupy them might land us into diplomatic
complications'.[8] If Germany were the attacking country, then the
question was raised if diplomatic relations with Italy should be
severed. Walshe was against this idea, saying that no such action
should be taken considering the large numbers of Irish nationals in ecclesiastical colleges and religious communities in Italian
territory.[9]

In February 1941 instructions were sent to the Irish mission
in Berlin. In the event of an invasion of Ireland by a country
other than Germany, Warnock was to send a formal note protesting the action of the invader. The representatives' primary
function would now become propaganda 'to foster sympathy and
counter invader's publicity justifying attack'.[10] The Irish legation
in Washington, considered a safe haven, was to become the centre
for propaganda, communication and instruction for all offices of
External Affairs. In the event of an invasion, Walshe believed it
would be necessary to ask some neutral country to take charge of
Irish interests. The United States was first choice as trustee, with
Spain as a possible substitute. However, the first choice would be
problematic if the United States became involved in the war or
if Britain happened to be the invading country. The problem was
put to one side, however, as Boland dryly noted in his memoirs:
'The question of the protection of Irish interests in the United
Kingdom if Britain were the invading power was left over for
a later decision.'[11] Nonetheless, Robert Brennan in Washington
was asked to make discreet enquiries as to whether the United
States would be willing to undertake this role if the case arose.
Clearly, the eventuality of a German invasion was thought to be
the more likely scenario.

If invasion came, the Irish population would also need instructions. This was predominantly the concern of the Department

of Defence and the military authorities, but Walshe was asked to consider the 'Draft Instructions to the Population in case of Invasion' in the light of international rules of law and practice. Assisting the Department of Defence in drawing up memoranda and advising on international law consumed a great deal of Walshe's time over the following months. In this case, Walshe thought that the language used in the civilian instructions, which were based on the Swiss version, should be simplified for the benefit of the less well-educated sections of the civilian population. He made a number of critical remarks about the text, but drew attention to a point relating to the proposed date of issue of the instructions from which, he said, 'it would appear that the Instructions may be intended for issue before any invasion of this country has actually taken place.' If this were the case then External Affairs would need time to consider the foreign-policy implications and the 'possible consequences of such action on the minds of the belligerent Governments at the present time'.[12] Without the proper diplomatic preparation, the distribution of instructions preparing the civilian population for an invasion could cause either of the belligerents to become suspicious of Ireland's position.

Irish preparations for invasion clearly did not allow for much resistance to the aggressor. In the event of the country becoming occupied, Walshe envisaged that most civil service staff would remain at their posts to carry out their normal work, provided that this work did not involve assisting the enemy. However, he did argue that in certain instances assisting the assailant would result in less destruction and hardship on the civilian population:

> It may appear questionable whether anything would be gained from a military point of view by giving the enemy a pretext for resorting to the indiscriminate and ruthless requisitioning of supplies instead of acquiring supplies in a regular manner in consultation with the Department concerned.[13]

Walshe further saw the 'maintenance of the internal discipline and cohesion' of civil service staff in occupied territory as a matter of 'primary importance', and therefore advised that a single authority should be appointed to act as 'guide, philosopher and friend to the Civil Service'. He was adamant that the appointee

should be a member of the government, and believed that 'the post could hardly be filled by a Civil Servant'.[14]

Michael Rynne, legal adviser to the Department of External Affairs, responded to draft orders that were to be enforced in the event of hostilities, proposed by the Taoiseach's department. Rynne's response highlights the resentment at the omission of proposals that had been specifically recommended by Walshe:

> It is clear that [Walshe's] attitude of extreme caution, combined with insistence on close coordination between this Department and the Department of Defence, in relation to incidents in any way likely to involve this country in war, was not fully adhered to by the Department of the Taoiseach when drafting their proposed instruction.[15]

Rynne suggested that these omissions were no mere oversight by the Taoiseach's office, and he outlined how the Taoiseach's department proposals represented a departure from specific recommendations that Walshe had been at 'pains to implement in recent months'. Lack of agreement on the role of the Department of External Affairs was a primary concern for Walshe, whose residual fears concerning the stature of the department were never too far away.

Later in the year, Walshe, accompanied by Rynne, attended a conference on wartime preparations held at the Department of Defence. Concern was raised that in the event of an invasion, the Gárda Síochána would be considered part of the 'armed forces' rather than the 'civilian population', considering that a large proportion of the gardaí at the time was armed with revolvers. Walshe and Rynne agreed that the possession of these weapons was for protective reasons as part of their policing duties, and did not make them part of the 'armed forces'. Thus, it was envisaged that External Affairs would contact the belligerent powers to inform them of this distinction regarding the armed gardaí who were part of the 'civilian population' and not part of the 'armed forces'.[16] The gardaí would have to remain in the occupied territory to carry out their normal functions. Walshe also thought it important from a political point of view that 'some remnant of the Government framework should continue to exist in occupied territory if possible'.

Some felt that these preparations were not being considered with enough haste. The Department of Defence wrote to Walshe to urge swifter attention to a number of matters:

> With reference to this Department's minutes of the 10th January last, and subsequent reminders on the question of plans of action for Irish diplomatic representatives abroad in the event of hostilities, I am directed by the Minster for Defence to enquire if you are now in a position to forward the desired information.[17]

Walshe was quick to point out that his department was prepared for any eventuality, and he was somewhat annoyed by the interference. External Affairs was ready, and had been for some time:

> Our Legations and Offices abroad have had in their hands for over 18 months complete instructions as to what to do if they have to close their Offices and withdraw.

These instructions also outlined the three most urgent steps to be taken in case of Ireland becoming involved in the war:

· to provide for the closing and withdrawal of our Legation … in the enemy country;
· to provide for the closing of the Legation of the enemy State here;
· to ensure that our Legations and Offices abroad have instructions and funds to enable them to carry on, even if communications are totally disrupted.[18]

Walshe also proposed that a note to the hypothetical invading country be drafted. This 'draft note', when written, was wrought with pride, defiance and historical overtones, and it committed the Irish people 'to defend, with God's help, their ancient sovereignty and the measure of independence their fathers so hardly won'.[19] Reflecting Walshe's stated policy inclinations, this draft included two versions, depending on whether 'the attacking country is Britain' or 'the attacking country is any country other than Britain'.[20]

Apart from these preparations, intelligence and censorship were also integral to Walshe's measures for maintaining neutrality during the war. The Irish representatives abroad were involved in the gathering of intelligence, while Walshe's staff paid particular

attention to local newspaper articles which referred to Ireland.[21] Reports on articles carried by the press in Germany, Britain and the United States were considered vitally important by Walshe; he needed to be well informed of all wartime developments that affected Ireland, and it was the Irish censorship and intelligence authorities who ensured this through regular reports.[22] Detailed files were kept in Walshe's office on issues such as the whereabouts of German nationals in Ireland; espionage activities; internees; newspaper reports on Ireland and Irish neutrality; incidents of belligerent aircraft landing in Irish territory; and the movements, mail and telephone conversations of diplomatic staff based in Dublin.

In May 1940 the Irish censorship intercepted a report by the Czechoslovakian consul, D. K. Kostal, who was based in Dublin. Reporting to his superiors, Kostal described the majority of the Irish people as anti-British and said that Ireland's censorship was biased and controlled in order that the German embassy could not be accused of acting incorrectly. Walshe was referred to in the memorandum as having refuted the allegations of favouritism towards Germany. According to Kostal, Walshe said, 'We have a big secret service and we know about everything that is going on.' Walshe continued that, 'the German Ambassador Dr Hempel is a gentleman, surrounded by spies. We do not allow anything that would be against Great Britain and we watch the Germans better than you imagine.'[23] The External Affairs files contain large quantities of documents, many of them letters to Walshe from Colonel Liam Archer or Colonel Dan Bryan, director of the Irish intelligence unit, G2, who related information on a wide variety of matters.[24] Most of the correspondence deals with issues of minor importance, but it provides an insight into the type of information Walshe received, and in some cases Walshe's views on various matters are revealed.

G2 kept a close watch on IRA activities, and Walshe was informed of any major developments.[25] Dan Bryan apprised Walshe of any communist activities in Ireland, but in effect this was of little concern to the department.[26] The gardaí and the Department of Justice also cooperated closely with Walshe and External Affairs. The protection of all foreign representatives in Dublin was the responsibility of the Irish authorities. Hempel was on occasion threatened and intimidated. In one case, he informed

Walshe that he was receiving anonymous phone calls at his home, but he decided to drop the issue when the Irish authorities suggested that they listen to all his calls as a countermeasure.[27]

Closely linked to the Irish intelligence service was the Irish censorship, which provided Walshe with valuable information.[28] For example, Walshe was sent a transcript of a telephone conversation between James Dillon and David Gray that had been intercepted and recorded by the censor. The Department of External Affairs' interest in censorship lay primarily with matters relating to diplomacy. Walshe realised that public comment on Irish neutrality or on the wartime affairs of the belligerent states could endanger Ireland's position. He had a particular interest in the monitoring of communications between foreign representatives in Dublin and their headquarters. Diplomatic correspondence was not directly interfered with but was 'observed', and its contents made available to Walshe.[29]

Walshe directed that any information that could affect neutrality be vetted in consultation with his department. He was primarily concerned that press reports regarding attacks on Irish ships and vessels in or near Irish territorial waters not be released for publication without his knowledge. It had been arranged, for example, that reports of attacks on British ships be suppressed to avoid the charge of being a source of information for German interests. Walshe wrote to the controller of censorship, Joseph Connolly, informing him of his principal concerns:

> No news regarding any incident which affects our neutrality or which is likely to be the subject of representations to a foreign Government should be published without prior reference to this Department.[30]

Walshe insisted that this level of control was necessary as any mistimed or misinformed statement could lead to a diplomatic disaster. Connolly was left in no doubt as to the seriousness of his task:

> The success of any diplomatic negotiations which we may have to have with regard to such incidents may be seriously prejudiced by the premature publication of particulars of the occurrence.

News regarding Irish shipping was of particular importance and

singled out by Walshe, who stated that External Affairs required immediate notification to consider if an official statement was necessary. With a view to preventing the charge that Ireland was a source of information, Walshe sought the suppression of any news regarding attacks on, or the sinking of, British ships.

Walshe's interest in censorship was not confined to matters directly affecting his department and Irish neutrality. His close connection with the censorship process gave him influence beyond his normal brief, and he was quick to offer opinions on subjects that could not be considered in his direct area of responsibility. He supported the office of the censor, for example, in its decision to prevent the sale of a book entitled *The Persecution of the Catholic Church in the Third Reich*. His opinion on this publication was in no way influenced by any sympathy with Nazi ideology and neither did he wish its sale to be prevented due to the state's diplomatic relations with Germany. Rather, the reason he gave was his concern for the 'real moral harm' that this publication could effect. The authors of the book reproduced explicit illustrations and quotations of Nazi propaganda that sought to incite hatred and contempt for the Church. Despite his agreement with the general opinion of the book, Walshe believed that 'you cannot be indecent in order to show up the indecency of others.'[31] He opposed the book, therefore, because of his own sense of decency. The moral welfare of the Irish public was hardly the direct concern of the secretary of the Department of External Affairs, yet having the ear of the censor, Walshe would not forego the opportunity to make his views on such matters known.

While Walshe abhorred the idea of information falling into the wrong hands, he was not, it seems, reluctant to circulate information to journalists when it suited his needs. Liam Archer of G2 sent Walshe a copy of a letter entitled 'Memo on Dublin News Routine and Sources', which had been intercepted by the postal censorship.[32] It was written by a British press correspondent who had been based in Dublin and who was now advising his or her successor on the best sources of information in Dublin. In a section entitled 'Miscellaneous Sources and Contacts', there is a reference to Walshe:

> Joseph P. Walshe, secretary, department of external affairs, Upper Merrion Street. He keeps up to the minute on all important Irish

news and cooperated with me on several good dope stories on Irish attitude, etc., such as 'informeds say…'

The reporter described Walshe as 'highly informed' and 'awfully decent', but warned that Walshe's private phone number should be used sparingly.[33] Walshe, however, could never have been considered a really useful source of information. He was secretive in the extreme and kept many of his own colleagues in the dark on various matters, and it is unlikely that he divulged information of any real importance to the press.

While Walshe found his contact with the office of the censor useful primarily as a source of information, he also came to value its discretion. He trusted its judgement when it came to informing him of matters of possible relevance to External Affairs, and at times he drafted in their assistance to deal with matters of some delicacy. In April 1941, for example, Walshe wrote to Thomas Coyne informing him that since the beginning of the war he had been allowing the Loretto nuns send occasional messages to their convent in Madrid through the diplomatic bag.[34] Walshe explained that the letters were handed in to the department unsealed, and that upon general inspection they had proven to be innocuous. However, Walshe was somewhat embarrassed by one particular letter. He does not recount its contents but Coyne's reply is sufficient to understand Walshe's predicament. 'I think that this good lady might have confined herself to personal matters and Loretto affairs', he said, concluding, 'it smacks of the *News of the World*.' The Irish External Affairs staff stationed abroad were also allowed to use the diplomatic bag for sending and receiving correspondence from home. This, too, caused some difficulties; in one case, the mother of an Irish official at the legation in Vichy directly referred in her letter to the use of the diplomatic channel to send a number of packages to her daughter.[35] Correspondents had been asked not to mention the use of the diplomatic bag as it would cause some embarrassment if the British authorities found out.

On another occasion, Walshe turned to the censor for his own personal reasons when he sought the interception of a 1941 edition of the *Reader's Digest*. It appears that Walshe was directly referred to in one of the articles and he wished to prevent its distribution in Ireland.[36] Coyne hoped the secretary for External

Affairs could see the lighter side of the article, and his reference is a clue to the nature of the remarks made about Walshe:

> I trust that the personal publicity which you are having in this matter will enable you to collect large fees for lecturing to the farmers' wives in the Middle West when an ungrateful country finds that it has no further use for your services.[37]

Walshe was not shy in asking for the intervention of the censor. On another occasion, he wrote seeking the removal of certain material from circulation in Ireland. Following complaints from the German minister, he wrote seeking the recall of a magazine entitled *Everybody's*. Coyne pointed to the impracticality of banning such publications:

> I am afraid that we could hardly justify banning it unless indeed we were to ban about 90% of the journals that arrive here from Britain.[38]

Walshe had also raised some questions concerning de Gaullest pamphlets that were on sale at some outlets. It is not clear whether this query was based on Hempel's objections or on Walshe's own political viewpoint, which would have been more disposed towards the Pétainist perspective.

The charge has been made that Walshe used censorship to play down the consequences of Germany's accidental bombings in Ireland. This is true to the extent that Walshe did not wish to incur further pressure from the Allies to join the war. It does not, however, indicate a pro-German policy. At the outset of the war, close Anglo-Irish intelligence cooperation was established following meetings between Walshe and Britain's military intelligence agency, MI5.[39] For the most part John Maffey was satisfied with the Irish censorship arrangements although, at times, friction with Walshe occurred. Maffey did at one point complain to Walshe that the censorship of mail between Britain and Ireland by the Irish censorship authorities was leading to long delays in post reaching its destination. Walshe took exception to the comment and, following investigation, found that censorship on the Irish side was not the source of the problem but rather the much more extensive censorship on the British side. Maffey suggested that the British authorities could help the Irish postal authorities

by carrying out the censorship for them or by sending representatives to help with the work. Walshe spoke to Joseph Connolly
about the situation. Connolly, the Controller of Censorship,
believed that the representation by Maffey had been inspired by
certain people in Britain who did not like the idea of the contents
of their correspondence being made known to the Irish government. On the basis of the complaint, Connolly was convinced
that Irish censorship should be extended further, and he made the
following enquiry of his chief postal officer, J.J. Purcell:

> I was wondering if we could do a more particularised selective
> censorship. There are, for instance, in a great many areas definitely
> known residents whose views, connections and influence could be
> reasonably estimated.[40]

Purcell replied outlining the details of Irish postal-censorship
procedure. He explained that only 10 per cent of all mail was
stopped by the Irish censors for examination and that the mail
that was stopped was released the same day. The chief postal censor was adamant that if there were any grounds for complaint
they did not relate to his office. He laid the blame with the British
censorship, and noted with some irony Maffey's suggestion that
'to overcome the delay the British Censorship would be willing
… to do our job for us or … to incorporate us in their organisation to do the job.'[41] Walshe was annoyed by the suggestions of
inefficiency but absolved Maffey of the criticism, telling Purcell
that the British minister had been 'somewhat shamefaced' about
the matter, implying he had been acting under orders.[42]

Further friction over the matter of communication and censorship occurred when the British authorities at Swansea seized from
an Irish boat the Department of External Affairs' diplomatic bag
addressed to the Irish legation in Lisbon. Walshe was incensed
by the action, and refuted all claims by the British that the bag
had been taken accidentally. This was nonsense, claimed Walshe,
who explained that the front of the bag was clearly identified
with a brass plate with the address of the Lisbon legation. Prior
to this incident, Walshe explained, the British had on seven other
occasions seized Irish diplomatic bags. While all were eventually
returned, Walshe was deeply concerned that no such infringements
occur again. A new system was promptly initiated. Future mail

would be sent in diplomatic bags under the special charge of the captain. This, hoped Walshe, would help to secure the 'uncensored and speedy passage' of Irish diplomatic correspondence.

Despite these differences with Maffey, it was from the German side that Walshe received most of the complaints with regard to censorship. This was not surprising, according to Donal Ó Drisceoil, who, in his study of Irish censorship during this period, points out that the heavy reliance of Irish newspapers on Anglo-American news sources and the widespread availability of English newspapers in Ireland resulted in a strong pro-Allied slant in the Irish newspapers.[43] Hempel argued that the Irish public was at a considerable disadvantage by receiving its news through these British and American agencies, thus resulting in a general bias against the Reich.[44] Walshe agreed to make some efforts to curb the bias, but there was little enthusiasm for making a serious attempt in response to these protests. Hempel and the Axis representatives largely understood and accepted this situation with regard to English newspapers, and their protests were more often than not merely perfunctory.[45] This was noted by Thomas Coyne, who explained that while the complaints by the German minister were understandable, he believed they were prompted by the desire to 'get something on the record at a time when the Swiss and Swedish press have just been taken to task by the Wilhelmstrasse.'[46] Coyne's assessment of the press censorship was that it was not unduly unfair to Germany as Irish papers had been prevented from being completely pro-Allied. Walshe did not allow the censorship process to serve solely the protection of Allied interests, and he was anxious that British and American propaganda not be allowed to circulate freely around the country.

Due to his efforts to remain impartial, Walshe had to endure some criticism from the Allied side. In certain cases, their complaints were valid, but Walshe felt that neither side had been allowed a free hand. Walshe had previously spoken with the Italian representative to Ireland, Vincenzo Berardis. Following a number of propaganda articles, Walshe reminded Berardis that Ireland was on friendly terms with Britain and the United States and therefore could not allow such attacks contained in the Italian bulletin to continue. Walshe felt this kind of propaganda to be insulting to the intelligence of the Irish people, arguing that 'It was only fit for natives or aborigines.'[47] This comment was

imperious in itself, but Walshe thought it adequate to describe what he saw as a blatant interference in Irish internal affairs. Walshe wrote to the Irish legation in Rome charging Berardis with 'violating all rules of hospitality and neutrality' by continuing to publish attacks on Britain, the people of the United States and the Jews.[48] Walshe felt that Berardis was having a disastrous effect on the friendship between Italy and Ireland:

> You have taken no notice of my request to you to abstain from these activities so harmful to the interests of the Irish State. In recent bulletins your comments on the distinguished head of the American people, the American people themselves, and on the Jews, are not merely in the worst of bad taste, but they display an attitude towards the Government of this neutral country which can only be described as a gross breach of the privileges of hospitality which you enjoy.[49]

Walshe would brook no further interference from Berardis, whom he regarded as inept, and he certainly would not allow Irish neutrality to be put in jeopardy by the Italian minister.

At the beginning of the war Walshe's department provided the ideological justification for the imposition of strict censorship. A memorandum entitled 'Neutrality, Censorship and Democracy' was drafted in preparation for opposition criticism that censorship was 'neither necessary nor democratic'. It sought to prove that censorship was both 'legitimate and necessary'. The document recognised the division within the country regarding support for either of the belligerents, and noted that neutrality was not a universally agreed policy. Thus, if a certain section of the people were allowed to vent their opposition towards Germany, it was more than likely that 'others would try to express in even more offensive terms their detestation of British morality.' The memorandum, therefore, based its justification of strict censorship on the premise that without this restriction the escalation of discussion would inevitably lead to civil war. The memorandum is political in its refutation of the arguments in favour of free speech:

> If we were a nation of Dillons words would only lead to words. But we are not. And if a competition of this sort were allowed to start between gentlemen who would confine themselves to words, they would very quickly get supporters who would wish to use stronger

arguments, and it might very well be that we would have a civil war to decide the question as to which of the European belligerents we should declare upon.[50]

The document makes a number of interesting commentaries on the nature of neutrality itself:

> In our own interests and according to our declared policy we must suppress propaganda against the nearest belligerent and are thus led naturally to prevent propaganda against the other.

In this way, Irish foreign policy in relation to censorship was outlined by clear reference to the delicate position that Ireland was in. Neither Axis nor Allied side could be allowed preference without risking recrimination from the other. Over the years, Walshe developed a good working relationship with those in charge of the Irish censorship and intelligence. The efficiency of the Irish military-intelligence section, in particular, in apprehending German agents as they arrived was of great assistance to Walshe in persuading the Allies that Ireland was not a centre of Axis espionage against Britain. This was particularly important as Irish–Allied relations continued to deteriorate during 1941.

In February 1941 Éamon de Valera sent the Irish Minister for Co-ordination of Defensive Measures, Frank Aiken, to the United States in an attempt to acquire arms and supplies for the Irish government. The previous year, Gray had been willing to assist Ireland in acquiring arms and munitions. Since then, however, his attitude towards Irish neutrality had changed significantly, as had his relationship with Walshe. Despite admitting that he had no specific instructions on the matter, he told External Affairs that he would advocate that no armaments be given to Ireland unless de Valera were 'ready to engage himself'.[51] Gray realised that this stance would not be popular, but he thought it important that the Irish understand that the United States had little sympathy with what he described as de Valera's 'academic contentions' in relation to Irish entry into the conflict. Gray believed that it was for its own good that the Irish government got to grips with the reality of the situation, even if it meant that he himself became unpopular.

At the start of the year Gray and de Valera met, and Walshe wrote a synopsis of their conversation. The main point of contention

was the issue of the potential value of the Irish ports to Britain's war effort. Gray suggested that if it could be conclusively shown that the use of these ports was vital to Britain's survival, then the United States could not criticise the British if they seized them. Walshe could not comprehend this attitude as he saw the US being equally reluctant to suffer any physical consequences of the war. He pointed to a recent refusal by the US to accede to Britain's urgent request for more destroyers, saying, 'so it would appear that America is not ready to sacrifice even a part of her fleet efficiency' while at the same time 'she asks us to make incalculable sacrifices.'[52] Walshe admitted that the ports might be a factor in Britain's success or failure, but he was adamant that they were only one among many possible causes. He was weary of US demands and especially of Gray's temerity, protesting that 'we are getting tired of America's vicarious heroism at our expense.' Walshe then compounded his argument by drawing the following analogy: if the US decided not to enter the war but Britain acquired Japan as an ally, would the US government then be willing to hand over to Japan the ports of New York, Philadelphia and Baltimore in order to ensure British victory? Apart from the fact that before the end of that year Japan had bombed the US naval installation at Pearl Harbour, this was hardly the most compelling of arguments made by External Affairs.

Despite a number of misunderstandings, Gray hoped that his relationship with Walshe could remain on cordial terms even though differences between them on matters of policy would continue. He stated that he maintained a sympathetic regard for the Irish point of view:

> With people whom I respect and admire, it is difficult for me to have reticences or reservations on matters of common concern that may come up between us. I prefer to have open differences of viewpoint.[53]

While he personally believed that armaments should only go to countries that were actually involved in the fighting, he said that this was not a criticism of Irish neutrality and that there was no lack of friendliness on the part of the US government. This alleged respect for the policies of de Valera was, however, wearing thin with Walshe.

Gray reported that a bad economic situation was imminent in Ireland, and that he hoped a change of policy would ensue, as petrol and coal shortages demoralised the country's industries and caused severe hardship and mass unemployment. 'If the government has no more imagination and foresight in coping with this than they have shown in regard to the shortage of supplies they are in for a bad time which the Opposition will let them enjoy to the full.'[54] He wrote to Eleanor Roosevelt on 10 February 1941:

> It is obvious that the Irish Government is not going to get from the United States the things they would like as long as the prevailing sentiment of the country is against our aid to Britain policy ... For months I have tried to prepare Mr De Valera for this but they have not believed me.[55]

Gray held Walshe to blame for the intransigent position of the Irish government. He described the Department of External Affairs as 'very weak', and pointed out the secretary's over-reliance on Irish-American pressure: 'they have evidently relied on what they have heard from the Irish American pressure groups which were out to beat the President in the recent election.'[56] Considering the state of their relations and the refusal of Gray to consider sending arms to Ireland, it was perhaps unwise of de Valera to send Aiken to the United States. From an Irish point of view, however, it was hoped that an envoy appealing directly to the President would have a more positive effect than making any further requests through the unsympathetic Gray. The plan was not discouraged by Gray, who hoped that a direct refusal from the State Department would serve to educate the Irish government. Thus, from the outset the venture was doomed to failure and could do nothing to improve relations between Walshe and Gray.

At this time, Walshe was having similar diplomatic difficulties with the British representative. From a meeting with John Maffey in February 1941 he concluded that, 'the British representative had never been so frank about British dislike for our neutrality, and I feel that his frankness is a presage to a suggestion of some kind, whether good or bad I cannot guess.'[57] Maffey admitted that 'Irish matters were the most delicate that the British Government had to deal with.' He sought to know how this suspicion had grown, to which Walshe, always liable to raise the subject of

Britain's past subjugation of Ireland, replied, 'that the atmosphere of suspicion had been built up over centuries and had continued very active down to the betrayal on the Partition issue in 1924.'[58] Within a couple of months he reported that Maffey had issued the warning that 'the time might come – indeed he believed it certainly would come – when Britain and/or America would have to bring serious pressure to bear on us.' Walshe pointed to British reluctance to help Ireland defend herself and asked Maffey, 'what kind of preparation were the British now making to secure our goodwill for themselves … they were holding back supplies from us, they refused to give us arms.'[59] Maffey admitted that the arms were deliberately withheld, and Walshe deduced that it would not be long before new proposals and demands from the US and Britain would be received. The previous year, Britain's offer of unity had been rejected, but British desire to use the Irish ports had not subsided. During this period there was much criticism of Irish neutrality in the British and US press, and pressure was mounting to forcibly take the ports. David Gray became a supporter of this demand, and neither he nor Maffey did much to assuage the fears of Walshe, who in this context may have welcomed the effort to seize the diplomatic initiative by sending Aiken to the United States.

When de Valera first told Gray of his plan to send Frank Aiken as special representative to Washington, the US minister replied that, 'it was very desirable to send such a representative, as he would have the Irish point of view clearly established in his mind and would be able to bring back authoritative information in respect of the position of the United States.'[60] Gray expected that following such a visit Walshe might finally realise that it was wartime pragmatism rather than any malevolent influence inspired by him that primarily influenced the State Department policy regarding the arming of Ireland. The Secretary of State, Cordell Hull, he believed, would point out that US munitions were in heavy demand and that the American government had obligations and other priorities to fulfil before it could give the Irish government any consideration.[61] However, Gray remained hopeful that the visit would serve to increase understanding between the two countries, and he wrote to Eleanor Roosevelt introducing Frank Aiken:

If he will talk to you frankly, as I am sure he will, you will get a better idea as to Mr de Valera's position in the present crisis than you could get from anyone that I know.[62]

Greater understanding between Ireland and the US was also what Walshe was hoping for, as he believed that Gray had been misrepresenting the Irish government's position to Roosevelt and the State Department. Gray himself gave no indication that there was any serious tension developing over these differences. In fact, despite disagreement, relations remained cordial:

These are very difficult times for everyone here, but the courtesy, kindness, and fine manners of all the Members of the Government make it possible for the American representative to have a happy time here, even though he is obliged to differ fundamentally with the Irish Government on many questions.[63]

However, he was not optimistic about Aiken's chances of acquiring arms, and clearly warned that:

Although your mission may be able to place some orders under contracts for delivery within a reasonable time, it must contemplate the likelihood of being able to get quick delivery on a substantial quantity of material unless it should obtain the cooperation of the British Purchasing Commission.[64]

While there may have been some anxiety in the US, there was no official State Department objection to the Aiken visit.[65] The Irish Minister for Co-ordination of Defensive Measures would be granted meetings with the relevant authorities. Gray believed that de Valera had understood his warnings, and the Taoiseach had thanked him for the arrangements that had been made to facilitate the visit.[66]

Gray had arranged with the State Department that Aiken's mission be given official status, but Walshe soon became anxious when the Press Association in Washington reported on a recent statement by Roosevelt in which he stated that he had not received official notification about the proposed visit. Walshe immediately contacted the Irish representative in Washington, Robert Brennan:

There is implication of discourtesy which might make Aiken's

situation awkward. American Minister in Dublin conveyed to Taoiseach reply of approval from State Dept but you should see them immediately and request correction.[67]

Walshe did not hide his inclination to blame Gray for the confusion, and he criticised what he saw as Gray's somewhat puerile desire to have all official Irish-American business related to the United States through the Dublin legation:

> The request was made originally through Mr Gray in order to give him the satisfaction of being the first to convey to his Govt the news of a project which [he] had been for months encouraging.[68]

The incident was based on a misunderstanding, and Walshe was for the time being satisfied that no deliberate discourtesy was meant. However, this would soon change as the first reports arrived from Brennan commenting on the progress of the Aiken visit.

Brennan reported that they had seen the President but all had not gone well. Roosevelt believed that Aiken had previously stated that Ireland had nothing to fear from Germany.[69] The statement was not unjustified but Walshe believed it was a misconception that Gray should have prevented. Similarly, Walshe was extremely annoyed on hearing that Roosevelt believed that part of the difficulty in sending armaments to Ireland was that no assurance had been given that such provisions would not be used against Britain. Later, Brennan reported that the atmosphere in Washington was changing for the worse and that senators he had been working with, though still willing to help, were not so enthusiastic.[70] Aiken's visit was not going according to plan, and dignitaries who were to be present at meetings and conferences to be attended by Aiken now absented themselves.

From Gray's point of view, the first reports of Aiken's visit were not pleasing. If Aiken had been sent to the US to get supplies, he asked, then why was he making speeches from New York to San Francisco? He reflected on the statements that implied that the Roosevelt administration was, for political reasons, holding back on supplies for Ireland:

> If that is the allegation, does the Minister really mean to indict the American Government in their own country while he is that Government's guest?

Clearly Aiken's mission was not as diplomatically astute as it might have been. Gray also took exception to de Valera's St Patrick's Day broadcast on 17 March 1941 in which the Taoiseach stated that 'both sides in blockading each other were blockading us.' Gray said that the facts known to the US government did not support the view that Britain was blockading Ireland, and that the statement had the effect of undermining popular support in the US for the policy of aiding Britain. He issued the warning that Irish matters would not take precedence over the Anglo-American alliance, and concluded that, 'It is obvious that, in the present emergency, policies antagonistic to the British war effort are antagonistic to American interests.'[71] Walshe and de Valera were disappointed to learn that Aiken had been understood to be expressing a hostile attitude to Great Britain. De Valera said that Aiken was, 'one of the clearest headed members of the Irish Government and that he very well understood the probable significance of a German victory for Ireland, and that, although he had taken the field against England, his intelligence had made him understand the desirability of letting anti-British feeling die down as quickly as was possible.' He explained that Aiken, in attempting to clarify the Irish position regarding Irish neutrality and through his statements outlining the effect of partition upon Irish feeling in the present situation, may have created an impression that had not been intended. Gray agreed that this was the case, and admitted that his information regarding Aiken's visit had come solely from the newspapers.[72]

Gray reasoned with de Valera and said that the US was not asking Ireland to abandon neutrality but only to inaugurate what he described as 'an attitude of helpful cooperation within the limits of neutrality'. In other words, 'not to manifest an attitude which impressed American opinion as being hostile to Britain'. He was satisfied to hear de Valera reply that it was not Irish policy to show hostility to Britain but that when the Irish people were called upon to fight 'it was more natural for them to fight England than any other nation.'[73] It was because of this historical legacy that Gray felt he could not recommend that Ireland be supplied with arms unless some explicit undertaking were given that the weapons would not be used against Britain. At the same time, de Valera maintained that he could not give any such

undertaking unless he received a reciprocal guarantee that Britain would make no attempt to seize the Irish ports.

John Maffey agreed with Gray's assessment that the economic restrictions that had been introduced in Ireland would soon have the country in 'a bad mess'. He reported that there was little resentment towards Britain and that the hardships were blamed on de Valera's government. On an official level, however, Anglo-Irish relations were at a low:

> Walshe, for instance, says, 'that we are being punished, etc., etc.'. Leydon, who feels that he has been badly let down by his opposite numbers in the Board of Trade with whom he has negotiated in happier days, spoke to me with considerable violence about our policy and added that he hoped 'Never to go to London again'.[74]

Walshe was under considerable pressure. Britain was taking a tough stance and Maffey was not offering any sympathy. The two men met in March 1941, and Walshe, in his own words, put all the cards on the table. Maffey had initially been preparing his statement for a tête-à-tête with de Valera but decided on using Walshe as the more expedient means of conveying his message.[75] Maffey had many previous discussions with de Valera and had found him to be as elusive as his reputation in London had suggested. Walshe, however, was more inclined to listen to the arguments and offer some agreement. Maffey felt that if some of his arguments prevailed, Walshe would have more of a chance of influencing de Valera than if he went to the Taoiseach himself.

German espionage in Ireland was one of Maffey's primary concerns while stationed in Dublin. He expressed to Walshe grave reservations at the recent landing of another German agent in Ireland. Gunter Schultz had landed by parachute in Wexford on 12 March 1941, but was arrested shortly after.[76] Of even greater significance was the detection of a wireless set in operation in the Dublin area that was suspected of being used by the German minister. Maffey reminded Walshe of de Valera's promise that Ireland would not be used as a base of attack on Britain. This was not being fulfilled, he said, pointing to Hitler's use of Ireland as a cover for his submarines. Maffey directly challenged the way in which policy was formulated in Walshe's department, arguing that the pace of events had moved too fast for the Irish Government:

In these circumstances had the Government of Éire got a policy, or were they content to leave everything to chance when some accident of the struggle might determine policy for them? Did the Department of External Affairs realise the risk they ran, if they were not constructive now, of being suddenly stampeded into rash decisions when there would be no chance to act with deliberation on prepared lines?[77]

Walshe, he said, was receptive to this line of argument. Maffey indicated his belief that Ireland would sooner or later be forced into the war. He could not accept that the Germans would continue to respect Ireland's neutrality, and Germany would use the country when it suited it to get a foothold against Britain. He was weary of Ireland sitting on the fence, and asked Walshe if they had decided to accept Hitler's New Order. That, at least, would be a policy he said, 'but if they felt that Éire's proper place was in association with the Anglo-American and democratic group they had better start moving or they would find themselves nowhere.' Walshe used partition as a reason for not entering the war, but Maffey countered by raising Malcolm MacDonald's offer of unity the previous year, which de Valera had rejected out of hand. Walshe said the problem was that the offer was based on a commitment that would be honoured after the war, which had raised 'a familiar bugbear in the long history of Irish disappointments'. While the Irish government may have had some objections to the plan, Maffey argued that it had offered no alternative proposals. Therefore, a more plausible explanation for the rejection was that the Irish government at that time firmly believed that Britain would be defeated, and that this had been confirmed by the recent fall of France:

> Walshe demurred to this unheroic suggestion (which is the true one) and said that certainly our chances looked poor then, much poorer than they do today.

Maffey added that Britain was on the road to victory and that this could be detected in the great uneasiness felt by the people of Ireland towards their government's policy. Neutrality, he said, was an enforced policy and that the strict censorship had prevented the people from deciding the issues on the basis of moral judgement. Walshe greatly resented the lecture, and refused to accept

that Britain was fighting for any cause but its own, arguing that 'England was fighting for herself, for her life, and nothing else. America was thinking of nothing but her own interests. Ireland would fight for herself and for nobody else.' Maffey continued his assault on Irish policy, and claimed that Britain was protecting Ireland's freedom but was receiving nothing in return. Ireland, he said, was fast losing the sympathy of the nations of the world to which she once belonged, and the policy of isolation was based on 'a petty and parochial policy', with de Valera drawing his inspiration from the old Anglo-Irish hatred. Maffey cited some of the Taoiseach's speeches and said to Walshe that in light of the atmosphere these created he had found it difficult to make any progress in London on matters on which Ireland sought assistance. Walshe argued that the British Prime Minister's refusal to give a guarantee not to invade Ireland had left de Valera no option but to remain suspicious. Maffey countered by pointing to the Continental experience of neutral countries that had been given promises of a similar kind. There was no point in Britain giving such a promise. It had no wish to invade Ireland but strategic factors may have made this aspiration an impossibility. Maffey was a skilled tactician and he transferred the moral pressure back to Walshe with great ease:

> The predicament in which the unforseen policy of Éire had placed us was a tragic dilemma. On the physical side the possession of facilities in Éire might become a matter of life and death to us. On the moral side the principle of respecting the rights of small liberty loving nations was a matter of life and death to us.[78]

Walshe was in a difficult position, and realised that Ireland's current status did not present him with a suitable opportunity of giving Maffey his views on Britain's respect for 'small liberty loving nations'. He simply stated that there should be no doubt that de Valera was 'a sincere friend of Britain' who hated 'the German policy of aggression'.

Walshe suggested that a meeting be arranged with de Valera, but Maffey refused on the grounds that neither he nor anybody else could make any progress with the intransigent de Valera. It was his aim to persuade Walshe of the merits of his argument, who in turn, he hoped, would persuade the Taoiseach. Walshe

asked what specific measures should be taken in order to make progress, and it was suggested that an invitation should be issued to a member of the British government to come to Dublin to discuss what facilities Britain required. Maffey believed that the first part of his strategy had worked, but he overestimated the meaning of Walshe's comments. Even if Walshe was in agreement with the idea of a major shift away from neutrality, there was no guarantee that he would be able to convince de Valera. Maffey optimistically reported to his government that he believed de Valera would alter his position on neutrality. He therefore advised the urgent preparation of documents to illustrate the importance of Ireland to the protection of Allied shipping in the Atlantic, a document on the scale of protection that would be given to Ireland, as well as a definition of Britain's attitude towards partition. Maffey believed that a proposal along these lines had merit and a chance of success. If not, then at least Britain would have this 'honourable approach' on the record. If Britain found it necessary to invade, it would lessen Ireland's case for grievances. Basing his comments on Walshe's statements, Maffey believed that a 'genuinely forthcoming attitude on the subject of Ulster' could promote rapid progress on the issue and lead to the strategic unity of the British Isles. The time for vacillation was over. If de Valera rejected a new move then the British representative recommended that Britain 'clap on one hundred per cent economic restrictions without a single qualm and see what emerges from the mess'.

Due to the deterioration of Anglo-Irish relations, de Valera correctly suspected that Maffey was in favour of implementing a policy of indirect economic coercion. Gray told de Valera that he did not know whether this was true as Maffey had not mentioned it, but he could understand how Britain felt:

> It was to me quite conceivable and logical, in view of the great difficulties which Britain encountered in supplying herself with necessities and in view of the fact that the Irish Government made no contribution to the safety of ocean-borne commerce.[79]

On hearing this, de Valera remarked that many felt Gray to be more pro-English than the English themselves, and he advised the US minister that he would be better off looking after US interests. Gray retorted that, due to their alliance in the present

emergency, American and British interests were one and the same. At this point, Gray detracted from his initial criticism of Aiken's visit to the US and wrote saying that the press reports had given the impression that Aiken had associated himself with anti-British groups in America. Now Gray was passing on press clippings that presented the other side of the story, and that made him feel that he had possibly been unfair to Aiken. He was 'very glad, in common fairness, to present the other side to you', adding, 'You are, of course, at liberty to use it in any way you see fit.'[80] Kathleen O'Connell, de Valera's personal secretary, replied on the Taoiseach's behalf, saying, 'he feels confident that you will agree, that newspaper comments on the one side or the other, at a time like this, are no fair index of either Mr Aiken's views, or of the manner in which he is carrying out his mission.'[81] This did nothing to alleviate the tension, however, and soon Gray became annoyed when he learned that de Valera had told General Mulcahy, an opposition member of the National Defence Council, that Gray had been, 'misrepresenting Ireland to Washington', and that if he had not been a friend of Roosevelt's he would ask for the US minister's recall.[82]

Gray thought that de Valera was getting into a 'very ugly mood', and described how the Taoiseach, in a fit of rage, refused two vessels that Roosevelt had offered him. He believed de Valera had assumed dictatorial powers and was influenced only by Walshe. 'You must realize that there is no discussion of Irish policy permitted in the press, on the platform, or on the radio.'[83] In his opinion the Irish people were not fully informed of their Taoiseach's policies, and he believed that if they were told of the non-cooperative attitude towards the US, they would not be so supportive of neutrality. He thought that even the Irish Cabinet was ignorant of aspects of de Valera's policies: 'To the best of our knowledge and belief, the Prime Minister has confided to no member of his cabinet our request for an explanation as to the significance of his implied statement regarding British blockade of Ireland and probably his own version of the communication regarding Mr Aiken.'[84] Thus, when Roosevelt made a token gesture towards fulfilling Irish supplies, Gray was delighted that de Valera had been shown up in front of the Irish public:

Mr D.V. has I think never experienced such a fast one as you put

over with the two ships and the Red Cross wheat ... I had just
received a copy of his peevish declination of the ships and his
announcement that he was sticking by Aiken when the papers carried the news of your 'Generous Gift to the Irish People'. There has
been no official statement about it but it went over big with the
public which of course was what was wanted.[85]

Gray believed that bitterness towards Britain and cowardice were the
main reasons why the Irish government did not want to get involved
in the war. He also included partition in the following points:

1. They don't want to give any help to Britain under any
    conditions.
2. They don't want to get into the war for fear of the bombing.
3. They want to use the war to end partition. But this is a con-
    cern of the leaders rather than the rank and file. The masses
    are not actively stirred up by partition.[86]

It was now clear, therefore, that Gray would no longer view any
Irish request for munitions with any degree of sympathy.

Walshe was anxious to talk to Gray about the arms situation in the aftermath of the Aiken visit. Gray explained that he
had changed his initial attitude of favouring arms being sent
to Ireland when he realised the extent of anti-British feeling
throughout Ireland. Walshe confided in him that an undertaking was given that in the event of an invasion by Germany,
Ireland would join the war and give every assistance it could to
the Allies. Gray, however, was distrustful and told Walshe that he
believed the Irish government was not opposed to a German victory. 'The aftermath of the recent bombing', he said, to illustrate
his point, 'discloses the fact that there is no resentment against
Germany.' However, he explained that it was 'a very lively fear of
the Germans' and 'a definite unwillingness to make any sacrifice
to help England' rather than any pro-German sentiment. He later
watered down his remarks and admitted that a majority of people
in Ireland, including the government, would rather see a British
victory. In the early part of the war, Walshe may have given Gray
cause to believe that he favoured a German victory. While he
grudgingly accepted that the Irish people were not pro-German,
Walshe himself would remain under suspicion.

Gray was annoyed with the Irish position and became increasingly inclined towards the idea of using force to acquire the Irish ports that were so badly needed by the British:

> I am beginning to think that if any port seizing has to be done it could be done without serious trouble by us if there were a landing in force with a display of air force over Dublin dropping leaflets.[87]

Here we see the origins of the American note which was based on his belief that de Valera would not change his position unless forced to: 'He either has an understanding with the Germans on which he relies or what is more likely he is blindly taking the thousand to one chance that he can escape involvement, get a free ride and no fare collected after the war by a forgiving Britain.' Gray believed that Aiken had made contact with radical elements of Irish-American nationalists while in the US. He warned of the dangers to US–Irish relations that such association with these groups could create. In one meeting, de Valera questioned Gray's distrust of the Irish government and asked him about a statement attributed to Roosevelt to the effect that he had not received any guarantees that any arms given to the Irish government would be used against a German attack. The Taoiseach pointed out that it was the stated Irish policy to repel any aggressor. Gray felt this comment was a criticism of the US legation in Dublin, and insisted that he had reported accurately on Irish policy to the Department of State.[88] In July 1941 Gray complained that he had been misrepresented in the Dáil when de Valera stated that it was he who had first suggested sending an Irish Cabinet member to Washington to negotiate for arms and supplies directly with the American government. Gray was anxious to avoid any responsibility for the failure of the Aiken mission, and reminded de Valera that, on suggesting the visit, he had also warned that this procedure was unlikely to achieve significant results but was more likely – as well as being more diplomatically acceptable – to be successful than broadcasting to American pressure groups.[89]

Gray accepted that there was no general anti-American resentment in Ireland but insisted that a number of the Cabinet were bitter towards the US President. He saw de Valera and Walshe, in particular, as leading the charge against Roosevelt, and was

exasperated by what he saw as Walshe's inability to understand the reality of the American situation. He also recognised that his first year in Dublin had caused Walshe to become resentful of him. 'There is no doubt that Mr DeValera is very bitter, also Walshe the permanent secretary for External Affairs'. In addition, Gray saw that part of his task was to educate Walshe:

> I am continually hunting for a way of framing the questions: How can you expect to wage a subversive campaign against my Government's aid for Britain's policy in United States Territory and not expect my Government to resent it?[90]

He thought Walshe had little reason to be annoyed regarding the Aiken situation, and believed that it was on the American side that the insult had been felt:

> We have never asked anything of you except friendly cooperation and you show friendly cooperation by sending a Cabinet minister to America who addresses meetings of organizations opposed to Government policy and identifies himself with their aims. We have … let you have twenty thousand rifles which were need by those fighting Hitler but never a word of thanks because they were earmarked to you through the British.[91]

This, however, was not the way Walshe assessed the situation, and relations between the two were to continue to deteriorate.

Raymond, in his article on the controversy relating to the Aiken mission, believes that Gray has been wrongly victimised by 'conventional Irish nationalist historiography', which was strongly influenced by the writings of Professor T. Desmond Williams in the 1950s.[92] He claims that the blame for the failure of the Aiken mission cannot be levelled on Gray, and investigates why Gray's goodwill towards Ireland disappeared so quickly in the summer of 1941, saying that the reason most likely lies in the fact that the Irish administration tried to make Gray a scapegoat for the failure of the trip. Others have pointed out that US administrators saw Aiken as being fanatically anti-British, and that he further irritated officials by his domestic interference in appealing to Irish-Americans, some of whom were bitter critics of the Roosevelt administration.[93] Raymond suggests that, as the failure of the Aiken mission became evident, de Valera initiated a vicious

attack on Gray, saying he had suggested the mission to discredit the Irish government. 'Gray was innocent', says Raymond, who maintains that this incident poisoned Gray's relationship with the Irish government for the duration of his tenure.[94]

While this incident was a deep source of bitterness between Gray and the Irish government, to conclude that it was the cause of all Gray's future diplomatic discord is to oversimplify the matter. Gray's performance as US minister to Ireland up to that point had already been fraught with difficulties and disagreement, and the origins of his failure to achieve his potential in Dublin can be seen long before the Aiken mission. Walshe, in particular, realised that Gray was not fully attuned to the obligations of a resident diplomat. Gray was not a career diplomat but a writer and journalist who received the post through political favour.[95] His British counterpart, Sir John Maffey, on the other hand, was a shrewd and tactful diplomat who understood Walshe better, and knew how to disagree while avoiding confrontation. Walshe did not resent difference of opinion but found it difficult to use Gray as a means of communicating Irish opinion to the State Department. Despite any bitterness Gray may have felt in the aftermath of the Aiken mission, it was his task to facilitate reasoned communication between the US and Irish governments. Walshe may have felt, however, that such lines of communication had never been properly established. His relationship with Gray was substantially less cordial than his meetings with Maffey, even though British policy towards Ireland was often equally, if not more, exacting than that of the United States.

During this time, Britain maintained its surveillance of German activities in Ireland. From the outbreak of hostilities, the War Office greatly feared German U-boats exploiting Ireland's neutral shores. Robert Fisk has pointed out that because British intelligence activities around Ireland were regarded as particularly sensitive during the war, even today many of the official records that would normally be open to historians are still closed.[96] The Admiralty records, however, provide some insight into the nature and extent of an intelligence operation along the south and west coasts of Ireland upon which a British naval vessel, disguised as a trawler fishing off the Irish coast, went in search of German U-boats. Walshe and de Valera were well aware that German submarines were using Irish territorial waters, and they agreed with Maffey that the Irish

authorities would wire news of the U-boats' presence 'to the world', but obviously to the benefit of the British Admiralty.[97] The British trawler could have been seen as a logical extension of this arrangement, but Walshe and de Valera would not have appreciated this risk to their neutrality. Fisk says that there is some doubt that the British government itself was aware of this intrigue.[98] It is likely, however, that the Irish authorities had information, or at least suspicions, of British naval activities in Irish waters. Walshe would have been naive to think that Britain would do nothing to counteract what it saw as the unrestricted freedom allowed to German submarines. In July 1941 Fred Boland met with the German chargé d'affaires, Herr Thomson, who claimed that a German reconnaissance plane had noted a number of trawlers in Irish territorial waters that had new aerials and appeared to be travelling too fast to be fishing trawlers.[99] Thomsen, who claimed that he was not making a complaint but simply bringing the matter to the attention of External Affairs, clearly desired a satisfactory explanation. Boland brought the matter to the attention of M.J. Beary, assistant secretary at the Department of Defence, who reported that the trawlers had been spotted but that nothing suspicious was noted. It was explained that the speed of the vessels was due to the fact that the area in question was not a fishing ground. The trawlers may have been en route to fishing grounds or may, as Thomsen suspected, have been British reconnaissance vessels sending wireless messages to the Admiralty. If the Irish defence forces genuinely had no previous misgivings concerning the trawlers, then it would have been extremely naive had their suspicions remained dormant after the German approach.

Despite Maffey's protestations to the contrary, it may have been possible that the British military went farther than its political authorities would have officially allowed. One British military agent, Charles Tegart, reported a high level of German activity in Ireland. He assessed that up to 2,000 insurgents had been landed in Ireland and had prepared the way for a German-inspired IRA revolution.[100] The British, however, had other sources of information, and John Maffey ensured that exaggerated reports of German activity did not gain too much credibility. Maffey's American counterpart also had his own sources of information, and it would prove a difficult task to persuade Gray that Ireland was not overrun with German spies.

Further difficulties between Walshe and Gray ensued when, in September 1941 Gray informed Walshe that in order to clear up misunderstandings with the US press, he was giving 'off the record' information to visiting correspondents.[101] Gray's lengthy memorandum caused a degree of consternation in External Affairs, and prompted Walshe to send an equally lengthy reply in response. Walshe answered Gray's statements point by point. Gray's 'off the record' disclaimer was an immediate source of contention for Walshe, who explained that this was particularly precarious when dealing with the press. The information that Gray was divulging was not only highly sensitive but was also largely unsubstantiated. Gray stated, for example, that there had been a German-sponsored revival of the Irish Republican Army. From this he had drawn even more speculative conclusions:

> The Germans must presumably have tried unsuccessfully to inter-est the Irish Government before turning to the Irish Republican Army movement.[102]

Walshe explained to Gray that basing such stories on presump-tion and prefacing them with 'must presumably' was dangerous, as 'journalists leave out these little trimmings when passing on the news.'[103] Gray had also outlined rumours surrounding a deal between Germany and the IRA:

> The Irish Republic with German assistance is to have the whole of Ireland, north and south, and two English counties as a bridgehead for the control of England.[104]

Walshe was understandably aghast at the US minister's belief in the 'inherent probability' of this story, and felt that even the journalists would find it difficult to use such an outrageous anec-dote. Gray also claimed it fair to presume that many parachutists – a number of them IRA agents – had landed in Ireland without being captured. Walshe was perplexed; no IRA parachutists had been captured, so how could Gray assert, without proof, that such landings had occurred? He described Gray's logic as 'twisted', and believed it to be damaging to Irish–US relations.[105] In the following paragraph Walshe continued to assess Gray's logic and method of argument:

Once you make convenient assumptions, the rest of your romanc-
ing becomes relatively easy ... You begin by assuming that there is
an organisation of German Secret Agents in Ireland and you say
immediately afterwards that you have very little information as to
their method of operation. You 'think it is correct to say that they
probably finance such I.R.A. groups and activities as have escaped
internment by the Government;' but after the semi-colon, you leave
the realm of assumption and opinion and you say quite definitely
'they stir up anti-British feeling whenever possible'. Then you return
to your innuendo ...[106]

Walshe continued in this way to refute each argument made by Gray.
In response to the statement that support for the policy of neutrality
was based on the fear of being bombed, Walshe replied: 'It can't be
that your opinion of the Irish people is so low as to believe that
their Government has to base its policy on the principle of fear.'
Gray described how the *Irish Press* ('the Government-owned Irish
newspaper') had shown resentment towards US aid to Britain,
and claimed that this had made it difficult for him to get aid
and support for Ireland.[107] At this, Walshe openly expressed his
disdain towards Gray:

If it is this non-existent attitude of the Irish Press which prevents
you getting things for Ireland which you would like to get, clearly
our chances of getting anything from the United States through
you are exceedingly poor.[108]

According to Walshe, the attitudes contained in Gray's memorandum were based on 'insinuation and innuendo', and were
inimical to 'harmony and friendship' between the two governments, and he suggested that Gray resign from his post:

If you really feel that your interest in this ... is limited by the pas-
sions and prejudices of the present moment, perhaps you ought ...
review your position. This is, of course, a purely personal suggestion, but the whole character of your notes forces the conviction
upon me that your prejudices make it impossible for you to be the
instrument through which a proper balance of goodwill can be
established between our two Governments.[109]

Walshe was increasingly uncompromising in his view of Gray.
Relations were strained, and even their overt courtesy subsided.

The Canadian High Commissioner in Dublin, John Kearney, warned Gray that Walshe had blamed him for all the trouble regarding the Aiken mission and its attempt to procure arms. Gray believed Walshe to be bitter against him 'for refusing as an individual to take the responsibility of recommending that they be armed without receiving some undertaking as to Éire's position in case of invasion'. He was well aware of his isolation, and thought it unlikely that he would be used by Walshe and de Valera if they decided to accommodate the US. However, Gray maintained that he held no grudges and that he was even in favour of saving de Valera's 'face' if it meant cooperation could continue.[110]

Following the Japanese attack on Pearl Harbour in December 1941, de Valera expressed the view that it would be unnatural for the Irish nation not to sympathise with the people of the United States. Conscious of this new pressure to enter the war on the Allied side, he reaffirmed the position of the state by saying, 'We can only be a friendly neutral.'[111] While attempting to reaffirm Ireland's determination to remain neutral, his choice of phrase 'friendly neutral' – wholly ambiguous if not a complete self-contradiction – was most unfortunate for Walshe's task. Hempel immediately requested an explanation for the remarks. Walshe explained that the reference to the vast numbers of Irish in America was at the heart of the statement: 'There could not but be a certain very real sympathy for America', he said, 'in a fight in which so many people of Irish blood would be taking part.'[112] Hempel inquired whether this latest declaration meant that British and US requests for use of the Irish ports would be acceded to, but Walshe assured him that neutrality was the only policy under consideration. Walshe felt his best defence in response to these criticisms was to raise Irish concerns about Germany's attitude towards Ireland. Hempel repeated assurances that so long as Ireland remained neutral, Germany would not infringe that policy. Hempel's instructions on the matter were definite and clear, and he had no doubt about their 'unchangeable character', and said that 'no matter what nations went into the war, Germany would not interfere with Irish neutrality.' Hempel, however, did not trust Walshe's own assurances that American entry into the war would leave Irish neutrality unaffected.

When referring to this incident in the 1960s, Professor Nicholas

Mansergh, in his *Survey of British Commonwealth Affairs*, caused some controversy when he stated that apologies had been made to Hempel and the German Foreign Office for de Valera's protest against the invasion of Holland and Belgium. Fred Boland believes that no apology was made, and refers to Hempel's own telegraphic report on the matter.[113] Boland comments:

> While it is difficult to be sure of what I said to him at this interval of time, I would not challenge the accuracy of Herr Hempel's report, although its terms, which are his own, are obviously chosen in such a way as to make them as acceptable to his own authorities.[114]

This is a commentary on diplomatic procedure in general, where many factors influence the tone and content of reports. William Warnock, the Irish representative in Germany at the time, spoke to a Dr Ullrich, head of the archives section of the German Foreign Office, concerning the dispute of the alleged de Valera apology:

> Dr Ullrich said to me that in reading through Dr Hempel's reports, and Dr Woermann's memoranda, we must bear in mind the context. Dr Woermann and others, with the desire to smooth things out and avoid unnecessary [un]pleasantness with foreign countries, sometimes drafted reports in a way calculated to calm down Herr von Ribbentrop or Hitler himself.[115]

The reports of diplomats and officials were sometimes prone to presenting a more favourable account of events in order to keep their superiors content. This is confirmed by Boland, who in his memoirs comments that Maffey was rarely disagreeable, despite the impression one may get from the official archives:

> Maffey (the British Ambassador) was fine, but you can see from British state papers what used to happen was his reports, by the way, were not in accordance with fact. I mean, he had Reports in which he had conversations in which he dressed down De Valera, told him that it was disgusting that Ireland should be neutral. He never said that at all! This was to keep the old man quiet. Actually the position was, Churchill of course, felt we should be in the war; but the Military, they didn't want us in the war at all. They had nothing to give us.[116]

In this way, we must read the diplomatic correspondence of the time circumspectly. In Dublin, Walshe's statements had failed to please Hempel, officially at least. Hempel, however, was willing to give Walshe some leeway. This was in stark contrast to Walshe's correspondence with Gray, who was unconvinced that Ireland genuinely hoped for an Allied victory and that the Irish government would do everything in its power to prevent Ireland being used as a base for attack against Britain.

Towards the end of the year, Walshe, on the advice of Michael Rynne, apprised de Valera of the situation regarding captured espionage agents. The memorandum dealt specifically with the 'Case of Mr X', which was more than likely a reference to the German agent, Herman Goertz, who was captured and interned by the Irish authorities towards the end of 1941 but who had been at large since May of the previous year. The question of his punishment caused Walshe some difficulties based on the following corollary: Irish dependence on one belligerent nation would increase in direct proportion to the severity with which the offending country was punished.

> One strong reason why small neutrals do not punish foreign agents with severity is the fact that they could not do so without screening themselves behind the other belligerent and becoming more dependent on it for future protection. They would, moreover, be exposed to the accusation of acting on behalf of the other belligerent, since the activities concerned are usually directed in the last resort against that Power. It is a generally accepted custom that small Powers in their international dealings should not take measures involving great Powers out of proportion to their capacity to defend themselves, whether by diplomatic or military methods. Without the very gravest cause, they do not expose themselves to reprisals which would oblige them to seek the protection of the other belligerent.[117]

Thus, the memorandum offers an interesting perspective on Walshe's state of mind at that point in time. He advised against a public trial for Goertz as it would attract attention and give American newspapers further grounds on which to attack Irish neutrality on the basis that the country was a German spy centre. At the same time, the Allied authorities would have to be satisfied that justice had been done, and Walshe suggested issuing a strong

note to Germany protesting at such infringements on Irish neutrality. The difficulty with this, however, was that the German authorities had recently shown generosity in response to a plea made by the Irish government to release some 300 Irish citizens from internment camps in France. Generally speaking, Walshe concluded that the German government had taken special pains to obtain information about Irish citizens in the occupied countries.[118] This was the finely balanced situation that Walshe found himself in at the start of 1942.

CHAPTER 6

WALSHE AND THE CHALLENGE TO NEUTRALITY 1942–1943

AS THE WAR progressed, pressure mounted on the Irish government. The treatment of the German espionage agents found in Ireland was a particular source of difficulty. David Gray believed that the Irish authorities were incapable of providing the resources needed to control Axis espionage activity. He had long predicted that the Irish government would be forced to enter the war, and his plans for a 'note' demanding the closure of the German legation in Dublin was designed to break de Valera's obstinate adherence to neutrality. Walshe fully realised that the discovery of German agents would be used by the Allies as a pretext for making demands on Irish neutrality. He believed that the Irish intelligence agency, G2, had the situation under control. His concern, therefore, was not with the exploits of these agents but with the reaction of the Allied powers to their existence in Ireland.

In a letter to Roosevelt in early 1942, Gray suggested that a token gesture of arms should be made available to the Irish government.[1] This, however, was only one of the approaches Gray suggested with the specific aim of coercing the Irish to enter the war. In February Sumner Welles wrote to Dublin rejecting Gray's more aggressive suggestion that an oil embargo be placed on Ireland and that Irish ships should no longer be allowed travel in Allied convoys.[2] The following month, Gray adopted a more reasoned approach, reporting that the recent transfer of material from the British army had produced favourable results, and suggested that the US should do something similar.[3]

In January 1942 the Irish government protested against the landing of United States troops in Northern Ireland, although the Government of Northern Ireland welcomed this development. The previous month, it had decided to record its wartime activities in order to provide an official account of its assistance to the United Kingdom's overall war effort. This would be done to provide information of general interest but also 'to prevent the possibility that the efforts and sacrifices of Ulster should hereafter be discredited or belittled'.[4] It also served to highlight its loyalty to Britain in its time of need, in contrast to the government south of the border. Walshe told Gray that the decision not to consult the Irish government prior to the sending of the Expeditionary Force had 'deeply wounded the feelings of all Irish who thought along nationalist lines'.[5] Gray expressed both his regret and his surprise at Walshe's disclosure, and said that, on a diplomatic level, they were both to blame. He admitted that he should have anticipated the reaction of the Irish government and accordingly informed the State Department. Walshe, he thought, should have warned him of the attitude of the Irish government. Walshe did not fully agree as he felt he could not be expected to anticipate the plans of the US government. Gray's defence was that he had received no notification of the arrival of the troops until he was informed by Maffey, by which time notification had already been sent to de Valera. Privately, Gray felt that the approach had, 'relieved the Irish Government of the possible embarrassment of making a protest at a time when it might have caused serious trouble instead as of now being but the registration of a claim after a *fait accompli*.'[6] Walshe, of course, could not subscribe to this method, which precluded the Irish government from making a protest, even if, in Gray's view, it had saved them the embarrassment of being turned down.

From a diplomatic point of view, it was a crude move by a large power. Gray was able to plead ignorance – the best defence in this case – and he promised to speak with his government to see if anything could be done about the situation. There was little more Walshe could do or say. Gray's rendition of the events to Walshe was disingenuous. He personally supported the landing of US troops, and reported to his government that the Irish were aggrieved at the move on account of their missed chance to 'entrap the American Government into recognition of their claim of

sovereignty over the Six Counties'. He thought Walshe was unwise in his support of the protest against the landing:

> Neither Walshe nor prominent Irishmen to whom I have talked in the last two days appear to have any appreciation of the unfortunate effect on American opinion which the Prime Minister's statement seems to me likely to make. They seem unable to understand that, unlike the English, we are not used to protests of this kind at actions by which they are likely to be direct beneficiaries.[7]

Throughout this time, Gray questioned Walshe's motives and ideological beliefs. Soon after his arrival in Dublin, he became suspicious of Walshe, believing him to have strong pro-German tendencies. In August 1941 Mr Smale, the American consul in Cork, wrote to Gray outlining the recent movements of Hempel in and around that area.[8] He mentioned that the German minister had visited Waterville the previous month and that Walshe had stayed in the same hotel at the same time. The report was quick to draw the conclusions that need hardly have been mentioned to Gray:

> I should like to believe that Walshe may have been there to keep an eye on the Minister, but it is generally believed that such was not the case.[9]

Later, in February 1942, Gray was told by the Brazilian consul in Dublin that the German legation was without doubt the centre of propaganda and was also in control of the Italian legation:

> It is his impression that the Germans have very direct communications with Berlin, presumably by wireless, and a large staff of Irish paid agents.[10]

The Brazilian consul cited Fred Boland in particular as being definitely pro-German, and alleged that he turned in 'all information to the Axis Legations which may be of interest to them'.[11] Gray also learned 'from a most secret but entirely reliable source' that in a conversation with the Italian minister in Dublin, Vincenzo Berardis, Walshe had expressed the opinion that while no immediate danger of a British invasion seemed likely at that particular time, he reserved the judgement that it might be seriously considered in the future. All the more shocking was the report for Gray when he read that Walshe had advised that:

A decisive attack by the Axis on the British islands should not be too long delayed and not later than the beginning of next Spring, because the main concern in governing circles in Éire lay in the possibility, which was considered to be more and more certain, that America would intervene in the war, which would render the position of Éire even more critical than at present.[12]

While admitting that Berardis was not a reliable source, Gray nevertheless took the allegations seriously and conveyed them to Roosevelt as proof of the difficulties of his task in Dublin:

> The Italian Minister is extremely unreliable, but as it confirms the impression gained from previous reports you may care to show this message to the President for his strictly personal information as showing the unsatisfactory attitude of some at any rate of the Irish authorities in regard to this country.[13]

He concluded that, even under the most favourable interpretation, this conversation indicated that Walshe's support lay with the Axis.

Some of Gray's sources for his belief that Walshe was pro-Nazi were more unreliable than others. When Gray first arrived in Dublin, he was impressed by the ambience of his Phoenix Park residence. Although it needed a good deal of renovation, he and his wife Maude liked what he described as 'its home-like atmosphere ... the view of the mountains across the Park meadow and the memories and ghosts that are here'.[14] Gray was intrigued by the fact that the house could be considered 'the former seat of British tyranny' in Ireland:

> Arthur Balfour was here eight years nearly, James Bryce, Agustine Birrell, George Wyndham, the long succession of English liberals who ruled Ireland on its way to Home Rule.[15]

Gray was to be significantly influenced by the ghosts that occupied the house. Arthur Balfour, in particular, would soon 'communicate' with Gray. The deceased former British Chief Secretary for Ireland, who had once dwelt in the same residence, had an important message for the new American minister.

T. Ryle Dwyer has outlined David Gray's interest in matters of the occult. During his student days and after, he had made a number of inquiries into the subject. It is not surprising, then, that

he took a great interest in Geraldine Cummins, described as 'one of the two most noted writing mediums in Europe', who lived in Cork.[16] Gray had a number of private sittings with Cummins in which the spirits of Theodore Roosevelt, Sarah Roosevelt (Franklin D. Roosevelt's mother) and Arthur Balfour, among others, allegedly communicated with him. He transmitted to the President sections of transcripts of these conversations. On one occasion, in November 1941, Gray sat with Cummins in the US legation. Sarah Roosevelt, the President's deceased mother, was first to speak. She would not give her name through the medium but described herself as Sarah R., whose 'son is the most important man in the world today'. She was evidently worried about the President and sought Gray's intercession: 'Can any one induce him to lay off – relax?'. Perhaps one of the more significant communications came through Arthur Balfour, who had an important message regarding Joseph Walshe. Balfour's purported spirit asked:

> I saw a man here, dark with a strong face in the last six months. Some name like Walsh. Is there a Joe Walsh? (Joe Walshe is the Permanent Secretary of External Affairs).[17]

Balfour's ghost told Gray that Walshe and his colleague Seán Murphy could not be trusted. The alleged spirit advised, 'If you meet those two again lay false tracks for them. Never let them know the slightest inkling of your real intentions.' This intercession came at a time when the relationship between Walshe and Gray was already strained, and it is interesting to read Gray's subsequent memoranda in light of this new source of 'information'.

Gray was also told that German spies were well organised in Ireland, and that the IRA was ready and prepared to be used on Hitler's command, and would then form a quisling Cabinet. In this scenario, Walshe was more than a German sympathiser; he was 'a leading Quisling', according to Cummins, or the ghost of Balfour. Gray was impressed by these ethereal communications. He wrote to Roosevelt commenting on the fact that there had been quite a lot of advice 'purporting to be from Arthur Balfour', and concluded that 'most of it seems pretty sound'. Gray informed Roosevelt of what he had been told about Walshe's pro-German tendencies, and told of German plans to install a quisling government in Ireland, adding that he had received confirmation of a more traditional kind

for this other-worldly information. On mentioning his suspicions about Walshe to William Cosgrave, he received the reply that 'this bore out his secret information and he mentioned the two names that Balfour mentioned. Later I checked in the same way with the vice Premier O'Kelly and got the same answer, though no names were mentioned.'[18] Some time later, Theodore Roosevelt, the former President of the United States, contacted Gray from the 'other world' and told him that 'I think Franklin will hold the Japs for a while.' Four days later, Pearl Harbour was attacked by Japan. At this point, Gray was forced to sound a note of scepticism in his assessment of this new-found source of intelligence:

> I suspect that if these communications come through pretty much as given our friends on the other side don't know very much more than they did on this side.

In a later letter to the President concerning the phenomenon, Gray commented on how these sources should be treated:

> Assuming these comments do come from friends who have passed on I think they should be treated exactly as advice from friends who are still here.[19]

It is difficult to determine to what extent Gray was influenced by these other-worldly consultations. He had already been suspicious that Walshe had strong pro-Nazi tendencies, and he regarded the information he received through the medium as strong confirmation. Balfour's advice may have unduly influenced the United States' representative to Ireland when he pleaded, through Cummins, 'If only your people would occupy the island before the blow falls.' Soon after, Gray would begin a series of consultations with the State Department and British officials to have the Irish government presented with a note demanding the use of the ports. These initial suggestions formed the basis of his demands for what became 'the American Note'.

Whether Balfour's ghost had good knowledge of the situation in Ireland or not, he certainly knew what Gray wanted to hear. On Gray's own performance, Cummins – or Balfour – commented:

> You have been very useful because you were so blunt in the past ... The fact that De Valera asked some time ago for your removal

from Éire was the highest compliment any American diplomat in this country has ever been paid. There is undoubtedly going to be trouble among the civilian population soon in this country. There are signs of unrest in the collective mind.

Perhaps Cummins was a mind-reader rather than a medium. Roosevelt replied to the communications with an attempt to render them harmless:

Those are real contributions and I hope you will continue ... I rather like your thought of treating these communications as advice from friends who are still here.

Ryle Dwyer has pointed out that one of Gray's final messages came from his father, who warned that the greatest danger was in his own country and that moves were afoot to discredit Roosevelt. Gray was determined to play his part in helping the President by discrediting de Valera in order to prevent him from adversely influencing Irish-American opinion.[20] It is difficult to definitively assert to what extent Gray trusted these clairvoyant bulletins, but considering his subsequent demands for tough action to coerce Ireland into the war, it is clear that he was significantly influenced by them. Whether they were the inspiration or the confirmation of what he already believed, Gray's attitude towards Ireland was moving into a new and more aggressive phase. Walshe, in Gray's eyes, had been further tarnished by this information, which confirmed his previously held suspicions. This would make Walshe's diplomatic task more difficult in the following year when the American note was conceived and developed.

On a more elementary level, Maffey and Gray complained to Walshe about the circulation of foreign propaganda in Ireland, and sought the suppression of the German bulletin. While Walshe was always conscious of not displeasing the Allies, he was equally determined not to let them have it all their own way. He defended the German bulletin, saying it was relatively objective. Maffey stated that the publication of the bulletin was not a serious concern in itself, but suggested the Irish government should consider the publication with English public opinion in mind. Walshe, annoyed at this arrogance, reminded the British representative that Irish public opinion was his priority:

Our people would consider it strange from the point of view of our neutrality if we suppressed the relatively insignificant German propaganda and continued to allow the vast stream of British propaganda to pour into the country.[21]

Gray suggested to Walshe that both Allied and Axis bulletins be submitted to External Affairs for approval. This was completely impractical, and Walshe felt he exercised considerable restraint in not telling Gray what he thought of the idea: 'I felt it was a cheap trick, but I did not say so.'[22] Both sides knew that the Irish government could not take responsibility for the approval of the views expressed in either Allied or Axis propaganda.

From this point on, the meeting became increasingly heated. Walshe's report listed a number of what he described as Gray's 'extremely irritating remarks':

America is in a lynching humour with Ireland because she does not give up the ports.
Ireland owes all her supplies to the British and American Fleets.
Ireland is very careful not to send a single thing to Great Britain of which she herself has the slightest need.

Maffey made matters worse by saying to Gray that the important thing to remember was that they had not succeeded in convincing Ireland of the justice of their cause. Walshe recalled with some sarcasm:

He (Maffey) objected to Gray's mention of the ports because it seemed to make a trivial aspect of what was really a great moral cause.[23]

Soon after this confrontation, Walshe spoke to both the German and Italian ministers, asking them to shorten their bulletins due to the nationwide shortage of paper.[24] This was indicative of his approach: recognising the need to placate the Allies but unwilling to give their respective representatives the opinion that he would accede to their every demand. He defended neutrality but recognised the need to make concessions. However, on the issue of German espionage in Ireland, Walshe would find Gray and Maffey more difficult to placate.

Walshe believed that Irish intelligence and security arrangements were adequate and professional.[25] Gray, however, remained

sceptical that the Irish authorities had German espionage under control. As we have seen, his suspicions of Walshe's pro-German sentiments had increased greatly following his sessions with Geraldine Cummins. He had astounded Walshe by claiming there had been a German-sponsored revival of the IRA and that Germany must have tried to engage the Irish government in some sort of arrangement.[26] This issue of Axis espionage and the Irish authorities' handling of it was to be a major point of friction between Walshe and Gray over the coming years. Walshe was normally quite calm and measured in his correspondence with representatives of foreign governments, but the frankness of his language in treating of Gray's allegations of an organised spy network in Ireland show the level of irritation he had now arrived at:

> Although you say you have no means of knowing whether the Axis spy system is effective, you tell your journalists that there is every reason why it should be efficient and extremely important … What a pretty story! and all founded on acknowledged ignorance.[27]

These suspicions were the genesis of Gray's insistence that the American government demand the removal of Germany's legation from Dublin on the basis that it was a security threat to the Allies. The note that was eventually handed to the Irish government in February 1944 was considerably watered down in comparison to Gray's original proposal, which also sought the use of Irish ports for the Allied war effort. Gray had informed the State Department that Ireland was the centre of an organised Axis spy network. Walshe found Gray's 'very exaggerated idea about German agents and activities in Ireland'[28] extremely unhelpful, and later described his obsession as 'spymania'.[29] But Gray had received decisive information on the matter. Following another session with the medium Geraldine Cummins, Arthur Balfour had again sought to advise Gray on how he should approach this question:

> The German spies in this country have conveyed to the German authorities the information that some little time ago Fianna Fáil party officials in the inner circle urged an agreement with the U.S.A. … and it is held in German H.Q. that there have been negotiations to this effect and that on conditions of delivery of supplies De Valera will come in with U.S.A. or is inclined to do

so. The German minister has therefore been directed to put on the psychological screw and threaten again.[30]

Walshe complained that Gray thwarted US–Irish security arrangements, and said that his reports on the perceived danger of Axis agents in Ireland were wildly exaggerated. Yet, despite Gray's reticence, Walshe, it seems, was able to circumvent this negative attitude and form a number of important links with US government and security officials. It was important that the State Department had other sources of information to draw upon in its assessment of the Axis threat, and the Office of Strategic Services (OSS) filled that gap by sending a number of trained agents to Ireland to assess the situation. This provided Walshe with an important alternative connection to the United States government. He would use the route to good effect in his effort to bypass what he saw as the obstructive influence of Gray.

Throughout the war, the OSS collected and collated a wide variety of information on Ireland.[31] From the information it received, reports were compiled on the Irish situation.[32] Many included an assessment of the sociopolitical situation in Ireland as well as strategic military data. Politics, economics, Axis propaganda, and German military and submarine activity in and around Ireland were chief among the interests of the OSS. Assessment of Irish public opinion through censorship of correspondence and close scrutiny of the press was another primary concern of this intelligence agency. Walshe established good relations with these agents, who were inclined to file more realistic reports concerning espionage in Ireland. In an External Affairs telegram to the Washington legation in 1944, reference is made to 'our good friends in Security Service' who were, it seems, satisfied with Irish–US security arrangements.[33] Walshe was convinced that the OSS had counteracted Gray's spurious allegations: 'We are convinced American Government does not fear serious espionage from here.' A document dated 1946 retrospectively accuses Gray of actively discouraging 'normal official contacts between the staff of the American Legation … and the officials of the Department of External Affairs to the point of securing the transfer to other posts of American service officers who continued to maintain such contacts.' Walshe believed that by 1943 Gray was opposed to all such cooperation, and said that he 'openly

criticised and obstructed official arrangements between the two
countries approved by the respective Governments'.[34] Many of
the concerns of the OSS agents overlapped with the responsibilities of David Gray. Ideally, they should have complemented each
other, but tension arose between the two parties. The detailed
intelligence reports should have enhanced Gray's ability to report
on the Irish situation, but the difference between their respective
versions was sometimes too significant to ignore.

The files of External Affairs and the military archives show
that G2 was well informed of the arrival and movement of foreign agents. Most were apprehended within days of their landing
in Ireland. Walshe, in turn, was kept abreast of all developments;
good intelligence information was crucial in presenting a competent picture of the work of the Irish authorities. Walshe was
in regular communication with Dan Bryan and Liam Archer,
although it seems that much of the information was conveyed
verbally via telephone and person-to-person meetings.[35] Later in
the war, Walshe wrote a memorandum outlining his ideas on
intelligence and security, and on his own experience with the
Irish intelligence officials:

> A water-tight Security Department, keeping all its activities to
> itself, would be of no use to the State. It might very easily become
> like any imperium in imperio – a source of danger … In our coun-
> try at any rate, the liaison between Security officials and the foreign
> Affairs officials is so close, so interwoven, as to form almost one
> Department.[36]

This is further testimony to the close level of cooperation between
External Affairs and G2 that led Walshe to consider that they work
as one department. It was also an expression of Walshe's incredu-
lity at the State Department's apparent lack of questioning of the
contradictory intelligence reports on Ireland from both Gray and
OSS officials in Ireland.

Walshe was convinced that any German espionage activity in
Ireland was closely monitored, but the Allies required more tangible guarantees. David Gray would not be persuaded that Irish
security measures were satisfactory. As a result, Walshe formed an
alternative relationship with United States security officials who
were satisfied that Irish intelligence was doing all in its power to

maintain adequate security. It was to prove an important channel of communication in the years to come, although it did not
prevent the delivery of the American note. Walshe became particularly close to Ervin 'Spike' Marlin, an OSS agent who was
posted to Ireland in 1942, ostensibly as an economics adviser to
the Dublin legation, and was given the title 'Special Assistant to
the Minister'. Marlin admitted that one of the reasons why the
State Department continued with the American note, despite
the cooperation with the Irish intelligence authorities, was on the
basis of Gray's assessment that Ireland was overrun with German
spies. This was partly caused by a lack of communication between
the State Department and the Intelligence Department.[37] Marlin
said that there was a great deal of confusion between departments,
and clearly Gray's point of view was winning out.

Before Marlin's arrival, Gray had seen the potential for conflict
with his own position but received specific assurances in this
regard. He was told that, although Marlin would receive his
instructions from the OSS, 'all subjects of interest to the Department of State will be made known to the Legation.'[38] Gray was
not satisfied, and felt he would have no control over Marlin's work.
He sought further information on Marlin's mission to Ireland, but
this was refused by the Secretary of State for reasons of secrecy:

> it is not customary for the Department to receive copies of detailed
> instructions to representatives sent on missions similar to that of
> Marlin; however, the latter's principals have cabled him to acquaint
> you fully with the purposes of his assignment.[39]

Marlin's real task was to verify the veracity of the press reports on
the alleged freedom and frequency with which German agents were
operating in Ireland.[40] His assessment would not tally with Gray's
reports of a vast and organised spy network. He later recounted that
he believed such rumours to have been without foundation:

> I spoke to J.P. Walshe who told me that there were between fifty and
> a hundred thousand British sympathizers in Éire who were strain-
> ing at the leash to report anything they heard about German spies. I
> didn't discover any spy centres. I assumed that Irish intelligence had
> the place buttoned up; once they realized it was in their interest to
> keep us informed, they were very good to us.[41]

Marlin was soon transferred to London because he felt the security situation to be satisfactory. Gray was not in agreement with this prognosis and gravely resented the interference; in particular, he begrudged Walshe's apparent alliance with Marlin.

Gray later wrote to William Phillips, who was attached to the US embassy in London, concerning the appointment of OSS agents, as he had been informed that the State Department proposed to withdraw its agents from Ireland. He told Phillips that he would be willing to retain Marlin as a 'special assistant' provided that he would be kept in the picture of all events and information gathered.[42] Gray said he was not opposed to US intelligence agents working in Ireland, so long as he would be fully involved and had authority over their actions. He spoke to Walshe about possible cooperation between Irish and US intelligence agents concerning IRA activities. Walshe had no objections to the idea, and Gray suggested to Phillips that, 'if your man comes over he [should] come prepared to meet and cooperate with the Irish Secret Service people on my introduction through External Affairs.'[43]

OSS interest in Ireland did not end with Marlin's departure, and over the coming years, Walshe would host a number of visitors interested in gathering information. In March 1943 Gray informed Walshe that a Colonel Bruce and Captain Stacey Lloyd were 'very well satisfied with your kindness and cooperation and hopeful that some mutually useful arrangement may come of it'.[44] However, he expressed resentment about a proposed visit by Marlin, saying, 'I am not responsible for Mr Marlin', and he remained unconvinced that the Irish authorities ran a tight ship as far as security was concerned.[45] Walshe recognised it was a significant failure for Gray to prevent Marlin's involvement as he was dependent on these espionage threats as justification to proceed with his American note.

In stark contrast, Maffey was not overly concerned with German espionage in Ireland. In November 1942, for example, he learned of the Irish government's decision to intern a Polish airman, Sergeant Zenit, who had recently crash-landed in Wexford. Maffey used all the usual arguments to plead for the release of the airman, but to no avail. Walshe explained that de Valera had made the decision under considerable political pressure due to criticisms of having unneutral tendencies. This was coupled with

increased IRA activities, including the escape of six IRA prisoners from Mountjoy Jail, which appeared to have been assisted
by official collusion. Walshe was anxious, therefore, that Maffey
would not push this particular case:

> 'Let this case go. It will enable us to help you in the long run.' I
> think this is probably true and sincerely meant. For that reason I
> regretfully advocate not further challenging the decision.[46]

Maffey, therefore, assented to Walshe's request but expected considerable leniency with regard to future cases of Allied internees.

About this time, the Dominions Office suggested that if
Walshe so wished, he would be welcome to visit London. Eric
Machtig recommended that Walshe should not be extended a
formal invitation, but that he could come not for any specific purpose but to renew personal contacts with his British counterparts
and also to get a feel for the atmosphere in London at that stage
of the war.[47] Machtig said that the Dominions Office would do all
it could to facilitate the visit and arrange for Walshe to meet anyone he wished. Walshe was more than willing to make the trip,
which took place in November 1942. Machtig displayed considerable enthusiasm for the visit, and a suitable schedule was arranged.
He hoped that Walshe would have the opportunity to meet the
Secretary of State, Emrys Evans, among others.[48] He promised
to do his best to arrange any other meetings that Walshe considered desirable, with people such as Lord Cranborne, Anthony
Eden and Sir Stafford Cripps. He cautiously asked the Irish High
Commissioner in London, John Dulanty, if he was making any
arrangements, realising that Walshe might wish to remain the
centre of attention for the duration of his visit.

Machtig attempted to generate some excitement and possibly sympathy for Britain's cause as he arranged a tour of various
aspects of the 'war effort', including a night visit to a bomber
operational unit.[49] The proposed schedule was put before Walshe,
who replied enthusiastically. Maffey felt that the visit could be
used to put pressure on the Irish position. He suggested that
Walshe was most amenable under the following conditions:

> In conversations with Walshe in high places when the trend is
> towards a sympathetic attempt to understand Irish neutrality and

appreciate what the Department of External Affairs is trying to do for us against a difficult background…

That Maffey practised this strategy with some skill is borne out in the archival evidence. While Gray was busy creating conflict, Maffey would apparently appease Walshe with some ease. Having gained his confidence, Maffey would accrue significant concessions from Walshe. For the coming visit, Maffey believed that the following were the main points that should be put to Walshe:

· That the loss of strategic facilities has meant bitter losses to us at sea;
· That the presence of Axis Legations in Dublin keeps and must continue to keep us on tenterhooks, since whatever the Irish authorities may do, new and subtle means of communication exist in these days and valuable sources of information are available;
· That nothing exacts greater resentment in the popular mind of the United Nations than the internment of our airmen, and all matters … relating to them touch a sore point.[50]

The first point referred to the refusal to grant the Allies the use of strategic bases in Ireland which, Maffey asserted, had led to significant British losses at sea. By this time, however, the emphasis of the war had moved east to Russia and the need for such bases had lost its urgency. The subsequent issues, however, were more pressing. Even at this stage of the war, Walshe was mindful of postwar politics, and he recognised that if he did not deal adequately with these points of contention, Ireland's position after the war could be adversely affected.

That Walshe was becoming increasingly concerned with Ireland's postwar position can be seen in his handling of the questions surrounding a radio transmitter that was known to be in use in the German legation. Walshe came under repeated pressure from Maffey and Gray to have it removed. They claimed its presence was a very real danger to the Allied war effort. Its existence lent credence to Gray's claim that Ireland was a base for Axis espionage. Walshe, however, proved his diplomatic skill in recognising this danger and by his successful disposal of the potentially offending transmitter. When the British first

learned of the presence of a radio transmitter sending signals to Germany, they informed the Irish authorities. Immediately, Walshe asked Michael Rynne to investigate the legal obligations of a neutral state in time of war with regard to communications. Rynne reported that neutral governments were obliged to 'ensure uninterrupted communications in wartime ... between foreign diplomatic missions (belligerent or otherwise)'. However, Walshe was glad when Rynne referred specifically to the position in relation to radio transmitters:

> Notwithstanding the nature of their own municipal laws, neutral states are absolutely forbidden to permit the erection of private wire-less transmitters by or on behalf of belligerent authorities. (Articles 3 and 5 Hague Convention No. v.)[51]

Clearly, if either belligerent breached this rule it would be the government's duty to put an end to the abuse and prevent its recurrence. Rynne believed that the best course would be to locate the set by technical means and then to request the owners to dismantle it and to hand over the components, or serious consequences for Irish neutrality could accrue. When Dan Bryan of the Irish military-intelligence agency wrote to Walshe in 1941 regarding covert messages that were being sent from Ireland, he suggested that Ireland and Britain should 'exchange information on suspicious signals heard in either country so that the network of the intercepting services can be widened to catch signals emanating from Éire'.[52] However, it was not until 1943 that Walshe made any definitive demands on the German minister. The relatively long period between the discovery of the wireless transmitter and Walshe's ultimatum to Hempel to destroy it may have been due to advice from the British, who might have found it more useful in the early stages to allow the transmissions to continue. In this way, they could monitor Hempel's information. Now, however, with the war approaching a crucial stage, the Allies insisted that the Irish authorities close in on Hempel's illegal radio transmissions. When Walshe eventually approached Hempel, he said that it constituted a positive threat to Ireland's neutrality, and that both Britain and America requested its removal. Hempel said that if he gave it up, he would feel that he had given up everything, but Walshe replied that it was a 'luxury' and some-

thing to which he was not entitled in the first place. Claiming that they both remained in good humour, Walshe concluded: 'I should venture the opinion that, if they do not allow him to get rid of the wireless, it will be a sign that our neutrality has ceased to have any value to them.'[53] A week later, however, events had led Walshe to become much more animated on the subject. Two Abwehr parachutists, O'Reilly and Kenny, had landed in Ireland, complete with wireless sets.[54] Although they had been captured immediately, it did not stop Walshe from emphasising the fear that such actions by Germany caused. He linked this latest infringement with the transmitter issue, and cited Allied pressure as the reason for his demand that the wireless set be destroyed:

> … the mere fact of their arrival would of necessity give an opportunity to the other belligerents to question once more the expediency of respecting our neutrality.[55]

Perhaps earlier in the war, Walshe may not have been as ready to confiscate Hempel's transmitter. However, as Allied fortunes changed, so too did his attitude towards Germany, and he reminded Hempel that Ireland would not be used as a base against Britain. He had a distinct air of superiority when he asked Hempel to warn his government 'of the folly of thinking that parachutists could be landed here without escaping arrest'. Walshe predicted that these recent German parachutists would provoke an ultimatum from Britain and the United States regarding the transmitter, and as a pre-emptive measure delivered his own ultimatum, telling Hempel to hand over or destroy the set.

Walshe believed that Hempel had neither supported nor been informed of the sending of the latest parachutists. The German minister was apologetic, and claimed that he had previously warned his superiors of the serious consequences for relations between the two countries caused by such incidents, and of the difficulties it caused for the Irish government in maintaining neutrality. He decided to relinquish his transmitter and proposed that it be placed in the safe of his local bank. The safe was to have two keys – one he would keep and the other to be in the possession of the Department of External Affairs. Neither party could open the safe in the absence of the other.

Walshe accepted this arrangement and, soon after, the wireless

transmitter was rendered harmless in a Dublin bank. Maffey was informed and appeared satisfied with the outcome. He wrote to Walshe saying he had informed London of the situation, and declared that he had 'accepted' this solution. Walshe, not liking his tone, however, annotated on Maffey's letter: 'He was not asked to accept. He was simply told because of his representations to the Taoiseach. I made it quite clear that the matter was concluded before he made representations.'[56] Irish policy may have been strongly driven by Allied concerns and pressures, but Walshe was going to ensure that an element of freewill be maintained. This would prove more difficult when Walshe was forced to consider the fate of both Axis and Allied crew members who were downed in Irish territory.

Maffey's reservations regarding the internees were also an important concern for Walshe. Robert Fisk has pointed out that within minutes of war breaking out, Britain impinged on Irish neutrality when an RAF flying boat landed off the coast of Dublin. The Irish authorities reacted by refuelling the aircraft.[57] This was only the first of many such landings, but Irish collusion with Britain was complicated by the fact that Hempel watched closely for any pro-Allied treatment. Ultimately, Walshe and the Department of External Affairs designed a policy that strongly favoured the release of Allied air crews but which discriminated against the release of Axis internees. Hempel's initial concern was that the conditions of German internees would be good, and that any benefits given to the British internees would also be given to them.[58] With this in mind, Walshe and a number of External Affairs officials received a delegation from the German legation where it was agreed that all benefits – which allowed considerable freedoms – would be applied equally to all internees.[59] Hempel's concerns were soon to change, however, as he received reports of British aircraft making forced landings and being allowed to depart without internment. Suspecting anti-Axis discrimination, he put pressure on Walshe to clarify Irish government policy with regard to the internment of belligerent aircraft and crew.

In one report, Hempel had heard reports that a British military aircraft, which had landed near Strokestown, County Roscommon, had subsequently been released. Boland alleged that he had not heard of the incident but promised to make enquiries. He had already been quizzed by Henning Thomsen, secretary to

the German legation, on another suspected release of a British military aircraft. In this case, his defence was that the aircraft had been a passenger plane due to the fact that fourteen people had been killed and that some of the victims had been women.[60] Boland felt these replies would only suffice as a stop-gap measure. He was anxious to speak with Walshe in order to clarify the legal position and formulate a more satisfactory response for future cases. Hempel was correct to seek clarification on the Irish position as he was given a variety of explanations as to how internment policy was decided. Towards the end of 1942, it was explained to him that it was not a question of Irish policy but one of international law:

> We interned aircraft which landed here when we were obliged to do so, but we could not intern aircraft if we could not point to a clear and decisive authority for our so doing.[61]

These explanations became vastly less satisfactory when it became clear that the Irish authorities had far fewer misgivings when it came to the internment of German personnel.

As the United States became increasingly involved in the European war theatre, Gray's interest in internment grew. Adding to Walshe's problems, he reported the possible increase in US air forces in Northern Ireland. He was attempting to clear the way for a potential increase in accidental landings on Irish territory. As most of these flights were allegedly for training purposes, he hoped that the Irish government would accept the distinction between 'combatant' and 'non-combatant' flights. Walshe preferred to use the terms 'operational' and 'non-operational' to make the distinction, but Gray was more interested in what the Irish position would be in the case of an accidental grounding of an operational flight. When Gray remarked that the US government did not question the Irish right to intern such flights, he was being unusually sensitive. However, he got to the real point when he asked, 'whether, in principle, the Irish Government would recognise the presumption that German planes which grounded on Éire territory were engaged in operational flights, whereas the presumption that American planes based in Northern Ireland were engaged in non-operational flights.'[62] Walshe's reply reflected the reality of the situation. The Irish government wanted to avoid

interning any US airmen if at all possible, but he was unwilling to formalise that position. The State Department was keen to assert the analogy between aircraft and surface vessels, which were entitled to twenty-four hours delay before internment. Walshe wasn't opposed to discussing the issue, but advised that such consultations should take place after the war. 'In practice', outlined Walshe, 'our attitude of friendly neutrality towards the United Nations results normally – insofar as aircraft and their crews are concerned – in the internment of only such crews as are on operational flights.'[63] Walshe felt it best to leave the existing situation as it was, saying that to initiate formal agreements or regulations would lead to difficulties. What Gray did not recognise, but what Walshe hinted at, was that the ambiguity was useful, whereas a definitive agreement could lead to a less favourable situation for the Allies.

It was a mistake for Gray to push the issue, but he continued to seek written confirmation of acceptance for the distinction between 'operational' and 'non-operational' flights. He felt that Walshe's letter had not sufficiently emphasised the point, but he finally settled on a formula suitable to both their points of view: 'I agree to your suggestion that we do not formalise the understanding by an exchange of notes but only by memoranda that will make it clear to my Government that I have not misunderstood or mis-reported the facts.'[64] Gray had become more cautious in his dealings, and he sent Walshe the text of his aide-memoire outlining his views on the issue in an attempt to prevent future misunderstanding. Despite their previous differences, Gray also hinted at the advantages of a favourable response to these US government concerns:

> I find I neglected to record what I remember making very clear – that is that my Government would be most appreciative of the attitude of the Irish Government and that I considered it a cooperation which, when it could be divulged to the American people, would have far-reaching influence for good.[65]

Walshe insisted, however, that he had already covered the situation appropriately. He was unwilling to clarify the situation further, and concluded the matter verbally with Gray. In a handwritten note, he rather cryptically updated the record: 'After a

further conversation with Mr Gray he agreed that my letter of 11th Dec. dealt adequately with the situation and that nothing further was required.[66] Regrettably, from Walshe's point of view, the matter did not finish there. In March 1943 Gray thanked Walshe for the refuelling of an American Flying Fortress that had recently landed in Irish territory and was helped on its way after the passengers had spent the night in Ireland. He was curious to know what the situation would be if a German aircraft sought similar refuelling privileges. Walshe again told him that this would not occur, and that any German aircraft would be deemed to be on an operational flight. Gray suggested that petrol companies that supplied American airlines should earmark specific quantities of petrol in Ireland for American purposes. He suggested that as Germany would have no petrol stocks in Ireland this would preclude the Irish government from according the same privileges of refuelling to them. Walshe was growing weary of these thinly veiled attempts to formalise the benefits that the Irish government was already providing the Allies:

> Mr Walshe took the position that there was no need to have any apprehensions in regard to this matter and that he would prefer that we trust the Irish Government implicitly, as the British had done, and rely on verbal assurances that in no case would petrol be supplied to German aircraft.[67]

Despite Walshe's assurances, Gray still thought it better to have something formally agreed on the matter, and it was only when he discussed the issue with Maffey did he take the view that the suggestions he had advanced regarding a 'definite understanding' were unnecessary.

In the meantime, further incidents of British and US aircraft landings in Irish territory and their subsequent release became widely known. Hempel again approached the Department of External Affairs. This time he was told that the planes concerned – and the Strokestown landing in particular – had been engaged in purely passenger duties. Hempel had also heard of an Allied aircraft, containing four generals, making a landing on Irish territory. There was even a rumour that General Eisenhower was included in the group. Boland's initial remarks were flippant and unconvincing, and the German minister became increasingly

worried about their significance. Boland initially attempted to persuade him that such rumours were designed to put pressure on Irish neutrality. He told Hempel not to listen to rumours, as 'the way rumours travelled around here was simply extra-ordinary and there was always the possibility that some of them were put around for the express purpose of causing difficulties to our neutrality.' Hempel, who had heard the story on good authority, pressed Boland, who was ultimately forced to admit that there was some justification to the report. It was explained that a plane containing a number of high military officers had landed and was subsequently allowed to depart again:

> I said that we did not allow military passengers on the civilian air services from Foynes and that, probably in view of this restriction, the British operated services to and from the Six County area on which military personnel probably constituted the bulk of the passengers carried. Very occasionally, these passenger planes made forced landings here and we had spoken to the British about them but, of course, in view of their passenger character, there was no question of our being able to intern them.[68]

Boland's explanation shows that External Affairs was not as prepared as it should have been. When faced with questions on the issue, Walshe seems to have been nonplussed, initially at least, when attempting to explain this apparent anomaly in Irish neutrality. In order to rectify the situation, Walshe drafted a memorandum later that month in which he outlined the general problems concerned with internment. He admitted that the warfare rules formulated in The Hague in 1923 clearly stated that if belligerent aircraft enter neutral territory they must be interned. However, he also pointed out that with the enormous increase in the number of aircraft being used, the subsequent burden on neutral countries would be too great if they all had to be interned. The situation was a learning experience, wrote Walshe, who outlined some of the most practical rules derived from the logic of Irish circumstances. Borrowing a phrase he had often used with Gray, he said that 'the custom is slowly emerging of confining internment to planes and crews actually engaged on strictly operational flights.'[69] Thus, internment policy evolved – slowly, but more specifically in response to Hempel, Gray and

Maffey's queries and complaints. In conclusion, Walshe outlined the fundamental principle as being not to do anything that could be interpreted as taking part in the war.

It is now clear that Irish policy in relation to internment discriminated greatly in favour of Allied aircraft. It is also evident that Walshe's efforts to stave off German accusations of bias were not working. In May 1943 Hempel conveyed his dissatisfaction with the situation, and warned that he would be forced to address a formal note to the Irish government regarding the recent case of a Flying Fortress that had landed at Collinstown and was subsequently allowed to depart.[70] Hempel knew that this was only one incident among many, and he indicated that a formal protest would have been made earlier had it not been for a delay by his superiors in giving specific instructions on the matter. Boland's defence was that the principles of internment were uncertain, and that the Irish government was following principles that seemed appropriate and that appeared to be far stricter than those used by other neutrals. Hempel escalated the issue to Walshe, who explained the principle of only interning planes deemed to be on 'operational' flights. The statistical discrepancy between Allied and Axis internee numbers was explained by the fact that the British and the Americans 'were much more likely to come within the exemption category than the Germans who could only find themselves over our territory in the course of an operational flight.'[71] Hempel did not dispute Walshe's assertion that there would be more chance of German flights over Ireland being 'operational', but he sought explanations for six specific incidents of aircraft that had landed in Ireland and were later released. Walshe failed to confront the issue, and for months he neglected to give Hempel a reply. Having raised the issue in May, Hempel now told Walshe in September that if he did not receive a reply within a few days he would report the matter to his government. If Walshe was worried about the threat he did not show it. In fact, he appeared nonchalant in his response:

> I told him that we could not complain about that attitude. He was, of course, perfectly free to report to his Government on his failure to obtain a reply but he should remind his Government about the much more serious matters relating to which no reply had been received by the Irish Government from them.[72]

Hempel insisted on being given a reply to the six specific cases mentioned in his protest. Having had enough of Walshe's vacillation and constant reference to general principles, he now sought precise justification for specific occurrences of what he believed was a serious abrogation of Irish neutrality. External Affairs drafted a response that claimed Irish internment policy was stricter than that of other neutrals. The various nuances of international law had to be taken into consideration, and therefore, in individual cases, 'a neutral state must consider the question of internment not merely from the point of view of the question whether international law, as established by definitely adopted rule or general practice of neutrals, gives it a right to intern.'[73] In the specific cases mentioned, it was asserted that after examining all the factors – including the type of plane, the equipment it carried, and the circumstances in which it came to land on Irish territory – and taking into account the principles outlined, a decision to intern could not be made. Thus, it was believed there was no reason why a reply on these lines would not be satisfactory to the German minister. However, Walshe and Boland knew that the reply should be made quickly, before the planned release of a number of British internees, as the justification for this action might not be so easily illustrated. It was also their plan to argue that Germany had little cause for objection considering its own failure to reply to an Irish note concerning Axis bombings of Irish ships and ships with Irish-bound cargoes. On hearing the reply, Hempel insisted that his government considered the release of Allied planes and their passengers as a serious infringement of the neutral policy. He sought the immediate execution of internment policy on an equitable basis, and further demanded compensation for previous transgressions through the release of a corresponding number of German personnel.[74] Walshe believed the matter had been adequately addressed and, it appears, gave little further thought to the question. As the Third Reich's chances of victory began to wane, Walshe became less sympathetic towards Hempel's complaints that the Allies were receiving more favourable treatment.

Walshe's changing attitude to the Allies was first noted by Maffey in late 1942. He had been discussing Ireland's postwar position with Gray, who told him that a recent Chicago newspaper had carried an article from London stating that Walshe,

who was in London at the time, had requested representation for Ireland at any postwar reconstruction commission, on the grounds that Ireland would be vitally interested in its decisions. Maffey noted that 'a great change had been worked in the viewpoint of the Irish Government since the recent Allied victories.'[75] This was a natural reaction to world events, especially since 1943 was a significant period in the war for Allied successes. In January a German offensive against Russia ended in failure when the German forces surrendered. July saw another victory for the Russians at the Battle of Kursk. Britain had its successes in Africa, and the United States sank twenty-one Japanese transport ships taking troops to New Guinea, while both were involved in the landing of troops in Sicily. The war was far from over, but certainly there was a new air of optimism among the Allies. As Germany had more pressing problems at hand than the matter of internees in Ireland, Walshe would not hesitate to capitalise on Hempel's difficulties.

Walshe's enthusiasm for the Allied cause found expression in a plan to release twenty of the thirty-three British internees held at the Curragh internment camp.[76] Maffey and Walshe had previously attempted to organise the simultaneous release of both British and German internees, but the British military authorities rejected the plan on the grounds that the German internees had by now learned much about Ireland that could be of use to the German Abwehr if the prisoners were sent home. The release of both sets of internees would have been a relief to Walshe, but he acceded to this reasoning. Instead, Maffey urged Walshe to consider the principle that only those airmen who were deemed to be on 'operational flights' should be interned. This would mean, by Maffey's reckoning, that only thirteen of the thirty-three British internees should remain in captivity. The policy was obviously biased against Germany, which was extremely unlikely to be able to justify any non-operational flights in this region.

The postwar position of Ireland was of great concern to Walshe, and it greatly influenced his position on the issue of internees and the internment of aircraft. However, he was conscious also of the fact that, while cooperating closely with Britain on many matters, it was possible that the Irish government would not get full credit for the positive role it had played in assisting the Allies. Maffey had maintained his view that Irish neutrality

had allowed serious threats to Britain. This inspired some rather obsequious, though perhaps necessary, attempts by Walshe to remind Maffey of the benefits that had accrued from Irish neutrality. He showed Maffey a number of American news reports that stated that Spain was organising a league of neutrals to work in close harmony with the Vatican and to 'stand together for the purposes of European reconstructions and to safeguard the neutral's position in the post war world'. Walshe said that, despite some reports to the contrary, Ireland had not accepted an invitation to join such a league. The Irish representative in Madrid, Leopold Kearney, had reported that a number of suggestions had been mooted, including that, as Catholic nations, Spain and Ireland could help one another. Considering the position Ireland was in, it may have been a tempting offer to acquire an ally to face any reticence from the victors after the war. Walshe, however, rejected the idea, and attempted to demonstrate how far Irish statehood had travelled since independence:

> Mr Walshe said that they were convinced that Spain was in a very imbalanced post-revolutionary and pre-revolutionary position and certainly the idea of collaboration with her would meet with no favours here … Mr Walshe told me that Mr Kearney had been instructed not to let this matter develop in any way. Éire is already, in its own opinion, collaborating with the Vatican and sees no point with special collaboration with Spain or anybody else for the purpose stated.[77]

Walshe was at pains to point out that there was no such collaboration, and that if at any time in the future the Irish government decided to move in that direction, the British would be kept fully informed. This was the start of many attempts by Walshe to garner favour for Ireland in the postwar situation.

Maffey, meanwhile, maintained strong pressure on Walshe to reassess Irish neutrality. In May 1943 he sent Walshe a further memorandum on the internee situation, but it was really a broad attack on Irish neutrality. He began by stating that 'Nations genuinely neutral are influenced by their geographical proximity to powerful neighbours.' To Walshe, this had been patently obvious, but Maffey was trying to make the case for further leniency towards Britain:

Neutrality today is a relatively fluid term. Each neutral nation endeavours to formulate a workable interpretation, and these interpretations vary not only because of the new and devastating methods of war but because of pressures which cannot be resisted and of ideological sympathies with a belligerent power.[78]

This was an accurate assessment of Irish neutrality, and Maffey hoped that the Irish government would see fit to make further adjustments in light of the fact that some of the rules of Irish neutrality laid down in 1939 were now found to be impractical. He described the internment of British airmen as 'unneutral and unjustifiable', while at the same time he believed the internment of German air crews was a necessity. The excuse might be used that at the start of the war the implications of internment on Britain may not have been realised, but that now this defence no longer existed. Maffey described how he and his government had been shocked by Irish neutrality and at Ireland's refusal to fight for its own freedom. While stating that Britain had never threatened Ireland, he admitted that this course may not have been too far away:

> There were many good reasons requiring the maximum restraint on our side when the question of the internment of British airmen arose in practical form in 1940. We had preoccupations so immense that we could not afford to enlarge the field of controversy.[79]

Maffey was in an accusatory frame of mind, and asserted that Irish neutrality was formulated on the basis of a fear of Germany and a fear of a British defeat. It was probably an overstatement but he insisted that internment had been 'a most gravely hampering factor' to Britain, and that 'the number of lives and aircraft lost by airmen in distress seeking to avoid internment in Éire ... is known to be grievously high.' Thoughts about Ireland's plight after the war were never far from Walshe's mind, and he was again reminded of this when Maffey stated that Ireland's internment policy was 'casting long shadows' throughout the Commonwealth. He believed that the decision to introduce the distinction between 'operational' and 'non-operational' flights was taken by Walshe and de Valera in an effort to alleviate the injustice of the policy.

Maffey's arguments were excessive. The Irish government had

operated a generous policy towards the internment of planes and crews from Britain. Only a small fraction of those British airmen who had landed on Irish territory were interned. Many of those who were interned were subsequently released.[80] Even as early as 1942 it had become so commonplace for the Irish authorities to refuel downed British aircraft that an agreement was reached in which the British government would refund to Ireland the fuel used by the aircraft along with a 100 per cent bonus.[81] Michael Rynne pointed out that Maffey's arguments had little basis in international law, and that the Irish government had already stretched the bounds of generosity in this regard:

> Our present internment policy, under which we are still able to keep a few Britishers in an internment camp, has already been indignantly attacked by the German Minister in a Note of formal protest (27 July 1943). We were unable to answer that note because it took as its headline those legal rules which we have been gradually forced by British pressure (tacit as well as overt) to leave far behind.[82]

Rynne's comments outline the nature of the policy developed by Walshe, which was based on keeping to a minimum the number of British airmen interned in Ireland while at the same time interning all German air crews. Walshe clearly felt the injustice of the comments, but Maffey showed him little sympathy:

> He is, of course, highly sensitive. On analysis he did not make much of a case against me. He professed to be shocked at my statement that after the war there would be revelations of axis underground activities in Éire during the war. He had understood that the liaison between their Security branch and ours was most effective, and he felt that the Éire Government had been very forthcoming in the matter. I agreed, but said that neither he nor I nor any of the Security people could shut their eyes to the probability (which in my view amounted to certainty) that many things are going on quite outside our ken.[83]

Walshe was disheartened by the meeting, and believed that German espionage attempts in Ireland had been highly incompetent and completely observed by the Irish authorities. He shied away, however, from the subject of the British internees, as de

Valera planned to speak with Maffey directly on the subject. Walshe, perhaps, would have found it difficult to maintain his good relationship with Maffey had they discussed the matter at that particular time.

Following a visit to Ireland in the early part of the war, one British official, Herbert Shaw, had concluded that Walshe ran an efficient department and believed he had at his disposal a competent staff and sources of information that, under happier circumstances, might well have supplemented the foreign missions of the British government.[84] This view was reiterated by Maffey. Despite their differences, he felt comfortable in asking Walshe 'if he saw anything through his European window which would interest me and which he could tell me I should be grateful.'[85] Walshe admitted that his representatives abroad did not say much, as they knew that their communications could be tapped. However, he did inform Maffey that William Warnock had reported severe destruction in Berlin as a result of Allied bombing raids. Warnock had raised fears for himself and his family, and reported anxiety in Germany over the Russian front but said there was no general 'demoralisation', and that there were no signs that food was running short. Walshe told Maffey that from his sources he had got the impression that, 'Hitler was obsessed by the Russian front and treated everything else, including Africa up to date, as a side show, even to the extent of withholding help in the latter zone which might affect the issue.'

The quality and accuracy of Warnock's reports were of importance to Walshe, who would take them into account when formulating policy towards Germany and in his conversations with Hempel. In October 1943 Walshe sought Warnock's assessment as to how long more he thought the war would continue. It was a difficult estimate to make. However, taking into account a large number of factors, he cautiously suggested that he would be surprised if the war had ended by the same time the following year.[86] It was an important assessment nonetheless, and realistic in not being over-optimistic in the light of the continued advances of the Allies.

The administration of External Affairs continued to be of considerable interest to Maffey. He wrote to the Dominions Office seeking information from the Foreign Office concerning the relationship between British and Irish diplomatic representatives in

various missions around the world. He believed 'individual personality' was the major influence on any of the Irish missions,
and that Walshe exerted very little organisation or discipline.
'Dulanty', the Irish High Commissioner to London, he said, 'was
a law unto himself', and described him as somewhat of a loose
cannon.[87] 'I get the impression', he reported, 'that his visits here
do not promote goodwill between nations.'[88] In 1942, when the
Dominions Office was arranging a visit for Walshe to London,
Machtig realised that Dulanty may not have been consulted
about the visit and that Walshe would not have appreciated being
upstaged by his subordinate.[89] Despite their intermittent rivalry,
Walshe and Dulanty maintained a cordial and professional
relationship. Walshe had no cause for complaint as Dulanty's
reports were regular and comprehensive. Regular telephone contact was maintained, and the files of the Irish archives contain
a large amount of Dulanty's wartime reports from London.[90]
Unfortunately, these contain very little, if any, correspondence or
instructions from Walshe, although from Dulanty's comments
certain inferences can be made about Walshe's instructions.[91]
Maffey believed that the strict censorship indicated the basic
Irish policy, which, he thought, set the standard for the Irish representatives. He asserted that the major conforming and unifying
factor was that the Department of External Affairs was regarded
as the 'chief agent for establishing full independence and foreign
status in the eyes of the world', and that neutrality had bestowed
unforeseen importance on Walshe's department.

Maffey continued to maintain pressure on the Irish government for the release of the British internees, and he met Walshe
in August 1943 to repeat his objections. Walshe, however, had
his own grievances to vent. As he went on the offensive, he said
he was annoyed by 'the general welter of injured feelings created
by the suspicion that England was now showing definite spite
to Ireland in many directions'.[92] Walshe cited as an example the
fact that Ireland had not been included in a list of neutral states
to which a note was being sent concerning the harbouring of
'Axis delinquents'. He had heard that Ireland had originally been
included on the list but was removed by London. What had really
rankled Walshe was that American newspapers had hinted at the
reason for Britain's intervention, suggesting that 'Éire was under
the Dominions Office'. Walshe said that Britain's 'hostile' policy

was becoming clear as it became increasingly difficult for Irish ships to obtain warrants to load their cargoes. Maffey denied any deliberate punitive policy and said that the measures were based on war restrictions. Next, Walshe 'waxed hot about "that old man" the American Minister'. Gray had recently published a letter he had sent to Cardinal MacRory in which he had spoken of the Axis legation in Dublin using fuel that had been transported to Ireland in Allied convoys, while the Irish government interned those airmen who protected those sea routes. Maffey agreed that Gray had broken diplomatic etiquette by publicly circulating the letter, but insisted that Gray's main point was correct. On the question of civil aviation, Walshe had heard that discussions had been going on but that Ireland had been excluded. These incidents were critical to Walshe's apprehensions that Ireland was going to be left out in the cold after the war. He detected a feeling of hostility emanating from the Foreign Office, but Maffey insisted that very friendly associations had been established and would be maintained. Walshe agreed that this was true to an extent but felt that not everybody understood this, and that Ireland's contribution during the war was not known or appreciated:

> He said that he was concerned at the danger of these cumulative and growing resentments going too far and digging a ditch between the two countries when in the light of the experience gained during the war there would be a great opportunity of building the bridges and starting a new chapter.[93]

Maffey admitted that many people in Britain believed that Ireland should have joined them in the war. They had been through a period of great danger and sacrifice, and some, he said, resented the fact that Ireland refused to help them at a time when Irish help was considered a vital factor. 'This was not forgotten', said Maffey, 'but fortunately we had got along without them [the ports].' Despite this, he believed that Walshe was exaggerating the force of such resentment:

> However at the head of affairs there was some appreciation of the particular difficulties affecting Éire's freedom of action at the outbreak of war, and I did not think that he would find that resentment provided the driving force in the British policy towards Éire.

He then suggested that Walshe should travel to London to meet his 'old friends at the Dominions Office' if he thought this would help to re-establish good faith. Walshe believed that the war was 'almost all over bar the shouting', and this prognosis had created a new set of problems. Not only did he fear that Ireland would be left out of the reconstruction of Europe, he feared for the future ideological make-up of Europe itself:

> Finally he spoke with obvious anxiety of the dangers now facing western civilisation from a mighty and triumphant Russia. In the manifesto issued by the National Committee of Free Germans in the U.S.S.R. he saw the first move towards the bolshevisation of Germany. After that what?[94]

Machtig read Maffey's lengthy report and refused to contemplate Walshe's accusations, saying, 'suspicions of our every action (or inaction) seem to grow like weeds in Walshe's mind.' The meeting had, however, provided a useful purpose. It had put Walshe somewhat at ease, and had cleared the air of suspicion for the time being. Machtig was anxious that all Walshe's questions be answered fully and as openly as possible.[95] While all the answers may not have been to Walshe's liking, this attitude was indicative of the frank communication between the British and Irish representatives.

In September 1943 Walshe met Hempel, who expressed an optimistic outlook for the outcome of the war. He felt that while Germany could not keep on fighting the combined Allied forces, he hoped that they would soon see that Russia was already a greater threat to their civilization, and would opt to throw in their lot with Germany to defeat the communists.[96] Considering what he had said to Maffey about his fear of Russia, this idea may not have been totally repugnant to Walshe. However, coinciding with Germany's diminishing war chances, Walshe's attitude towards Hempel continued to change. The following month, Hempel called on External Affairs to request confirmation or denial of information he had received that asserted that a number of British internees had been released subsequent to their transfer to Gormanstown. He was frankly informed that his information was correct and that the airmen had been released because it was deemed that the aircraft in which they had landed was not engaged

in operational duties at the time. Hempel objected strongly to the move and put his official position in a 'pro-memoria' handed to External Affairs in December 1943. He noted with dissatisfaction that a change had taken place in the original Irish position of interning all planes and crews. Hempel was neither consulted nor informed, but learned of the change somewhat by chance:

> The German Minister has only learnt gradually of the release of allied planes allegedly engaged on non-operational flights and only when he mentioned the matter at the Irish Department of External Affairs, was he informed of the new practice of the Irish Government.[97]

Hempel had good cause for complaint. The biased nature of internment was becoming more overt, and Walshe appeared unperturbed by Hempel's threats. The following month, when Hempel sought the release of a German plane and crew, the emphasis of the question had changed. Rather than the Irish government seeking to prove that the plane had been on an operational flight, as had been the case for Allied flights, it was now up to the German government to establish that it had been non-operational. The German minister was told that there was no evidence that the aircraft in question had been a training plane and therefore on a non-operational flight.[98] Walshe was quick to point out that the crew had destroyed the plane and that the explosion had indicated significant munitions – more than was needed for a training plane.[99] Britain, however, had been allowed more of a benefit of doubt, with planes known to be on operational missions given freedom, whereas Germany had no chance to prove its innocence in individual cases. Walshe told Hempel that the Department of External Affairs could not regard any German plane that landed on Irish territory as being on a training or non-operational flight.

Departmental records confirm the biased nature of Irish internment policy. Detailed accounts – compiled by the Irish military-intelligence agency, G2 – were kept of US, British and German aircraft and crews compelled to land on Irish territory during the war. From a chronological list of forced landings of belligerent aircraft, it can be seen that the Irish authorities practised selective internment that strongly favoured the release of

Allied aircraft and personnel. Of a total of 267 US aircrew forced to land on Irish territory from the beginning of the war up to 30 September 1944, nine were killed and the remaining 258 were released or allowed to escape. None were interned. Over the same period, 406 British airmen found themselves downed in Ireland. Of these, 109 were killed, 192 were released and forty-three interned. In contrast, of the eighty German crew members forced to land on Irish territory over the same period, some twenty-four were killed, one escaped, one was released and the remaining fifty-four were interned.[100] These figures, while they do not account exactly with the total number of airmen who landed, do outline the discrimination that was now obvious to both Hempel and Walshe. Adding further insult to Hempel was the decision in October 1943 to release another twenty British airmen who had been interned while on non-operational flights over Irish territory. While Maffey expressed the appreciation of the British government for this amnesty, he sought another change of policy by seeking the release of all those airmen remaining in captivity. He also suggested that the Irish authorities refrain from interning any future stranded British pilots. Walshe reported that Maffey had been rather arrogant about the matter, and had threatened that 'if we interned any American airmen, we might get a very "bloody" Note.' Walshe believed such a statement ungrateful and unnecessary, and replied that 'if we got a "bloody" Note, we'd send back a Note more "bloody" still.'[101] This was a clear warning to Walshe that diplomatic and political pressure on Irish neutrality from the Allies had not yet run its course.

CHAPTER 7

WALSHE AND THE AMERICAN NOTE
1944

ON 21 FEBRUARY 1944 Gray handed de Valera a communiqué entitled 'American demand for the expulsion of the Axis representatives in Ireland'.[1] This statement, often referred to as the 'American note', outlined that even though Irish policy was designed to be that of a 'friendly neutral', it had ended up as operating 'in favour of the Axis Powers against the United Nations on whom your security and the maintenance of your national economy depends'.[2] Gray initially proposed that the US government send a note to de Valera demanding Allied use of the ports. This approach was generally seen by Washington as being too severe.[3] Gray revised the note but felt a minimum demand should be to insist on the closure of the Axis offices in Dublin.

The origins of the American note can be seen as early as 1941. Maffey pointed out to Gray that the Germans were concentrating their attacks on convoys 'on a region which put the width of Ireland between them and English protective air bases'. Following these comments, Gray got the idea to send the Irish government a note about neutrality:

> As Dev had promised that Ireland would never be used as a base of attack against Britain was this not an infringement of the spirit of that promise. I got quite excited and said I thought he had something and that perhaps a note was in point.[4]

As we have already seen, Gray had sent numerous reports describing how a highly organised Axis agency enjoyed 'almost unrestricted opportunity for bringing military information from Britain ... into Ireland and from there transmitting it by various routes and

methods to Germany.'⁵ With continued Irish intransigence over the lending of the ports to the Allies, and the persistent refusal to compromise on the policy of neutrality, the US government considered coercing the Irish administration into compliance through economic means. One document described US policy as 'a refusal to allow any but the barest food essentials to be exported', thereby hoping to induce 'acute economic distress in Éire and force the de Valera government to abandon its neutrality policy'.⁶ While this belief had underpinned US policy towards Ireland, its reliability was called into question by certain sections of the US State Department. While the strategy of economic coercion succeeded in causing hardship, there was little evidence to show that the de Valera government was going to capitulate. One report from an American military attaché in Dublin stated that economic affliction would only serve to 'render a people susceptible to propaganda which promises to right all their grievances and endow their country with economic prosperity and political prosperity'.⁷ This was particularly true of the Irish, who 'have always turned to the enemies of England for help'. Thus, it was concluded that the current policy was turning the Irish away from the Allies and into the Axis camp. The report was sceptical about British motives, saying that the, 'British wanted us to appear more harsh to the Irish than they so that by contrast British treatment of Ireland would appear more considerate of Irish interests.'⁸ Ireland had been a traditional friend to the US in Europe, and the report warned that the British Foreign Office may have been 'once more practising its balance of power policy and attempting to divide two traditionally friendly powers for future post-war profit'. The report fell into the hands of Walshe, who was soon to receive a disclaimer through the Irish legation in Washington:

> I have been informed by the official who prepared the report that the report had been taken into consideration by the competent authorities … who made the criticism that he was incorrect in his assumption concerning American economic policy towards Ireland. There is no such policy; indeed no defined policy whatsoever; and there was no desire on the part of the United States authorities to penalise Ireland.⁹

Thus, while US authorities claimed the report had no official sanction, and stated that it did not reflect the official policy of the United States towards Ireland, it is not clear whether it was withdrawn due to inaccuracies or because of an excess of candour in certain aspects.

Clearly, there were differing opinions in the State Department concerning Irish policy. Gray confirmed many of the assertions of this report, and thereby contradicted the official denial that there was a policy of economic coercion towards Ireland. Like the author of the report, he too was not confident of British willingness to cooperate in the effort to maintain pressure on Ireland. He was suspicious of its attitude towards the sending of supplies to Ireland, believing that for economic reasons the British were being more benevolent than their stated policy and, therefore, making the United States seem more severe. His suspicions were strong enough for him to advise his government not to continue the current 'restricted supplies to Éire when British trade interests are procuring very generous allotments to Éire and refuse to let us know what they are'.[10] This recurring distrust towards Britain was an 'old cancer' that poisoned Anglo-American relations. However, his main fear at this time was that his proposed note to de Valera would be put in jeopardy by British intransigence.

Roosevelt was initially supportive of Gray's note, and he wrote to Secretary of State Cordell Hull: 'I think Mr Gray is right in his desire to put de Valera on record. We shall undoubtedly be turned down. I think the strongest fact is that we are losing many American and British lives and many ships in carrying various supplies to Ireland without receiving anything in return, and without so much as a 'Thank You'.'[11] Hull replied in agreement:

It appears to me that without question air and naval facilities in Ireland would be of considerable usefulness to the United Nations war effort. The Department has been informally advised by a high officer of the War Department that these facilities would be enormously useful from a military standpoint.[12]

This view was later contradicted by other military advice, but for the moment Hull felt that if the request were accepted then the US would have much-needed facilities, and if it were rejected then an official refusal would have been put on record. It appeared

to be a win-win situation, but it was based on misguided diplomatic guidance.

Following a general election in Ireland in 1943, Gray reported that while de Valera lost Dáil seats, he was able to remain in government, and that there was no popular repudiation of the policy of neutrality. Gray was not disappointed with the result but felt it right and proper that de Valera stay in power long enough to accept the responsibility for his wartime policies:

> From our point of view I think it desirable that he should continue in office if only to take the responsibility for the consequences of his misjudgment of the world situation and for his policies based on that misjudgment.[13]

Perhaps he was afraid that if Cosgrave came to power, he too would pursue the policy of neutrality, making de Valera appear less intransigent. Alternatively, if Cosgrave joined the war effort, then Ireland would get the best of both worlds, having earned part of the glory and having missed the greater part of the war. Gray wanted neither, and seemed more concerned with proving a point to de Valera than hoping for a change of policy. The continuation of the status quo would mean he could continue with his 'note'.

Soon, however, the whole basis for Gray's demands was nullified by the opinion of US army and navy advisers, who could see no substantial benefit in acquiring the Irish ports. The State Department adjusted its stance accordingly, and explained to the minister in Ireland:

> It may be stated at this point that the War and Navy Departments believe that it is not possible to visualize just now what military value might lie in having bases in Éire or if we actually would want to utilize such bases as the war progresses. It is their belief, however, that in making plans for our strategy of the war it would be desirable now to know whether we could rely on being able to use such bases should they be required.[14]

Gray would not have read with any satisfaction Hull's recommendation that the Irish government be approached on the matter with this watered-down version of his note. 'The War and Navy Departments feel that it is preferable to approach the Irish

Government in this manner rather in the manner outlined in the draft which was drawn up by you during your visit here.' This was a resounding rejection of Gray's proposals. Roosevelt saw the logic of the arguments put forward by his navy advisers, and approved a new message instead of Gray's version. 'It was the President's thought', explained Hull, 'that some parts of the former might possibly be incorporated in this new draft, but he has no strong views in that respect.'[15] Hull was attempting to explain in diplomatic language that the proposed message was too aggressive, that Roosevelt didn't support Gray's draft but would, if possible, like to appease his uncle by putting something of that draft into this new version. The Assistant Secretary of State, E. R. Stettinius, further outlined that following discussions between State Department officials and the Chiefs of Staff with a view to agreeing a new note, it was concluded that a more limited approach than that contemplated by Gray was desirable 'in view of their military estimate and of their desire to make no commitments of any kind at this time'.[16] Stettinius assured Roosevelt that Gray was kept fully informed of this decision, and that he had expressed his complete agreement with the new proposals towards Ireland.

Despite official acquiescence, Gray was furious with this decision. He replied to Hull saying that the revised approach 'leads us into a position where we get neither the promise of the desired facilities nor the record of a refusal'.[17] Furthermore, he felt the 'extremely mild phrasing' would mislead de Valera and Walshe into thinking that the demand was half-hearted. For him it was important to emphasise that the State Department regarded the Axis missions as an intrusion into what he considered a US defence zone.[18] He explained that while on his recent trip to the United States he had been told to write the draft of the note himself. He presented that version to Roosevelt and the visiting British Prime Minister, who approved the idea.[19] Happy with this level of endorsement, Gray returned to Dublin, and was pleased to hear that Maffey had been called to London to discuss the matter. Now, however, as he was side-stepped politically back home, he felt completely hard done by.

Meanwhile, Gray's relationship with Walshe found little cause for improvement. While Gray was in Washington and New York, the second secretary of the US legation and chargé d'affaires *ad*

interim, T. A. Hickok, had a minor altercation with Walshe. The source of the disagreement was Hickok's relationship with a Dr Wilson, a leading throat specialist in Dublin who had been involved the previous year in an attempt to assist the escape to Northern Ireland of interned British airmen who had abandoned their enclosure at the Curragh. Gray asked Walshe if he was satisfied that Hickok and the US legation were in no way compromised by the incident, to which Walshe replied that he was. However, soon after, it became clear that the matter had not been resolved:

> Early in May there were indications that Mr Walshe was disinclined to receive Mr Hickok officially and had unceremoniously cancelled a dinner invitation with the British Representative at which Walshe had learned that Mr Hickok was to be present.[20]

Walshe admitted that he was avoiding Hickok in public as he had affronted the Irish government by appearing publicly with the Wilsons at a party at which Irish military officers were present. Hickok wrote to Walshe in an effort to clear up any misunderstanding, and explained that no offence had been intended.[21] Walshe's argument was that as an official of the American legation Hickok's association with the offending Dr Wilson would be interpreted as approval for his action. He asked Hickok to imagine the fate of an Irish official in Washington who publicly consorted with a person in a similar position to that of Dr Wilson:

> We have recently heard that the State Department complained of an indiscretion in conversation of one of our officials in the United States. The accusation turned out to be without foundation. The example will serve to show you that a great country like yours attaches quite a lot of importance to the behaviour of foreign officials within its borders. A small country like Ireland must be at least as careful.[22]

Walshe was unbending on his requirement for diplomatic protocol, and would not be dissuaded that Hickok had not understood the need not to be publicly identified with Wilson. Hickok maintained that he had never knowingly flaunted his friendship with Wilson, but he regretted that the incident had marred their relationship, and in an effort to make amends he invited Walshe to lunch to discuss the matter and restore good feeling. Following

their luncheon, Hickok reported that 'everything was sweetness and light'. However, on being shown Walshe's correspondence on the matter, Maffey condemned it as 'stupid and ungentlemanly and indicative of Walshe's mentality'. He objected, in particular, to Walshe's description of the events as 'an act of defiance and hostility', and pointed out that it would be impossible for anyone in Washington to be in a position comparable to that of Wilson.[23] Maffey believed that Walshe had taken advantage of Gray's absence, and claimed Walshe's letter constituted a diplomatic affront. He asked Hickok for a copy of the correspondence to send to London as a means of indicating to his own superiors 'the mentality of the people with whom we have to deal'.

On his return to Dublin, Gray explained that Maffey's concern was partly due to his feeling responsible for Wilson and also because of his resentment for Walshe's attack, which he believed had been directed at him as much as at the American official.[24] Gray commended Hickok on his handling of the situation, and assured him that the matter was closed. Later that year, however, when faced with an order for staff reductions in Dublin, Gray recommended that Hickok should be the one to be relocated. He said that while Hickok had been unfairly treated by External Affairs, the resulting effect was 'detrimental to the cultivation of that mutual confidence and understanding which is desirable between the senior secretary of this Mission and the Irish Government'.[25] Hickok's career in the US legation in Dublin, therefore, was effectively finished by Walshe's intervention, and Gray saw the incident as further confirmation of Walshe's intransigence towards the American point of view.

When Gray learned that US military opinion was against his original note, which sought the removal of the German legation from Dublin as well as the use of the Treaty ports, he advised sending no note whatsoever rather than sending the revised version, which he saw as being inadequate. The military opposed Gray's note because it felt the ports were of limited value but also on the basis that de Valera might accept the offer contained within it, which provided substantial gain for the Irish government. Gray believed that this 'if and when' approach would lead to diplomatic defeat for the US government. He admitted that the army and navy's objection on the grounds that Ireland might acquiesce would be valid 'if there were any likelihood that our

proposal would be accepted'.[26] Gray completely ruled out this possibility, and admitted that the note was designed not as a genuine offer but rather as a means to another end. Seán Cronin has argued that the primary objective of Gray's note was not to prevent German espionage but rather to put 'de Valera on record in such a manner as would strengthen our defence against pressure group attempts to involve the United States in the partition question'.[27] This is borne out by the archival evidence. Gray saw no possibility of de Valera joining the war and giving the United States use of the ports. Yet, he was adamant that the proposal should go ahead:

> We must look forward to an indefinite period of bitter agitation over Partition and the main objective of our Irish policy should be to protect the Anglo-American relation from the menace of Éire inspired anti-British pressure in the United States.[28]

Gray believed that de Valera and Britain were on a collision course over partition, and that this could have domestic repercussions for Roosevelt through a 'long range war policy' in which he visualised the Irish diaspora in America being mobilised in an effort to mount pressure on US administrators to become involved in partition.[29] With this in mind, the specific aims of the note were thus outlined:

> To spread the truth about Éire and her obligations to Britain and to the United Nations on the record and let the world know that de Valera is biting the hand that feeds him; that is to say, discredit him and his group in America and put the Fenians on the defensive.[30]

The note was designed, therefore, to negate any justification for the Irish to seek their help in trying to solve partition after the war.

It is significant that contact between Gray and Walshe was minimal during this period. Gray could not be stopped, and Walshe thought it impossible to convince him that the Irish authorities had the security situation under control. As we have seen, the German legation in Dublin was not the real motive behind the note, and Walshe would have guessed that it was only a pretext on which to make demands on the Irish government.

Despite his objections to the sending of a watered-down message, however, Gray continued with the plan. In November 1943, anxious to get the delivery of the note under way, he reported that the British were stalling: 'Why the British have held up action on your Irish note all this time I have not been able to find out. Sir John Maffey says he does not know and I think if he did he would give me a hint at least.'[31]

Gray felt Ireland was now a soft target for his demands due to the precarious economic situation in the country:

Éire is in the position of begging for crumbs from the United Nations and bringing in a few odd lots through Spain and Portugal … Éire's dependence on the outside world is standing out more and more clearly as her trade position is more closely examined in spite of her attempts to avoid admitting that dependence.[32]

In a letter to the Secretary of State in December 1943, Gray sent further testimony that the Axis representatives in Dublin were a menace to Allied military security. He referred to the presence of a wireless transmitter in the German legation and also made reference to the presence of the IRA, who had declared war against the USA and Britain and were, allegedly, still rampant despite many of them having been interned: 'They are in the civil service, in the army, and everywhere in civil life.'[33] In both of these cases, however, the Irish government had acted in an exemplary fashion, and had cooperated with US and British intelligence. Walshe had sought to impress this view on Gray, but without success. Clearly, at this stage Gray would not rule out any level of exaggeration if he thought it would gain support for his impending diplomatic assault.

Gray's suspicions at this time about Britain's reluctance towards the planned demands on de Valera were correct. Maffey was indeed reticent about the initial proposal, and in August 1943 he wrote to the Dominions Office concerning the idea that the United States would request to lease one or two of the Irish ports. Maffey understood that this was not based on 'paramount need' but on the desirability of 'making the record right'. He had serious reservations as to the wisdom of this course of action:

A straight refusal by Mr de Valera would certainly simplify matters. But we cannot count on that. He is sufficiently astute to put forward general queries in regard to heavy preparatory defensive

arming of Éire forces, arguments regarding Partition, confusing the issue and getting the best of both worlds whatever happens.[34]

Maffey did not underestimate de Valera's coyness, and believed that some other, more satisfactory, formula could be found that would serve the same purpose. His worry was that the suggested approach could backfire, and he was apprehensive that Gray would convince the State Department to proceed without Britain's agreement. Gray reasoned that the British were slow to approve the demarché on the basis that 'having got along without the Irish thus far [they] do not want to have us put De Valera in the position of claiming post war consideration by giving us facilities at this late date.' He personally could not understand this view, and believed the Allied request for the expulsion of the Axis legation implied no reward; rather, he regarded it as the 'remedying of a long standing wrong'.[35] There were no reasons for British fears as he was certain that de Valera would refuse the request, and this was the most important facet of the approach.

When it was finally delivered, the primary demand of the American note itself was couched in diplomatic terms, though direct nonetheless:

> We should be lacking in candour if we did not state our hope that this action will take the form of severance of all diplomatic relations between Ireland and … [Germany and Japan].[36]

One of the primary demands in the note was the request for the Irish government to remove the Axis legations based in Dublin. Gray related that as de Valera was reading the document his immediate response was to reject it, saying, 'Of course our answer will be no; as long as I am here it will be no.'[37] He needed no time to consult Walshe and his other advisers. The following day Maffey issued British concurrence and support for the American initiative. De Valera saw the demand as an ultimatum, despite assurances that the US had no intention of invading Ireland if a negative response was received. Brennan voiced similar concerns in Washington, and Walshe requested confirmation of the oral assurances Gray had given de Valera a few days previously. It was, perhaps, part of their policy to dramatise the most belligerent aspects of the note. Gray, conscious of his previous

misunderstandings with Walshe, was at pains to reassure them
that the guarantees he had given were the same as those he had
been instructed to impart by the State Department:

> I then told you that in order that there might be no variation
> between my instructions and the assurances I was about to give
> you I would read you the paraphrase of that portion of the tel-
> egram which set forth the nature of the assurances.[38]

Gray, already terrified of being put on the back foot, repeated
that if the Irish government did not accede to the US request
there would be no military repercussions. His method of persuasion was to attempt to transfer to the Irish government 'moral
responsibility' for any consequences such as the loss of US soldiers caused by the transfer of Axis information through Ireland,
and said that 'if American lives were lost in this way American
mothers and the American press would most probably conduct
just such a campaign of publicity against Éire as you and I would
least desire.'[39]

Walshe helped draft the initial reply to the note. While
expressing appreciation for the assurance of no military repercussions, the inherent anger at Gray's role in the breakdown in
communications between the US and the Irish government is
explicit:

> [The Irish government] doubted that such a Note could have been
> presented had the American Government been fully aware of the
> uniformly friendly character of Irish neutrality in relation to the
> United States and of the measures which had been taken by the
> Irish Government, within the limits of their power, to safeguard
> American interests.[40]

It pointed out that to remove the Axis representatives would be
the first step towards participation in the war. This step was therefore impossible, as the policy of neutrality represented 'the united
will of People and Parliament'. The note was soon to become
public, and each side selectively published correspondence. Gray
told Maffey that in view of the information that had already
leaked out, the State Department had decided to publish the
exchange of notes between them and the Irish government. The
Dominions Office followed suit, deciding to publish their note

with Maffey's covering letter and also de Valera's letter of reply. Maffey was instructed to warn Walshe that these publications were going to take place.[41] Walshe was aware that Maffey and Gray were trying to blame the leaking of the note on the Irish government, but he was ready to rebut that accusation, citing as proof the fact that the 'B.B.C. made the first positive announcement in London at 6 o'c on March 10th, almost simultaneously with Hull's statement in Washington.' He suspected that the leaking of the story was connected with some greater scheme to apply further pressure on Ireland, and referred to the recent Churchill demarché:

> One fact was absolutely certain – our Censorship was not given the chance of stopping the story. In any case, the campaign against us in Britain and America, and the provocative tone of Churchill's speech, could not be explained away without some prior intention to let the cat out of the bag.[42]

At this stage the note was already beginning to lose its potency. Maffey reported that the Irish newspapers were commenting on the travel ban imposed by Britain, giving it a punitive background and putting it in the same context as economic sanctions. This was a disastrous line for Britain, thought Maffey, who warned that it should be made clear that any such restrictions should be treated as being derived from the increased risks due to retention in the war zone of the Axis Dublin representatives.[43]

On 14 March 1944 Walshe met with Maffey. The degree of tension was not as high as it might have been. Maffey urged calm and restraint, and assured Walshe that there would be no sanctions imposed on Ireland. Walshe, however, had been given good reason for concern. The previous day, Churchill announced the cessation of travel and trade between Ireland and the UK for 'military reasons'. Walshe maintained that Churchill's statement would 'envenom British public opinion' against Ireland, but he was assuaged by Maffey's unofficial assurances that no sanctions would be imposed. Walshe thanked Maffey, saying the Irish government was 'very grateful' to him for the work he had done in helping to maintain good relations between the two countries.[44] With the US channel closed, Walshe did not wish to do anything to alienate Maffey at this time. The following day, Walshe again raised his concern at the deterioration in Anglo-Irish relations caused by the

'sharp tone' of Churchill's statement in the House of Commons and by the widespread indications in the British press of a punitive economic policy. Maffey admitted that the Irish government had been more than helpful during the course of the war, based on a 'friendly interpretation of neutrality', but told Walshe that they could never dispose of two basic grievances. Firstly, 'the denial of the use of the Ports had caused us heavy losses at sea', and secondly, the Axis legation 'remained a grave source of danger' to Britain.[45] However, having said all this, Maffey insisted that the current restrictions were necessary for military reasons and had nothing to do with political or economic sanctions. Certain shortages or hardships might come about because of the measures, but again this was a side effect rather than an objective.

Walshe pointed to some of the coverage in the British and American newspapers, and Maffey was forced to admit that many of them carried stories that were far from the truth. He told Walshe that the Irish government was lucky to have an effective censorship that it could now use to control public opinion towards Britain. He would later complain that the head censor was anti-British, but for the moment an effective censorship was favourable if it could serve interests beneficial to Britain. As there had been rumours of closing the northern border and of stopping the migration of Irish labour to the UK, he warned Walshe that Ireland should take no measures that would appear to be in retaliation. Admitting that such sanctions might be imposed, Walshe said that they had felt compelled to do this until it became clear what action Britain proposed to take. If economic sanctions were imposed, as had been suggested by Churchill, then all able-bodied men would be needed in Ireland for agricultural and industrial work.[46] Sensing Walshe's urgency, Maffey pushed for immediate action from London. He saw no need for relations with Ireland to sour over the issue, and he reported to his superiors that there was no pro-German feeling in Ireland. He understood there was resentment over Churchill's statement as its inherent economic threat was regarded as 'bullying'. However, he maintained that public opinion was generally favourable towards Britain, and that when it became clear that any moves were based on military necessity, the Irish would accept them with 'reasonable calm', and would be sure to continue the cooperation that already existed.

The following day, Walshe met both Gray and Maffey at

separate times. His talk with the US minister was marked with
tension. The recent events created a major crisis in Irish–US relations. It would have been normal for the two to have met soon after
the presentation of the note to clarify and discuss the issues. Yet,
Walshe gives his meeting with Gray a coincidental air, saying that
on arrival for lunch at the US legation 'I was placed next to David
Gray and it was inevitable that he should talk about the situation.'
He described Gray as being 'perturbed at the hornet's nest which
he has stirred up'. The exchange was marked by a lack of frankness
and Walshe's comments could hardly be seen as constructive:

> I said quite frankly that there was a lot of the 'big bully' about the
> end of it, and Gray immediately said 'That is the part I had noth-
> ing to do with.'[47]

The conversation retraced old ground, and Walshe asked Gray
why 'he always seemed to be able to turn mere possibilities into
positive facts'. Walshe personally blamed Gray's misconduct for
the ill-feeling generated by the American note:

> He misinformed his Government with regard to Irish policy and
> conditions in this country, and was thereby primarily responsi-
> ble for what might have been a serious rupture in the relations
> between Ireland and the United States.[48]

At the same luncheon, Walshe spoke with Maffey and reasserted
his objections to the state of suspense the Irish government had
been left in. Maffey assumed a placatory role, smoothing over the
turbulence created by recent events. Walshe reported that 'Maffey
completely agreed with me', and that the 'situation from his point
of view was most unsatisfactory ... He was ready again to give
every possible assurance, but he could understand that was not
enough in such a serious situation.'[49] Following this, Maffey wrote
to his superiors, again pressing for some action that would clarify
the Irish labour situation. Walshe had told him that there was a
labour pool of over a thousand men already holding permits and
assembled in Dublin ready to sail. Considering the present tension, Walshe felt that the Irish government could hardly encourage
them to go. Churchill had stated that the restrictions imposed
on travel were the first step towards isolating Great Britain from
Ireland. Walshe sought assurances that no specifically punitive

measures were being contemplated. Maffey was sympathetic to Walshe's position, and reaffirmed to his superiors that the Irish authorities would not only continue in their cooperation with Britain but would greatly increase it. He warned that:

> Unless scope of measures is defined, the Éire Government will be in genuine difficulties on this point. Walshe further offers on behalf of the Éire Government all cooperation possible to the British Government in any plans designed to effect closer control of axis activities.[50]

These recent moves had caused Walshe considerable anxiety. He feared that as the Allies looked more and more certain of victory, Irish cooperation would be played down. While Gray may have wanted the American note to prevent a strong anti-partition lobby in the US after the war, Walshe may have seen the demand as an attempt to rule Ireland out of any postwar negotiations.

Gray, at this point, was of the opinion that the note had been a success as far as the long-range primary objective was concerned, as he believed de Valera would have little chance of making trouble over partition. He reported that Irish officials were taken aback that such a note was contemplated despite the Irish-American lobby.[51] He repeated the message to John Winant of the US embassy in London, suggesting that following the presentation of the note: 'We are in a very good position for both short and long range if we don't spoil it. As long as we keep the record clear I do not think Mr De Valera can make much or serious trouble in America for Anglo-American relations over the Partition question during the post-war period.' However, he was not completely satisfied with the Irish reply, and became suspicious of Walshe's tactics, referring to what he described as 'Walshe's proposals'. Here, Gray may have been referring to an invitation by Walshe to US security officials to come to Dublin for a conference to discuss security matters:

> I trust you will inform me as to the British view of another note to Éire. I am anxious to have De Valera's reply answered for the American public but think it unwise to send another note to De Valera. I fear it would be playing into his hands. I know that you saw through Joe Walshe's move and trust that you agree with my recommendation contained in the telegram referred to.[52]

British reaction to Gray's suggestion for a follow-up message
to de Valera was not favourable. In a letter to Churchill, Lord
Cranborne related the view that Gray appeared to be suffering
from a bad attack of cold feet. He had learned that Gray had
sought State Department authorisation to announce that the
United States had no intention of instituting military or economic reprisals against Ireland. To demonstrate the sincerity of this
statement, Gray further sought the release of certain supplies that
had hitherto been denied to Ireland. While the British and the
United States both wanted to exert a certain amount of pressure
on Ireland, neither wanted to shoulder the blame alone. Cranborne
did not look kindly on what he saw as Gray's attempt to shift the
bulk of the blame to Britain:

> I cannot imagine any action less likely to ease the present situation.
> It would make the United States' Government look remarkably
> silly, and it would put us, who have loyally supported them, in the
> position of acute embarrassment.

This was all the more important in view of Churchill's statement
that Ireland would have to be isolated from the rest of the world:

> If, at the moment when we impose these restrictions, the United
> States Government makes a public announcement that they do
> not intend to indulge in economic reprisals, there would be many,
> both in Southern Ireland and outside, who will get the impression
> that we are taking advantage of the American note to squeeze the
> Irish Government.[53]

Cranborne sensed the negative mood in Ireland, and he cautioned
Churchill that their measures could be interpreted as an attempt
by the British government to bring pressure on de Valera. Gray's
suggestion was therefore regarded as extraordinarily inopportune
from Britain's point of view.

Walshe continued to probe Maffey on the threat of sanctions,
but both he and Maffey admitted that the American note was
receding into the background. Walshe still feared, however, that
Ireland would be isolated economically and politically, and felt
that the explanation that certain restrictions were necessary due
to impending operations was only an excuse to mask sanctions.[54]
He was not convinced by Maffey's assurances, who replied saying

that he personally felt sure there would be no undue negative economic measures imposed. He caused Walshe some further anxiety by hedging the question with vague replies and by eventually saying that the possibility could not be ruled out completely. Walshe was further alarmed when it seemed to him that Maffey was preparing the way for British sanctions on Ireland to be camouflaged under the guise of military measures. He was completely dissatisfied with this situation and with Churchill's speech, which he described as being of an 'extremely ungracious character'. John Kearney, the Canadian High Commissioner in Dublin, told Walshe that Churchill had made the comments 'tongue in cheek' and that they would be taken in context by those who knew. Walshe disagreed with this sentiment:

> How many people, even amongst the very best informed, would know that his tongue was in that position? It was a most unscrupulous and a most damaging speech.[55]

Walshe was ill at ease, and Maffey realised that he had no means by which to reduce this anxiety. He wrote again to his superiors, admitting that he had not been able to calm Walshe and that the air was full of doubt and suspicion. He relayed what Walshe had told him on a number of occasions – that the Irish government was willing to cooperate in any restrictions deemed necessary for military purposes provided that it knew the nature of the restrictions.[56] Walshe felt the British were getting away with a certain duplicity over the restrictions, emphasising their punitive or non-punitive aspect according to what suited them at the time, and he therefore called for Cranborne to make a definite statement that no sanctions would be taken against Ireland. He was not willing to let the British authorities criticise the Churchill speech in private while at the same time allowing such statements to go ahead with their tacit approval:

> The mere one-sided announcement of the measures, whatever the Dominions Office might say, was enough in itself to give them a strong flavour of sanctions. The British always wanted it both ways. Now, apparently, they wanted us to believe that Churchill's speech was or was not a sanctions speech according as it suited their particular needs.[57]

Walshe insisted that the pool of Irish workers ready and waiting to travel to Britain were necessarily restricted until the Irish government had a better idea as to the measures Britain meant to take against Ireland. He was deliberately uncompromising on this issue, and intended to force the British to give some indication one way or another regarding the sanctions. Maffey had indicated to him that the 'restrictions' might easily turn into 'sanctions', especially in relation to shipping. Based on this, Walshe went so far as to warn de Valera that unless a statement to the contrary was received, it was better to assume that a substantial percentage of shipping carrying Anglo-Irish trade would be withdrawn.

Afraid that any subtle reservations on his part would be picked up on, Maffey wanted to avoid Walshe until he had received further and more definite instructions from London. Maffey reckoned they could count on continued Irish cooperation, and pressed his authorities for some clarification, especially with regard to the labour question. It was 'undeniably a matter of practical concern to them calling for a decision', argued Maffey, who pointed out that any clarifying statement need apply only to the present situation and would not cover later unforeseen contingencies. It was a small price to pay, he believed, because, in his opinion, 'a small bridge would do a great deal'.[58] He felt sure that Britain's Foreign Secretary, Anthony Eden, at least, appreciated the need for treating Ireland fairly. However, a couple of days later the issue was in danger of escalating when the Irish government decided to close down recruitment of Irish labour for the United Kingdom. Maffey attempted to convey the view that this action would not cause any serious inconvenience to the United Kingdom, and Walshe was keen to express the view that the action was in no way retaliatory:

> Step has not been taken in any combative spirit, but because departure of able bodied men must be avoided in view of unknown scope of our restrictive measures. For instance, cutting of turf in Éire may be vital to economic life of the country.[59]

Walshe believed that the Irish move reflected a position that the British government had allowed to develop. He was now more convinced than ever that economic sanctions were a certainty.

Walshe's worst fears were fortunately not realised, and at the

end of the month Maffey was able to convey more positive news
to de Valera. Having waited 'under the sword of Damocles' for so
long, he reported that both de Valera and Walshe showed 'great
relief' when they were informed of British intentions, which
included giving Ireland the opportunity to cooperate 'in measures
designed to serve the needs of our Military security'. De Valera
was equally conciliatory, and said that Anglo-Irish relations had
suffered but that he now looked forward to re-establishing goodwill. By Maffey's account, de Valera wanted to help Britain to the
utmost, but this was not always easy, and while Britain's precau-
tions would cause great difficulties, Ireland would 'readily bear
any necessary hardship in a spirit well disposed to our cause'.[60]
The Taoiseach also used this meeting with Maffey to register his
resentment towards the American note, especially in the light of
their mutual cooperation. He believed that joint security efforts
had meant that the German legation had been given little chance
to damage Britain. Maffey replied that history would prove that the
Allied request had been fully justified. While sceptical that the note
would bear any real fruit, Maffey now began to change his view.
Whether it was due to the American note or not, it now appeared
to him that there was a sea change in opinion in Dublin:

> Later I also went over the ground with Walshe, who expressed
> appreciation of the consideration now shown to Éire suscepti-
> bilities. It is clear that no question would be raised regarding the
> continuance of our air service.

This was further confirmed for Maffey from the advanced levels
of cooperation now being touted by Walshe who, along with Seán
Leydon, planned to travel to London with Maffey in the following days to initiate dialogue and further contact with British
officials. Walshe was anxious to re-establish good relations with
Britain, and he may have been somewhat overeager in his expression of this attitude to Maffey:

> Walshe asks as a great favour that conversations between Leydon
> and Departments concerned should if possible take place at the
> D.O. not in technical department atmosphere. I said that I would
> pass this on, but could guarantee nothing, as departments are very
> busy.[61]

Maffey also expressed the hope that the Secretary of State would make time to meet with Walshe directly as he believed he was in a pliable mood, saying, 'he will find him most anxious to do everything possible.'

This Irish delegation travelled to London with the main aim of finding out what restrictions were to be placed on Ireland, but it was clear from the outset that some tough bargaining would have to be done. They learned, for example, from John Stephenson, assistant secretary at the Dominions Office, that shipping to Ireland was to be greatly reduced; coal, in particular, was to be cut by a massive 50 per cent.[62] Walshe spoke of the isolation of Ireland, and he highlighted his resentment at the lack of a proper explanation for the interruption of the Aer Lingus service between Dublin and London. He repeated his suspicion that the British wished to give the appearance of sanctions, and he reported the following to de Valera:

> Although it is very difficult to be very definite about their purpose, the British, without actually imposing sanctions, would like to be able, if the occasion arose, to give the impression that they had done so.[63]

When Walshe met Cranborne, he spoke of the harshness of the American note and of Churchill's speech, believing they were unjust in view of the past years of friendship and cooperation. He even made the case that if Britain maintained a colony in the United States – Virginia or Massachusetts for example – the United States would have taken a very different attitude towards the war. Walshe feared that the 'sanctions' were a reaction to the increasing attitude that, in the postwar world, Ireland should be punished for refusing to enter the war. To remedy this he proposed that a new era in Anglo-Irish relations be inaugurated, and suggested that Irish unity be established so that 'the regularisation of good relations between Britain and Ireland' could be established. Walshe added that, so long as partition remained, 'the abnormality of that factor would affect all our relations.' He conveyed to Cranborne de Valera's hope that Britain would 'see Ireland in its proper perspective' when it came to appraise the postwar situation. Walshe clearly saw Ireland playing its part in building a new world society, and indicated that Cranborne had been receptive to his comments:

They wanted Ireland to be friendly, as we did, and the need for closer collaboration in the world we had all to face after the war required a completely new outlook.

Walshe did not hesitate when Cranborne gave him the opportunity to express his ideas on the subject of Ireland's place in the postwar world:

> He gave me an opportunity of talking about British subjectship and the desirability of eliminating the elements of British supremacy from any future groupings of which Ireland and Britain might happen to be members.[64]

While he sought the removal of partition and the independence of Ireland, he maintained the view that Ireland could benefit from continued membership of the Commonwealth. While Walshe remained optimistic – at least for the sake of these conversations – his British counterparts were not quite so sanguine about the establishment of a new balance of power. He reported that they were depressed by the prospect of Russia playing a dominant role in Europe, and thought that this would benefit Ireland, saying, 'this aspect of the situation rather inclined them to be somewhat more friendly with us.' They gave Walshe great satisfaction by criticising Churchill's handling of the international situation, and also by expressing their recognition and appreciation for the part played by the Irish authorities in maintaining intelligence integrity in favour of Britain. From Walshe's point of view, these talks were a success in re-establishing good relations with Whitehall. In truth, little else was achieved apart from giving Walshe the chance to increase Ireland's standing in the eyes of Britain.

When Walshe was given the opportunity to discuss intelligence and security matters with two US security officials, he used it to prove Ireland's willingness to cooperate. The two security chiefs – referred to as 'Mr X. and his colleague'– are named as Hugh Wilson, US ambassador to Germany at the outbreak of the war and Colonel Fagan, deputy to Colonel Bruce.[65] In this meeting, Walshe was critical of Gray, and Wilson agreed that in order to preserve Ireland's friendship with the US, a new channel of communication would have to be established. Walshe displayed his desire that Ireland should not be denied its place in

the postwar society, and he expressed the readiness of the Irish government to be 'even more helpful in the sphere of intelligence during the critical months ahead'. This could be facilitated by the appointment of some suitable agent in Dublin over which Gray should have no control. Walshe was greatly impressed by Wilson, and felt that a new era in Irish–American relations would ensue:

> He left me with the impression that he regarded the final settlement of the Irish problem as a vital factor in the future relations of the English-speaking peoples of the world. He has a very high esteem for the organisation and influence of the Catholic Church.[66]

Walshe said he had rarely met someone with such a 'balanced objective out-look of the world of the future'. This was not surprising considering the extent to which they appeared to be in agreement.

This continued contact between Walshe and US security officials in the aftermath of the American note caused Gray much annoyance. Marlin had continued to insist that the Irish authorities had German activities under control, and Gray therefore sought to have his involvement in Irish affairs permanently terminated. Gray had heard from a local British consular and security agent, Captain Collinson, that Marlin on his most recent visit to Ireland had said that he was 'perfectly satisfied' that the Irish had every point adequately covered.[67] That Gray was receiving these reports about Marlin from British officials was a source of great embarrassment to him:

> The British Visa and Security Officer here lunched with me today and I find that he has the same view of Marlin that I have and that Marlin expressed to him the same fatuous confidence in the complete efficacy of the Irish Intelligence that he did to me.[68]

Gray levied the charge that Marlin had done the United States great harm in Ireland, and for that reason thought he should be removed from London and taken 'out of the picture'. If Marlin could be moved far enough away, then Gray would make no further investigation into the matter:

If he moves this fellow out to Chungking or beyond without
objection, I would say it was best to let the whole matter drop. I
feel strongly though that Marlin is a danger as long as he is in his
present position.[69]

Gray admitted that he had a personal dislike for Marlin but
insisted that recent events had convinced him that Marlin was
'too coloured with the Irish viewpoint [to] effectively ... serve
American interests in such a crisis as still exists'. With Marlin out
of the way, Gray's assessment of the security situation in Ireland
would be left unchallenged. Gray spoke of when Marlin first arrived
in Ireland: 'Very soon he made me feel uneasy. He was persistent
in his efforts to inject himself into situations which were not his
affair and to undertake activities which we had not contemplated.'
Gray found Marlin to be 'ingeniously evasive' and 'extremely difficult to pin down', and finally, when Marlin refused to disclose
the source of some 'unimportant information', Gray asked for his
removal.[70] Their major differences, however, originated when
Marlin appeared to establish good relations with Walshe:

> Shortly after he left, the Permanent Secretary for External Affairs,
> Mr Joseph Walshe, spoke very highly of him to me and I find that
> he spoke in the same terms to Sir John Maffey, a circumstance which
> should have put me on my guard.

Such a recommendation of approval from Walshe confirmed the
demise of the OSS official. Soon after the presentation of the
American note, Marlin again saw Gray:

> He [Marlin] said that he had been conferring with Mr Walshe and
> that Walshe was willing to continue cooperating with us. As the
> British Representative and I had never any doubt about the con-
> tinued and more energetic cooperation of the Éire Government
> after the delivery of the note, I failed to grasp the meaning that
> he evidently meant to convey, namely, that he had negotiated this
> cooperation from an unwilling Irish Government.[71]

Gray referred to a proposal by Walshe to cooperate by means
of a security conference to be held in Dublin. The Secretary of
State said that the proposal could be accepted but that it had
to be made clear that this did not nullify the demands made

in the note. Gray, however, was highly suspicious of Walshe's motives:

> I then pointed out that Mr Walshe's approach was evidently a device to manoeuvre the Department of State into accepting a substitute for the dismissal of the representations and thus nullify the effect of the Irish Government's refusal of our request. The implication that Walshe already had an understanding with Marlin and was trying to score against the Department of State is strong. Otherwise Walshe would have followed the usual diplomatic practice of taking the matter up either with this Legation or through the Irish Minister in Washington.[72]

For Gray, conclusive evidence of Walshe's scheming was that before any definite assurance regarding the proposed security conference had been given, Walshe had asked Brennan in Washington to seek an announcement by the President to say that the Irish government was cooperating with the United States government for security reasons. The request was refused by the US government, which did not wish to 'waive the refusal of the Irish Government to our request regarding Axis representations'. Walshe may have received some unofficial assurances that such an invitation would be welcome, and Gray felt that Walshe would not have instructed Brennan in this regard had he not received some assurances that the request would be acceded to. He surmised, therefore, that it was Marlin who had encouraged the idea.

Gray was correct in suspecting that Walshe was using Marlin as his primary means of communication with the US at this time. He had in fact met Marlin and discussed the possibility of a security conference in an effort to subvert what he saw as Gray's misinformation to the State Department. Walshe had got wind of Gray's plan to send a further note to the Irish government, and he told the US security official that in a recent article in the *New York Herald Tribune* it was stated that government officials were 'documenting a vigorous reply to Mr de Valera with evidence supporting American belief that he is not really master in his own household'. Walshe was worried that the information they had shared in cooperation with Marlin would now be used to 'document' a case against his government. In his description of these

apprehensions, Walshe describes the level of trust built between
them in the course of this cooperation:

> I said that, if any information which we gave to him in confi-
> dence, as part of our secret arrangement for securing the safety
> of American interests in this country, were used for the purpose
> of trumping up a case against us, there would be a catastrophic
> breach, not only in the friendly relationship between our two
> Intelligence Services, but also in the wide relations between the
> two Governments which naturally required a considerable degree
> of trust in each other.[73]

Marlin told Walshe that his honour would oblige him to resign
if these fears proved correct, but he was clearly apprehensive that
Irish–US relations could be damaged further.

Walshe had for some time suspected a divergence of opinion
in Washington over Irish policy. He had long expressed the view,
for example, that the American note was a shock considering the
ongoing cooperative efforts between the two governments. He was
further perplexed by the move in view of Marlin's estimation that the
methods used by the Irish authorities in combating Axis espionage
activity were 'effective and fully satisfactory'. If there had been security
deficiencies, then he could not understand how the US government
had made no effort to make any suggestions as to how any such
loopholes could have been closed. Walshe had therefore come to the
conclusion that the American note was an entirely political move.
Marlin was able to throw some light on what had gone wrong, and
he shocked Walshe by telling him that the State Department may not
have contacted the Intelligence Department to validate Gray's reports
of espionage activity in Ireland, that there was a great deal of confusion between departments, and 'nobody had enough control to see the
whole picture.' Walshe derived some satisfaction in hearing this:

> I expressed the view that – since, after all, if we in our very small
> Department could maintain the closest liaison with our Intelligence
> Services – surely a great Department like the Department of State
> would not fail to maintain the closest contact with all the information
> coming from the intelligence side.

Walshe, whose experience had taught him 'the absolute need for
secrecy', clearly took some satisfaction in being able to reproach

Marlin in this way. It gave him an interesting insight into how and why the American note came to be, despite the cooperation they had undertaken. Ultimately, it all came down to inadequate communication and the misinformation passed on by the State Department's Dublin representative:

> I spoke to him about David Gray and the petty charges which he was now making about the supposed existence of a wireless which conveyed even the speeches of Bishops to Haw-Haw. And I reminded him of the great reluctance with which David allowed him to remain in Ireland and to have any separate contacts with us. I reminded him also of Col. Bruce's remark that we should not take any notice of Gray's idiosyncrasies in this matter.[74]

Marlin planned to go to London to discuss these matters with his superior, Colonel Bruce. Walshe's suggestion that they establish closer contacts by holding a 'friendly conference' was seen as the best way of 'forestalling Intelligence difficulties in relation to the Second Front'. Marlin reported back to Walshe, saying he had seen Gray who expressed the hope that the whole controversy would die down. Marlin believed that Gray was the source of the misunderstanding between the United States and Ireland, and he suggested to Walshe that the Irish government publish these 'calumnies' and immediately refute them. Thus, Gray would be forced to send these reports to the State Department, which would be unlikely to allow Gray to remain in Dublin for much longer following the unsuccessful attempt to have the Axis legation removed. Marlin felt that despite Gray's assurances to the contrary it was still a possibility that the State Department was considering another note to the Irish government. He hoped this was not the case, and he gave a personal assurance to Walshe that he would do his best to prevent it.

Marlin was not sent to distant foreign climes, as Gray had advocated, but he was prevented from returning to Ireland in June of that year due to what was described as a 'misunderstanding' with Gray.[75] His work was not abandoned, however, and two other security-service officials, Hubert Will and Ed Lalor, came to support the security cooperation inaugurated by Marlin. This was hardly a vote of confidence in Gray, and Walshe was keen to stress to the visitors the positive impact of Marlin's work:

> But for his patriotism in the interests of America and his complete understanding of this country, the liaison between our Security officials would never have been established … Mr Marlin and I came to the conclusion that a lot of doubts and difficulties between our two countries could be effectively removed by the establishment between our Security services of a free, easy and friendly intercourse.[76]

In a subsequent letter, Walshe thanked Marlin for helping to mend relations 'at a point where misunderstanding seemed likely to go on increasing', and assured him that the 'good work' would continue through Lalor and Will. It is important to note that the friction between Walshe and Gray was not solely based on a difference of opinion or a clash of ideals on the neutrality issue. Walshe was very well disposed to Spike Marlin, but they had clear differences: 'I know you always held tenaciously, and strongly expressed the view, that we were wrong to be neutral.'[77] Despite their disagreements, Walshe regarded him as a friend and an ally with whom he could work for greater cooperation and mutual benefit.

It is true to say that Gray did little to improve Irish–US relations during this time. He believed that continued pressure on Ireland was crucial if the American note was to get the reply it deserved. He believed de Valera misrepresented the note to the Irish public for political ends, but gained some satisfaction by predicting that this would backfire on the Taoiseach when they realised that they had been duped: 'It is a very ignorant electorate but it cannot be continuously misled.'[78] As proof of this, he relayed the story of how the Irish Defence Council was in session the night following the presentation of the note. It was in the process of making plans to repel an Anglo-American invasion, which they were led to believe must follow the rejection of the American demand:

> The telephone rang and it proved to be the British Military attache who had not been told of the note enquiring where the Irish Army would take delivery of five hundred motorbicycles which had been procured for them. It naturally rocked the meeting. The Opposition while standing by neutrality are getting ready to attack this misrepresentation of our request and the gratuitous hostility which De Valera has stirred up against us.[79]

That situation was to some extent comical, but Gray seemed to miss the point that despite the note Anglo-Irish relations would remain on a cooperative footing. Indeed, Gray seemed unable or unwilling to put his diplomatic relations in Dublin back on an even keel. To the contrary, the continued cooperation between Maffey and Walshe was another source of resentment for Gray, who would become increasingly suspicious of British motives.

When de Valera announced in the Dáil that aircraft landing in the course of operational missions would be interned, Gray called on Maffey to discuss the matter. He was of the opinion that the Irish authorities would be reluctant to intern any US aircraft and personnel but was worried by the statement. Maffey gave Gray the following analysis of the internment situation: 'Since Éire is geographically within our defense area, the impartial treatment of Axis and Allied airmen is in fact not neutral but pro-Axis.' Gray was sceptical of Maffey's hardline stance:

> For reasons which I have never been able clearly to understand, the British even after we came into the war suppressed or minimalized publicity as to their airmen interned in Éire. Correspondents were kept away. When we began discussing the question with the Éire Government, I made it clear to Mr Walshe that in the case American airmen were interned I could never take the responsibility of preventing American correspondents from interviewing them as the British did and that he could judge as to the effect of such publicity on Irish–American relations as well as I could. In my opinion, this rather than any diplomatic representations has been the chief factor in our success in keeping our men out of the wire cage. Maffey now appreciates that it was the useful line for us to take, though he is now debarred himself from taking it.[80]

Gray, however, would not be dissuaded from his task by Maffey's apparent duplicity. He had a vendetta against de Valera, and believed that vigilance should be maintained lest he 'wriggle out' of his current difficulties. His approach was disingenuous. He referred to a recent speech in which the Taoiseach described the English language as 'a badge of servitude' and a language that Ireland should cast off. Gray planned to store this quotation for future use, describing it as 'an insult to a hundred and thirty million Americans'.[81] Gray misunderstood the Irish position with apparent ease.

Gray received some support from the State Department

when on 21 September 1944 he handed de Valera another note from the US government appealing to Ireland not to grant asylum to Axis war criminals.[82] This request was not directed solely towards Ireland, as Switzerland, Sweden, Portugal, Spain and Argentina were all solicited in a similar fashion. In his advice to the Taoiseach, Walshe was precise in the category of reply to be given. An 'aide-memoire' rather than a 'note' was the preferred choice. A note, Walshe thought, while allowing the opportunity to explain one's case, would also leave one open to analysis and criticism. The reasoning behind this argument shows something of Walshe's diplomatic style. When dealing with Gray, it was best to be clear, concise and prepared for confusion. The aide-memoire, he said, 'becomes definitely an official document when it is handed by you to the American Minister as a resumé of your conversation with him and can therefore, if necessary, be ultimately published'. This was important in case of future dispute. Walshe claimed that an aide-memoire had another advantage, 'namely that of brevity' (the less said the better) and 'as an Aide-Mémoire, its real sense becomes apparent only in the course of the conversation of which it is supposed to be a resumé.'[83] In this way, a suitable degree of ambiguity could be introduced. The broad outline of a reply was to be presented in a written format accompanied by a verbal explanation and possibly supplemented by a candid off-the-record exchange of views. This would make clear the position of the Irish government but would leave little of substance for the US to criticise.

Gray pressed Walshe for a reply to this latest request. He believed that this note had had a profound effect on Walshe: 'He appeared depressed but said "In a couple of days". Five days have passed and no answer. It is hard to believe that Dev will say "No" but I think he will hedge his reply so that it will further strengthen our hand against pressure group action.' Gray's greatest fear was that after the war de Valera would be able to claim that Ireland's benevolent neutrality had greatly helped the Allied cause, and that Ireland had a right to some credit for the role it had played:

> De Valera has never broken with Vichy. When Vichy disappeared the Irish Minister went to Paris. Now he wants to get solid with de Gaulle because he knows De Gaulle is out to make trouble, and in a general way to obtain credit for humanitarian action.[84]

When it eventually came, the reply to the American request regarding Axis war criminals was, as Walshe had advised, brief. The Irish government pointed to difficulties with the request due to the absence of 'a comprehensive international code applicable to the subject matter of the request of the United States Government'.[85] The reply also stated that it was not the policy of the Irish government to grant admission to aliens whose presence would be 'at variance with the policy of neutrality, or detrimental to the interests of the Irish people, or inconsistent with the desire of the Irish people to avoid injury to the interests of friendly States.' While this was not a negative response, it was not sufficiently positive for the US government, which was puzzled by its ambivalence. It failed to understand how the Irish government could feel that 'justice, charity, honour and the interest of the nation could require the admission of axis war criminals'.[86]

Some time later, Maffey informed Walshe of a question due to arise in the House of Commons on the character of the Irish reply. Due to the reply's 'cagey' nature, the Dominions Office found itself in some difficulty in trying to indicate its acceptance of the Irish reply while not displeasing the US government or the House of Commons. Walshe felt the proposed Dominions Office statement to be too threatening, and his description of Maffey scuttling off to secure some alteration is, perhaps, somewhat exaggerated:

> Sir John Maffey agreed without hesitation and he immediately left for his office in order to secure from the Dominions Office some modification which would indicate an acceptance of our reply.[87]

No change was made. Maffey later said that the statement was regrettable but felt that it would not affect the good relations between the two countries. Maffey tended to blame the weakness of the Parliamentary Secretary of State for the Dominions, who was, he suggested, susceptible to US and House of Commons pressure:

> It was his [Maffey's] misfortune to have such a poor representative in the House of Commons. Evans, he thought, was no good, very weak, and, in fact, a b..... f... [sic] [bloody fool] Extremists in the House knew that and their tactic was to play on his desire to appear strong.[88]

Walshe trusted Maffey but was cautious when he noticed contradictions between the attitudes of Britain and the United States towards Ireland:

> The Americans, who had sent us a somewhat fierce Note with a fiercer reaction to our reply, when it came to a public statement were in fact almost amiable and certainly infinitely less objectionable than the British who disapproved of the Americans' action in sending us a Note.[89]

Maffey attempted to put the ambiguities of Britain's attitude towards Ireland into context and assure Walshe that relations would not be damaged. Walshe needed to be placated regularly, but his respect for Maffey allowed him to be persuaded. Thus, despite tensions between Britain and Ireland caused by a myriad of problems, relations on a diplomatic level remained open.

While Walshe and Maffey were communicating on the same wavelength, relations between Walshe and Gray reached a new low. When informed of the Irish government's decision to publish the text of the aide-memoire responding to the US request regarding Axis war criminals, Gray reacted violently and threatened to talk to the press himself and publish the US reply to the Irish response. This misunderstanding was easily cleared up when the Irish legation in Washington approached the State Department. Gray was later apologetic, and explained to Walshe that 'he had to go the whole hog in the absence of precise instructions from his Department.'[90] The incident may seem trivial but it does serve to illustrate the lack of easy and frank communication between Walshe and Gray. This was in stark contrast to Walshe's association with Maffey, with whom problems of a more profound nature could be discussed.

Gray understood the reasons behind the divergence of views between himself and Maffey. He had often expressed his distrust when British policy towards Ireland appeared to less harsh:

> From time to time I have encountered entirely unwarranted assumptions on the part of the British Mission, which I have somewhat bluntly challenged. It appears difficult for the British Foreign and Dominion Offices' personnel to learn that we cannot freely spend our armed and economic resources in a common cause and accept reserved areas on which the 'no admittance' sign is exhibited.[91]

However, he admitted that his relations with Maffey were 'happy and frank', and that a little bluntness with the Irish had done no harm. Maffey may have had a little success in altering Gray's attitude. They agreed that at this time it was in both their respective governments' interests 'to have an Ireland prosperous and friendly toward us and toward all other nations'. Gray said that in his view Britain's policy of forbearance toward Éire and of 'maintaining Irish economy at considerable sacrifice' suited the US as it weakened attacks of anti-British opinion on Anglo-American cooperation. However, he remained somewhat resentful of Maffey's lecture on the special status of Anglo-Irish relations: 'Sir John Maffey has often pointed out to me the desirability of recognizing clearly the special relation existing between Ireland and Britain due to propinquity and to economic and historic associations of longstanding.'

Maffey outlined to Gray the following points, which he believed would form the basis of their policy towards Ireland:

· No reprisals, no threats, no coercion;
· Clarification of Éire's constitutional position in regard to Britain;
· Complete freedom of choice accorded to Éire as to what her status shall be, but insistence on the exercise of choice without equivocation;
· If the choice be for association, suitable engagements to that end;
· If the choice be for separatism, and ending of Éire's special Commonwealth preferences;
· Reliance on good will and the operation of enlightened self-interest with regard to the economic factors involved to work out a solution for Northern and Southern Ireland and of their relation to Britain and to each other.[92]

Gray recognised that this was an attempt by Maffey to avoid 'drift' and to initiate a constructive policy towards Ireland. These points are noteworthy as they signified a conciliatory policy by Britain, and Maffey's comments may have helped Gray to follow suit. For Walshe, the coming year would prove all important in ensuring that Ireland was not left out in the cold in the postwar era.

CHAPTER 8

WALSHE AND POSTWAR DIPLOMACY 1945–1955

IN JANUARY 1945, as the outcome of the war looked more certain, Walshe had good reason to fear that the victorious Allies would adopt a punitive approach towards Ireland. The governments of the United States and Britain had persistently criticised Irish neutrality, and following the American note Walshe believed it possible that Ireland would be omitted from any reconstruction plans for Europe. However, both Maffey and Gray stated that postwar policy towards Ireland should be based on cooperation rather than coercion. Gray was at this stage following Maffey's lead, and indicated that while the issues surrounding the American note had not been forgotten, future US policy towards Ireland would be based on collaboration. 'American policy toward Ireland was basically the same as towards all other friendly countries; that is, the good-neighbor policy', he said, adding that 'We felt it to be in our interest to have an Ireland prosperous and friendly towards us and towards all other nations.'[1] The newly appointed Secretary of State, Edward Stettinius, confirmed that, while the Roosevelt administration had felt 'bitter disappointment' at Ireland's refusal to remove the Axis diplomats, the long-range policy towards Ireland was to be that of 'good neighbor'.[2]

This new-found goodwill, however, would not diminish the demands made on the Irish government. With victory in Europe for the Allies almost complete, the logical policy for Walshe to follow was to facilitate any US or British requests. While his efforts were primarily directed towards this aim, Walshe also remained mindful of Axis diplomatic rights and privileges. In

January 1945, for example, when Gray sought certain assurances regarding the internment of Axis warships, he was surprised not to find Walshe more receptive to his petition. Gray explained that as the end of hostilities drew near German ships and aircraft might try to take refuge in neutral countries. It was hoped that Ireland would recognise its 'special responsibility to intern such vessels and aircraft and to keep them intact until such time as they might be finally disposed of by the United Nations'.[3] Walshe was not well disposed to the request; however, it was not the request itself that he objected to, but rather the manner in which it was made. Considering his grave concerns that Ireland would not be included in postwar reconstruction plans, this was a dangerous approach to adopt. He may have allowed his resentment towards Gray to affect his judgement. The following month, for example, when Maffey sought permission for the British government to establish a radar post on Irish territory, Walshe did not object, and pointed out that Ireland already provided a similar favour to Britain at Valentia.[4]

Despite his support for a policy of cooperation, Maffey did not refrain from strongly criticising the Irish government. He told Walshe and de Valera that Irish policy during the war was 'a neutrality with teeth in it', and said that Irish censorship had adversely affected England. Indeed, it seemed to him that the censor must have had a text at his bed head saying 'No credit for England'. It was Maffey's next comment, however, that worried Walshe most, as it did nothing to remove the threatening atmosphere surrounding Anglo-Irish relations at that time. 'I was sorry to see this tendency. It did not bode well for the future', said Maffey, who qualified his remarks with the suggestion that the Irish censorship should appoint a 'friend of Britain' with a watching brief to help prevent any negative public comment from poisoning international relations.'[5] Maffey believed his conversation had a positive effect, and reported that Walshe had taken this idea quite well. Under the circumstances, however, Walshe had little choice but to acquiesce in the matter.

In April 1945 the Allies became interested in obtaining the property that had housed the German legation in Ireland. Gray expressed the view that following the collapse of the German government it was the desire of the United Nations to take possession of the German legation and archives. The US State Department wanted these orders carried out before

any consultation with Britain. Maffey resented this secretive approach, and thought the instructions were pointless because if Hempel had not already done so, the Irish government would be sure to destroy any incriminating documents contained in the German legation before allowing Allied access to them.[6] At the end of the month, Gray reiterated the demand, stating that their primary concern was to appropriate any information in Hempel's offices that could be important in combating German submarine warfare, which was expected to continue for some time. He was naturally worried that any such archives would be destroyed by the German minister. Gray admitted to Walshe that the request was probably 'out of the ordinary', but considering the imminent collapse of Germany and the impending announcement of VE Day, he thought that an exception could be made.[7] Walshe, however, explained that there were certain legal and technical difficulties in handing over the legation before a formal declaration of victory had been made.[8] Gray was once again affronted by Walshe's lack of acquiescence, and interpreted these remarks as an indication of Dublin's pro-German sentiment.[9]

The British government ultimately supported the American demand for access to Hempel's offices, and Maffey pointed out that there was little to be gained by refusing to cooperate. He reminded de Valera that the benefits of neutrality lessened as those who were to be the victors and the losers became apparent:

> If he were struggling in the ditch with an enemy who was trying to kill him and asked me, a bystander, for help as an old friend, I might have the right to say, 'I am sorry, but I am neutral,' but nevertheless such a reply would not create a favourable impression on him.[10]

De Valera would have to consult his legal advisers before giving any answer, but Maffey argued that while the legal precedent might not have been clear, the opportunity to show friendliness towards the Allies should not be lost: 'In this world one got what one gave. If one gave friendship, one received it.' Maffey believed that the policy of neutrality had been 'embraced wholeheartedly by Éire for a narrow political reason – that is to say for the sake of establishing the fact of independence and in order to emphasise the political estrangement from England'. As a result, Maffey

maintained, the instructions to the Irish representatives abroad were based on how best to exploit this situation:

> Dublin today is a propaganda centre for the dissemination of the doctrine that Éire's neutrality was in all respects justifiable [*sic*] and indeed virtuous, any other policy being unthinkable so long as the Irish Motherland is mutilated by Partition. The vehemence with which this is asserted is perhaps some indication of an uneasy conscience.[11]

Any attempts, therefore, by Walshe to justify Irish neutrality on idealistic foundations would be derided by Maffey on the basis that the policy was formulated on political expediency.

Boland described the general feeling at the time in relation to neutrality when he said, 'Well, we're lucky if we can stay neutral and get away with it!' He explained that when Walshe and he had established 'techniques which ensured increased confidence in the relations between ourselves and the British', their belief in neutrality grew. This confidence was augmented when Germany attacked the Soviet Union, thus lessening the danger of a German invasion of Britain or Ireland.[12] One memorandum described the difficulties of war from a neutral perspective:

> Neutrality is not like a simple mathematical formula which has only to be announced and demonstrated and respected … Instead of earning the respect and goodwill of both belligerents it is regarded by both with hatred and contempt; 'He who is not with me is against me.' In the modern total warfare it is not a condition of peace with both belligerents, but rather a condition of limited warfare with both … In cold economic and military fact it is becoming more and more difficult to distinguish between the seriousness of the two emergencies called war and neutrality.[13]

To describe neutrality as 'not a condition of peace' but rather a condition of 'limited warfare with both' belligerents is accurate. For example, despite Maffey's periodic cynicism, the Department of External Affairs believed that certain factors made neutrality more advantageous to Britain. Ireland did not have the means to defend itself or to conduct a war, and if neutrality had been abandoned this would have placed extra pressure on scarce British resources. In this way, Boland explained, Ireland's neutrality

enabled Britain to increase her resources in a way that she could not have done if her neighbour had not been neutral:

> Ireland was able to send her a substantial supply of food, which otherwise she would have had to import across the submarine-ridden seas of the Atlantic and the Bay of Biscay. Moreover, Britain was at that time, intensely concerned to increase her own supply of armaments to render her campaign in North Africa possible. This was largely a question of man-power, and she derived considerable help from Ireland in the shape of workers who were unemployed in Ireland and … a considerable number of people – calculated by experts at as many as 325,000 – flowed into the English armament factories, and helped to supply and to expedite Britain's own re-armament.[14]

These efforts to defend neutrality, however, were soon nullified when de Valera incited Allied fury by extending his condolences to Hempel on the reported death of Hitler.

When de Valera consulted Walshe on the matter of the German legation, he was told that the statement that the German government had ceased to exist was 'belied by the negotiations for surrender'.[15] He indicated that the Irish government was obliged to hand over the legation but had no such responsibility with regard to the contents being intact. Walshe believed it was purely mischievous for Gray to suggest that the Irish government was deliberately delaying matters in order to give Hempel time to destroy certain documents. Walshe stated that only when the German government announced a surrender would the legation be handed over. Walshe also invited further pro-German suspicion when he proposed that Hempel would be allowed to reside in Ireland as a private citizen.[16] Maffey, meanwhile, reiterated the point that while VE Day had not yet been officially announced, it was obvious that on a de facto basis the German government had ceased to exist. Walshe replied that the Irish government was waiting for Britain's announcement of victory. On this basis, Maffey claimed the episode was a minor diplomatic success. It was unlikely, he felt, that any documents of value would be found in the German legation, but the request had ensured cooperation from the Irish government after victory was announced. It was also another 'on-the-record' refusal of the Irish government to cooperate with the Allies on a friendly basis, which could be used against de Valera at

a later date.[17] Maffey, like Gray, was compiling a catalogue of evidence for use if needed after the war. Later that same day, de Valera provided Maffey and Gray with an unexpected addition for their dossier on the pro-Axis stance of the Irish government.

On 2 May 1945, following reports of Hitler's death, de Valera, accompanied by Walshe, visited Hempel to express their condolences to the German minister. The next day, Gray telephoned Walshe to ask if the reports in the national press were accurate. As Walshe confirmed the story, the Irish embassies and legations relayed the deluge of negative international reaction to the visit. Robert Brennan, in Washington, reported the strength of hostility felt in the United States, and Gray could not have wished for better or stronger condemnation from the American press.[18] In response, Walshe requested clarification as to the protocol followed by other neutrals. An External Affairs telegram to the Irish legation in Berne on 4 May conveyed the urgency felt in Iveagh House: 'Did Swiss Government take any measures of condolence or official mourning on Hitler's death? Please telegraph immediately.'[19] Walshe hoped that Ireland could point to similar actions by the leaders of the other neutrals. The message was also sent to the Irish representative in Madrid, but there was little support forthcoming. The Irish legation in Berne reported that as no official notification of the death of Hitler had been received, the Swiss government had not acted regarding the presentation of condolences. Brennan pointed out that the German representative in the US had attended the inauguration of the US President in 1941 on the invitation of the Secretary of State, despite the fact that Poland, Denmark, Norway, Luxembourg, Holland, Belgium and France had been overrun. While this was a possible defence, Brennan cautioned Walshe that it may be unwise to prompt further controversy given the current volatile situation. Brennan felt that the visit to Hempel had attracted more attention than anything else arising from Irish neutrality.

Walshe himself felt the brunt of the criticism that the visit prompted. He was personally criticised by an agitated Irish-American who was horrified at de Valera's gesture. That the Taoiseach had been accompanied by Joseph Walshe was of particular concern:

My name is WALSH and, when I read that a Joseph WALSH

accompanied you, I wanted to take the first steps to have my name changed. Joseph WALSH has brought dishonor to the House of Walsh [*sic*].[20]

Much has been written on this incident, yet Walshe's own stance remains unclear. Dermot Keogh states that it is likely that the secretary supported the visit to Hempel, based on Walshe's past strict adherence to protocol.[21] Tim Pat Coogan, however, has said that both Walshe and Boland strongly opposed de Valera's move.[22] In his memoirs, Fred Boland states that even Hempel himself was surprised by the visit, saying 'he was delighted to be rid of him [Hitler]; they all were.' Boland believes that de Valera was encouraged by Frank Aiken and Frank Gallagher, but insists that both he and Walshe violently opposed it: 'Literally on bended knees, we asked him to remember all the Irish-Americans who had lost their lives, but because he had been to the United States Embassy two weeks previously to condone on the death of Roosevelt, he was afraid of being accused of being partisan. It was a ghastly mistake.'[23]

Despite the furore it caused, de Valera showed little sign of regretting his action. Writing to Robert Brennan, he pointed out that 'So long as we retained our diplomatic relations with Germany to have failed to call upon the German representative would have been an act of unpardonable discourtesy to the German nation and to Dr Hempel himself.' He realised that he could have avoided that task by feigning a 'diplomatic illness', but this was abhorrent to him, and his personal respect for Hempel had sealed the decision not to add to the German representative's humiliation:

> During the whole of the war Dr Hempel's conduct was irreproach-able. He was always friendly and invariably correct – in marked contrast with G.[Gray].[24]

He explained that had he not made the visit, a bad precedent would have been set, arguing that it was 'of considerable importance that the formal acts of courtesy paid on such occasions as the death of the head of a State should not have attached to them any further special significance, such as connoting approval or disapproval of the policies of the State in question or of its

head.' He was adamant that he had made the right decision, and refused to explain his reasoning publicly lest this indicate regret. Despite the worldwide criticism, he maintained that he had acted both 'correctly' and 'wisely.' The British Prime Minister, Winston Churchill, incensed by de Valera's action, openly condemned Ireland and accused de Valera of collaborating with the Axis powers. He congratulated Northern Ireland and the British people for their restraint towards what he saw as Southern Ireland's treachery:

> With a restraint and poise to which history will find few parallels, we never laid a violent hand upon them, which at times would have been quite easy and natural, and left the de Valera government to frolic with the German and later the Japanese representatives to their heart's content.[25]

Maffey believed this speech was a major blunder, and said that it had placed de Valera back in the limelight. He recognised that the British Prime Minister had felt the need to vent his fury, but was certain that it was not the correct course to follow:

> I sympathise very deeply with the Dominions Office. This country needs quiet treatment and a patient, consistent policy. But how are you going to control Ministerial impressions into your china shop? Phrases make history here.[26]

Maffey maintained that the 'absent treatment' policy advocated by the Dominions Office was a more effective strategy. On many occasions, Walshe had aired his fears that Ireland would be left out in the cold after the war. It was Maffey's view that this anxiety should be used to Britain's advantage and to gain future Irish acquiescence, and the more Ireland was ignored the better:

> The Prime Minister, handling world problems on a vast stage, finds it expedient from time to time to come into collision with that policy, thereby producing local reactions here which may seem regrettable to those on the spot but which no doubt serve a useful purpose in another higher dimension.[27]

Maffey's effort to see Churchill's point of view was no more than a lightly veiled attempt to hide his own annoyance. He pointed

out that initiating this 'world radio contest' and attacking the Taoiseach personally had given prominence to the Irish leader. De Valera had responded with gusto, and his return radio speech had given the Irish nation a renewed sense of self-esteem, as well as a profusion of reverence for their leader.[28] Churchill was never likely to win the war of words, and had succeeded only in making de Valera 'as great a hero as is the Irishman who wins the winning try at Twickenham'. Maffey repeated that 'absent treatment' would not have presented de Valera with this opportunity of escape from 'the eclipse which had closed down on him and the Irish question'.

For Maffey, the timing of Churchill's assault on the Fianna Fáil leader was also inopportune because de Valera had been coming under political pressure at home. After the collapse of the Reich came the relaxation of censorship, and with it the beginning of public knowledge of the atrocities committed under Hitler. In the public mind, de Valera's action took on a 'smear of turpitude, and for the first time, and at a critical time, a sense of disgust slowly manifested itself', explained Maffey, who cited as proof the disgust registered by the traditionally pro-Irish John Kearney, the Canadian High Commissioner to Ireland.[29] Kearney wrote to his superiors saying he had met Walshe and told him that he regarded de Valera's visit to Hempel as 'a slap in the face', and said that there would be serious consequences resulting from the visit. He had found the Department of External Affairs to be 'profoundly depressed', and said that Walshe had 'vaguely mooted some idea of apology'. Kearney agreed with Maffey's assessment of Churchill's speech. 'We had him on a plate', he exclaimed. 'We had him where we wanted him. But look at the papers this morning!'[30]

Gray believed that de Valera's visit to Hempel was motivated by some political end such as cutting the final links with the Commonwealth. He also speculated that he himself had prompted de Valera to act rashly and do 'a foolish thing' following a 'rather stiff discussion which I had with him on the day that I made our request (May 31) and presented the aide-memoire'.[31] Maffey proffered a similar explanation, saying that while the Taoiseach was 'mathematically consistent' in making the visit, he believed it was possible that the request for the possession of the German archives might have propelled de Valera's actions. The Allied

request, explained Maffey, was to de Valera's mind another assault on the principles of neutrality, and his action was in defiance of their demands. According to Maffey, de Valera wanted to show that he was no 'bandwagoner' in light of the Allied victory.[32]

Gray was not keen to let de Valera off the hook on this issue. Having explored his recollection, he identified another possible insult towards the US government. The issue concerned the conduct of Michael MacDunphy, the secretary to the Irish President, who had offered his condolences to the German minister on Hitler's death. From his research, Gray found that MacDunphy had made no call to him following the death of Roosevelt:

> Examination of our records at the time of the death of President Roosevelt disclosed that fact that although Mr de Valera, Mr Walshe, Permanent Secretary for External Affairs, and leading members of the Government and Opposition had called to this Legation, the Secretary to the President did not call.[33]

The fact that MacDunphy called to Hempel was now regarded as a slight by Gray. He wrote to Walshe asking him whether an affront to the US government was deliberately intended as it was evident that two different procedures had been followed. Walshe did not answer the query, from which Gray deduced that the offence had been intentional. According to Gray, MacDunphy was generally regarded as 'an officious ass', and while he claimed that he did not want to be a stickler for protocol, he thought it important that the Irish government confirm or deny whether the discourtesy was deliberate. Gray went as far as to suggest that the matter warranted his withdrawal from Dublin, but this suggestion was not appreciated by his authorities. The acting Secretary of State, Joseph Grew, mentioned the proposal to President Truman but emphasised that it was Gray's idea:

> When I spoke to you this morning about the withdrawal of Mr Gray from Dublin I did so on the basis of a telegram from the Minister himself, who suggested it. Since this morning I have re-examined all the steps taken by the Irish Government on the deaths of President Roosevelt and Hitler.[34]

Following the death of President Roosevelt, the Irish President sent a telegram of sympathy to President Truman. De Valera had sent his condolences to the Secretary of State, and the Irish

representative in Washington sent a message of sympathy to Mrs Roosevelt. De Valera called on David Gray, and the Dáil was adjourned as a mark of respect. Having looked into the matter, Grew found that there was no evidence of disrespect towards the United States government; the State Department did not regard MacDunphy's actions as having any significance. Gray had clearly misread the situation and had failed to grasp what Maffey had more acutely understood: that while the visit to Hempel was abhorrent to him and to many others, the Taoiseach was 'mathematically correct' and consistent in making the visit. Gray's superiors correctly decided that, as far as protocol was concerned, it was not a matter on which to base the withdrawal of the US representative in Dublin. Gray's proposal was indicative of his diminutive approach to diplomacy. Roosevelt had died on 12 April 1945, and Harry Truman took over as President. Gray confided to Maffey that 'the State Department seemed to get more and more like a "mad house" since the Star business expert had taken over the controls.'[35] Apart from the sense of personal bereavement at the loss of his nephew, Gray was feeling politically isolated.

In the meantime, Gray continued his efforts to secure Walshe's support with regard to the repossession of the German legation building in Dublin. He described Walshe as having an 'engaging personality' as well as possessing 'great skill in shifting the discussion to other grounds than those upon which it is based'.[36] Walshe was certain that no documentation or archives would be found at the German legation. Gray agreed, believing that such documents would have contained evidence of German proposals to Ireland. Both he and Maffey were of the opinion that Walshe would never allow access to the legation until he could be sure that all such data had been destroyed. When Walshe suggested that he would at any time of the day or night telephone as soon as any decision on the legation had been made, Gray replied with some disdain:

> Since you still recognise the German Government as diplomatically extant, I feel that there no longer exists a possibility of finding the archives in a condition that would be of use to the United Nations, and I suggest that both of us enjoy our sleep without having immediate nocturnal action on our minds.[37]

On 9 May 1945 Walshe arranged for handing over of the German legation. Gray now thought the matter was one of routine since the potential value of searching the premises had been lost.[38] He believed this episode was a further insult and a deliberate move to prevent the retrieval of any archives or other incriminating evidence regarding Irish–German relations during the war.

When Walshe handed over the keys of the legation, he stated that an inventory of the contents of the building had been made earlier that day by an External Affairs official. Gray said it was obvious that the offices had been stripped and that the incinerator showed signs of recent and extensive use. He felt that the Allies were taking over the legation not from Germany but from the Irish government, which had 'ample time to remove anything it wished'.[39] Ed Lalor of the OSS came from London to search the German legation but had found little in the way of important archives. However, one letter was found in the cellar, crumpled into a ball, which had evidently escaped from a container with material bound for the incinerator: 'It is on Dáil Éireann stationery and seems to be written by a prominent supporter of the De Valera Government and Dáil member in the spring of 1943 to the German Minister congratulating him on Hitler's birthday and wishing the German army success.'[40]

Gray attached some importance to the find and believed it supported his contention that there had been significant pro-German activity in Ireland.[41] This was further confirmed for him when Walshe indicated that he was unwilling to abandon Hempel and his staff, as well as a section of the German internees, to the mercy of the Allies. While the military internees were swiftly dispatched, it was decided that the spies and espionage agents should remain in captivity in Ireland until a suitable arrangement for their repatriation could be found. Carolle Carter suggests that External Affairs saw the need to mollify Britain, but maintains that if spies such as Goertz had been sought by the British for trial as war criminals, the Irish government would have refused as this would have weakened neutrality. This, Carter says, is borne out by the fact that de Valera refused to agree to conditions for the disposal of war criminals that had been accepted by other neutrals.[42]

At the end of May 1945 Maffey told Walshe that he would soon be going to London to discuss the question of German

internees under Irish jurisdiction. He warned that any 'laxness' on
the part of the Irish government would not be looked on favour-
ably, and suggested that all the internees could be sent to England
as prisoners of war. Walshe thought there would be difficulties
with this as the prisoners were being held for offences committed
against the Irish government, and there was no apparent reason for
handing them over to Britain. The proposal might be acceptable,
however, if an undertaking were given that the prisoners' position would not be worsened by their transfer. It would have been
of considerable embarrassment to the Irish government if any of
the internees under its charge should be executed following their
relocation to Britain. Maffey did not raise the question of the staff
of the German legation at this meeting but it was a matter with
which he was deeply concerned and would return to later.[43] Despite
the tensions, Anglo-Irish relations were somewhat improved when,
in response to a Parliamentary question, the Under-Secretary of
State for Dominion Affairs, Emrys-Evans, stated that:

> I need not add to what the Prime Minister has said as to the danger
> involved to our security, and, indeed, our existence, by the attitude
> of neutrality adopted by the Éire Government in the war. There
> are, however, no grounds for suggesting that the Éire Government
> committed un-Neutral acts to the disadvantage of this country.[44]

Ireland's assistance during the war was not directly acknowledged,
but it would have seemed to Walshe and others that there was
some element of recognition in this statement. When Maffey
returned to Dublin, he stated that he could give no assurance
that the ultimate punishment of the internees would remain the
same if they were handed over to Britain. He insisted, however,
that their continued presence would lead to 'political trouble', and
added that Gray and the Americans were also getting 'worked up'
about the matter. Walshe did not doubt the importance attached
to the issue, considering the repeated warnings of the possibility
of an 'unpleasant political situation' developing. Nonetheless, he
risked the anger of the Allies by frustrating their demands by
including conditions to ensure the wellbeing of the prisoners.

  While Walshe had initially given the impression that the Irish
authorities would willingly surrender the agents on the undertaking
that the position of the prisoners would not be made worse while in

British hands, Maffey now found that this was unacceptable to the Irish government. He had put the proposal to his government, but when he returned to Dublin the Irish government absolutely refused to release the spies. It is possible that Walshe was culpable for the confusion, and certainly Maffey believed this to be the case:

> My own opinion is that Walshe of External Affairs tentatively agreed to the surrender of these men on conditions and exceeded his authority, and that Mr de Valera was most unlikely to have given them up even if the British Government had accepted the conditions.[45]

Gray was somewhat offended that he had not been consulted on this matter. He thought it inevitable that de Valera would resist any requests made by the Allies, and suggested that while Ireland should be given supplies it should be placed on a low priority listing.

On 4 July 1945 Walshe acknowledged a British offer that placed a ship at the disposal of the Irish government for the repatriation of the German military internees. With regard to the espionage agents, however, Walshe indicated the government's continued unwillingness to concede to British demands on the issue:

> It is intended to keep them under detention until such time as, after consultation between the two Governments, it is agreed that they are no longer a menace to the security of either country and can, therefore, safely be restored to liberty.[46]

The following month, the Department of Justice wrote to External Affairs concerning the matter. In his reply, Walshe was clear as to the attitude to be shown to the internees:

> We are not free to let out any of the men in Athlone unless they are prepared to return to their respective countries. The British and American Governments believe that the activities of these men were directed ultimately against British and American interests, and they would regard it as unfriendly on our part to release them without securing their agreement to that course.

Despite the clarity of Walshe's instructions, the following week the Department of Justice – without consulting External Affairs – ordered the release of the spies and announced that Ireland would grant them asylum.[47] The ex-spies were released on parole

by the Minister for Justice, Gerald Boland, who was somewhat sympathetic to their cause. Months later, however, he reluctantly signed their deportation orders.[48]

The position of Hempel and the personnel at the German legation was also given prolonged consideration. Maffey warned that the Irish government would receive a note from the United Nations regarding the status of the German legation personnel in Dublin, but Walshe continued to support Hempel's request to reside in Ireland: 'I told him that the late German Minister was now a private individual residing here with his family and we did not consider it appropriate to take any steps to have him transferred to Germany until such time as he himself expressed a wish to go there.'[49] Maffey felt it would be detrimental to relations if the Irish government insisted on allowing the German legation staff residential status. Walshe did not succumb to Maffey's warnings, and protested that the sending of notes was a 'barren method' of communication. He did not regard the German staff as a problem, and believed that Maffey's comments on the subject represented 'a somewhat unhealthy interest in our internal affairs'. Walshe's statements were a bold notification that even in the postwar world the tenets of neutrality would be maintained to safeguard Irish independence.

Gray was displeased when the British Foreign Office eventually accepted Walshe's view that the German agents in Ireland had broken Irish law rather than United Nations law. He was of the opinion that the issue should be pursued, and regretted that the matter had 'tended to blur the outlines of the United Nations' plan of action now being formulated'.[50] What this 'plan of action' consisted of, Walshe could not be sure, but his reaction was indicative of his attitude towards Allied requests throughout the war. While generally meeting their requirements, he was adamant that neither Britain nor the United States would dictate terms to the Irish government. The Allies may have been of the view that Ireland was wrong in not joining them in the war effort, but Walshe insisted that the Irish government was well within its rights to remain neutral. Ireland, in fact, had done more than just remain neutral, but had risked that policy by acceding to successive Allied requests. Walshe and de Valera's postwar stance was a brave but risky strategy that demonstrated a courageous self-belief at a time when it would have been easier to side with the victors.

When assessing Walshe's role, we must remember that, while his own views were influential, he always took his lead from de Valera. However, the methods by which he implemented government policy were largely of his own making. Now, as the war came to a close, it was clear that a review of Walshe's administration of External Affairs would be required. With this in mind, a conference of all the heads of External Affairs missions was organised for September 1945. The aim was to initiate an assessment of its own foreign policies and procedures as it was recognised that it was important to analyse and reassess the organisation of External Affairs in light of the new international environment. The role played by Walshe at this conference is not clear, but it is likely that he used the occasion to air many of his strongly held views on both departmental and policy matters. The memoranda and conclusions of the conference provide a pertinent assessment of the department at a time when Walshe was nearing the end of his twenty-four-year reign.

At the time, the External Affairs infrastructure was lacking in a number of areas. The conference attendees concluded, for example, that the foreign missions were inadequately staffed. Heads of missions found themselves spending a large amount of their time attending to routine clerical work, and their libraries were inadequate for cultural propaganda tasks. However, this was not seen as sufficient excuse for the lack of propaganda work, and the conference's concluding memorandum suggested that Ireland's foreign representatives needed 'to be roused energetically to the consciousness that their main work abroad is to spread the knowledge and esteem of Ireland'. The war had created many difficulties for the Irish representatives, but the work of promoting Ireland, it was concluded, should continue despite such hardships. Nothing less than absolute dedication was sought from the 'Apostles for this country' who were commanded to seek every opportunity to promote the name of Ireland. It is likely that these comments came directly from Walshe, who had waited for some time to tackle what he saw as a malaise among the foreign diplomatic corps. As an example, reference was made to one representative who had carried out no cultural propaganda because he had no cultural secretary. This was far from the ardent enthusiasm sought:

They have been too static, too routine, too little conscious of the fact that we are in the pioneering stage and that their work of propaganda, in the good sense, should go on and should have gone on notwithstanding material difficulties.[51]

This was strong criticism of Irish representatives who were left in no doubt that greater effort, initiative and enthusiasm would be required in the future. Walshe may have been preparing to lead by example, as he planned to transfer to a new position in Rome. In the early part of the war, he had written a comprehensive portrait of what the Irish representative to the Vatican should look like. It depicted a dedicated diplomat living a somewhat frugal lifestyle. It was a role that Walshe would embrace with enthusiasm.

Following the conference, Thomas Kiernan – who had been assigned to the Vatican during the war – wrote a lengthy memorandum with suggestions for the improvement of the Irish foreign service. The question of staffing levels was foremost in Kiernan's mind, and he emphasised the need to develop the commercial side of their work.[52] This sentiment was echoed by the secretary of the Department of Finance, J.J. McElligott, who also addressed the conference. The heads of missions were briefed on the general economic situation that faced Ireland in the postwar world. The pressures on government resources were great, so in addition to providing budgetary and economic information on various countries, the diplomatic corps would be expected to identify new trade and financial opportunities.[53] As well as spreading propaganda about Ireland around the world, Kiernan suggested that the department itself should develop an awareness among the Irish people of the work of External Affairs, as there was a tendency to regard it as a 'decorative department'.[54] Kiernan had a particular interest in the means of disseminating propaganda, and put forward a number of novel and innovative ideas concerning the use of press, radio and film.[55] Already, it seems, there was a new air of energy and optimism permeating Iveagh House.

Gray reported what he had heard of the conference's proceedings, and said that de Valera had spoken of the possible effect of declaring an Irish republic and of Ireland's relationship with the Commonwealth. Concern had been expressed over the increasing influence of Russia in European affairs, and the diplomatic corps was advised to keep in contact with the views of the Holy

See. This reflected Walshe's attitude, especially now that he was to take up the Vatican position, rumours of which were now widespread in diplomatic circles:

> In connection with the Conference, it was rumoured that Mr J. P. Walshe, Permanent Secretary External Affairs, would be transferred to the Holy See and his place taken by Mr Hearne, now High Commissioner for Canada.[56]

Maffey said that Walshe had long awaited the end of the war in order to realise this 'dream'. He believed the conference would lead to a shake-up of the department, and predicted much change for many of the Irish diplomatic incumbents:

> Dulanty is hardly likely to stay much longer in London. There are rumours that Walshe will now achieve his heart's desire and that Kiernan from Rome will take his place in the Department of External Affairs.[57]

Walshe's appointment would take some months to complete, and he continued to use this time to influence the Allies' postwar attitude towards Ireland. Within a week of the conclusion of the conference, Walshe was in London to meet British officials. There he met John Stephenson, who was acting Under-Secretary of the Dominions Office, in place of Eric Machtig, who was ill. Walshe had known Stephenson throughout the 1930s and 1940s, and their meetings had been influential in bringing about the Anglo-Irish settlement in 1938.[58] Stephenson, however, was on this occasion 'most unfriendly' towards Walshe, and warned that any Anglo-Irish friendship was limited by the intense 'hatred' in Britain towards Ireland. Walshe reflected on how he had previously found Machtig unwilling to admit the 'real Dominions Office attitude'. He therefore delighted at the chance that Stephenson had given him for 'a good row'. Walshe told Stephenson, bluntly, that he should read Irish history in order to prepare himself to deal with Anglo-Irish relations:

> I also went back on the immediately pre-twenty-two period, and made it clear to him that the bad anti-Irish attitude of Sir Edward Harding and his Colonial office mind in regard to us had left a deep impression on the Dominions Office ever since.[59]

From the tone of this conversation, Walshe expected that his meeting with the newly appointed Dominions Secretary, Lord Addison, scheduled later that day, would be contentious. He envisioned a rebuke of some sort for Ireland's neutrality but found instead a cordial reception. Addison asked Walshe to tell de Valera 'I am his friend' and that 'Friendship for Ireland will be the policy of my Department so long as I am in it.'

Walshe, keen to engineer a new era in Anglo-Irish cooperation before his departure to Rome, told British officials that the Minister for Industry and Commerce, Seán Lemass, was willing to travel to London for talks. Addison replied that they had already been thinking along those lines. Walshe, somewhat taken aback by the Dominions Secretary's reiteration that the Irish government was 'pushing an open door', believed that the new Labour government that had come to power earlier that year under Clement Attlee was a sign of a new and more friendly relationship with Britain. Walshe indicated Ireland's support for Attlee's domestic policies: 'If the advent of a Labour Government indicated a definite phase of a social revolution, we in Ireland could only rejoice that what had long since taken place in Ireland had at last become a fact in England.' In Addison, Walshe concluded, Ireland had an ally in the British Cabinet. He could only hope that the Dominions Secretary would be able to circumvent a traditional 'anti-Irish animus' held by some in the Dominions Office. From the difference in their reactions, Walshe thought that Stephenson's hostility had meant that the acting Under-Secretary had little knowledge of Addison's views towards Ireland. In light of these apparent differences, therefore, Walshe was concerned that the newly appointed Dominions Secretary would be able to persuade Dominions Office staff that to establish friendly relations with Ireland was the best policy to pursue. However, after his talk with Lord Addison, Walshe had another meeting with Stephenson, who he now found more receptive to the proposed visit of Seán Lemass. Walshe urged that such ministerial contact was crucial and of benefit to both sides. He warned Stephenson:

> ... to be careful not to stake the responsibility upon himself (by giving wrong advice to his Minister) of creating a wider gap between us, and thus postponing, perhaps indefinitely, those personal contacts upon which so much depended for all of us.

My Minister had made a generous gesture. It would be extremely unwise to reject it.[60]

According to Walshe, this statement had the desired effect as Stephenson seemed eager to discuss the details of the proposed visit. Walshe suggested a routine strategy for the talks, proposing that Lemass would come to London for a couple of days. The civil servants and officials would take over, and at the end of these consultations the ministers could meet again in either London or Dublin.

Stephenson, in recounting his version of these events to Maffey, believed that Walshe's visit had come at a very opportune time as the Cabinet was due to discuss proposals on Britain's relations with Ireland.[61] He thought that Walshe had been very pleased with the visit and said their talks had been very general. Walshe, for example, mentioned that, as part of the expansion of External Affairs, Ireland planned to exchange High Commissioners with Australia. Stephenson, for his part, had raised the issue of Ireland's air agreement with the US, saying the British Air Minister had felt somewhat let down. Walshe responded, however, that for years the Irish government had sought agreement on this matter but had been 'fobbed off' with excuses that 'wouldn't convince a bushman', and he now thought Britain's jealousy somewhat childish.[62] The two men also discussed lend-lease, petrol, and the availability of hard currency. Walshe was impressed with Stephenson's detailed knowledge of the subjects they discussed, saying, 'He mentioned their generosity in dollars, and in this connection, he seemed to be completely *au courant* not only with total amounts but with individual transactions, a fact which contains a lesson for us.'[63] He saw this as proof that a more centralised and powerful Department of External Affairs, with greater influence over other government matters, would serve to improve the quality of Irish diplomatic representation. Walshe, meanwhile, planned a further visit to the Dominions Office for later that month.

Walshe's endeavours to re-establish Anglo-Irish relations on a more constructive level caused some tension between Gray and Maffey. Gray had drafted a new note to be presented to the Irish government concerning the Germans still resident in Ireland. Maffey took a dim view of this new approach and remarked,

'As you will see, it is pretty bad. It may do for America, but it would not do for us ... Gray has cabled this draft to the State Department. I cannot think that they will like it. Anyhow, I made it quite plain that we should follow our own line.'[64]

However, Gray was planning a trip to London and, knowing what a 'grand person' he was, Maffey requested that the US representative be shown due respect during his visit. Cognisant of the issues that mattered most to Gray, Maffey asked that Gray be included if 'there is anything on under the auspices of the Foreign Office or otherwise, by virtue of which a little attention could be shown to him'. Gray's efforts did little to derail Walshe's latest diplomatic initiative, and on his next visit to Whitehall he made it obvious, in a lengthy conversation with Sir Basil Newton, that he greatly wished for closer ties with the British Foreign Office.[65] It seemed to British officials that Irish policy had undergone a sea change, with Walshe expressing some enthusiasm for the idea of establishing a Western and American bloc:

> He evidently favoured the development of the British Common-
> wealth to include nations with similar interests, mentioning as
> particular examples, Egypt, Scandinavian countries, Belgium and
> Holland ... [These countries] with their own Kings could be asso-
> ciated with the British Commonwealth, he evidently thought the
> development would be a happy one, though he did not actually say
> Éire would like to participate on the same associate basis.[66]

Walshe's ardour for the idea was largely based on his anxiety that, following the end of the war, Russia would exert inordinate influ-ence over Europe and propagate the spread of Bolshevism:

> I had the impression that Mr Walshe was considerably preoc-
> cupied by the spread of Russian domination and that the Éire
> Government might be glad to contribute to any system of defence
> against a threat to Western security. From a previous remark by
> Sir John Stephenson I understood that motives such as those just
> indicated might play a useful part in solving the problem of mili-
> tary bases in Éire.

Walshe's remarks were, perhaps, 'off the cuff' and may have been ill-advised, but he clearly thought that this declaration would appeal to Newton. Walshe also mentioned that there were 5,000

Jews in Dublin and that 'the ostentatious behaviour of some of them was not making them popular'. Newton received the strong impression that Walshe did not wish to see any considerable immigration of Jews into Ireland, and 'after mentioning a visit he had made some time ago to Tel Aviv and the Middle East, showed no great sympathy for Jewish aspirations in Palestine'. Newton remained tactfully reserved and any comments he made were 'off the record'. He was clearly interested in hearing Walshe's views but did not wish to divulge much information in return. However, he felt that some of Walshe's misconceptions ought to be cleared up:

> I did not offer more than were necessary to illicit Mr Walshe's views. As however I did not wish our conversation to seem to be pointed against Russia I remarked that in my opinion it would no doubt remain the principal aim of British policy to continue during peace the policy of close co-operation with Russia as well as America followed during the war. I appreciated nevertheless that in any case some grouping of countries with kindred economic, cultural or other interests might prove natural and convenient in the West as well as in the East.[67]

Newton undertook to arrange further meetings for Walshe, who was anxious to return to London as soon as possible. From his apparent eagerness, the Foreign Office could confirm that Ireland was seeking a 'reconciliation' with Britain and the Commonwealth. Newton realised that there would be public criticism of any move to bring Ireland back into the fold but, happily, he believed such a development both possible and desirable.

Newton's memorandum also sheds light on the Foreign Office attitude towards Ireland in the postwar period. As Maffey had predicted and advised, a policy of friendliness and conciliation was prevalent. Newton's response had been measured, but not everyone would have appreciated Walshe's frank confessional:

> I am glad that Sir B. Newton made it clear to Mr Walshe that the principal aim of British policy was still to co-operate with Russia. There can be no question of our basing a reconciliation with de Valera on a common anti-Soviet or anti-Semite policy, which seems to be Mr Walshe's conception of what he calls 'a Western and American Block'.[68]

At the end of this note is a handwritten addendum exclaiming, 'Mr Walshe is a little rat and violently anti-English.'[69] Stephenson thought Walshe's comments were a useful guide to the feelings not only of Ireland but of other European countries.[70] Walshe was not alone in suspecting Russian aims, and this distrust was a primary motivating factor for support of a Western bloc. Walshe would soon get the chance to air these views on a larger stage, where his concern at the spread of communism would, he believed, ensure that his mission to the Vatican would be treated as a priority by Iveagh House.

Throughout his career, Walshe regarded the Vatican as a guide and model for External Affairs, and he believed his proposed new position in Rome would allow him a continued contribution to the formulation of Irish foreign policy. In the past, he had demonstrated extreme sensitivity with regard to that post. William Macaulay, for example, who was serving as the Irish chargé d'affaires at the Holy See in the early years of the war, was reprimanded for leaving his post for medical treatment.[71] This countermanded Walshe's specific instructions that the Irish legation at the Vatican should under no circumstances be left unattended. Most of the Irish diplomats abroad had at one time or another received instructions to seek the views of the Holy See's representative. If they had no specific instruction on an issue, they would be safe if they followed the line taken by the nuncio. To cite a typical example, in August 1944 Walshe wrote to Berlin:

> Keep in close touch with Nuncio and generally while using your own discretion you could follow his line … Perhaps you could ascertain what his instructions are. You can tell him our policy is to keep as closely as possible to lines of Vatican policy.[72]

During the war, External Affairs drafted a document which stated that the mission to the Holy See was Ireland's most important diplomatic post. The memorandum is interesting in the context of Walshe's proposed appointment, as it was probably written by him, and in it he continually emphasised the importance of the mission over all other posts. The position called for the 'highest degree of care and self-sacrifice' by the incumbent, who was expected to alter his or her life to the environment of the Vatican:

> Unless he sets out of deliberate purpose to become an observant Churchman in detail, he is courting failure. He must acquire, not only

a serious knowledge of the history of the Church, but also an intimate acquaintance with the day to day work of governing the Universal Church from its centre. His purpose must always be to establish such close relationships with Vatican officials that there will always be a receptive atmosphere for his requests and advice in relation to Ireland.[73]

The Irish representative was to listen patiently to the problems and comments of all the Irish ecclesiastics, and he was to study the organisation of the Vatican in order to determine the best way in which Irish interests could be augmented. The Irish representative was also charged with reminding officials of the righteousness of Irish national aims; this was particularly important bearing in mind the strength of the papacy over the Catholic Church in the United States and the British dominions. It would be a mistake for the Irish representative to think that 'slow movement or inaction can achieve anything', especially at the Vatican, where 'only constant pressure brings success'.

Throughout the war, Walshe had often justified Irish neutrality by reference to Vatican policy. Maffey had recognised the existence of this close affinity between the Vatican and Ireland, but thought that Walshe exaggerated the point: 'Here and there, and more particularly in the Department of External Affairs, there is constant emphasis on the close relationship to Rome, and the power of the Irish College in Rome, and the good work achieved by Irish Priests.'[74] Walshe was of the opinion that Irish priests and missionaries, in view of their Catholic faith and of the neutrality of their country, were able to act as 'powerful intermediaries on behalf of suffering humanity' and were of 'particular service to people of Allied nationality in the Far East'. In September 1945 Maffey sought from his British counterpart at the Vatican an assessment of Ireland's standing at the Holy See. From his interest in Ireland's relationship with the Vatican, he developed the idea that Ireland's representatives there could be of use to Britain. Maffey was intrigued by the special position occupied by Ireland at the Vatican and was curious about the 'contacts and avenues of approach' this allowed Ireland but which were denied Britain. Maffey pointed out that the Church had no great influence over general government policy but that the opposite was true when it came to the workings of individual departments. This was especially true in Walshe's case, and he described it as probably 'the

most significant feature in the working of Irish diplomacy'. For example, it fascinated Maffey that the Department of External Affairs would 'exclude major subjects from consideration while they move heaven and earth for the repatriation by air of a young priest'. This was largely due to Walshe who, he believed, 'operates in this line of business *con amore*, but the pressures would be there whether he liked it or not'.[75]

When the British Foreign Office received a request from its representative to the Holy See, Sir d'Arcy Osborne, for an assessment of Ireland's new delegate at the Vatican, the task fell to Maffey to write an 'appreciation' of Walshe.[76] Maffey's report is illuminating, as he comments on aspects of Walshe's character as well as their personal and professional relationship. Despite their many differences during the war and the strong objections by him towards neutrality, Maffey ultimately believed that Walshe was pro-British:

> During all the years of the war, and especially during its darkest days, I found Mr Walshe helpful and friendly. He was certainly anti-German (mainly for religious reasons), and in negotiating some awkward corners in the interpretation of Éire's neutrality.[77]

Maffey realised the difficulties of Walshe's position, and with the benefit of hindsight he understood Walshe's adherence to neutrality, though he did not agree with it. It was de Valera, Maffey thought, who remained obstinately inflexible, and in this regard Walshe's influence on the Taoiseach was of crucial importance. They had a close personal relationship; Walshe was a regular visitor to Maffey's home and part of the same social circle, where he was known as 'Joe' to one and all.

Maffey's 'appreciation', however, reveals a pragmatic and somewhat utilitarian approach towards his friendship with Walshe. 'He evidently likes coming to our house and being admitted to the family circle', seems a cold way of describing his 'friend'. As one would expect, Maffey's loyalty to his country came first, but he further described Walshe as having an 'inferiority complex' and said that this was the key to understanding his whole character. It was asserted by Maffey that this flaw was one that was common in the Irish psyche. The whole spectrum of Anglo-Irish relations was dogged by it, and Walshe, in particular, was susceptible. 'Does

London take our Department of External Affairs seriously? Am I not the equal in stature to the top rank of their Foreign Office?' were the questions that, according to Maffey, constantly plagued Walshe. This, he explained, led to some difficulties in dealing with External Affairs as Walshe would be liable to take offence at the least thing and his paranoia led to 'constant watchfulness for affronts and to petty manifestations of *Saeva indignatio*'. In this way, Maffey believed that Walshe was sometimes a bad influence on de Valera, as he would continually pass on to the Taoiseach any matter that was derogatory towards Ireland, such as adverse comment in the British press.

Maffey believed it was time for Walshe to move on and get away from what he termed, 'the '98 motif and the bigotry and *Kleinstädterei* [provincialism] of Dublin'. Walshe was vain and constantly worried about his health, and he was not popular in political circles, explained Maffey, who also stated that he was regarded as 'too much of a trimmer'.[78] This was in reference to the change of government in 1932 when Walshe changed from being 'pro-Cosgrave and bitterly "anti-Dev"… [to being] anti-Cosgrave and hotly "pro-Dev".' Maffey had long been fascinated with the influence of the Catholic Church in Ireland, and Walshe was no exception in this regard. He would sometimes shock Maffey by his devotion:

> Often when we had to discuss grave and urgent practical problems of wartime he would neglect them to press for my help for some Jesuit priest held up in the antipodes of war.

Thus, Maffey believed that Walshe's mission to the Holy See would have to be judged in this light. It was a new era for Walshe and for Ireland, said Maffey, who believed that Ireland's 'mood of self satisfaction has suddenly undergone a crescendo' in the light of Britain's postwar difficulties, such as the continued economic hardships. 'Events, it is claimed, have proved how right she has been. Her noble neutrality has been blessed by Heaven.' The whole country had an air of renewed self-confidence and new-found pride in the contribution of the worldwide Irish diaspora. This was the tide, explained Maffey, on which Walshe was going to Rome. It was important to remember this because, he predicted, it would not last and soon Walshe would find that

Ireland's esteem in the eyes of the Vatican did not count for as much as he thought. Maffey believed that Walshe's mission would be to ensure Vatican support for a worldwide campaign against partition. D'Arcy Osborne would have to be aware of this but Walshe could be useful nonetheless:

> He will certainly meet more than half way any consideration coming from us and he will appreciate it more from us than from anybody else. At well selected moments he will talk freely and indiscreetly.

Walshe himself was no Anglophobe, and he moved quickly to establish good relations with his British counterpart in the Vatican. He wrote to John Maffey, telling him that Sir d'Arcy Osborne had been extremely kind to him and expressed the hope that British–Vatican relations would soon be placed on a higher footing. It was important, he said, for all sides to unite in the fight against Bolshevism.[79] This was to be a recurring theme throughout Walshe's tenure in Rome.

David Gray also provided an 'appreciation' of both de Valera and Walshe when, in the years after the war, he wrote his memoirs. That Gray was deeply embittered by his experiences in Ireland during the war is clear from his accounts in this unpublished manuscript:

> The date on which de Valera made his fateful decision to throw in his lot with Hitler and help destroy Britain and the English speaking world, we do not know. We know only that the captured German Foreign Office files show that on August 26th, a week before World War Two began, Mr de Valera made secret proposals to Berlin.[80]

Gray came to despise not only de Valera's stance during the war but also the Taoiseach's whole career. Based on further research, he identified a close affinity between de Valera and Hitler, and juxtaposed the careers of the two leaders without difficulty or apology:

> In 1932 de Valera came to power in Ireland. In 1933 Hitler became Chancellor of the German Reich. de Valera in that year, had already begun the unilateral revision of the Anglo-Irish Treaty

by repudiating the Annuities. In 1936 Hitler denounced the re-armament provisions of the Versailles and Locarno Treaties and reoccupied the Rhineland. In February 1938 he seized Austria and Czechoslovakia. In 1938 de Valera seized nothing. He lacked power but he obtained by trickery from the British Government what he lacked power to compel.[81]

Gray now believed that Irish neutrality had been calculated from the start to aid German victory, and Walshe was also implicated in that conspiracy. He recounted his arrival in Dublin in 1940, saying he had been met by Walshe: 'I had no suspicion at this time that Mr Walshe was already working harmoniously with the German Minister to hamper American preparedness.' Gray came to realise this only when he went to the Hempel's residence for lunch:

> The Hempel children appeared for a few minutes before lunch and made their manners to the guests. What struck us especially was that they addressed Mr Walshe as 'Uncle Joe', indicating his status as a family friend.

What made matters worse, however, was that Walshe was seated to the right of Frau Hempel, 'though according to Éire protocol he was a civil servant and ranked after all foreign diplomats.' Gray remembered with shame that he had not noticed this insult to the United States until weeks after the event. Gray later recounted another lunch with Walshe:

> He had an attractive little town house and when we came we agreed that it had been the jolliest party we had been to in Dublin … Joe was shortly to take his holiday with Herr Hempel on the Kerry shore. In view of the impending 'German victory', and the possible landing of German paratroopers, to be with Hempel was a good idea. But he did not talk about his holiday.

Gray himself recounts that he had spoken with Hempel that day, saying 'we agreed that we must be civilized whatever happened and remain personal friends.' For Gray, however, Walshe's arrangement represented something sinister, and in his memoirs he concluded that:

> Joe was a lovable man if one was not bothered by the thought that out of love for Ireland he might push you over the brink. He was perhaps the only man I ever knew who attained his heart's desire.

He wanted to live in Rome in an Irish-owned Italian palace and wear an Ambassadorial uniform. In 1940 Éire owned no Roman palace nor maintained ambassadors. But he achieved both aspirations and served with competence and credit.

Clearly Gray had been deeply embittered by his experiences in Dublin, and even after the war had ended he persisted in his belief that Walshe, de Valera and the policy of Irish neutrality was definitively pro-German.

Conor Cruise O'Brien, who joined the staff of External Affairs towards the end of the war, provides an interesting account of Walshe's convictions and beliefs. However, as O'Brien was to have little significant contact with Walshe, the account may be somewhat flawed. While they make interesting reading, it seems many of his memories are based not on first-hand experience but on accounts he heard while a junior official in the department, as well as reports he learned of subsequently. For example, according to these accounts, Mussolini was Walshe's hero, and Walshe's apparently pro-Axis sentiments are mentioned.

O'Brien was initially surprised at Walshe's acceptance of his application. He had attended a nondenominational school and then Trinity College, and he expected Walshe to consider this 'the most disreputable and morally contagious collection and environment that one could find in Catholic Ireland'.[82] He states that his curriculum vitae would, therefore, have been repugnant to Walshe, who he describes as 'an exceptionally devout Catholic, even by the exacting standards of the Ireland of the first half of the twentieth century'. This is disputed by Boland, who states that, while he was 'dying to get to the Vatican', Walshe 'wasn't particularly pious'. Boland explains that Walshe's attitude towards going to the Vatican was that 'he thought that the Church was making some mistakes, and if he could only get there and talk to them frankly, he could save them from their blunders!'[83]

When Walshe departed for the Holy See, one of his main objectives was to make Ireland more influential at the centre of the Catholic Church, which he believed was too closely connected with Italy and its politics. In his view, the papacy should have been more concerned with strengthening international faith, especially in the face of the growing threat of communism.[84] Walshe believed that the papal offices needed reorganisation. The system was outmoded and

the Holy Father's statements were criticised for their 'turgid style', and even the monsignori found it 'a penance' to read them. He charged the Church with neglecting its central beliefs, arguing that it had 'gone back to a kind of materialism in religion, as well as in morals'. For this, he blamed world politics and especially the rise of communism, which had horrified the Church into the 'pathetic belief that they can win back people to the faith by giving them bread'. Walshe argued for a vibrant worldwide Church, and in his view Ireland would have its part to play, especially in regard to infiltrating the upper echelons of the Vatican. To this end, he suggested the building up of an elite of young priests to take their place in the secretariat. It was a period of great change, and Walshe found his new post challenging. 'In this welter of views and abnormalities', he concluded, 'it is difficult to steer a clear course as Vatican Representative.'[85]

In June 1946 Walshe presented his credentials to the Pope. Addressing his remarks in Italian, he referred to Ireland's long history of devout worship and missionary zeal. This faith in the Church, he assured the Holy Father, would continue, and the Irish people would 'never cease to be fervently united with him in unfailing prayer for the triumph of the Kingdom of God, not only where there had been the greatest work of destruction, but above all in the minds and hearts of men.' He asserted that it was his hope that 'the divisions that existed between the nations might disappear, and all people followed the principles of social reconstruction so humanistly expounded by the Supreme Pontiff; so that the much desired Christian revival may become the true foundation for a just and lasting peace.'[86] To this, the Pope responded in kind, and said that the history of Ireland 'in its alternating vicissitudes which had carried her successfully to splendid heights and calamitous depths, shows consistently what greatness which has remained unchanged through the course of the centuries: unshakable fidelity and unfailing attachment to the See of St Peter.'

The Holy Father further stated that no country could surpass the 'supernatural riches in faith' of Ireland, which was 'so rich in spiritual vitality as to be able to transfuse its super abundance … to other peoples'. The work of the millions of sons and daughters of Ireland had caused a new and flourishing Catholic life to arise and develop in many countries. He thanked Walshe for reconfirming the 'unshaken loyalty' of the Irish nation.[87] Walshe

believed that the ceremony was a success, particularly when the Pope had told him that 'if statesmen would follow Mr de Valera's example in public and in private, the solution of the world's problems would become much easier.'[88] He was gratified to learn that the Pope intended to appoint an Irish cardinal, and he felt that it was a time of great opportunity for the Irish in Rome.

During his audience with the Pope, Walshe learned of some startling news. The Holy Father, on replying to Walshe's specific enquiries, said that an Irish cardinal would be appointed at the next consistory, but then added, 'I was going to make Dublin a Cardinal but the *Americans* were opposed to it. I yielded because, after all, they are the *same as yourselves.*' Walshe could not help but suspect David Gray's involvement.[89] De Valera, however, was not as inclined to read any malicious intent into the matter, believing that the Americans 'had pressed for an extra Cardinal for themselves and had suggested that as the person they were pressing to be appointed was of Irish origin, and as Armagh was vacant we could wait.'[90] Walshe did not report this matter to Dublin immediately, as he hoped to be able to return home for a brief visit. By August, that trip looked unlikely, and he felt obliged to report his findings through the normal diplomatic means. This was typical of Walshe's style. The preferred option was always to deal with sensitive matters in person and 'off the record'. This matter further inspired Walshe to set about his task of meeting all the cardinals of the Curia. He was immediately struck by the 'very remarkable calibre' of these men who 'in culture and distinction … seem to be of an incomparably superior type', and were 'living proof of the essential superiority of Roman training and culture'. To Walshe's satisfaction, some expressed their admiration for the work of de Valera and others had a good knowledge of Irish history. They saw Ireland as a traditional Catholic nation, and would look to establish a 'very special form of cooperation'. This helped to confirm Walshe's view that the Irish had a unique opportunity to increase their influence within the Church in Rome.

The greatest encouragement Walshe received was from Cardinal Pizzardo, who said that Ireland would soon receive a nuncio 'of the first order', and that Ireland could be made 'the centre of a world revival of Catholic life'. Pizzardo criticised the Irish community in Rome for not learning the Italian language and for criticising everything Roman and Italian. Walshe

agreed with this assessment and suggested that the best policy would be to become 'more Roman than the Romans'. It was a policy he pursued vigorously himself as he expended considerable effort studying Roman and Church history. While he was already able to speak Italian, he strove to make himself more fluent, and reported that this had a very positive effect in his meetings with Vatican officials. Walshe believed that the Vatican would become one of the most important global political institutions. He established good relations with the Secretary of State, Monsignor Montini, who expressed a desire to educate himself about Ireland. Montini agreed that the Holy See had neglected to send the right sort of candidate to the Dublin nunciature, and Walshe found him agreeable to his suggestion to have a number of young Irishmen at Vatican headquarters.[91]

The length and detail of his frequent memoranda are an indication of the enthusiasm with which Walshe had taken up his post. At times, he was, perhaps, over-enthusiastic. From his meetings, Walshe gained the impression that Ireland was perfectly poised to make a significant impact on the Vatican. He received favourable replies to his efforts from Boland and de Valera, who were aware that Walshe needed encouragement. 'It is a great pleasure to see how energetically you have set to work', wrote de Valera. 'Keep it up and do not allow yourself to be discouraged.'[92] This support was of crucial importance to Walshe, who often felt isolated from headquarters. He responded with thanks for these words of support. Replying in August 1946 to a letter he had received from de Valera earlier that month, he expressed his extreme gratitude for the Taoiseach's kind words. They had given him 'the consolation and encouragement' that, he confessed, he had needed 'very badly'. Walshe admitted that during the opening months of his tenure, he had felt he was sending his reports into a 'vacuum'. He believed that, due to the pressures of work on de Valera back home, Boland must have been reluctant to bother the Taoiseach with reports from the Holy See. Walshe was used to a different system of operating, and was clearly missing the authority he once had when he was able to contact de Valera directly on any matter that needed attention:

> No doubt, also, the fact that I was no longer able to pick up the phone and report at once on national interests or my own troubles,

was too sudden a change for me, and I allowed myself to become too worried about an 'iron curtain' between myself and my superior which, in effect, did not exist, except in my imagination.[93]

De Valera, in support, wrote in a similar vein. 'I often wish that you were at the other end of the phone and that we had only to press a lever to get in immediate contact with one another.' However, he clearly outlined to Walshe that the proper channels should be used for all official business and memoranda: 'There is one thing I must ask you: never rely on any direct letter to me to get anything except something very special done. Make sure to duplicate it, as I think you do, in a formal letter to the Secretary, so that it may be immediately attended to.'[94]
De Valera, therefore, was making it quite clear that he did not want Walshe to bypass Boland and the Department of External Affairs on official matters.

Walshe had gone to great lengths to ensure that the Vatican's reply to his letter of credence was acceptable to the Irish government. Despite its apparent interest in Ireland, he found considerable ignorance concerning the constitutional position of the Irish Free State. He was astounded, for example, that the Secretary of State, Cardinal Montini, did not know that Ireland had a president or that the office of the Governor General no longer existed.[95] This prompted him to commission a new Italian translation of the Irish Constitution. De Valera complimented him on these efforts, and was at pains to reassure Walshe that he was keeping up to date with affairs in Rome by reading all the reports:

> Do not forget that although I may not write to you I read with interest every report you send, and I am constantly with you in spirit in the efforts you are making to secure for Ireland her rightful place in the Eternal City.[96]

Walshe admitted that the first eight months in Rome had left his nerves 'a bit ragged'. However, now that relations had been established and a system of communication was in place, he looked forward to a healthier lifestyle.[97] 'I have lots of reports to send on various aspects of the situation here', he reported, 'especially the growing strength of Communism and the anxiety of the Holy See in regard to it. It is flowing over the country like a wave after an earthquake.' The threat of communism was his greatest fear,

and he concluded that 'one could not safely prognosticate about future developments without coming to the conclusion that both Italy and the Church are facing a really serious crisis.'[98]

One of Walshe's other concerns was that the Irish embassy should have a suitable residence in Rome. At the time, the embassy building was in an undesirable part of town and was noisy and busy.[99] When he found the Villa Spada, it was not without other suitors. Gray, in Dublin, was warned by one US official:

> Don't mention the Villa Spada as we are trying to get it for ourselves, and Boland is in the way of interfering with this acquisition on account of Joe Walshe's wanting it so badly.[100]

The Villa Spada was, however, worth the wait. This seventeenth-century villa had a far superior location than the existing residence, and was surrounded by extensive grounds. Walshe wrote to Dublin seeking sanction for the purchase of the Villa Spada, and he was allowed a budget of $150,000 by the Department of Finance.[101] Using the help of Prince Pacelli, the legal adviser to the Vatican, Walshe secured the purchase of the property within his financial limit. However, the current tenant of the villa was not inclined to leave his place of residence. Walshe wrote concerning his difficulties over the removal of Robert Sulzer, secretary to the Swiss legation. 'He hates going, it is gall and wormwood for him to leave the place of his revels where he used to entertain the golden youth of Rome like a minor emperor.' Despite this problem, Walshe was satisfied that things were going to plan, and he did not appreciate criticism from subordinates at Iveagh House on the matter:

> On [Saturday evening] having worked all day and up to a late hour on the Spada for a long time I get a [telegram] from the [Department] (no doubt Gallagher) suggesting that the payment of the ⅔ to Bonanni was the cause of the delay in getting out Sulzer and that I had acted without consulting Prince Pacelli ... all that *in clear*, to a country where every telegram is scrutinised by the British, American and Italian authorities.

Walshe insisted that he had acted in consultation with Pacelli, and added in the margin of the letter that it looked likely that Sulzer would leave within a short time. He concluded with the following plea to Boland:

Above all, Fred, I beg of you as a good friend never to let either Leo [McCauley] or Gallagher fire off letters or telegrams to me suggesting I am neglecting or have neglected the interests of the State. That is the one thing I cannot stand. It would cause such a collapse in my psychological relations with home that I could not physically go on. That may indicate great weakness of character but I can't work without the understanding and sympathy which you have created between us and I am sure between yourself and the other rep[resentative]s abroad.[102]

Walshe may have been having some difficulty in adapting to his new position as a subordinate within the overall External Affairs hierarchy, but the department in Dublin was also feeling the effects of Walshe's departure. Perhaps not so much because he was missed, but because it was now realised how much work needed to be done. Walshe was told by one visitor that External Affairs was 'frightfully badly off for men', and that the 'situation seems to be quite desperate'. Walshe suggested to Boland, with just perhaps a little irony, 'Could you bring back some of the older men for a while to the [Department] until you had a good selection of young fellows trained?'[103]

On the question of the new nuncio for Ireland, Walshe sought instructions. He suggested that an Irish-American would be suitable, but he was at this stage open to other suggestions: 'Things may have happened since I left home which would warrant the type of strong Italian who would understand the desires of the Holy Father and carry them out.'[104] Walshe was somewhat out of touch with headquarters, which was of the view that someone of Irish origin would be more suitable for the job. Walshe quickly came into line with opinion in Dublin. The following year, he told Montini that 'the appointment of anybody but an Irishman would be most unwelcome.'[105] He believed that the appointment of a nuncio to Ireland would be a test case, and concluded that 'the mere appointment of an Italian even if he were a saint, would be resented by the Hierarchy and would be a defeat for the [Government] on a most important issue external and internal.'[106] In such an eventuality, he suggested that his withdrawal from the Holy See be given serious consideration. Later, on hearing rumours that Monsignor Panico was showing interest in the Irish post, Walshe lost no time in telling Montini why he would not

be a suitable nuncio for Ireland. Not only was Panico an Italian, but Walshe also mentioned his 'extreme worldliness ... his greed for gold ... [and his] notorious cupidity'.[107] Panico had been noted as an antagonist of the Irish while in Australia, and was deemed wholly unsuitable by de Valera.[108] Walshe was horrified by the unsuitability of this proposed appointment, and said that it was 'only in a system where the human and the divine get so inextricably mixed up ... and often without a serious effort to diag-nose which is which ... that such ghastly errors can be perpetrated'.[109]

When Walshe came to the end of his first year in Rome, he expressed the hope that he would make considerably more pro-gress in his second year. He was deeply committed to his work, and explained that it took some time and effort to get to know the workings of the Vatican; he also admitted that he was still 'at sea' about a number of matters. 'In truth', he said, 'every month I spend at this post, the more convinced I am that you must nearly live with the Monsignori and with the lay follower in order to do the job properly.'[110] The nuncio question would remain at the top of his agenda, and he was unwilling to make a trip home at this stage as he believed that he was not in the Villa Spada long enough to have the system 'well oiled'.[111] He believed, however, that some progress was being made on a number of issues, and that Cardinal Montini was beginning to see things from the Irish perspective.

Early the following year, in 1948, de Valera lost the general election and relinquished power to an inter-party government, with Fine Gael's John A. Costello taking over as Taoiseach. Before his departure, de Valera paid tribute to the department that Walshe had managed for most of the Free State's two-and-a-half decades of independence:

> In the Department of External Affairs the nation is magnificently served. I was often amazed by the fact that they were able, small in numbers as they were, to do the work they did.[112]

Seán MacBride, leader of Clann na Poblachta, took over as Minister for External Affairs. Walshe would have been sorry to see de Valera go, but he did not let this affect his work at the Vatican, which he continued with unstinting enthusiasm. By the end of

1948, he firmly believed that previous Irish approaches to Vatican diplomacy had been too timid and that a more forceful approach should be adopted.[113] This was partly based on his view that the Vatican could no longer ignore the vast contribution made by Ireland to the international Church.[114] In a letter to Boland on 13 November 1948, Walshe referred to the repeal of the External Relations Act by Costello, which made the Free State a republic. Walshe discussed the matter with Cardinal Montini, and in his report to Dublin stated:

> He understands the motives for the repeal perfectly and he expressed his astonishment that we could have allowed the anomaly to continue so long. I explained again Mr de Valera's motive for retaining the tenuous link when the Act was passed as well as the fact that he and his whole party now completely supported the Minister's policy of repeal. Moreover the whole country was unanimous in its desire to break the last constitutional link.[115]

Walshe's report was discreet in his respect for de Valera while remaining deferential towards the new government.

In August 1949 Walshe wrote to Dublin to remind Iveagh House of the need for secrecy in all important diplomatic matters. This was based on the fact that public knowledge of some issues or statements would be detrimental to the normal workings of diplomacy:

> As I have always tried to give most faithfully in my reports everything that I hear of the slightest Irish interest and my own reactions thereto, I have sometimes to write … material of a somewhat explosive character, as is almost everything concerning the Irish Clergy. Otherwise, I should become a useless limb of the Department deserving only to be cut off at the first opportunity. And I certainly should not be following the principle of *uberrima fides* if I were to doctor my reports by exaggerations, additions or subtractions.[116]

Walshe rightly believed that confidentiality was of the utmost importance if he was to induce Vatican officials to speak freely and frankly with him. He expressed the hope that his reports would remain within 'the narrowest possible circle', but believed that this was already the case as he was sure that only Boland and

the minister would be privy to his reports. In this case, he was correct in saying that 'the very slightest breath or rumour that the Cardinals had criticised our Hierarchy, even in the most friendly fashion, would destroy all possibility of our helping to bring about that collaboration which is so great an interest for the future of our country.' Walshe's difficulty, however, lay in recognising that some information was of more general concern. In seeking to limit his reports to the departmental secretary and the minister or the Taoiseach, Walshe was intruding into a matter on which he could no longer dictate.

Walshe was finding it difficult to relinquish the reins of power and adapt to his new position as a single spoke in the wheel of the Irish diplomatic service. Believing that the Vatican was the model for Irish foreign policy, he had also presumed that his reports would be crucial to Dublin. This was not always the case, and when he received Boland's request for ideas on how to improve the propaganda of the diplomatic service he was only too happy to use the opportunity to give his views. He enthusiastically suggested the use of a pamphlet giving the history of Ireland's glorious past. It would be a most important asset to have in Rome, which he saw as 'the most potentially fruitful centre of propaganda in the world'. Referring to Ireland's contribution to Catholicism and also to the recent declaration of a republic he said:

> At a time when Protestantism is going to pieces, and Catholicism is clearly destined to be accepted, as the only true form of the Christian Faith, the Republic can shake off its historic attachments to a tradition which was really never naturally ours, and go back to its only solid claim to the gratitude of the Civilized world, namely, that we have never ceased to be the defenders and advocates of Christian beliefs and principles in their highest form.[117]

As a means of heightening Ireland's prominence, he suggested the use of the modern tools of propaganda such as film and audio recording. He explained to Boland how 'The voice ... is recorded electrically on a wire without any trouble whatsoever and can be immediately reproduced on the same instrument.' Walshe was not shy about utilising the opportunities such new technology afforded:

People love to hear themselves reproduced on the wire with almost

miraculous speed and we can make use of the fact to slip in a statement of the Minister before or after. I use this failing to make them listen to 'Dun do Shuile' or 'Caoineadh na dtri Muire'.

He suggested that it might be especially useful for Seán MacBride, who could make statements regarding partition in French for dispatch abroad.

Walshe had a number of suggestions to make in regard to improving the position of Irish ambassador to the Holy See. Since his arrival in 1946, he had found it difficult to carry out his duties on the salary and expenses provided. In 1941 a Department of External Affairs memorandum, which was probably drafted by Walshe, outlined the duties and responsibilities expected of the Irish representative to the Vatican. The position called for the 'highest degree of care and self-sacrifice', and any Irish representative there was expected to alter their lifestyle in order to fit the environment of the Vatican. Attendance at social functions was to be kept to a minimum and the temptation to become too involved with the Roman community outside the Vatican was to be resisted. The Vatican and its resident diplomats provided ample opportunity for social contact. The Irish representative was not precluded from entertaining guests, but a careful balance between generosity and flamboyance had to be maintained:

> His emoluments are sufficient, but only sufficient, to maintain through his own household a modicum of entertainment suited to the modest dignity which should characterise Irish representation abroad.[118]

Now, however, Walshe discovered that 'modest dignity' was, in practice, not sufficient to host the hoards of guests he felt obliged to entertain. This became a major part of his job, and much of his own salary went towards supporting that task. Apart from establishing contacts with Vatican officials, Walshe was obliged to receive a multitude of visitors from Ireland. The fact that he was a single man made his task all the more difficult.[119] Walshe was now experiencing first hand some of the problems of the diplomat, which he had shown little sympathy with when he was ensconced in Iveagh House. 'It has become a fully proven fact of my experience that if you want to maintain and create contacts of value for the work of the mission, you must do so round your

own dinner table', and he estimated that he entertained over two thousand people each year.[120] The cost of this was high: 'Each person for lunch costs, as an absolute minimum twenty two shillings ... and, generally, it runs much higher depending on the individual capacity for consumption of wines, liqueurs, cigars etc.' To assure Boland that he was not personally contributing to these expenses, Walshe reported that he had given up both wine and cigars. He had to maintain four servants and complained that each had a large appetite. He told Boland that he did not want to exaggerate the situation, but went on to say:

> I am quite ready to reduce all expenditures, even these minimal essentials for my work; but if I had to do so, would it not be better to close down for a year or so; and try to do the exclusively official Vatican contacts from a flat of a few rooms with one servant. It would be still better to send me elsewhere to help in the present campaign against the partition of our country.[121]

To suggest the temporary closure of the Irish embassy was sensational. It is clear that, apart from the lack of sufficient finances, he was obviously depressed about the Vatican's poor response to Irish advances in a number of areas. He suggested therefore that the closure could be portrayed as a protest, but admitted that overall the consequences would be detrimental to Irish influence and esteem. His suggestion was a dramatic device and one that he himself did not take seriously. For the sake of the nation, he would struggle on with what he had at his disposal: 'So we have to try and combine essential economies with the continued maintenance of the present Embassy, and the softpedalling scale on which I try to run it.' Walshe argued, therefore, for preferential treatment for the post of Irish ambassador to the Holy See. He had always believed it to be the most important of all the diplomatic posts, and now sought increased remuneration to help meet the vast expenses of the mission.

Despite these financial restrictions, Walshe greatly enjoyed his time in Rome, and he continued his dedicated devotion to his task. He had grave concerns over international affairs and was constantly worried about the spread of communism:

> Here the feeling is growing more pessimistic every day and some

of the colleagues have made their plans for a sudden exit by plane should the war suddenly start. What a desperately wrong attitude! But we should take due note of it. It seems to be useless to try and judge Russian reactions by ordinary standards. They may even believe, in their almost religious fervour, that the chaos of a new war, no matter who won, might be the best road to universal bolshevism. Their provocative conduct seems to have no other explanation.[122]

Throughout his time at the Holy See, this attitude did not change. In December 1951, for example, he hoped that de Valera, now back in power after a three-year absence, would make a visit to Rome in order to show solidarity with the Holy Father in the build-up to what he described as the 'coming crisis'.[123] He aired the question of whether the Pope should remain in Rome in the case of a Russian occupation, and suggested that the Irish authorities would have to 'consider the possibility of His wishing to come to Ireland'.[124] He thought it would be an enormous coup for Ireland if that eventuality came to pass:

> It would indeed be a strange and wonderful event in the story of our Country, if the Successor of St. Peter had to take refuge amongst us from what threatens to be the greatest of all the persecutions, not only of the Christian Church, but of all free institutions.[125]

Despite the hard work Walshe put into his efforts at the Holy See, there is no doubt that he was happy in Rome. This was borne out by his plans to remain there following his retirement. One contemporary account depicts Walshe in Rome when the American author, Mary Bromage, made her way to the Villa Spada to meet him. Upon arrival, she was greeted by Luigi, 'young and gamesome and strutting in his green livery', who showed her to the garden:

> His Excellency awaited us, standing on the gravelled walk by his small swimming pool … Still, we saw, in the moment of reunion, the correct and humorous bachelor of his country's foreign service. He was, however, more celibate than bachelor, wedded only and forever to Rome … Though more unchanged than changed, he was a thousand times at home here.[126]

Walshe, it seems, was never short of company at the Villa Spada,

for 'Luigi hovered as a frolicsome, perhaps naughty, much-loved companion.' Bromage also described how Walshe, for company, 'had the young priests studying all around him in the Ambiente, for he would invite them in the afternoons to swim in this pool'. Considering his normal penchant for privacy, the tone of the article, published some years after his death, would not have been appreciated by Walshe.

By the end of 1953, Walshe was reaching the end of his tenure at the Vatican, and was soon due to retire altogether from the service of the Department of External Affairs. He had mixed feelings about his achievements as Ireland's ambassador to the Holy See. He wrote to de Valera commenting on the fruition of the one great hope he had held at the start of his tenure: 'I think we have reached the end, or almost the end of the grave neglect by Rome of the mass of Catholic opinion in the West.' He described it as an extremely interesting post, and thanked de Valera for having sent him there. With some sadness he concluded:

> This is my last Christmas in Rome. I have become an obstacle to the promotion of a whole group of young fellows, and that is the last thing I want to do. P.G. [Please God] before I leave, I shall be able to tie up a few more loose ends, so that I can have the consolation of feeling that I really tried hard to do what you sent me here to do.[127]

This last paragraph of Walshe's letter somewhat shocked de Valera as it reminded him of Walshe's imminent departure. He congratulated Walshe on his service, saying, 'I do not know of anyone who could throw himself as energetically into the work, or feel as you feel how great the work was in the interest of the two great Causes to which you have devoted yourself. I am sure your work will bear perennial fruit.'[128] De Valera felt genuine sadness as he enquired of Walshe as to his future plans. Those plans were only vaguely defined at this stage. For health reasons, he had been advised to spend time in a dry climate and therefore South Africa was where he expected to spend the first eight months of his retirement. There he could decide what to do, but he already had it in mind to settle in Rome. This plan was liable to change depending on the international situation or if there was a radical currency change that would have affected his standard of living,

as his source of income derived from Ireland. Rome, he said, was the next best place after Ireland to live in. With the many Irish priests and nuns resident in the Holy City, there was never any danger of being lonely. It was also near enough to Ireland for an annual visit home.

Over the years, Walshe had built up a large collection of books on Roman and Church history, which he believed were necessary for his work there. 'I could get nowhere until I had penetrated beyond the surface of their culture, and had contrived in some small degree, at any rate, to become one of themselves.' Walshe had not only succeeded in going native but enjoyed every minute of it:

> I do not regret all the long hours of study I have given to achieve this end. I have derived the enormous personal advantage, from these years spent in Rome, of becoming a much more serious student of the essentials of our civilisation ... I still have a mass of reading to do – and I have the books available for it. So I am looking forward with joy and tranquillity to the years which may still lie before me.[129]

Joseph Walshe retired on 2 October 1954. For a time, he resided in Kalk Bay, Cape Province in South Africa, as he had planned. Unfortunately, he was not allowed as much time as he might have wished for to enjoy his retirement. He had little opportunity to fulfil his hopes of further research and writing, although it seems he enjoyed his brief sojourn. He died of cardiac asthma in February 1956 at the age of seventy. He had been on a visit to Egypt, and was buried in Cairo. A newspaper report of his funeral cites 'many mourners' in attendance, but the list makes no mention of family or friends from home. Walshe's home was Ireland, his spiritual home was Rome, and his life had been dedicated to the service of his country.

CHAPTER 9

WALSHE'S LEGACY

FRED BOLAND, IN his memoirs, emphasised the central importance of Joseph Walshe in the study of the history of Irish foreign affairs. The findings of this study confirm that view. From 1922 to 1946, Walshe was the single-most consistent influence in the management of Irish foreign policy. He played a pivotal role in the formulation and administration of that policy and in the building of the Department of External Affairs. While Walshe's arrival at the most senior position in the department was quite fortuitous, the archives show that he possessed the capabilities demanded by that exacting position. Boland states that Walshe had the advantage of 'intellectual and dialectical equipment which none of his fellow Heads of Department at that time could claim'.[1] His expertise was indispensable to successive Irish administrations. He held a degree in law, and possessed a strong grasp of international and constitutional law. This was evident from the role he assumed in the important constitutional debates during that time. Walshe identified opportunities for constitutional advancement, although his memoranda often counselled prudent strategies to temper the actions of those who sought unrealisable or unsafe objectives. Walshe encouraged political leaders to travel in order to foster alliances with other dominions, while his own regular visits to London helped in the establishment and development of closer links with British officials. It has been shown that these contacts were crucial in providing Walshe with a valuable channel of communication throughout his diplomatic career.

By the end of the 1920s, Walshe had established himself as the leading departmental adviser on foreign affairs. He had created a secure infrastructure for the department, but remained conscious of the need to continue to raise the stature of External

Affairs. Walshe's desire to see the department as a permanent entity stimulated his appreciation for the need for professionalism in every aspect of his work. In his early years, he quickly gained an exceptional knowledge of the diplomatic procedural precedent necessary for the successful fulfilment of his duties. With great alacrity, he assumed responsibility for ensuring that the government had the requisite expertise available to formulate informed foreign policy. Walshe also established himself as a somewhat distant and austere superior who was not always remembered with fondness by those who worked under him. He had a habit of keeping aloof from his fellow diplomats, and it has been shown that he under-utilised subordinates who were a valuable source of specialist knowledge. Walshe placed great demands on himself, and he expected diplomats to adhere to the same exacting standards of professional behaviour. It is clear that he sometimes expected unrealistic performances from Irish envoys abroad. The position of heads of missions under Walshe was often made more difficult by his practice of supplying them with vague or imprecise instructions. While that may have been the fault of his political superiors, it is more likely a reflection of his own conservative diplomatic style.

Notwithstanding his defects as a diplomat and chief administrator, Walshe held a central role during a number of critical periods in the development of the Irish state. During the transfer of power from Cumann na nGaedheal to Fianna Fáil, for example, his influence was pivotal. Despite having previously criticised the Fianna Fáil leader, the evidence shows that Walshe, by remaining at his post in 1932, helped to provide the administrative continuity that was instrumental in the success of de Valera's efforts to establish his government as a constitutional and rational administration. Furthermore, Walshe utilised de Valera's arrival as an opportunity to develop and expand the Department of External Affairs. De Valera had a keen interest in foreign affairs, and his dual portfolio meant that Walshe had a most powerful ally at the Cabinet table. Walshe had no difficulty in establishing a good working relationship with de Valera, who soon came to rely heavily on his advice.

Walshe was highly regarded for his negotiating ability – a skill that appealed greatly to de Valera. Boland explains that 'what made Joe such a formidable adversary ... and does more than

anything to explain his extraordinary ability to influence people and win them over to his own way of thinking, was the remarkable intuitive sense which enabled him to identify other people's human weakness and to play on them to his own advantage.[2]

Walshe was given plenty of opportunity to use those skills, particularly in the management of Anglo-Irish relations. It must be said, however, that Walshe as a negotiator had one major flaw: he had a tendency to gloss over points of contention in the minutes of critical meetings. This may have been a deliberate effort to get discussions started, but it often led to difficulties later. Having said that, Walshe's talent for 'persuasive eloquence' certainly made him an asset in any negotiating team, and this was demonstrated in an obvious way during the many Anglo-Irish discussions during the 1930s.

Walshe was instrumental in finalising the 1938 agreement with Britain, which settled the economic dispute, legitimised de Valera's constitutional changes, and paved the way for Irish neutrality. This was the result, in large part, of years of effort by Walshe, who had maintained regular contact with British officials throughout the economic war. Against the background of the approaching global conflict, Walshe understood which concessions Britain was most likely to accede to, and on that basis negotiated determinedly to ensure the closure of the agreement before the advent of war. Walshe, however, was sometimes out of touch with de Valera's latest thoughts on Ireland's position in relation to the coming war. During these negotiations, he indicated to British officials that the Irish government would be willing to accede to a defence arrangement with Britain in return for significant developments on the question of Northern Ireland. He also stated that neutrality was not being seriously considered in Dublin at that time. This was not the case, and the following year he travelled to London to seek recognition for Irish neutrality, the course chosen by de Valera. The outbreak of the Second World War, therefore, provided Walshe with the most serious professional challenge of his career. He helped administer a precarious neutral policy that was not clearly formulated. The documentation indicates that there were few guidelines for that policy's implementation, and decisions were made on a *pro re nata* basis. While declaring neutrality, the Irish government found itself compromised by British requests for assistance. This position was made more difficult by the lack of military power to defend the

country's integrity if attacked with force. Departmental papers make it clear that, while de Valera was in direct charge of foreign policy during this period, it was left to Walshe to formulate the best means of implementing Ireland's neutrality.

Walshe's wartime sympathies lay with Britain, and he encouraged much of the Irish government's covert cooperation with the Allies during this period. It is true, however, that he was pragmatic in his approach towards neutrality. Considering the bleak future that appeared to await Britain in the summer of 1940, Walshe saw no reason to tie Ireland to its ailing neighbour. While the decision to reject Britain's offer of a united Ireland in return for participation in the war was made by de Valera, Walshe's prognosis for the outcome of the war could not have failed to influence the Taoiseach.[3] Walshe was similarly pragmatic in his dealings with Germany. While accommodating in his conversations with Hempel, he held no genuine sympathy for Hitler. De Valera would not have tolerated such pro-German sentiment, and Walshe always acted under instructions. What are sometimes interpreted as pro-German utterances must be seen in the context of the mid-1940 period when it appeared to many that Germany would be victorious. Thus, it was natural for Walshe to consider the possibility of Ireland's position in a new world order, and his conversations with Hempel were designed to give that impression.

The records of Walshe's meetings with foreign diplomats based in Dublin during the war show the level of diplomatic acumen he possessed. At one point during the war, he was in the contradictory position of seeking from Germany 'special consideration' for Ireland's policy of neutrality, while at another level actively working to maintain Dublin's newly established relationship with Britain. It was Walshe who gave Boland specific charge of Axis affairs, while he remained responsible for Allied matters. The archives demonstrate, however, that this delegation of responsibilities did not preclude Walshe from attending meetings with Hempel at critical moments during the war. Axis and Allied diplomats alike were agreed on the importance of Walshe in dealing with de Valera. The sources show that Gray was the most sceptical of Walshe, but he nevertheless maintained close contact with the External Affairs secretary. Their sometimes acrimonious meetings placed an extra strain on Walshe, who expected the United States to display a more helpful attitude towards Ireland.

Walshe took a firm stand on Allied requests and advised de Valera to maintain neutrality. While his sympathies did not lie with Germany, Walshe was never willing to let the Irish government be dictated to by London or by Washington. This may not have always been the most prudent policy, especially later in the war when it became clear that the Allies would be victorious. It is paradoxical that Walshe was constantly worried that Ireland would be ostracised by the international community after the end of hostilities. During the course of the war, de Valera had come to question Walshe's judgement, and it became clear that a new manager of External Affairs would be appointed to oversee Irish foreign policy in the postwar period.

By the end of his tenure, there was a lack of a reforming atmosphere within Iveagh House, and it was clear that Walshe had been ineffectual in certain areas of administration. That External Affairs would be better served by a new secretary was evident when a conference of the heads of missions of the Irish diplomatic service took place immediately after the war. An atmosphere of new opportunity was palpable, as those who had felt cut off from head office were given the opportunity to air their views. Communications had been restricted not only by war, but also by Walshe's administrative style. Sensing that Walshe would not be head of External Affairs for much longer, many diplomats strongly criticised the organisation and procedures of the department. However, while Walshe had sometimes shown the strain of his work during the Second World War, his overall performance must be credited, considering the difficult circumstances under which he operated. Walshe was rewarded for his long service by being given the post he most desired, that of Irish ambassador to the Holy See. Throughout his career, he had regarded the Vatican's diplomatic corps as a model for Iveagh House, and believed that the mission there was Ireland's most important diplomatic post.

Clearly, Walshe would greatly miss being secretary of the department, but his new posting to Rome would give him the chance he always wanted to set the Church back on the right path. Boland recounts how Walshe believed he could influence the overall direction of the Church and 'save them from their blunders!'[4] Other than Boland's memoirs, there are few other personalised accounts of Walshe by contemporaries. Mary Bromage, however, on hearing of Walshe's death in 1956, wrote of her

meetings with him over the years. She had observed his fixation
with the Holy City, but noted that his reverence was not one
of sole Catholic piety, as he was also fascinated with its pagan
history. Bromage's account accurately described Walshe's satisfaction with his life in Rome: 'There, and perhaps in the Africa
of Augustine, was where his world lay; where his world had its
beginning and where it would, he hoped, have its end.'[5] It is evident that following twenty-four years as head of External Affairs,
Walshe warmly welcomed the opportunity to go to Rome. During
his time in Iveagh House, his health had suffered, although his
commitment to his departmental responsibilities had never
wavered. During periods abroad for treatment and recuperation,
he reflected on how thoroughly he enjoyed his work. De Valera
often soothed Walshe's insecurities by telling him that External
Affairs was not the same without the absent secretary. At these
times, his correspondence shows how dependent he had become
on the department, and he would have found it difficult to contemplate the idea of leaving the diplomatic service.

One reason why Walshe and de Valera had developed such
a close affinity was because of their shared value in secrecy. Unfortunately, this secretive diplomatic style has made it difficult
to assess Walshe's true contribution to Irish foreign-policy formation; it is likely that much documentary material relating
to Walshe was destroyed, possibly by the secretary himself. De
Valera, however, may have been equally to blame. Towards the
end of Walshe's career with External Affairs, the Taoiseach wrote
asking the former secretary if he would care to piece together an
official account of Ireland's wartime neutrality.[6] Walshe responded
by saying:

> Of course, I should be only too delighted to help in recalling the
> events of the war years. But you will remember, Sir, how extremely
> careful you always were, and it is doubtful if we have a single note
> in the Department, beyond perhaps something in regard to Gray's
> pernicious manoeuvres. However, when the other side have done all
> their work of publication, perhaps we could do something to fill the
> gaps, if circumstances and prudence permits.[7]

However, even where records exist, many difficulties are encountered.
The nature of the diplomatic documentation is problematic as it is

readily apparent that each diplomat wrote accounts of conversations from their own perspective. This was often done solely to satisfy their superiors. Furthermore, many of the departmental memoranda were unsigned and very often simply outline the policies that had been made, without illuminating how these decisions came about.

Walshe's heavy reliance on verbal communication makes a comprehensive picture of his role difficult. If the Minister for External Affairs is sometimes missing from the narrative, it is because much of their contact was oral and, often, little written correspondence passed between them. This is confirmed by Boland, who states that Walshe 'rarely committed his policy proposals to paper, preferring to try to persuade his Minister of their soundness by discussion'. This was particularly true during the de Valera administration. Walshe and de Valera had regular contact, meeting a couple of times a week or more, and having telephone conversations perhaps two or three times a day, or whenever the need arose.[8] Walshe would normally send de Valera a written memorandum only after they had already discussed what its content should be, and amendments would similarly be discussed in person or over the telephone. Similarly, when speeches and important policy documents needed to be written, de Valera would start by convening a meeting of his close advisers:

> We'd start to discuss the issue involved ... to decide what to put in, and Dev would dismiss various suggestions made until, suddenly, somebody would put forward an idea ... something would click with him and he'd say, 'Now, if you could write a speech on that theme, with that sort of note, I think we'd have what we are looking for.'[9]

Thus, the allocation of credit or blame, to particular people for certain ideas, is difficult. The numerous references to telephone conversations and statements such as 'I will speak with you on this matter in person' further frustrate attempts to accurately ascertain the level of influence Walshe had over policy matters. In this way, much of the Walshe–de Valera interaction is lost, but their *modus operandi* is significant in itself as it emphasises their highly confidential attitude towards their work.

While de Valera was always closely informed on important foreign-policy matters, Walshe was allowed a significant degree of

autonomy in dealing with departmental concerns. Boland tells us that Walshe never sought the limelight. This is true to the extent that he never wanted to be the focus of attention. However, his delegation of tasks within the department shows that he always maintained intimate involvement in all matters of significance. Walshe was, perhaps, over-protective of his position. While his closest assistants were permitted some involvement, they were never allowed to penetrate the highest levels of decision-making within the department. Walshe's substantial control over the administration of the department was largely due to de Valera's workload as Taoiseach, which meant that Walshe had the authority to attend to many issues of foreign policy and administration without significant consultation. However, on all matters of importance, de Valera's direction was paramount. Walshe's expertise was valued, but it is clear that 'de Valera was de Valera's primary foreign policy adviser', to use the words of Maurice Moynihan.[10] Therefore, while Walshe had a significant input into policy decisions, de Valera had his own ideas on foreign policy and would not always have been substantially swayed by Walshe.

Walshe, it may be concluded, held the central diplomatic position of influence during a momentous period in twentieth-century Irish history. By the time he was finally posted to the Vatican in 1946, the department had developed from its uncertain beginnings to become a valued agent in the Irish administrative decision-making process. Walshe had played a dual role as chief administrator and policy adviser. He had shaped the administrative culture of a department that endured many challenges: civil war, constitutional upheaval, transfer of power to former revolutionaries, economic war with Britain, and, finally, the Second World War. That had not been an easy task in the financially restrictive conditions of the time. Walshe's greatest contribution lay in his efforts to normalise Anglo-Irish relations in the 1920s and 1930s; he succeeded very well in that regard. While he may have shown signs of stress during the Second World War, it is to his credit as a professional diplomat that the department he established almost single-handedly withstood the strain imposed on it by the precarious policy of neutrality.

The continuity that Walshe brought to External Affairs was crucial to the state's development. During his tenure in charge of the department responsible for Irish foreign policy, Walshe acted

as the common thread, serving under six minsters before being appointed Ireland's first ambassador to the Holy See. From the available documentation, it is clear that Walshe exercised a disproportionate influence over almost every aspect of Irish foreign policy during his period in office. He personified the professionalism and dedication of that pioneering generation, and while his career was marked by both achievements and mistakes, his commitment to the administration of Irish foreign policy and the national interest was never in doubt.

BIBLIOGRAPHY

PRIMARY SOURCES

Ireland
National Archives, Bishop Street, Dublin
Department of Foreign Affairs
  Secretary's Office Files, A, P & S Series
  Secretary's Office Early Files
  General Registry Files – Pre-100, 100, 200, 300, etc.
  Confidential Reports
Papers of Desmond FitzGerald
  Letter Books
  Dáil Éireann Papers (Propaganda Department Files)
  Governor General Files
  Department of Foreign Affairs 1920s – Series D, EA, GR, LN, P
  D – Colonial and Dominions Office
  EA – External Affairs, general political files
  GR – General Registry, foreign affairs material
  LN – League of Nations
  P Series
Department of the Taoiseach
  S Files
Department of Finance
  Establishment Files
Department of Justice
  Office of the Controller of Censorship
University College, Dublin
  Papers of Desmond FitzGerald
  Papers of Patrick McGilligan
Franciscan Archives, Killiney, County Dublin
  Papers of Éamon de Valera (now housed in UCD Archives Department)
Military Archives, Cathal Brugha barracks, Dublin
  Papers relating to Censorship during the Second World War
  Departmental S Files
Public Record Office of Northern Ireland
  Cabinet Conclusions Files
  Papers of Sir Earnest Clark

England
Public Record Office, Kew, London
  Foreign Office (FO 371 Series)
  Prime Minister's Office (PREM)
  War Cabinet Papers (CAB)
  Dominions Office (DO)
Institute of Commonwealth Studies, Russell Square, London
  Correspondence relating to Land Purchase Annuities
  Correspondence relating to Oath of Allegiance
National Registry of Archives, Chancery Lane, London
  Index of Archives

United States of America
National Archives and Records Administration, Washington DC and Suitland, Maryland
State Department Records (Record Group 59 & 84)
Department of Defence, Office of Strategic Services (OSS) Files (Microfilm M Series)
Library of Congress, Washington DC
Papers of Myron C. Taylor, Diplomatic Service, Vatican
Papers of Robert Lansing, 1911–1928
Papers of Cordell Hull, United States, Department of State, Secretary of State
Papers of Clare Luce Boothe, 1903-1987
Franklin D. Roosevelt Library, Hyde Park, New York
Gray, David, Minister to Ireland 1940–47: Papers 1855–1962
Roosevelt, Franklin D, Papers as President, President's Secretary's File
Roosevelt, Franklin D, Papers as President, President's Official File
Roosevelt, Franklin D, Papers as President, Map Room Papers
Roosevelt, Franklin D, Papers as President, President's Personal File
State Department Dispatches
American Heritage Center, Laramie, Wyoming
The David Gray Collection (while some overlap occurred, this collection contained significantly different material to the Gray Papers housed in the Roosevelt Presidential Library. It includes Gray's draft autobiography)
Harry S. Truman Library, Independence, Missouri
Truman, Harry S, President's Secretary's Files
Truman, Harry S, Official File
Matthews, Francis P, Papers

OTHER PRIMARY AND CONTEMPORARY SOURCES

Bewley, C.. *Memoirs of a Wild Goose* (Dublin, Lilliput Press, 1989).
Boland, F., *Reminiscences of an Irish Diplomat: Frederich H. Boland, Ambassador to London, Permanent Representative at the United Nations and President of the General Assembly 1960*, compiled by his daughter Mella Boland (Crowley).
Bromage, M., 'Roman Love Story', *Michigan Quarterly Review* (Winter 1963), pp. 18–21.
Clarke, D.. *Seven Assignments* (London, Jonathan Cape, 1948).
Documents on German Foreign Policy 1918-1945 (DGFP) (London, HMSO).
Documents on Irish Foreign Policy (DIFP) (Dublin, RIA).
Foreign Relations of the United States (FRUS) (US State Department).
Maffey, Sir J., 'Lord Rugby Remembers', interviews with Terence de Vere White of the *Irish Times*.
Ó Broin, L., *Just Like Yesterday: an autobiography* (Dublin, Gill and Macmillan, [c. 1985]).
Ó Ceallaigh, S., *Seán T: Scéal a bheatha ó 1916 go 1923 á insint ag Seán T. Ó Ceallaigh* (Cló Morainn, 1972).
Van Hoek, K., *Diplomats in Dublin* (Dublin and Cork, The Talbot Press, 1943).
Woodward, Sir L., *British Foreign Policy in the Second World War*, Vol. I (London, HMSO, 1970).

SECONDARY SOURCES

Bailey, T., *A Diplomatic History of the American People* (ninth edition) (New Jersey, Prentice-Hall, 1974).

Barcroft, S., 'Irish Foreign Policy at the League of Nations 1929–1936', *Irish Studies in International Affairs* Vol. 1, No. 1 (1979), pp. 19–29.

Barrington, T.J., 'Public Administration 1927–1936,' in F. McManus (ed.), *The Years of the Great Test* (Dublin and Cork, Mercier Press, in collaboration with Radio Telefís Éireann, 1978), pp. 80–91.

Bell, J., *The Secret Army: The IRA 1916–1979* (second edition) (Dublin, Academy Press, 1979).

Bowman, J., *De Valera and the Ulster question, 1917–73*(Oxford, Clarendon Press, 1982).

Boyce, D., *Nationalism in Ireland* (London, Croom Helm, 1982).

Canning, P., *British Policy Towards Ireland 1921–1941* (Oxford, Clarendon Press, 1985).

Carroll, J., *Ireland in the War Years* (Newton Abbott, David & Charles, 1975).

Carter, C., *The Shamrock and the Swastika: German Espionage in Ireland in World War II* (Palo Alto, California, Pacific Books, 1977).

Chubb, B. (ed.), *A Source Book of Irish Government* (second edition) (Dublin, IPA, 1983).

Chubb, B., *The Government and Politics of Ireland* (second edition) (London, Longman, 1982).

Coogan, T.P., *Ireland Since the Rising* (London, Pall Mall Press; New York, Praeger, 1966).

Coogan, T.P., *De Valera: Long Fellow, Long Shadow* (London, Hutchinson, 1993).

Coogan, T.P., *The IRA* (London, Pall Mall Press, 1970).

Cook, C. (ed.), *Sources in British Political History, 1900–51. Vol. 2: A Guide to Papers of Selected Civil Servants* (London, Macmillan, 1975)

Cronin, S., *Washington's Irish Policy 1916–1986: Independence, Partition, Neutrality* (Dublin, Anvil Books, 1987).

Cronin, S., *Frank Ryan: The Search for the Republic* (Dublin, Respol, 1980).

Cruise O'Brien, C., 'The Roots of my Preoccupations', *The Atlantic Monthly*, Vol. 274, No. 1 (July 1994), pp. 73–81. [Also available online from: http://www.theatlantic.com/unbound/flashbks/cruise/cruis794.htm].

De Vere White, T., *Kevin O'Higgins* (London, Methuen, 1948).

Dooney, S. and O'Toole, J., *Irish Government Today* (Dublin, Gill & Macmillan, 1992).

Duggan, J., *Neutral Ireland and the Third Reich* (Dublin, Gill & Macmillan, 1975; first paperback edition, Dublin, The Lilliput Press, 1989).

Duggan, J., *A History of the Irish Army* (Dublin, Gill & Macmillan, 1991).

Dwyer, T., *Strained Relations: Ireland at Peace and the USA at War 1941–45* (Dublin, Gill & Macmillan, 1988).

Dwyer, T., *Guests of the State: The Story of Allied and Axis Servicemen Interned in Ireland During World War II* (Dingle, Brandon, 1994).

Longford, Earl of and O'Neill, T., *Éamon De Valera* (London, Arrow Books, 1974).

Fanning, R., *The Irish Department of Finance 1922–58* (Dublin, IPA, 1978).

Fanning, R., *Independent Ireland* (Dublin, Helicon, 1983).

Farrell, B., *Chairman or Chief: The Role of the Taoiseach in Irish Government* (Dublin, Gill & Macmillan, 1971).

Farrell, B., *Seán Lemass* (Dublin, Gill & Macmillan, 1983).

Finlay, I., *The Civil Service* Introduction to Public Administration, Series 6 (Dublin, IPA, 1966).

Fisk, R., *In Time of War: Ireland, Ulster and the Price of Neutrality 1939–45* (London, André Deutsch, 1983; reprint by Paladin Grafton Books, 1985).

Girvin, B., *The Emergency: Neutral Ireland 1939–45* (London, Pan Books, 2007).

Hancock, W.K., *Survey of British Commonwealth Affairs., Vol. I: Problems of Nationality 1918–1936* (Oxford, Oxford University Press, 1964 [1937]).

Harkness, D.W., *The Restless Dominion: The Irish Free State and the British Commonwealth of Nations, 1921–31* (London, MacMillan, 1969).

Harkness, D., 'Patrick McGilligan: Man of Commonwealth', *The Journal of Imperial and Commonwealth History*, Vol. VIII, No. 1 (October 1979), pp. 117–35.

Hickey, D.J. and Doherty, J.E., *A Dictionary of Irish History Since 1800* (Dublin, Gill & Macmillan, 1980).

Hinsley, F.H. and Simkins, C.A.G., *Security and Counter Intelligence*, vol. 4 of *British Intelligence in the Second World War* (London, HMSO, 1990).

Van Hoek, K., *Diplomats in Dublin* (Dublin and Cork, The Talbot Press, 1943).

Hopkinson, M., *Green against Green: The Irish Civil War* (Dublin, Gill & Macmillan, 1988).

Keatinge, P., 'The Formative Years of the Irish Diplomatic Service', *Éire– Ireland*, Vol. 1, No. 3 (1971), pp. 57–71.

Keatinge, P., *The Formulation of Irish Foreign Policy* (Dublin, IPA, 1973).

Kennedy, M., 'The Irish Free State and the League of Nations 1922–32: The Wider Implications', *Irish Studies in International Affairs*, Vol. 3, No. 4 (1992) pp. 9–23.

Keogh, D., 'The Origins of the Irish foreign Service in Europe (1919–1922)', *Études Irlandaises*, 7 (1982), pp. 145–64.

Keogh, D., 'Ireland: The Department of Foreign Affairs', in Z. Steiner (ed.), *The Times Survey of Foreign Ministries of the World* (London, Times Books, 1982), pp. 276–95.

Keogh, D., *The Vatican, the Bishops and Irish Politics 1919–1939* (Cambridge, Cambridge University Press, 1986).

Keogh, D., 'Éamon de Valera and Hitler: An Analysis of International reaction to the Visit to the German Minister, May 1945', *Irish Studies in International Affairs*, Vol. 3, No. 1 (1989), pp. 69–91.

Keogh, D., *Ireland and Europe 1919–1989: A Diplomatic and Political History* (Cork and Dublin, Hibernian University Press, 1990).

Keogh, D., 'Profile of Joseph Walshe, Secretary of the Department of Foreign Affairs, 1922–46', *Irish Studies in International Affairs*, Vol. 3, No. 2 (1990), pp. 59–80.

Keogh, D., *Twentieth-Century Ireland: Nation and State* (Dublin, Gill & Macmillan, 1994).

Keogh, D., *Ireland and the Vatican: The Politics and Diplomacy of Church–State Relations, 1922–1960* (Cork, Cork University Press, 1995).

Keogh, D. and Nolan, A., 'Anglo-Irish Diplomatic Relations and World War II', *The Irish Sword: The Emergency 1939–45*, Vol. XIX, Nos. 75 & 76 (1993–94).

Lawlor, S., *Britain and Ireland 1914–1923* (Dublin, Gill & Macmillan, 1983).

Lee, J., *Ireland 1912–1985: Politics and Society* (Cambridge, Cambridge University Press, 1989).

Lee, S., *The European Dictatorships 1918–1945* (London & New York, Methuen, 1987).

Longford, Lord and O'Neill, T.P., *Éamon de Valera* (London, Hutchinson, 1970).

Lynch, P., 'The Irish Free State and the Republic of Ireland, 1921–66', in T.W.Moody and F.X. Martin (eds), *The Course Of Irish History* (Cork, Mercier Press in association with Radio Telefis Éireann, 1984).

Lyons, F.S.L., *Ireland Since the Famine* (London, Fontana Press, 1973).

MacManus, F. (ed.), *The Years of the Great Test* (Dublin and Cork, Mercier Press in collaboration with Radio Telefis Éireann, 1978).

Maguire, M., *A Bibliography of Published Works on Irish Foreign Relations 1921–1978* (Dublin, Royal Irish Acadamy, 1981).

Mansergh, N., 'Ireland: External Relations 1926–1939', in F. MacManus (ed.), *The Years

of the Great Test (Dublin and Cork, The Mercier Press in collaboration with Radio Telefís Éireann, 1978), pp. 127–37.

Mansergh, N., *The Unresolved Question: The Anglo-Irish Settlement and its undoing 1912–72* (New Haven and London, Yale University Press, 1991).

McDowell, R.B., *The Irish Administration 1801–1914* (London, Routledge & Kegan Paul, 1964).

McMahon, D., *Republicans and Imperialists: Anglo-Irish Relations in the 1930s* (New Haven and London, Yale University Press, 1984).

McMahon, D., 'Ireland, the Dominions and the Munich Crisis', *Irish Studies in International Affairs*, Vol. 1, No. 1 (1979), pp. 30–7.

McManus, M., 'Ireland', in J.E. Kingdom (ed.), *The Civil Service in Liberal Democracies: An Introductory Survey* (London, Routledge, n.d), pp. 93–109.

Mitchell, A., *Revolutionary Government in Ireland: Dáil Éireann, 1919–22* (Dublin, Gill & Macmillan, 1995).

Mitchell, A. and Ó Snodaigh, P. (eds), *Irish Political Documents 1916–1949* (Dublin, Irish Academic Press, 1985).

Moody, T.W. and Martin, F.X. (eds), *The Course of Irish History* (Cork, Mercier Press in association with Radio Telefís Éireann, 1984).

Moynihan, M. (ed.), *Speeches and Statements by Éamon de Valera 1917–73* (Dublin, Gill & Macmillan, 1980).

Murphy, J.A., *Ireland in the Twentith Century* (Dublin, Gill & Macmillan, 1975).

Nolan, A., "A most heavy and grievous burden": Joseph Walshe and the Establishment of Sustainable Neutrality, 1940', in D. Keogh and M. O'Driscoll, *Ireland in World War Two: Diplomacy and Survival* (Cork, Mercier Press, 2004).

Ó Broin, L., *No Man's Man: A biographical memoir of Joseph Brennan: Civil Servant & first Governor of the Central Bank* (Dublin, IPA, 1982).

O'Carroll, J.P. and Murphy, J. (eds), *De Valera and His Times* (Cork, Cork University Press, 1983).

Ó Drisceoil, D., *Censorship in Ireland During the Second World War*, PhD Thesis, Department of History, University College, Cork, 1994, pp. 136–7.

O'Halpin, E., 'Aspects of intelligence', *The Irish Sword*, Vol. XIX, Nos. 75 & 76 (1993–4), pp. 57–65.

O'Halpin, E., 'Intelligence and Security in Ireland, 1922–45', *Intelligence and National Security*, Vol. 5, No. 1 (January 1990), pp. 50–83.

O'Halpin, E., *The Decline of the Union: British Government in Ireland* (Dublin, Gill & Macmillan, in association with Syracuse University Press, 1987).

Ó Muimhneacháin, M. [Maurice Moynihan], 'Functions of the Department of the Taoiseach', *Administration*, Vol. 7, No. 4 (Winter, 1959–60), pp. 277–93.

Palmer, A., *The Penguin Dictionary of Twentieth-Century History 1900–1991*, fourth edition (London, Penguin, 1992).

Patterson, R., *Uneasy Friendship: Ireland and France during the Second World War*, MA Thesis, University College, Cork, 1993.

Prager, G., *Building Democracy in Ireland: Political Order and Cultural Integration in a newly Independent Nation* (Cambridge, Cambridge University Press, 1986).

Raymond, R.J., 'David Gray, the Aiken Mission, and Irish Neutrality, 1940–41', *Diplomatic History*, No. 9 (1985), pp. 55–71.

Raymond, R.J., 'Irish Neutrality: ideology or pragmatism', *International Affairs*, Vol. 60, No. 1 (Winter 1983/84), pp. 31–40.

Rosenberg, J.L., 'The 1941 Mission of Frank Aiken to the United States: An American perspective', *Irish Historical Studies*, 22 (1980), pp. 162–77.

Salmon, T., *Unneutral Ireland: An Ambivalent and unique security policy* (Oxford, Clarendon Press, 1989).

Sexton, B., *Ireland and the Crown 1922–1936: The Governor Generalship of the Irish Free State* (Dublin, Irish Academic Press, 1989).

Stephan, E., *Spies in Ireland*. Translated from the German by Arthur Davidson. (Hamburg, Gerhard Stalling Verlag, 1961; trans. ed., London, Macdonald, 1963).

Townshend, C., *The British Campaign in Ireland 1919–1921: The Development of Political and Military Policies* (Oxford, Oxford University Press, 1975).

Whyte, J.H., *Church and State in Modern Ireland 1923–1979*, second edition (Dublin, Gill & Macmillan, 1980).

Williams, T.D., 'De Valera in Power', in F. MacManus (ed.), *The Years of the Great Test* (Dublin and Cork, The Mercier Press in collaboration with Radio Telefís Éireann, 1978), pp. 30–41.

Williams, T.D., 'Ireland and the war', in K.B. Nowlan and T.D. Williams (eds), *Ireland in the war years and after, 1939–51* (Dublin, Notre Dame University Press, 1969).

Williams, T.D., 'From the Treaty to the Civil War', in T.D. Williams (ed.), *The Irish Struggle 1916–1926* (London, Routledge & Kegan Paul, 1966).

Williams, T.D., 'A Study in Neutrality', *The Leader*, 28 February & 28 March 1953.

NOTES

INTRODUCTION

1 MacDunphy memorandum, 25 January 1935, Department of the Taoiseach (D/T), S6817, National Archives, Ireland (NAI).
2 Fisk, R., *In Time of War: Ireland, Ulster and the Price of Neutrality 1939–45* (London, André Deutsch, 1983; reprint, Paladin Grafton Books, 1985), p. ix.
3 When I first researched this work the de Valera papers were housed in the Franciscan archives in Killiney, Dublin. Subsequently these papers were transferred to the UCD archives department and have since been re-catalogued. The references in this work refer to their original location with their original file references.

CHAPTER 1

1 These early fragments of Walshe's life have been pieced together by Dermot Keogh's 'Profile of Joseph Walshe', pp. 59–62.
2 There are a number of rumours as to why Walshe left the order. Mary Bromage relates: 'Why he had, in his younger years, taken the Scarlet instead of the Black we did not know nor were we to discover. Was he, as friends would insist, just a trifle less acute of hearing than the Confessional required? Was he too committed to revolution and nationalism? Or was his chest, as a cough once or twice that evening suggested, not strong enough?' The author did not wish to enquire further, as Walshe had presented himself as a somewhat austere figure: 'This Irishman with his manifest intransigence, his passionate gnosticism, his iconoclastic wit, was not one to whom inquiries were rashly addressed on any subject.' See Bromage, M.C., 'Roman Love Story', *Michigan Quarterly Review* (Winter 1963), pp. 18–21. My thanks to Bernadette Chambers of the Department of Foreign Affairs for bringing my attention to this article.
3 O'Kelly's wife, Cáit O'Brien, had been Walshe's superviser in University College, Dublin. I have paraphrased these references from O'Kelly's autobiography, which is written in Irish. See Ó Ceallaigh, S.T., *Seán T: Scéal a bheatha ó 1916 go 1923*, Vol. II, as told to and edited by Pádraig Ó Fiannachta (Cló Morainn, 1972), p. 132.
4 For a full account of the establishment of the Propaganda, Publicity and Foreign Affairs Departments during this early period see Arthur Mitchell, *Revolutionary Government in Ireland: Dáil Éireann, 1919–22* (Dublin, Gill & Macmillan, 1995), pp. 99–110.
5 The nomenclature of the department should be clarified. The Department of Foreign Affairs was officially established in 1919. In 1922 it was renamed to become the Department of External Affairs. Subsequently, in 1971, it was renamed back to become the Department of Foreign Affairs.
6 For a brief biographical account of Brennan, Childers, Ginnell et al, see, Hickey, D.J. and Doherty, J.E., *A Dictionary of Irish History Since 1800* (Dublin, Gill & Macmillan, 1980).
7 De Valera to Robert Brennan, 28 February 1921, Dáil Éireann papers, DE 2/526, NAI.
8 De Valera to Brennan, 6 February 1921, Dáil Éireann papers DE 2/526, NAI.
9 Count Plunkett to de Valera, 6 February 1921, Dáil Éireann papers, DE 2/526, NAI.
10 Brennan [unsigned] to de Valera, 2 April 1921, Dáil Éireann papers, DE 2/526, NAI.

11 De Valera to Brennan, DFA, Secretary's Office early files, Dáil/Provisional Government/IFS, President's Office. File title: '1923 President's Subject Files', NAI.

12 De Valera to Brennan, 28 February 1921, Dáil Éireann papers, DE 2/526, NAI.

13 'General Directions' [Unsigned], 30 May 1921, Dáil Éireann papers, DE 2/526, NAI.

14 Unsigned memorandum, *Department of Foreign Affairs, Standing Orders, General*, n.d. [probably drafted by Brennan around June 1921], Dáil Éireann papers, DE 2/526, NAI.

15 Brennan to de Valera, 20 April 1921, citing letter from Seán T. O'Kelly, 18 April 1921, Dáil Éireann papers, DE 2/526, NAI.

16 Seán T Ó Ceallaigh to George Gavan Duffy, 1 February 1922, Documents in Irish Foreign Policy (DIFP) Volume 1. No. 235. NAI DFA ES Paris 1922–1923.

17 George Gavan Duffy, Dáil Éireann papers, DE 2/269, NAI.

18 Charles Bewley, *Memoirs of a Wild Goose*, ed. by W.J. McCormack (Dublin, Lilliput Press, 1989), p. 100.

19 Con Cremin in an interview with Dermot Keogh. See Keogh, *Ireland and Europe*, p. 11.

20 Walshe's curriculum vitae outlines his dates of service in Paris as being from 1 November 1920 to 31 January 1922. From 1 February 1922 he was appointed secretary to the Dáil, Ministry of Foreign Affairs until 1 September 1922 when he was appointed acting secretary, Department of Foreign Affairs. Although Walshe was not conferred with the rank of 'secretary' until 1927, he was effectively the secretary from 1922 and is, therefore, referred to as such throughout this text. My thanks to the Department of Foreign Affairs, and to Bernadette Chambers, in particular, for providing me with a copy of Walshe's curriculum vitae.

21 Hickey, D.J. and Doherty, J.E., *A Dictionary of Irish History Since 1800* (Dublin, Gill & Macmillan, 1980), p. 139.

22 David Harkness has described the memorandum as a blueprint for future Irish action in foreign affairs. See Harkness, D.W., *The Restless Dominion: The Irish Free State and the British Commonwealth of Nations, 1921–31* (London, Macmillan, 1969), p. 31.

23 George Gavan Duffy, memorandum entitled *The Position of Ireland's 'Foreign Affairs' at date of General Election, 1922*, June 1922, Department of Foreign Affairs early files, EA–D series, Dáil/ Provisional Government/Irish Free State, Miscellaneous papers, NAI.

24 The text of Walshe's letter was published in the Belgian press and sent to the British Foreign Office by Britain's representative in Belgium, Sir George Grahame. At this time Walshe was in the habit of signing many of his letters and memoranda with the Irish version of his name, Seosamh P. Breathnach. On this occasion it led to some confusion with Grahame misreading it as 'Mr. Breathbach'. In a precis of the letter written by a Foreign Office official the name is further misconstrued to read 'Mr. Breathback'. See George Grahame to the Marquess Curzon of Kedleston, 21 December 1922, FO 371/8246, PRO.

25 Gavan Duffy memorandum, June 1922, DFA, EA–D series, miscellaneous papers, NAI.

26 Memorandum entitled List of Addresses of all Foreign Representatives, DFA, EA–D series, Secretary's Office, Dáil/Provisional Government/Irish Free State, Finance/Accountant General/Accounts, NAI.

27 Keatinge, *The Formulation of Irish Foreign Policy* (Dublin, IPA, 1973), p. 76.

28 Deputy Gorey, 16 November 1923, *Dáil debates*, cited in 'References to External Affairs in An Dáil', P80/401. Papers of Desmond FitzGerald, Archives department, UCD.

29 Keogh, *Ireland and Europe*, p. 20.

30 S. MagCrait, accountant general, Department of Finance, to DFA, 29 April 1922,

NAI.

31 Walshe to secretary, Department of Finance, 27 March 1923, Secretary's Office – Early Files, Dáil/Provisional Government/Irish Free State, NAI.

32 Fanning, R., *The Irish Department of Finance 1922–58* (Dublin, IPA, 1978), p. 74, citing Department of Finance memorandum E 123/3, NAI.

33 Joseph Brennan memorandum, 5 October 1923, Department of Finance, F 826/5, cited by Fanning, *Department of Finance*, p. 642.

34 Harkness, *The Restless Dominion*, pp. 56–7.

35 Kennedy, M., 'The Irish Free State and the League of Nations, 1922–32: The Wider Implications', *Irish Studies in International Affairs*, Vol. 3, No. 4 (1992), p. 11.

36 *Irish Times*, 11 November 1926. Cited by Harkness, *Restless Dominion*, p. 95.

37 Unsigned memorandum, A Franco-Irish Entente, n.d., P35/158, McGilligan papers, UCD.

38 Unsigned memorandum, Department of Defence, Imperial Conference, 1926, Relation of Saorstát Defence Position to Locarno, Treaty of Mutual Guarantee, unsigned, McGilligan papers P35/158, UCD. This document also contains the following suggestion: 'Italian Immigration might easily solve the Ulster problem in a satisfactory way – replacing the Orange industrial workers by surplus hands from Turin, Milan, Genoa or other Northern Italian cities. The Italian would work at least as efficiently, would work harder, and would work for less. His cheerful character would make him fit in far better with the Southern Irishman than the Orangman ever would.'

39 Joseph Walshe, preliminary memorandum, to Minister Fitzgerald, Relations with Great Britain. Difficulties Summarised. DFA, Secretary's Office EA–D series, Dáil/Provisional Government/Irish Free State, 'Miscellaneous papers', NAI.

40 Walshe memorandum, Report on the 1926 Imperial Conference, FitzGerald papers, cited in Harkness, *The Restless Dominion*, p. 134.

41 Harkness, *The Restless Dominion*, p. 116.

42 Harkness citing E(IR\26)3, *The Restless Dominion*, pp. 134–5.

43 Walshe memorandum, Ratification of Arbitration Treaty with Siam and Treaty of Friendship with the Hedjaz, January 1927, FitzGerald papers, cited by Harkness, *The Restless Dominion*, p. 135.

44 Charles M. Hathaway to the Secretary of State, 10 January 1927, M580, Roll 223, State Department, National Archives of the United States (NAUS), Washington DC. His figures were based on an *Irish Times* survey that traced developments in this area. Hathaway concluded that the main reason for this regeneration of diplomatic interest in Ireland was the 'changed status' of the Irish Free State, pointing out that, following the Anglo-Irish agreement of 1922, Irish trade did not provide any substantially better opportunities.

45 Despite the fact that FitzGerald was one of the seven members of the Executive Council, it was still generally regarded that External Affairs was not equal with other departments. Newspapers such as the *Irish Times* and the *Irish Independent* often put forward the view that the department should be abolished and the Dáil itself did not regard its work with any great seriousness.

46 Charles M. Hathaway to the Secretary of State, 10 January 1927, M580, Roll 223, State Department papers, NAUS.

47 Hathaway to Secretary of State, 7 March 1927, M580, Roll 223, State Department papers, NAUS.

48 O'Higgins memorandum, FitzGerald papers, Archives department, University College, Dublin.

49 Walshe manuscript memorandum, n.d. [c. 1927], secretary's files, S.29(a), DFA, NAI.

50 *Ibid.*

51 Liam T. Cosgrave to Earnest Blythe, 30 August 1927, secretary's files, S.29(a), DFA, NAI.
52 Keogh, *Ireland and Europe*, p. 26.
53 Department of Finance to McGilligan, 17 February 1928, secretary's files, S.29(a), DFA, NAI.
54 Frederick Boland, *Reminiscences of an Irish Diplomat: Frederich H. Boland, Ambassador to London, Permanent Representative at the United Nations and President of the General Assembly 1960*, compiled by his daughter Mella Boland (Crowley). [Hereafter referred to as Boland memoirs.]
55 Kennedy, 'The Irish Free State and the League of Nations', p. 19.
56 Secretary's [Walshe] memorandum, 11 October 1927, McGilligan papers P35b/117, University College, Dublin.
57 Stephen Barcroft, 'Irish Foreign Policy at the League of Nations 1929–1936', *Irish Studies in International Affairs*, Vol. 1, No. 1 (1979), pp. 19–20.
58 *Ibid.*, p. 21.
59 Boland memoirs.
60 This table has been taken from memorandum entitled Estimates – Revenue etc. for Budgets. Details of Search for Economies. McGilligan papers, P.35a/10, UCD.
61 It should be noted that in this table the column titled 'Estimated Reduction' is not an official part of the original printed table but was added in pencil, probably by someone at the Department of External Affairs.
62 Item 1 involved the reduction by a flat rate of 10 per cent in the estimates presented by departments for travelling and subsistence. This would have adversely affected External Affairs in particular due to the nature of its work.
63 Smiddy to McGilligan, 5 March 1929, secretary's files, S.20a, DFA, NAI.
64 Walshe to Smiddy, 21 March 1929, secretary's files, S.20a, DFA, NAI.
65 Walshe to Smiddy, 23 March 1929, secretary's files, S.20a, DFA, NAI.
66 Smiddy to Walshe, 10 April 1929, secretary's files, S.20a, DFA, NAI.
67 T.J. Kiernan, Secretary for the Office of the High Commissioner, to Walshe, 27 March 1929, secretary's files, S.20a, DFA, NAI.
68 Walshe to Smiddy, 2 April 1929, secretary's files, S.20(a), DFA, NAI.
69 Smiddy to Walshe, 10 April 1929, secretary's files, S.20(a), DFA, NAI.
70 F.A. Sterling to Secretary of State, 13 June 1929, M580, Roll 223, State Department papers, NAUS. Sterling is citing Minister McGilligan's speech to the Dáil, June 1929.
71 Walshe manuscript memorandum, Vatican Appointment, n.d., McGilligan papers, P35(b)/112(1), UCD.
72 O.E. Sargent, 4 April 1929, memorandum with manuscript corrections and addenda by H.M. [Hubert Montgomery] dated 5 April 1929, FO 627/10, PRO.
73 Walshe manuscript memorandum, Vatican Appointment, n.d., McGilligan papers, P35(b)/112(1), UCD.
74 Sargent memorandum, 4 April 1929, FO 627/10, PRO.
75 Walshe manuscript memorandum, Vatican Appointment, n.d., McGilligan papers, P35(b)/112(1), UCD.
76 Hubert Montgomery to Henry Chilton, 5 April 1929, FO 627/10, PRO.
77 Batterbee to Hubert Montgomery, 27 May 1929, FO 372/2536, PRO.
78 Seán Murphy to Batterbee, 1 June 1929, FO 627/10, PRO.
79 Bewley, *Memoirs of a Wild Goose*, pp. 100–101.
80 *Ibid.*, p. 103. The contemporary documentation shows Walshe and Bewley to have been on a better footing than Bewley has given credit for.
81 Keogh, D., *Ireland and the Vatican: The Politics and Diplomacy of Church–State Relations 1922–1960* (Cork, Cork University Press, 1995), pp. 51–62. See pages 76–8 for details as to the expense incurred by the Irish government to make the residence

into a gift for the nuncio.

82 Dominions Office letter, 8 March 1929, FO 627/9, PRO. The British took a keen interest in these developments and Foreign Office files contain extracts from the *Irish Independent* of 9 March reporting that the Executive Council had decided to cut salaries by nearly 50 per cent of the Irish representatives abroad.

83 McGilligan to Amery, 14 May 1929, FO 627/9, PRO.

84 H.B. [Batterbee] memorandum, 17 May 1929, FO 627/9, PRO.

85 Memorandum entitled Imperial Conference, 1930, Summary of Proceedings, McGilligan papers, P35/172, UCD.

86 Walshe summarises the meeting in a memorandum entitled The Minister's Interview with General Hertzog, in which the '*inter se* controversy' was discussed. See Harkness, *The Restless Dominion*, Appendix D.

87 Walshe memorandum, The Convention Concerning the Succession to the Throne and the Right of Secession, 2 July 1930, McGilligan papers, P35/195, UCD.

88 Lyons, F.S.L., *Ireland Since the Famine* (London, Fontana Press, 1973), p. 509.

89 Walshe memorandum, The Convention Concerning the Succession to the Throne and the Right of Secession, 2 July 1930, McGilligan papers, P35/195, UCD.

90 Walshe memorandum, Change of Seals, FitzGerald papers, cited by Harkness, *The Restless Dominion*, pp. 233–7.

91 *Ibid.*, p. 147.

92 [Walshe] manuscript memorandum, The Privy Council, n.d., McGilligan papers, P35/196, UCD.

93 Walshe memorandm to McGilligan, n.d., McGilligan papers, P35/196, UCD.

94 Lyons, *Ireland Since the Famine*, p. 515.

95 Walshe memorandm to McGilligan, n.d., McGilligan papers, P35/196, UCD.

96 Walshe note, 8 January 1931, written on a memorandum by Dulanty, 6 January 1931, McGilligan papers, P35/196, UCD.

97 Lyons, *Ireland Since the Famine*, p. 509.

98 Conor Cruise O'Brien claims that the anti-de Valera 'dirty tricks' campaign was under the personal supervision of Walshe, citing Michael Rynne, legal adviser to External Affairs, as one of his sources of information. See 'The Roots of my Preoccupations', *The Atlantic Monthly*, Vol. 274, No. 1 (July 1994):, pp. 73–81. Also available online at: http://www.theatlantic.com/unbound/flashbks/cruise/cruis794.htm [Accessed 1 October 1997].

99 See Keogh, D., 'De Valera, the Catholic Church and the 'Red Scare, 1931–1932', in J.P. O'Carroll and J. A. Murphy (eds), *De Valera and his Times* (Cork, Cork University Press, 1983), pp. 134–59. This article contains an analysis of 'poster power' using illustrations to depict advertising campaigns of the rival parties during the 1932 general election.

100 Bewley, *Memoirs of a Wild Goose*, pp. 108–9.

101 Keogh points out that at the height of the 'Red Scare' de Valera visited Cardinal MacRory at Maynooth.

102 Whyte, J.H., *Church and State in Modern Ireland 1923–1979*, second edition (Dublin, Gill & Macmillan, 1980), pp. 43–8.

103 Walshe memorandum, The Church and the Present Position of the Saorstát: Dr. Byrne's Pastoral Letter, 18 July 1927, governor general files, D5464, NAI.

104 [Walshe] manuscript memorandum, The State, n.d., McGilligan papers, P35(b)/112(2), UCD.

105 McGilligan memorandum, The Department of External Affairs, [April 1931], D/T, S.2220, NAI.

106 See Dermot Keogh's 'Profile of Joseph Walshe, p. 59. Walshe is described as being 'secretive in the extreme' and we are told of his 'very restricted application of the "need to know" rule'.

107 McGilligan memorandum, 1930/31, McGilligan papers, P35/196, UCD.
108 Unsigned and untitled memorandum [dated sometime after March 1930], McGilligan papers, P35b/128, UCD.
109 Memorandum entitled The Irish Free State and the Commonwealth. Section II External Affairs, McGilligan papers, P35/196, UCD.
110 Harkness, *The Restless Dominion*, p. 147.

CHAPTER 2

1 Lynch, P., 'The Irish Free State and the Republic of Ireland, 1921–66', in T.W. Moody and F.X. Martin (eds), *The Course Of Irish History*(Cork, Mercier Press in association with Radio Telefís Éireann, 1984), pp. 327–8.
2 A copy of Walshe's declaration of allegiance to the Irish Provisional Government can be found in 'Home Department of External Affairs – 1923', Dáil/Provisional Government/Irish Free State, Secretary's Office – early files, D/FA, NAI.
3 Ó Broin, L., *Just Like Yesterday: an autobiography* (Dublin, Gill & Macmillan, [1985]), p. 98.
4 Keogh, D., *The Vatican, the Bishops and Irish Politics, 1919–39* (Cambridge, Cambridge University Press, 1986), p. 187.
5 See *Dáil debates* on the estimates for the year 1929–1930.
6 Keogh, 'Profile of Joseph Walshe', p. 71.
7 Cruise O'Brien, 'The Roots of my Preoccupations', *The Atlantic Monthly* [Available online from: http://www.theatlantic.com/unbound/flashbks/cruise/cruis794.htm [Accessed 1 October 1997].
8 Bewley, *Memoirs of a Wild Goose*, p. 114.
9 Walshe to de Valera, 12 March 1932, D/T, S2264, NAI.
10 Walshe, says Keogh, counselled against what has been described in more recent times as megaphone diplomacy. 'Profile of Joseph Walshe', p. 71.
11 Walshe to de Valera, 12 March 1932, D/T, S2264, NAI.
12 Keogh, 'Profile of Joseph Walshe', p. 72.
13 Mansergh, N., *The Unresolved Question: The Anglo-Irish Settlement and its Undoing 1912–72* (New Haven and London, Yale University Press, 1991), pp. 281–2.
14 Memorandum entitled Land Annuities – Chronology, secretary's files, S1, D/FA, NAI.
15 De Valera to the Secretary of State for Dominion Affairs, 5 April 1932, D/T, S2264, NAI.
16 Boland memoirs.
17 For copy of cablegrams received from Ottawa Imperial Economic Conference, August 1932, see secretary's files, S1, Part I, D/FA, NAI.
18 McMahon, D., *Republicans and Imperialists: Anglo-Irish Relations in the 1930s* (New Haven and London, Yale University Press, 1984), p. 79.
19 Keogh, D., *Ireland and the Vatican: The Politics and Diplomacy of Church–State Relations 1922–1960* (Cork, Cork University Press, 1995), pp. 95–6.
20 Mansergh, *Unresolved Question*, p. 286.
21 McNeill to de Valera, 7 July 1932. Published in *Irish Times*, 12 July 1932. Paraphrased by Brendan Sexton, *Ireland and the Crown, 1922–1936: The Governor-Generalship of the Irish Free State* (Dublin, Irish Academic Press, 1989), pp. 124 –8.
22 Walshe manuscript letter to de Valera, 8 July 1932, de Valera papers 1529, Franciscan archives, Killiney.
23 McMahon, *Republicans and Imperialists*, p. 64.
24 Walshe manuscript letter to de Valera, 8 July 1932, de Valera papers, 1529, Franciscan archives, Killiney.
25 [Walshe] manuscript memorandum, n.d., secretary's files, S22, D/FA, NAI.
26 Unsigned memorandum regarding conversation with Dulanty, 9 November 1932,

PREM 1/119, PRO.

27 Irish situation committee (32) 15th Meeting, Appendix I by H.F. Batterbee, 25 October 1932, CAB 27/523, PRO.

28 Irish situation committee, 15th meeting, 25 October 1932, CAB 27/523, PRO.

29 Memorandum entitled, Suggested Outline of Answer to Mr. Walshe, 8 November 1932, PREM 1/119, PRO.

30 Memorandum of conversation between Dulanty and Walshe with Lord Wigram, 17 November 1932, PREM 1/119, PRO.

31 McMahon, *Republicans and Imperialists*, pp. 93–4.

32 Walshe to de Valera, 2 May 1933, de Valera papers, 1529, Franciscan archives, Killiney.

33 Walshe writing from Cologne, Germany, to de Valera, 28 July 1933, de Valera papers, 1529, Franciscan archives, Killiney.

34 *Ibid.*

35 Lee, S.J., *The European Dictatorships 1918–1945* (London & New York, Methuen, 1987), pp. 178–80. Lee points out, however, that these and other figures have to be read with caution and he provides a more sophisticated look at German society and economy during this period.

36 Walshe writing from Cologne, Germany to de Valera, 28 July 1933, de Valera papers, 1529, Franciscan archives, Killiney.

37 Palmer, A., *The Penguin Dictionary of Twentieth-Century History 1900–1991*, fourth edition (London, Penguin, 1992), p. 101.

38 Dáil debate on the Department of External Affairs estimates, 11 July 1933, *Dáil debates*, Vol. 48, 2126–2141.

39 Walshe writing from Cologne, Germany, to de Valera, 28 July 1933, de Valera papers, 1529, Franciscan archives, Killiney.

40 Bewley, *Memoirs of a Wild Goose*, pp. 124–5.

41 Walshe to Bewley, 25 September 1937, D/FA Letter Book, Berlin 1936–37, NAI. My thanks to Dr Mervyn O'Driscoll for bringing my attention to this document.

42 Bewley, *Memoirs of a Wild Goose*, p. 173.

43 Walshe to Bewley, 25 September 1937, D/FA Letter Book, Berlin 1936–37, NAI.

44 Bewley rather caustically noted that 'many years before [de Valera's] ... zeal for Christianity had not prevented him from making a secret loan to Litvinoff and receiving a portion of the Imperial Crown Jewels as a pledge', *Memoirs of a Wild Goose*, p. 175.

45 *Ibid.*, pp. 166–7.

46 Walshe to de Valera, writing from Cologne, 13 June 1933, de Valera papers, 953, Franciscan archives, Killiney.

47 MacDunphy memorandum, 25 January 1935, D/T, S6817, NAI.

48 MacDunphy memorandum, 11 January 1932, D/T, S6232A, NAI.

49 MacDunphy memorandum, 25 January 1935, D/T, S6817, NAI. The original reads 'which may prove very awkward later when the folio of Minister for External Affairs is held by a Minister other than the President'. The 'if and' is a handwritten addition probably inserted to irk Walshe by reminding him that the department's independence was not fully established or possibly an expression of frustration at the President's double portfolio.

50 Years later, Maurice Moynihan wrote an article entitled 'The Functions of the Department of the Taoiseach', *Administration*, Vol. 7, No. 4 (Winter 1959–60), pp. 277–93.

51 Interview with Maurice Moynihan, 24 May 1996.

52 Walshe memorandum, 12 March 1936, D/T, S8749, NAI. [While this document has no specific signature, it is signed 'Department of External Affairs' and contains a number of hand-written additions and corrections all of which appear to be in

Walshe's hand.

53 Moynihan memorandum, Foreign Relations, 21 March 1936, secretary's files, S60, NAI.

54 Interview with Maurice Moynihan, 24 May 1996.

55 Moynihan memorandum, Foreign Relations, 21 March 1936, secretary's files, S60, NAI.

56 Walshe memorandum, Our Political Relations with the British: A chat with Sir Harry Batterbee, 2 May 1936, de Valera papers, 953, Franciscan archives, Killiney.

57 Batterbee memorandum, Talk at Mr. J.P. Walshe's house on Wednesday evening, the 29th April [1936], PREM 1/273, PRO.

58 Walshe memorandum, 2 May 1936, Our Political Relations with the British: A chat with Sir Harry Batterbee, de Valera papers, 953, Franciscan archives, Killiney.

59 Batterbee memorandum, Talk at Mr. J.P. Walshe's house on Wednesday evening, the 29th April [1936], PREM 1/273, PRO.

60 Malcolm MacDonald to prime minister, 10 September 1936, PREM 1/273, PRO.

61 E.J. Harding memorandum, 14 September 1936, PREM 1/273, PRO.

62 Memorandum on trade relations with Great Britain, secretary's files, S1, D/FA, NAI.

63 Walshe manuscript memorandum, 3 November 1936, de Valera papers, 953, Franciscan archives, Killiney.

64 Note attached to Batterbee memorandum of 4 December 1936, PREM 1/273, PRO.

65 Batterbee memorandum following talks in Dublin, 4 December 1936, PREM 1/273, PRO.

66 Mansergh, N., 'Ireland: External Relations 1926–1939', in F. MacManus (ed.), *The Years of the Great Test 1926–1939* (Dublin & Cork, Mercier in association with Radio Telefís Éireann, 1978), p. 133.

67 McMahon, *Republicans and Imperialists*, pp. 199–200.

68 *Ibid.*, p. 199. McMahon citing from interview with Sir Neil Pritchard, 21 May 1981.

69 Walshe to de Valera, 10 December 1936, de Valera papers, 953, Franciscan archives, Killiney.

70 Walshe memorandum, Report No. 2, 10 December 1936, de Valera papers, 953, Franciscan archives, Killiney.

71 Walshe to de Valera, 10 December 1936, de Valera papers, 953, Franciscan archives, Killiney.

72 Walshe memorandum, Report No. 2, 10 December 1936, de Valera papers, 953, Franciscan archives, Killiney.

73 Walshe memorandum, 11 December 1936, de Valera papers, 953, Franciscan archives, Killiney.

74 Mansergh, 'Ireland: External Relations 1926–1939', p. 134.

75 McMahon points out that de Valera had considered not reacting to the crisis at all. Batterbee told him, however, that if he did not provide for the succession then Edward VII would remain king of Ireland and that eventually Mrs Simpson would become queen. McMahon, *Republicans and Imperialists*, p. 200.

76 Walshe memorandum, Report of Conversation with High Commissioner at 5.20 p.m., on Friday the 18th December, 18 December 1936, de Valera papers, 953, Franciscan archives, Killiney.

77 Walshe to de Valera, 9 January 1937, de Valera papers, 953, Franciscan archives, Killiney.

78 See de Valera papers, files 1029, 1034, 1038, 1043, 1046, 1055, 1086, 1088, 1991 and 1995.

79 Keogh, D., *Twentieth Century Ireland: Nation and State*, New Gill History of Ireland

6 (Dublin, Gill & Macmillan, 1994), pp. 97–8.

80 Walshe's part in this episode has been dealt with elsewhere. See Keogh, *Ireland and the Vatican*, pp. 132–40; and also Keogh, D., 'The Irish Constitutional Revolution: An Analysis of the Making of the Constitution', in F. Litton (ed.), *The Constitution of Ireland 1937–1987, Administration* Vol. 25, No. 4 (1988), pp. 4–85.

81 Keogh, *Ireland and the Vatican*, pp. 137–9.

82 Copy of statement issued by British government, 30 December 1937, de Valera papers, 1043, Franciscan archives, Killiney.

83 Walshe to de Valera, 3 January 1938, de Valera papers, 953, Franciscan archives, Killiney.

84 Moynihan, *Speeches and Statements*, p. 276.

85 Walshe memorandum from Regent St., London to de Valera, 22 January 1938, de Valera papers, 953, Franciscan archives, Killiney.

86 Walshe memorandum from London to de Valera, 25 January 1938, de Valera papers, 953, Franciscan archives Killiney.

87 The position of 'Taoiseach' had been created in the 1937 constitution so de Valera was no longer referred to as the President of the Executive Council.

88 Walshe memorandum from London to de Valera, 25 January 1938, de Valera papers, 953, Franciscan archives Killiney.

89 De Valera to Franklin Roosevelt, 25 January 1938, de Valera papers, 1287, Franciscan archives, Killiney.

90 Roosevelt to de Valera, 22 February 1938, de Valera papers, 1287, Franciscan archives, Killiney.

91 Walshe memorandum from London to de Valera, 25 January 1938, de Valera papers, 953, Franciscan archives, Killiney.

92 'United Kingdom–Éire Negotiations'. Note by the government of Northern Ireland. Effect of the proposed treaty on Northern Ireland industry, 25 March 1938, CAB4/397, Public Record Office of Northern Ireland, Belfast.

93 Walshe manuscript letter from London to de Valera, n.d. [c. February 1938], de Valera papers, 953, Franciscan archives, Killiney.

94 Cudahy to State Department, 16 March 1938, State Department decimal files, RG 84, Box 2, NAUS.

95 Walshe to de Valera, 15 March 1938, de Valera papers, 953, Franciscan archives, Killiney.

96 Boland memoirs.

97 McMahon, *Republicans and Imperialists*, p. 283.

CHAPTER 3

1 Walshe to de Valera, writing from Khartoum, Sudan, 13 May 1938, de Valera papers, 953, Franciscan archives, Killiney.

2 Walshe to de Valera, writing from Cairo, 2 June 1938, de Valera papers, 953, Franciscan archives, Killiney.

3 Palmer, *Penguin Dictionary of Twentieth-Century History*, p. 427.

4 Walshe to de Valera, 24 September 1938, de Valera papers, 953, Franciscan archives, Killiney.

5 Walshe to de Valera, 28 September 1938, de Valera papers, 953, Franciscan archives, Killiney.

6 McMahon, D., 'Ireland, the Dominions and the Munich Crisis', *Irish Studies in International Affairs*, Vol. 1, No. 1 (1979), p. 37. However on 18 October 1938 the *Irish Press* reported de Valera as saying in the Dáil on the question of partition: 'It would be completely misleading to consider the present Irish divisions as racial … There is no real analogy between the position of the Sudeten Germans before the

recent crisis and the position in the Six Counties today.'

7   Walshe to de Valera, 28 September 1938, de Valera papers, 953, Franciscan archives, Killiney.

8   Fisk, *In Time of War*, pp. 71–3. Fisk indicates that while de Valera knew of these meetings he was fearful of an adverse domestic reaction if he should be seen to be cooperating too closely with Britain.

9   J.A. Stephenson to B. Cochrane, 'Defended Ports in Éire', 19 September 1938, DO 35/894/X31/18, PRO.

10 John MacVeagh memorandum, April 1939, State Department records, RG 84, Box 2, NAUS.

11 Walshe to de Valera, 22 April 1939, de Valera papers, 1287, Franciscan archives, Killiney.

12 Harry H. Balch to Hickerson, 10 April 1939, State Department records, US legation files, RG 84, Microfilm M1231, Roll 2, NAUS.

13 MacVeagh to State Department, April 1939, RG 84, Box 2, State Department records, NAUS.

14 Cudahy to Secretary of State, memorandum regarding conversation with de Valera, 16 March 1938, State Department records, RG 84, Box 2, 1938–3, NAUS.

15 Cudahy to Secretary of State, 29 May 1939, State Department records, RG84, foreign service posts of the Department of State, Dublin legation, 1939. 800–885.7. Box 6, NAUS (Suitland, Maryland depository).

16 Cudahy to Secretary of State, 15 August 1939, State Department records, RG 84, 300–810, Box 5, NAUS.

17 Boland memoirs.

18 Keogh, *Ireland and Europe*, p. 116.

19 Walshe memorandum on conversation with Herr Thomsen, 22 February 1939, de Valera papers, 953, Franciscan archives, Killiney.

20 Hempel to Foreign Ministry, 26 August 1939, *Documents on German Foreign Policy 1918–1945*, [*DGFP*] Series D., Vol VII, Doc. 303, p. 311.

21 Walshe note for a conversation with Hempel, 25 August 1939, de Valera papers, 1180, Franciscan archives, Killiney.

22 Hempel to Foreign Ministry, 26 August 1939, *Documents on German Foreign Policy 1918–1945*, [*DGFP*] Series D., Vol VII, Doc. 303, p. 311.

23 Hempel to Foreign Ministry, 31 August 1939, *DGFP*, Series D. Vol. VII, Doc. 484, p. 471.

24 State Secretary to Hempel, 1 September 1939, *DGFP*, Series D., Vol. VII, Doc. 527, p. 504.

25 Carroll, J.T., *Ireland in the War Years* (Newton Abbot, David & Charles, 1975), p. 15.

26 Longford and O'Neill, *De Valera*, p. 750.

27 Walshe memorandum on his visit to London, 6 to 10 September 1939, de Valera papers, 1180, Franciscan archives, Killiney.

28 Anthony Eden to prime minister, 9 September 1939, PREM 1/340, PRO. Handwritten in the margin is 'so far as it goes', indicating the scepticism attached to negotiating with the Irish delegation, and especially with Walshe.

29 Longford and O'Neill, *De Valera,passim*,

30 Memorandum dated 30 December 1937, DO 35/892/X11/4, PRO. Cited by McMahon, *Republicans and Imperialists*, pp. 235–6.

31 Anthony Eden to prime minister, 9 September 1939, PREM 1/340, PRO.

32 He came under the pseudonym 'Mr Harrison'. See Keogh, D. and Nolan, A., 'Anglo-Irish Diplomatic Relations and World War II', *The Irish Sword: The Emergency 1939–45*, Vol. XIX, Nos. 75 & 76 (1993–94), pp. 106–30; See also McMahon, *Republicans and Imperialists*, pp. 171, 235–6.

33 Maffey report, 25 September 1939, PREM 1/340, PRO. This is one of Maffey's first reports from Dublin. It is written in diary form beginning on 20 September 1939.

34 Warnock to Walshe, 25 September 1939, secretary's files, P24, D/FA, NAI.

35 Boland to chargé d'affaires, Berlin, 25 October 1939, secretary's files, P24, D/FA, NAI. It is interesting to note that Boland mentions that a special arrangement had been made for Hempel to send purely personal letters to Germany through External Affairs.

36 Cudahy to Secretary of State, 23 November 1939, State Department records, RG 84, foreign service post of the Department of State, Dublin legation, 1939. 800–883.7, NAUS.

37 Cudahy to Secretary of State, 29 December 1939, File 801.1, Box 5, RG 84, foreign service posts of the Department of State, General records, NAUS.

38 The High Court judge who ruled on the case was George Gavan Duffy, who had been Walshe's superior for a brief period in 1922 when he was Minister for External Affairs in the government of the second Dáil Éireann. See above, Chapter 1.

39 Cudahy to Secretary of State, 29 December 1939, File 801.1, Box 5, RG 84, foreign service posts of the Department of State, General records, NAUS.

40 The two men were eventually executed on 7 February 1940. The Department of External Affairs' efforts to obtain a reprieve for Barnes and Richards continued until the last moment. In January Walshe had been advised by Michael Rynne that Irish arguments should purport to rely on the doctrine of 'diplomatic protection' or international law. He suggested that the emphasis should be placed on the possible consequences for Anglo-Irish relations of the executions and of the nature in which some of the evidence at the trial, which would not normally have been allowed, was admitted. See secretary's files, S113(a), D/FA, NAI.

41 Cudahy to Roosevelt, 27 October 1939, Roosevelt papers, president's secretary's files, 'Diplomatic Correspondence Ireland: 1938–39', box 40, Franklin D. Roosevelt Library, Hyde Park, New York [hereafter FDRL].

42 Later, in mid-1941, Sumner Welles reported to Roosevelt that Cudahy had been interrogated by the British, who reported that the former US representative to Ireland had told them that Germany would win the war and that Britain was finished. Cudahy was expecting his recent interview with Hitler to be published in *Life* magazine. Welles to Roosevelt, president's secretary's files, safe file, State Department, box 5, FDRL.

43 Van Hoek, K., *Diplomats in Dublin* (Dublin and Cork, The Talbot Press, 1943), p. 43. Van Hoek first wrote these essays for the *Irish Independent*, which were later published as a collection of prose sketches of sixteen diplomats stationed in Dublin in the 1940s. For a further account of Gray's appointment see Raymond, R.J., 'David Gray, the Aiken Mission, and Irish Neutrality, 1940–1941', *Diplomatic History*, No. 9 (1985), p. 55–6.

44 Roosevelt would sometimes reply 'My Dear David' or 'Uncle David'.

45 Gray to Secretary of State, 29 April 1940, Roosevelt papers, official files 218, FDRL.

46 Bailey, T.A., *A Diplomatic History of the American People*, ninth edition (New Jersey, Prentice–Hall, 1974), p. 13.

47 Secretary of State Hull to Roosevelt, 6 February 1940, Roosevelt papers, official files 3904, FDRL.

48 Gray to Roosevelt, n.d., Roosevelt papers, president's secretary's files, diplomatic correspondence Ireland 1940, box 40, FDRL.

49 Van Hoek, *Diplomats in Dublin*, p. 46. Gray's book, however, was never completed but he later told Maffey that it would not have been very complimentary to Britain.

50 Raymond, 'David Gray', pp. 58–9.

51 External Affairs telegram to high commissioner to Canada, John Hearne, 31 October

1939, secretary's files, P.4, D/FA, NAI.
52 External Affairs to Hearne, 13 December 1939, secretary's files, P.4, D/FA, NAI.

CHAPTER 4

1   Sections of this chapter have been previously published in Nolan, A., "'A most heavy and grievous burden": Joseph Walshe and the Establishment of Sustainable Neutrality, 1940', in D. Keogh and M. O'Driscoll, *Ireland in World War Two: Diplomacy and Survival* (Cork, Mercier Press, 2004).
2   Walshe to de Valera, 1 May 1940, De Valera papers,1180, Franciscan archives, Killiney.
3   *Ibid.*
4   Memorandum on discussions between United Kingdom and Éire ministers, Mr Lemass and Dr Ryan with Mr Burgin, Lord Woolton and Sir Reginald Dorman-Smith, 30 April 1940, De Valera papers, 1180, Franciscan archives, Killiney.
5   Walshe memorandum on 3 May 1940 meeting with Eden, 6 May 1940, De Valera papers, 1180, Franciscan archives, Killiney.
6   Moynihan, M. (ed). *Speeches and Statements by Éamon de Valera 1917–73* (Dublin, Gill & Macmillan, 1980), p. 435.
7   Lee, J.J., *Ireland 1912–1985: Politics and Society* (Cambridge, Cambridge University Press, 1989), pp. 246–7.
8   *Ibid.*, p. 349.
9   Hempel to Foreign Ministry, 23 May 1940, *Documents on German Foreign Policy* (DGFP), Series D., Vol. IX, Doc. 310, pp. 422–4.
10 Gray to Roosevelt, 30 April 1940, Roosevelt papers, president's secretary's files, diplomatic correspondence, Ireland 1940, Box 40, Franklin D. Roosevelt Library (FDRL), Hyde Park, New York.
11 Gray to Roosevelt, 16 May 1940, State Department papers, M1231, roll 10, National Archives of the United States (NAUS).
12 For further information on German espionage in Ireland and German–IRA links during the war, see Carter, *Shamrock and the Swastika*; Duggan, J.P., *Neutral Ireland and the Third Reich* (Dublin, Gill & Macmillan, 1975; first paperback edition, Dublin, The Lilliput Press, 1989); Fisk, *In Time of War* and Stephan, E., *Spies in Ireland*. Translated from the German by Arthur Davidson (Hamburg, Gerhard Stalling Verlag, 1961; translated. edition, London, Macdonald, 1963).
13 NAI, D/FA A3. This section is based on the official minutes of the meeting contained in the secretary's files.
14 'Minutes of the First meeting between Representatives of the Government of Éire and Representatives of the Dominions Office and Service Departments of the United Kingdom, 23 May, 1940', A3, secretary's files, D/FA, NAI.
15 'Minutes of the Second Meeting Between Representatives of the government of Éire and Representatives of the Dominions Office and Service Departments of the United Kingdom, 24 May, 1940', secretary's files, A3, D/FA, NAI.
16 Clarke, D., Lt. Col., *Seven Assignments*, with an introduction by Field Marshal the Earl Wavell (London, Jonathan Cape, 1948), p. 182.
17 *Ibid.*, p. 183.
18 In the introduction to the published version of *Seven Assignments*, the Earl Wavell describes his employment of Clarke's services as being for 'less orthodox employment, the story of which cannot yet be told'. Clarke himself states that it was in the interests of a group of 'clear-sighted and courageous patriots' that he felt it best to 'cloak the episode with anonymity'.
19 Joseph Carroll recounts this story based on the original uncensored manuscript of Clarke's account of the episode. He claims that Clarke was ordered under the Official Secrets Act to strike out all reference to the country where the episode had taken

place. See Carroll, J., *Ireland in the War Years* (Newton Abbott, David & Charles, 1975), pp. 42–4.

20 Memorandum entitled Cooperation with the British Government in event of Attack, secretary's files, A3, D/FA, NAI.

21 Memorandum entitled Help given by Irish Government to the British in relation to the Actual waging of War, 24 May 1941, secretary's files, D/FA, NAI.

22 Fisk, *In Time of War*, p. 175.

23 In December 1940, the Irish government agreed to look after hundreds of women and children evacuated from London during the blitz. Fisk describes how the British government paid for a part of their lodgings. His reference to Walshe is not flattering. 'A rather miserly attempt by Walshe to get the British to pay for refugees' hospital treatment in Éire was "unfavourably received" in London.' D/T S12125 Walshe memorandum 20 November 1940. Cited by Fisk, *In Time of War*, p. 175.

24 Gray to Roosevelt, 31 May 1940, president's secretary's files, diplomatic correspondence, Ireland 1940, box 40, FDRL.

25 Walshe to Secretary, Department of Justice, S.A. Roche, 11 June 1940, secretary's files, A23, D/FA, NAI.

26 Walshe memorandum on conversation with Hempel, 17 June 1940, P3, secretary's files, DFA, NAI.

27 Hempel to Foreign Ministry, 17 June 1940, *DGFP*, Series D, Vol. IX, Doc. 437, pp. 601–3.

28 Hempel to Foreign Ministry, 21 June 1940, *DGFP*, Series D., Vol. IX, Doc. 506, pp. 637–40.

29 MacDonald memorandum, 17 June 1940, PREM 3/131/1PRO. Cited by Robert Fisk, *In Time of War: Ireland, Ulster and the Price of Neutrality 1939–45* (London, André Deutsch, 1983; reprint, Paladin Grafton Books, 1985), p. 193.

30 MacDonald memorandum, 21–22 June 1940, PREM 3/131/1, PRO. Cited by Fisk, *In Time of War*, p. 197.

31 British note to the Irish government, 26 June 1940, PREM 3/131/2, PRO. Cited by Fisk, *In Time of War*, p. 201.

32 Gray to Roosevelt, 28 June 1940, FDRL, president's secretary's files, Box 40, Roosevelt papers.

33 *Ibid.*

34 Unsigned memorandum, Comments of the foregoing, 1 July 1940, P13, secretary's files, D/FA, NAI.

35   *Ibid.*

36 Maffey memorandum, 14 March 1941, PREM 3/131/7, PRO. As cited by Fisk, *In Time of War*, p. 305.

37 Unsigned memorandum (Probably written by Walshe) Weekend Developments in the War Situation n.d. A2, secretary's files, D/FA, NAI.

38 *Ibid.*

39 Memorandum entitled Britain's Inevitable Defeat, undated and unsigned, secretary's files, A2, D/FA, NAI. This document is likely to have been written by Walshe not only because it coincides with his pessimism with regard to Britain's chances in the war but because there is also a handwritten correction that appears to be in his hand.

40 Boland memoirs.

41 Unsigned memorandum (probably written by Walshe), 11 July 1940, A2, secretary's files, D/FA, NAI.

42 Walshe memorandum, The International Situation and Our Critical Position in Relation to it, 15 July 1940, A2, secretary's files, D/FA, NAI.

43 Walshe handwritten addendum to memorandum, Help given by the Irish Government in relation to the actual waging of the War, secretary's files, n.d., A3,

secretary's files, D/FA, NAI.
44 Boland memoirs.
45 Unsigned memorandum (probably written by Walshe), 11 July 1940, A2, secretary's files, D/FA, NAI. Again we can see the difficulties in analysing Walshe's role. While this document is almost certainly Walshe's work it is impossible to draw this definite conclusion about this and numerous other unsigned documents contained in the archives.
46 *Ibid.*
47 Walshe memorandum, The International Situation and Our Critical Position in Relation to it, 15 July 1940, A2, secretary's files, D/FA, NAI.
48 Hempel to Foreign Ministry, 1 July 1940, *DGFP*, Series D, Vol. X, Doc. 79, pp. 89–90.
49 Ribbentrop to Hempel, 11 July 1940, *DGFP* Series D, Vol. X.
50 Walshe memo on conversation with Hempel, n.d., P3, secretary's files, D/FA, NAI.
51 Walshe memorandum, 9 August 1940, P3, secretary's files, D/FA, NAI.
52 Walshe memorandum on meeting with Hempel, 6 August 1940, secretary's files, P3, D/FA, NAI.
53 Walshe memorandum, 9 August 1940, secretary's files, P3, D/FA, NAI.
54 Case of Major Edward Reed Byas, British officer, secretary's files, A5, D/FA, NAI.
55 Telegram from Secretary of State for Dominion Affairs to the UK representative to Éire, 16 July 1940, secretary's files, A5, D/FA, NAI.
56 Walshe memorandum on conversation with Maffey, 15 July 1940, de Valera papers, 1180, Franciscan archives, Killiney.
57 Walshe memorandum, The International Situation and Our Critical Position in Relation to it, 15 July 1940, secretary's files, A2, D/FA, NAI.
58 Walshe memorandum to Taoiseach, 29 July 1940, secretary's files, A2, D/FA, NAI.
59 Hempel to Foreign Ministry, 31 July 1940, *DGFP* Series D, Vol X.
60 Walshe writing from Cologne to de Valera, 28 July 1933, 1529, De Valera papers, Franciscan archives, Killiney.
61 Hempel to Foreign Ministry, 31 July 1940, *DGFP* Series D, Vol X.
62 Estero circular telegram to foreign representatives, 5 July 1940, secretary's files, P2, D/FA, NAI.
63 *Ibid.*
64 Estero cablegram to Washington legation, 5 July 1940, secretary's files, P2, D/FA, NAI.
65 D/FA cablegram to Washington, 11 July 1940, secretary's files, P2, D/FA, NAI.
66 Washington legation to Estero, 15 July 1940, secretary's files, P2, D/FA, NAI.
67 D/FA cablegram to Washington legation, 16 July 1940, secretary's files, P2, D/FA, NAI.
68 Estero to Washington legation, 16 July 1940, secretary's files, P2, D/FA, NAI.
69 Estero to Ottawa legation, 21 July 1940, secretary's files, P4, D/FA, NAI.
70 Michael Rynne letter, 24 August 1939, secretary's files, S75, D/FA, NAI.
71 Vichy legation to Estero, 15 July 1940, secretary's files, P8, D/FA, NAI.
72 Estero to Vichy legation, August 1940, secretary's files, P8, D/FA, NAI.
73 Keogh, *Ireland and Europe*, p. 139.
74 Estero to Madrid legation, 5 November 1940, secretary's files, P12/4, D/FA, NAI.
75 Estero to Washington legation, 10 December 1940, secretary's files, P8, D/FA, NAI.
76 Washington legation to Estero, 18 February 1942, secretary's files, P8, D/FA, NAI.
77 Quirnal to Estero, 18 March 1941, secretary's files, P8, D/FA, NAI.
78 Secretary's files, P12/2, D/FA, NAI.
79 Walshe memorandum, The international situation and our critical position in relation

to it, 15 July 1940, secretary's files, A2, D/FA, NAI.

80 Estero to Washington legation, 21 July 1940, secretary's files, P2, D/FA, NAI.
81 Washington legation to Estero, 23 July 1940 (sent 22 July) secretary's files, P2, D/FA, NAI.
82 Estero to Washington legation, 21 July 1940, secretary's files, P2, D/FA, NAI.
83 Estero to Washington legation, 18 November 1940, secretary's files, P2, D/FA, NAI.
84 Washington legation to Estero, 20 November 1940, secretary's files, P2, D/FA, NAI.
85 Estero to Washington legation, 21 November 1940, secretary's files, P2, D/FA, NAI.
86 The many newspaper clippings and reports from Brennan to Walshe are contained in D/FA 219/3 & 3(a), D/FA, NAI.
87 France legation to Estero, 15 July 1940, secretary's files, P12/1, D/FA, NAI.
88 Estero to Vichy legation, 20 July 1940, secretary's files, P12/1, D/FA, NAI.
89 *Ibid*. It is interesting to note that when Spain suggested such an alliance it was rejected out of hand by Walshe. He was keen not to alienate the Allies, whose fortunes by that time appeared far more optimistic.
90 Estero to Vichy legation, 12 November 1940, secretary's files, P12/1, D/FA, NAI.
91 Vichy legation to Estero, 19 November 1940, secretary's files, P12/1, D/FA, NAI.
92 Murphy to Walshe, 3 December 1940, secretary's files, P12/1, D/FA, NAI.
93 Vichy legation to Estero, 1 December 1940, secretary's files, P12/1, D/FA, NAI.
94 Murphy to Walshe, 3 December 1940, secretary's files, P12/1, D/FA, NAI.
95 Walshe to Murphy, 7 January 1941, secretary's files, P12/1, D/FA, NAI.
96 Keogh, *Ireland and Europe*, p. 160.
97 Walshe to Murphy, 7 January 1941, secretary's files, P12/1, D/FA, NAI.
98 Vichy legation to Estero, received 14 January 1941, secretary's files, P12/1, D/FA, NAI.
99 Murphy to Walshe, 1 March 1941, secretary's files, P12/1, D/FA, NAI.
100 Keogh, *Ireland and Europe*, pp. 159–60.
101 Gray to Roosevelt, 13 July 1940, box 3, folder 7, Gray papers, AHC, Wyoming.
102 Gray to Secretary of State, 6 August 1940, president's secretary's files, diplomatic correspondence, Ireland, box 40, Roosevelt papers FDRL.
103 Gray to Roosevelt, 7 August [1940], president's secretary's files, FDRL.
104 David Gray, diary entries, 6 August [1940], Gray papers, box 3, folder 7, AHC.
105 Gray to State Department, July 1940, State Department records, RG 84, security segregated records, box 3, NAUS.
106 Gray to Roosevelt, 7 August 1940, Roosevelt papers, president's secretary's files, box 40, FDRL.
107 David Gray, diary entries, 6 August [1940], Gray papers, box 3, folder 7, AHC.
108 Gray to Robert Burgess Stewart, division of European Affairs, Department of State, 6 August 1940, Gray papers, box 3, folder 8, AHC.
109 Gray to State Department, July 1940, State Department records, RG 84, security segregated records, box 3, NAUS.
110 Gray to Robert Burgess Stewart, division of European Affairs, Department of State, 6 August 1940, enclosing Walshe's letter of appreciation dated 31 July 1940, Gray papers, box 3, folder 8, AHC.
111 Walshe to Gray, 9 August 1940, Gray papers, box 3, folder 8, AHC.
112 *Ibid*.
113 Gray to Walshe, 15 August 1940, box 3, folder 8, Gray papers, AHC.
114 Gray to Roosevelt, 14 August 1940, president's secretary's files, box 40, Roosevelt papers, FDRL.
115 Gray to Roosevelt, 25 August 1940, president's secretary's files, box 40, Roosevelt

papers, FDRL.

116 Gray to Secretary of State, 28 August 1940, 'No. 49 The Irish Political situation as of August 28, 1940', Gray papers, box 3, folder #8, AHC.

117 FDRL, Roosevelt papers, president's secretary's files, box 40, Gray to Roosevelt, 8 September 1940.

118 Ibid.

119 Walshe to Gray, 12 November 1940, secretary's files, P48, D/FA, NAI.

120 Gray memorandum on conversation with Walshe, [November 1940], secretary's files, P48, D/FA, NAI. The first page is missing from this file.

121 Walshe to Gray, 12 November 1940, secretary's files, P48, D/FA, NAI.

122 See newspaper clippings in secretary's files, P48, D/FA, NAI.

123 Sunday Review, 16 June 1958.

124 Untitled, unsigned and undated memorandum, secretary's files, P48, D/FA, NAI.

125 Washington legation to Estero, 9 November 1940, secretary's files, P2, D/FA, NAI.

126 Estero to Washington legation, 29 November 1940, secretary's files, P2, D/FA, NAI.

127 Estero to Washington legation, 4 December 1940, secretary's files, P2, D/FA, NAI.

128 Bowen to Dominions Office, 9 November 1940, FO 800/310, PRO. Cited by Fisk in In Time of War, p. 424.

129 Lee, Ireland, p. 247.

130 Walshe memorandum on conversation with Hempel, August 1940, secretary's files, P3, D/FA, NAI.

131 Lee, Ireland, p. 253.

132 Carter, Shamrock and the Swastika, p. 88.

133 Walshe memorandum on meeting with Maffey, 18 October 1940, secretary's files, A2, D/FA, NAI.

134 Walshe memorandum October 1940, A2, secretary's files, D/FA, NAI.

135 Hempel to Foreign Ministry, 29 November 1940, DGFP, Series D, Vol XI.

136 Ribbentrop to Hempel, 5 December 1940, DGFP, Series D, Vol XI, Doc 455.

137 Hempel to Foreign Ministry, 10 December 1940, DGFP, Series D, Vol XI.

138 Hempel to Foreign Ministry, 17 December 1940, DGFP, Series D, Vol XI.

139 It is not clear in what capacity Shaw was travelling. He has been described as a 'former southern Irish Unionist MP, a Protestant who had been Secretary to Lord French when he was Lord Lieutenant of Ireland in the closing days of British rule'. See Fisk, In Time of War, p. 413.

140 Notes on a visit to Ireland by Mr. Herbert Shaw 7–23 December 1940, FO 371/29108, PRO. The appendage is signed 'A.C.', Alexander Cadogan according to Fisk, see In Time of War, p. 425.

141 Ibid., for an account of Shaw's more general observations on Ireland see Fisk, In Time of War, pp. 413–42, passim.

142 Maffey to Machtig, 23 December [1940], PREM 3/128, PRO.

143 Robert Fisk interview with James Dillon, 10 July 1979, see In Time of War, p. 425.

144 Maffey to Machtig, 23 December [1940], PREM 3/128, PRO.

CHAPTER 5

1 Estero to Washington legation, 20 July 1940, secretary's files, P11, D/FA, NAI.

2 Third party memorandum on meeting between Walshe and Hempel, 3 January 1941, S11408, D/T, NAI.

3 Walshe memorandum on meeting with Hempel, 6 January 1941, secretary's files, A21, D/FA, NAI.

4 See file S10823, D/T, NAI.

5 Walshe to Moynihan, 25 October 1940, secretary's files, P22, D/FA, NAI.

6   Walshe to Moynihan, 27 November 1940, secretary's files, P22, D/FA, NAI.
7   Memorandum entitled Note of questions affecting the Department of External Affairs which would arise in the event of an invasion, secretary's files, P22, D/FA, NAI.
8   Boland memorandum on conversation between Walshe and de Valera, 5 May 1942, secretary's files, P22, D/FA, NAI. See also S279, military archives, Cathal Brugha Barracks, Dublin.
9   Boland memorandum, Note of questions affecting the Department of External Affairs, 21 January 1941, secretary's files, P22, D/FA, NAI.
10 Estero to Berlin legation, 25–28 February 1941, secretary's files, P22, D/FA, NAI.
11 Boland memorandum, Note of questions affecting the Department of External Affairs, 21 January 1941, secretary's files, P22, D/FA, NAI.
12 Walshe to Secretary, Department of Defence, 8 February 1941, S.249, military archives, Cathal Brugha Barracks.
13 Walshe to Moynihan, 21 April 1941, secretary's files, P54, D/FA, NAI.
14 Walshe to assistant secretary [Boland], 15 May 1941, secretary's files, P54, D/FA, NAI.
15 M.R. [Michael Rynne] to assistant secretary [Boland], 29 May 1941, secretary's files, secretary's files, P46, D/FA, NAI.
16 Minutes of conference held at the Department of Defence, 18 November 1941, departmental S [secret] files, S.249, military archives, Cathal Brugha Barracks.
17 Beary, Assistant Secretary, Department of Defence to Walshe, 12 December 1941, secretary's files, P22, D/FA, NAI.
18 Unsigned memorandum, 27 October 1941, secretary's files, P22, D/FA, NAI.
19 Unsigned memorandum, Draft Note, n.d., secretary's files, P22, D/FA, NAI.
20 *Ibid.* The difference in the two variations is very slight. If the invading country were Britain, the statement read: 'With the sympathy and support of other freedom-loving nations, and of the millions of the Irish race abroad, Ireland faces this *new* threat to her existence with the determination not to rest until freedom and peace have been restored to the Motherland' [emphasis added]. If the invading country was other than Britain the alternative statement omitted the word 'new'. This was the only difference but it seemed important that the world be reminded of Britain's past subjugation of Ireland.
21 See for example the confidential reports D/FA 200 series, NAI.
22 See secretary's files, A2, D/FA, NAI; memoranda such as 'Distortion of the German Press'; 'United States Radio and Press' and 'Our Neutrality: Statements from Press and Radio'.
23 D.K Kostal, Czechoslovakian consul in Dublin, report on the situation in Ireland (intercepted by the Irish censor) 31 May 1940, secretary's files, A8, D/FA, NAI.
24 See for example, 'Miscellaneous correspondence with Col. Archer and Col. Bryan, April 1940–June 1942', secretary's files, A8, D/FA, NAI.
25 See secretary's files, A12, D/FA, NAI.
26 See secretary's files, A55/I, D/FA, NAI.
27 Hempel to Walshe, 4 June 1941, secretary's files, A23, D/FA, NAI.
28 Censorship and intelligence are linked under the broader term 'security'. See O'Halpin, E., 'Aspects of intelligence', *The Irish Sword*, Vol. XIX, Nos. 75 & 76 (1993–94), p. 57–65, and for an examination of security from the foundation of the state, see his 'Intelligence and Security in Ireland, 1922–45', *Intelligence and National Security*, Vol. 5, No. 1 (January 1990), pp. 50–83.
29 Ó Drisceoil, D., *Censorship in Ireland During the Second World War*, PhD Thesis, Department of History, University College, Cork, 1994, pp. 136–7.
30 Walshe to Controller of Censorship, 9 October 1940, secretary's files, A9(1), D/FA, NAI.

31 Walshe to Controller of Censorship, 16 April 1941, secretary's files, A9(i), D/FA, NAI.

32 Secretary's files, A8, D/FA, NAI.

33 Letter to C.T. Hallinan, c. 25 Jan 1941, secretary's files, A8, D/FA, NAI.

34 Walshe to Coyne, 25 April 1941, censorship records 3/39, military archives, Cathal Brugha Barracks, Dublin.

35 Unsigned to Boland, 17 June 1941, censorship records 3/39, military archives, Cathal Brugha Barracks, Dublin.

36 My thanks to Diana James of the *Reader's Digest*, who has searched both British and US editions of the journal around this time for the article referred to. While a number of articles critical of Irish neutrality were published, no specific reference to Walshe was found.

37 Coyne to Walshe, 12 June 1941, secretary's files, A9(1), D/FA, NAI.

38 J. Connolly to minister [Frank Aiken], 14 February 1941, secretary's files, A9(1), D/FA, NAI.

39 Hinsley, F.H. and Simkins, C.A.G., *Security and Counter Intelligence*, Vol. 4 of *British Intelligence in the Second World War* (London, HMSO, 1990), p. 17. While Hinsley and Simkins do not name him specifically, the reference to 'the Éire Minister for External Affairs' is more than likely a reference to Walshe, who would not have objected to the use of the title. This has previously been pointed out by O'Halpin, 'Aspects of Intelligence', p. 60. Neither was it the last time that the term 'minister' would be used in reference to Walshe. See Fisk, *In Time of War*, p. 187.

40 J. Connolly, Controller of Censorship to J.J. Purcell, Chief Postal Censor, 11 July 1940, secretary's files, A9(1), D/FA, NAI.

41 Purcell to Connolly, 12 July 1940, secretary's files, A9(1), D/FA, NAI.

42 Connolly to Purcell, 11 July 1940, secretary's files, A9(1), D/FA, NAI.

43 Ó Drisceoil, *Censorship in Ireland*, p. 211.

44 Hempel, aide-memoire, 13 December 1941, secretary's files, P51, D/FA, NAI.

45 Ó Drisceoil, *Censorship in Ireland*, p. 212.

46 Coyne to Boland, 3 November 1942, censorship records, file 2/32, military archives, Cathal Brugha Barracks, Dublin.

47 Walshe memorandum, 1 April 1941, secretary's files, P36, D/FA, NAI.

48 Estero to Hibernia, Rome, 7 May 1941, P36, SDF, DFA, NAI.

49 Walshe to Berardis, 7 May 1941, secretary's files, P36, D/FA, NAI.

50 Unsigned memorandum entitled Neutrality, Censorship and Democracy, S11408 A/63, D/T, NAI. The memorandum contained in the Taoiseach's department files contains an appendix by the legal adviser to the Department of External Affairs, Michael Rynne, showing the censorship measures taken by other neutral countries. It is probable that the preceding document was also drawn up by External Affairs and it is further likely that Walshe wrote it or contributed significantly to its drafting.

51 Gray to Roosevelt, 6 February 1941, Gray papers, file: 'Roosevelt, F.D. and Eleanor (1930–41)', box 6, FDRL.

52 Walshe memorandum, Mr. Gray's Memorandum: Notes Thereon, 17 January 1941, secretary's files, P48, D/FA, NAI.

53 Gray to de Valera, 6 February 1941, Gray papers, file: 'de Valera, Éamon (1)', FDRL.

54 Gray to Roosevelt, 6 February 1941, Gray papers, file: 'Roosevelt, F.D. and Eleanor (1930–41)', box 6, FDRL.

55 Gray to Eleanor Roosevelt, 10 February 1941, Gray papers, file: 'Roosevelt, F.D. and Eleanor (1930–41)', box 6, FDRL.

56 *Ibid.*

57 Walshe memorandum on conversation with Maffey, 19 February 1941, secretary's files, A2, D/FA, NAI.

58 Walshe memorandum on conversation with Maffey, 14 March 1941, secretary's files, A2, D/FA, NAI.

59 *Ibid.*

60 Gray to Secretary of State, 24 February 1941, paraphrase of telegram sent, Gray papers, file: 'Hull, Cordell', box 4, FDRL.

61 Gray to de Valera, 3 March 1941, Gray papers, State Department dispatch 674–1098, box #10, FDRL.

62 Gray to Eleanor Roosevelt, 24 February 1941, secretary's files, P35, D/FA, NAI. Gray warned that Aiken was 'an interesting example of what Irish ideals do to people of non Gaelic origin, for his family … were Cromwellian settlers in Ulster'. Some time later, Gray admitted to Maffey that, following his first visit to Ireland in the early 1930s, he had planned to write a history of Ireland that would not have been sympathetic to the British viewpoint.

63 *Ibid.*

64 Gray to de Valera, 3 March 1941, Gray papers, State Department dispatch, 674–1098, box 10, FDRL.

65 For an account of the Aiken visit to the US see, Joseph Rosenberg, 'The 1941 Mission of Frank Aiken to the United States: an American Perspective', *Irish Historical Studies*, 22 (1980), pp. 162–77.

66 David Gray, Memorandum of conversation with Mr. De Valera, March 4, 1941, Gray papers, FDRL.

67 Estero to Washington legation, 15 March 1941, secretary's files, P35, D/FA, NAI. It is likely that the telegram was written by Walshe.

68 Walshe's handwritten addendum to Estero telegram to Washington, 15 March 1941, secretary's files, P35, D/FA, NAI.

69 Washington legation [Brennan] to Estero, 7 April 1941, secretary's files, P35, D/FA, NAI.

70 Washington legation to Estero, 1 May 1941, secretary's files, P35, D/FA, NAI.

71 Gray memorandum on conversation with de Valera, 26 April 1941, Gray papers, file: 'de Valera, Éamon (1)', FDRL.

72 David Gray memorandum of conversation with de Valera, 28 April 1941, Gray papers, box 5, folder 3, AHC.

73 *Ibid.*

74 Maffey to Machtig, 4 March 1941, DO 130/21, PRO.

75 Maffey to Machtig, 15 March 1941, PREM 3/131/7, PRO.

76 Duggan, *Neutral Ireland*, p. 156.

77 Maffey memorandum, 14 March 1941, PREM 3/131/7, PRO.

78 *Ibid.*

79 David Gray memorandum of conversation with de Valera, 28 April 1941, Gray papers, box 5, folder 3, AHC.

80 Gray to de Valera, 12 May 1941, Gray papers, file: 'de Valera, Éamon (1)', FDRL.

81 Kathleen O'Connell to Gray, 17 May 1941. Gray papers, file: 'de Valera, Éamon (1)', FDRL. O'Connell was replying to Gray's letters of 5 and 12 May regarding his conversation with de Valera of 28 April.

82 Gray to Roosevelt, 28 May 1941, Gray papers, file: 'Roosevelt, F.D. and Eleanor (1930–41)', box 6, FDRL.

83 Gray to Welles, 19 May 1941, Gray papers, file: 'Welles, Sumner', box 7, FDRL.

84 *Ibid.*

85 Gray to Roosevelt, 28 May 1941, Gray papers, file: 'Roosevelt, F.D. and Eleanor (1930–41)', box 6, FDRL.

86 Gray to Roosevelt, 27 May 1941, Gray papers, file: 'Roosevelt, F.D. and Eleanor (1930–41)', box 6, FDRL.

87 Gray to Roosevelt, 9 June 1941, Gray papers, file: 'Roosevelt, F.D. and Eleanor

(1930–41)', box 6, FDRL.

88 Gray, Memorandum of Conversation with Mr. De Valera, 19 July 1941, Gray papers, State Department dispatches 674–1098, FDRL.

89 Gray to de Valera, 22 July 1941, Gray diary entry, 27 February [1941], Gray papers, file: 'de Valera, Éamon (1)', FDRL.

90 Gray to Welles, 10 September 1941, Gray papers, file: 'Welles Sumner', box 7, FDRL.

91 *Ibid.*

92 See Williams, T.D., 'A Study in Neutrality', *The Leader*, 28 February & 28 March 1953.

93 Ryle Dwyer, T., *Irish Neutrality and the USA 1939–47*, p. 114.

94 Raymond, 'David Gray', p. 71.

95 His connections with Roosevelt are well known. See above, Chapter 3.

96 Files such as PREM 3/133/4 and PREM 3/133/6B relating to Ireland during this period, while having exceeded their extended release date of fifty years, have not been transferred to the Public Record Office, London.

97 Fisk, *In Time of War*, pp. 128–32, 135.

98 *Ibid.*, p. 137.

99 Boland to Beary, 19 July 1941, secretary's files, P47, D/FA, NAI.

100 Fisk, *In Time of War*, pp. 141–2.

101 Gray memorandum, Notes on Axis Activities in Ireland, September 1941, secretary's files, P48, D/FA, NAI.

102 *Ibid.*

103 Walshe letter to Gray, 11 September 1941, secretary's files, P48, D/FA, NAI.

104 Gray memorandum, Notes on Axis Activities in Ireland, September 1941, secretary's files, P48, D/FA, NAI.

105 Walshe to Gray, 11 September 1941, secretary's files, P48, D/FA, NAI.

106 *Ibid.*

107 Gray memorandum, Notes on Axis Activities in Ireland, September 1941, secretary's files, P48, D/FA, NAI.

108 Walshe letter to Gray, 11 September 1941, secretary's files, P48, D/FA, NAI.

109 *Ibid.*

110 Gray to Roosevelt, 21 October 1941, Gray papers, diplomatic correspondence, Ireland 1941, box 40, FDRL.

111 De Valera speech 14 December 1941, Moynihan, *Speeches and Statements*, p. 462.

112 Secretary's files, A2, D/FA, NAI.

113 See Hempel to Foreign Ministry, DGFP, series D.

114 Boland memorandum, 14 September 1962, de Valera papers, 1372, Franciscan archives, Killiney.

115 *Ibid.*

116 Boland memoirs.

117 Unsigned memorandum to de Valera, 28 November 1941, de Valera papers, 1180, Franciscan archives, Killiney.

118 *Ibid.*

CHAPTER 6

1 Gray to Roosevelt, 16 February 1942, Roosevelt papers, president's secretary's files, file: 'Marshall, George C., 1941 – 4/14/42', box 3, FDRL.

2 Welles to Roosevelt, 21 February 1942, Roosevelt papers, president's secretary's files, diplomatic correspondence, Ireland: January–April 1942, FDRL.

3 Gray to Secretary of State, 'Invasion and Defence of Ireland', 21 March 1942, Roosevelt papers, president's secretary's files, diplomatic correspondence Ireland: January–April 1942, FDRL.

4   Memorandum of the prime minister on the record of Northern Ireland's war effort, 3 December 1941, CAB4/493, Public Record Office of Northern Ireland, Belfast.

5   Gray memorandum, January 1942, Gray papers, folder 4, box 6, AHI.

6   *Ibid.*

7   *Ibid.*

8   Smale of the American consulate in Cork to Gray, 5 August 1941, Gray papers, box 5, folder 4, AHI.

9   *Ibid.*

10 Gray to Secretary of State, 23 February 1942 No. 293, transmitting memorandum of conversation with the Brazilian consulate in Dublin, 16 February 1942, Gray papers, box 7, folder 1, AHI.

11 *Ibid.*

12 Unsigned memorandum, n.d., Roosevelt papers, president's secretary's files, safe file: 'Ireland', box 3, FDRL.

13 *Ibid.*

14 Gray to Roosevelt, 30 April 1940, Roosevelt papers, president's secretary's files, diplomatic correspondence, Ireland 1940, box 40, FDRL.

15 *Ibid.*

16 The following section is based on David Gray's papers contained in the Roosevelt Library, New York and in the section of his papers based at the American Heritage Centre, Laramie, Wyoming. See also T. Ryle Dwyer's account of the United States minister's interest in these psychic revelations in *Strained Relations: Ireland at Peace and the USA at War, 1941–45* (Dublin, Gill & Macmillan; New Jersey, Barnes & Noble Books, 1988), Chapter 3.

17 Gray to Roosevelt, 15 February 1942, including sections of transcript of meeting with the medium Geraldine Cummins on 7 November 1941, Roosevelt papers, president's secretary's files, diplomatic correspondence, Ireland 1941, box 40, FDRL.

18 *Ibid.*

19 Gray to Roosevelt, 16 March 1942, Roosevelt papers, president's secretary's files, 'Diplomatic Correspondence, Ireland Jan–Apr '42', FDRL.

20 Ryle Dwyer, *Strained Relations*, p. 41.

21 Walshe memorandum, 31 March 1942, secretary's files, P36, D/FA, NAI.

22 *Ibid.*

23 *Ibid.*

24 Walshe note, 1 April 1942, added to end of his memo dated 31 March 1942, secretary's files, P36, D/FA, NAI.

25 Walshe's connection with G2, the Irish intelligence section of the military, and the Controller of Censorship was close. See secretary's files, A8, D/FA, NAI: 'Miscellaneous Correspondence with Col. Archer and Col. Bryan, April 1940–June 1942'. This file contains an enormous quantity of documents, with many letters for Walshe from Archer or Bryan transmitting information: 'with regard to …' or 'enclosed is an extract for your consideration …', and so minor pieces of information are contained in Walshe's replies, mostly dealing with matters of relatively little significance. This file also contains a large number of reports and memoranda. Collectively they show that Walshe was well informed of the activities of the Irish intelligence services.

26 Gray memorandum, 3 September 1941, secretary's files, P48, D/FA, NAI.

27 Walshe to Gray, 11 September 1941, secretary's files, P48, D/FA, NAI.

28 Walshe memorandum, 17 April 1942, secretary's files, P48, D/FA, NAI.

29 Walshe to Séan Leydon, 20 April 1942, secretary's files, P48, D/FA, NAI.

30 Gray to Roosevelt, 16 March 1942, Roosevelt papers, president's secretary's files, diplomatic correspondence, 'Ireland: Jan–Apr '42', FDRL.

31 The Germans too were busy gathering extensive intelligence information on Ireland. See Fisk, *In Time of War, passim.*

32 The State Department archives in Washington contain a large number of intelligence reports from Ireland. For example, record group 226 and records of the OSS, research and analysis branch divisions intelligence reports ('XL' series), 1941–46. See also microfilm M1499, roll 31, file 9847; roll 38, files 11962, 11963 and roll 92, file 12344 contained in OSS reports on Ireland, NAUS.

33 Estero to Washington legation, 17 April 1944, secretary's files, A53, D/FA, NAI.

34 Composite list of complaints against David Gray, D/FA memorandum, 24 April 1946, secretary's files, P48, D/FA, NAI.

35 My thanks to Comdt. Peter Young of the military archives, Cathal Brugha Barracks, for his assistance in this area.

36 Walshe memorandum, 23 June 1944, A60, SDF, DFA, NAI.

37 Walshe memo to Minister for External Affairs, 18 March 1944, DP1180.

38 Welles to Gray, 3 October 1942, State Department records, RG 84, Dublin legation, general records, 1942. 020 – 804.4, box 10, NAUS.

39 Hull to Gray, 10 November 1942, State Department records, RG 84, Dublin legation, general records, 1942. 020 – 804.4, box 10, NAUS.

40 See Fisk, *In Time of War*, pp. 530–1.

41 Robert Fisk interview with Ervine 'Spike' Marlin, London 14 March 1978. *In Time of War*, pp. 530–1.

42 Gray to Phillips, 7 December 1942, State Department records, RG 84, 820.02 – Marlin, Dublin legation, general records, 1942. 020 – 804.4, box 10, NAUS.

43 *Ibid.*

44 Gray to Walshe, 19 March 1943, Gray papers, box 10, folder 1, AHI.

45 *Ibid.*

46 Maffey to Secretary of State for Dominion Affairs, 3 November 1942, No. 92, DO 130/27, PRO.

47 Machtig to Maffey, 8 October 1942, DO 130/27, PRO.

48 Machtig to Maffey, 11 November 1942, DO 130/27, PRO.

49 *Ibid.*

50 Maffey to Machtig, 12 November 1942, DO 130/27, PRO.

51 M.R. [M Rynne] memorandum, Establishment of Belligerent Radio Transmitters on Neutral Territory, 7 August 1941, secretary's files, A25, D/FA, NAI.

52 Dan Bryan to Walshe, 'Secret and Urgent' memorandum, Interception of illicit Radio signals from Éire, secretary's files, 15 December 1941, DFA, NAI. Bryan makes reference to enclosing 'a copy of the proposals submitted by my visitor', which is probably in reference to the ongoing cooperation and consultations between Irish and British military officials.

53 Walshe memorandum, The German Wireless Transmitter, 15 December 1943, secretary's files, A2, D/FA, NAI.

54 Duggan, *Neutral Ireland*, p. 198.

55 Walshe memorandum on conversation with Hempel, 20 December 1943, secretary's files, A25, D/FA, NAI.

56 Maffey to Walshe, 22 December 1943, secretary's files, A25, D/FA, NAI.

57 Fisk, *In Time of War*, p. 104.

58 For an interesting account of the treatment of both Axis and Allied internees in Ireland during the war, see Ryle Dwyer, T., *Guests of the State: The Story of Allied and Axis servicemen interned in Ireland during World War II* (Dublin, Brandon, 1994).

59 De Valera papers 1180, Franciscan archives, Killiney.

60 Boland memorandum, October 1942, secretary's files, A26, D/FA, NAI.

61 De Valera papers 1180, Franciscan archives, Killiney.

62 Gray to Walshe, 1942, secretary's files, A26, D/FA, NAI.

63 Walshe to Gray, 11 December 1942, secretary's files, A26, D/FA, NAI.
64 Gray to Walshe, 1942, secretary's files, A26, D/FA, NAI.
65 Gray to Walshe, 22 December 1942, secretary's files, A26, D/FA, NAI.
66 Walshe handwritten note, 29 December 1942, inserted on Gray to Walshe, 22 December 1942, secretary's files, A26, D/FA, NAI.
67 Unsigned [Gray] memorandum of conversation with Walshe on 25 March 1943, Gray papers, box 10, folder 1, AHI.
68 Boland memorandum, 4 February 1943, secretary's files, A26, D/FA, NAI.
69 Walshe memorandum, Internment of Belligerent Aircraft and Airmen, 18 February 1943, secretary's files, A26, D/FA, NAI.
70 Boland report, 7 May 1943, secretary's files, A26, D/FA, NAI.
71 Walshe report, 10 May 1943, secretary's files, A26, D/FA, NAI.
72 Walshe memorandum on meeting with Hempel, 15 September 1943, secretary's files, A26, D/FA, NAI.
73 Unsigned External Affairs memorandum, 4 October 1943, secretary's files, A26, D/FA, NAI. While the memorandum is unsigned the reasoning behind the document very closely mirrors the explanations given by Walshe in his previous encounter with the German minister.
74 Unsigned memorandum, 29 November 1943, secretary's files, A26, D/FA, NAI.
75 Gray memorandum, Discussion of Anglo-Irish Problems at Ambassador Winant's Dinner, 28 November 1942, Roosevelt papers, president's secretary's files, diplomatic correspondence, 'Ireland: May–Dec 1942', box 40, FDRL.
76 Walshe memorandum, 24 April 1943, secretary's files, A2, D/FA, NAI.
77 Maffey letter, 24 April 1943, DO 130/33, PRO.
78 Maffey to Walshe, 12 May 1943, secretary's files, A50, D/FA, NAI.
79 Ibid.
80 By February 1944 there were nine airmen interned in Ireland. See Maffey to Walshe, 18 February 1944, secretary's files, A50, D/FA, NAI.
81 Walshe to Peadar MacMahon, secretary, Department of Defence, 9 November 1945, secretary's files, A26, D/FA, NAI.
82 Rynne memorandum, 11 April 1944, secretary's files, A50, D/FA, NAI.
83 Maffey to Machtig, 22 May 1943, DO 130/33, PRO.
84 Herbert Shaw, notes on a visit to Ireland 7–23 December 1940, FO 371/29108, PRO.
85 Maffey to Machtig, 2 April 1943, DO 130/33, PRO.
86 Berlin legation to Estero, October 1943, secretary's files, P12/3, D/FA, NAI.
87 Maffey to Machtig, 17 June 1943, DO 130/33, PRO. Dulanty had been a civil servant under the British government and was appointed by the Irish government as high commissioner to London in 1930. Deirdre McMahon explains that while Walshe and Dulanty held similar views on Anglo-Irish relations during the 1930s some degree of tension was caused when both vied for the role of deus ex machina in the negotiations between the governments. This attitude continued during the war years. McMahon, Republicans and Imperialists, pp. 24–5.
88 Maffey memorandum, 7 August 1943, DO 130/33, PRO.
89 Machtig to Maffey, 11 November 1942, DO 130/27, PRO.
90 See secretary's files, P12/14 (i) and P12/14 (ii), D/FA, NAI.
91 It would be impractical to go into any great detail regarding the contents of these reports except to say, perhaps, that it is clear that Dulanty was well connected at Whitehall.
92 Maffey memorandum, 7 August 1943, DO 130/33, PRO.
93 Ibid.
94 Ibid.
95 Machtig to Maffey, 19 August 1943, DO 130/33, PRO.

96 Walshe memorandum, The German Minister: His view on the present state of the war, 15 September 1943, secretary's files, A2, D/FA, NAI.
97 Hempel, 'Pro-Memoria', secretary's files, A26, D/FA, NAI.
98 Boland cumulative report, 6 November 1943, secretary's files, A26, D/FA, NAI.
99 Walshe memorandum, The German Minister: His view on the present state of the war, 15 September 1943, secretary's files, A2, D/FA, NAI.
100 Secretary's files, A26, D/FA, NAI.
101 Walshe memorandum, 14 October 1943, secretary's files, A2, D/FA, NAI.

CHAPTER 7

1   Generally referred to as the 'American note', a copy of which is contained in secretary's files, A53, 'US request of February, 1944, for removal of Axis Representatives in Ireland', D/FA, NAI. For newspaper cuttings and further background material, see S13450, DT, NAI.
2   'American Note', secretary's files, A53, D/FA, NAI.
3   Cronin, S., *Washington's Irish Policy 1916–1986: Independence, Partition, Neutrality* (Dublin, Anvil Books, 1987), pp. 131–3.
4   Gray diary entry, 27 February [1941], Gray papers, file: de Valera, Éamon (1), FDRL.
5   'American Note', secretary's files, A53, D/FA, NAI.
6   Report A ['Consideration of American Economic Policy towards Éire'], secretary's files, A46, D/FA, NAI. A copy of this document was sent to Walshe by the Washington legation on 7 December 1942.
7   MA [military attaché] report, 133, 18 May 1942, cited in 'Report A', [1942], secretary's files, A46, D/FA, NAI.
8   'Report A', [1942], secretary's files, A46, D/FA, NAI.
9   Dennis Devlin, Washington legation to Walshe, 31 December 1942, secretary's files, P46, D/FA, NAI.
10 Gray to Winant, 15 June 1943, Gray papers, file: 'Winant, John G', box 7, FDRL.
11 Roosevelt memorandum for the Secretary of State, 15 June 1943, Roosevelt papers, president's secretary's files, diplomatic correspondence, file: 'Ireland: 1943', box 40, FDRL.
12 Cordell Hull to Roosevelt, 29 June 1943, 811.34541D/11b, *FRUS*, Vol III, pp. 142–3.
13 Gray, Memorandum on Irish Elections held June 22, 1943, 27 June 1943, Gray papers, file: 'Ireland (1938–47)', FDRL.
14 Secretary of State to Gray, 18 September 1943, Gray papers, No. 103, file: 'Hull, Cordell', box 4, FDRL.
15 Hull to Winant, 19 September 1943, Gray papers, file: 'Hull, Cordell', box 4, FDRL.
16 Stettinius memorandum to the President, Status of Proposed Approach to Ireland, 11 October 1943, Roosevelt papers, president's secretary's files, diplomatic correspondence, 'Ireland: 1943', box 40, FDRL.
17 Undated by Gray in reply to Secretary of State's letter of 18 September 1943, Gray papers, file: 'Hull, Cordell', box #4, FDRL.
18 Secretary of State to Gray, 18 September 1943, Gray papers, No. 103, file: 'Hull, Cordell', box 4, FDRL.
19 Gray to Winant, 25 September 1943, Gray papers, file: 'Winant, John G', box 7, FDRL. Gray refers to the prime minister but mentions the name 'Eden' and is therefore possibly referring to the British Foreign Minister, Anthony Eden.
20 Gray to G. Howland Shaw, Assistant Secretary of State, 27 November 1943, Gray papers, box 11, Folder 6, AHC.
21 T.A. Hickok to Walshe, 31 May 1943, Gray papers, box 10, folder 3, AHI.

22 Walshe to Hickok, 10 June 1943, Gray papers, box 11, folder 1, AHI.
23 Hickok to Gray, 19 June 1943, Gray papers, box 11, folder 1, AHI.
24 Gray to Hickok, 30 June 1943, Gray papers, box 1, folder 11, AHI.
25 Gray to G. Howland Shaw, Assistant Secretary of State, 27 November 1943, Gray papers, box 11, folder 6, AHC.
26 Gray to Winant, 25 September 1943, Gray papers, file: 'Winant, John G', box 7, FDRL.
27 Cronin, *Washington's Irish Policy*, p. 149.
28 Gray to Winant, 25 September 1943, Gray papers, file: 'Winant, John G', box 7, FDRL.
29 Gray to Winant, 15 June 1943, Gray papers, file: 'Winant, John G', box 7, FDRL.
30 Gray to Winant, 25 September 1943, Gray papers, file: 'Winant, John G', box 7, FDRL.
31 Gray to Roosevelt, 4 November 1943, Gray papers, box 11, folder 6, AHI.
32 Gray to Secretary of State, 6 December 1943, Gray papers, No. 752, State Department dispatches 674–1098, 'Outgoing July 1943–July 1945', box 10, FDRL.
33 Gray to Secretary of State, 13 December 1943, Gray papers, No. 756, State Department dispatches 674–1098, 'Outgoing July 1943–July 1945', box 10, FDRL.
34 Maffey to Machtig, 24 August 1943. No. 79, FO 371/36602, PRO.
35 Gray to Roosevelt, 13 December 1943, Gray papers, file: 'Roosevelt, F.D. & Eleanor (1942–47)', box 6, FDRL.
36 *Ibid.*
37 Gray memorandum on meeting with de Valera, cited by Cronin, *Washington's Irish Policy*, p. 154.
38 Gray to de Valera, 2 March 1944, secretary's files, A53, D/FA, NAI.
39 *Ibid.*
40 Memorandum entitled Reply to American Note of the 21st February, as cabled to Washington, 6 March 1944, secretary's files, A53, D/FA, NAI.
41 Dominions Office to Maffey, 11 March 1944, FO 371/42679, PRO.
42 Walshe memorandum entitled Sir John Maffey Sanctions, 18 March 1944, de Valera papers, 1180, Franciscan archives, Killiney.
43 Maffey to Dominions Office, 13 March 1944, FO 371/42679, PRO.
44 Walshe memorandum, 14 March 1944, secretary's files, A53, D/FA, NAI.
45 Éire Rep. [Maffey] to DO, 15 March 1944, No. 47 secret, FO 371/42679, PRO.
46 *Ibid.*
47 Walshe memorandum on talk with Gray, 16 March 1944, secretary's files, A53, D/FA, NAI.
48 DFA memorandum of composite list of complaints against David Gray, 24 April 1946, secretary's files, P48, D/FA, NAI.
49 Walshe memorandum on conversation with Maffey, 16 March 1944, secretary's files, A53, D/FA, NAI.
50 Éire Rep. [Maffey] to Dominions Office, 16 March 1944, No. 50, FO 371/42679, PRO.
51 Gray to Roosevelt, 24 March 1944, Roosevelt papers, president's secretary's files, diplomatic correspondence, file: 'Ireland 1944–45', box 40, FDRL.
52 [Gray] to Winant, 14 April 1944, Gray papers, file: 'Winant, John G', box 7, FDRL.
53 Lord Cranborne's minute to the prime minister, 17 March 1944, FO 371/42679, PRO.
54 Éire Rep. [Maffey] to DO, 18 March 1944, No. 51, FO 371/42679, PRO.
55 Walshe memorandum, 18 March 1944, Sir John Maffey Sanctions, de Valera papers,

1180, Franciscan archives, Killiney.

56 [Maffey] to Dominions Office, 18 March 1944, No. 51, FO 371/42679, PRO.

57 Walshe memorandum, 18 March 1944, Sir John Maffey Sanctions, de Valera papers, 1180, Franciscan archives, Killiney.

58 Éire Rep. [Maffey] to DO, 18 March 1944, No. 51, FO 371/42679, PRO.

59 Éire Rep. [Maffey] to DO, 20 March 1944, No. 53, FO 371/42679, PRO.

60 Éire Rep [Maffey] to DO, 29 March 1944, No. 64, FO 371/42680, PRO.

61 *Ibid.*

62 The issue of coal was an important one for the country as a whole. Following these discussions, Walshe sent a circular to the diplomatic corps in Dublin telling them that their coal allotments would have to be reduced. Gray had made his own arrangements for the importation of coal for the coming year. However, he was worried about his 'friend and neighbor across the park' and suggested that he apply for his quota anyway and allocate it to the nunciature. Walshe took umbrage at the suggestion: 'The Nuncio has been able to get on pretty well so far. As you know, he is in a very special position here, as the personal representative of the Holy Father, and we should not let him want for essential supplies no matter how great the difficulty.' See Gray to Walshe, 31 May 1944, Gray papers, box 12, folder 5 and Walshe's reply, 7 June 1944, folder 6, AHC.

63 Walshe to de Valera, [30 April 1944], de Valera papers, 1180, Franciscan archives, Killiney.

64 *Ibid.*

65 Walshe memorandum, 3 April 1944, de Valera papers, 1180, Franciscan archives, Killiney.

66 *Ibid.*

67 Unsigned [Gray] to Bruce, 25 May 1944, Gray papers, 'General Correspondence', box 23, folder 1, AHI.

68 Gray to Robert B. Stewart, division of British Commonwealth affairs, Department of State, 25 May 1944, Gray papers, 'General Correspondence', box 23, folder 1, AHI.

69 Gray to Robert B Stewart, division of British Commonwealth affairs, Department of State, 25 May 1944, 'General Correspondence', Gray papers, box 23, folder 1, AHI. Gray was possibly referring to Chongquing in China.

70 *Ibid.*

71 *Ibid.*

72 *Ibid.*

73 Walshe memo to Minister for External Affairs, 18 March 1944, de Valera papers, 1180, Franciscan archives, Killiney.

74 *Ibid.*

75 Walshe memorandum on meeting with Will and Lalor of the US security service, 23 June 1944, secretary's files, A60, Security Correspondence etc. with Great Britain and USA, D/FA, NAI. The memo does not expand on the nature of this misunderstanding between Marlin and Gray. Marlin's contradiction of Gray's assessment of the Irish spy situation, however, had previously disingratiated him with Gray. In an interview with Robert Fisk in 1978 Marlin placed some belief in the rumour that Gray had requested his recall. See *In Time of War*, p. 531. It is probable that Walshe had this rumour in mind when in 1946 he claimed that Gray actively discouraged friendly contacts to the point of securing the transfer of those who continued to maintain such contacts.

76 Walshe memorandum on meeting with Will and Lalor, 23 June 1944, secretary's files, A60, D/FA, NAI.

77 Walshe letter to Ervine Marlin, 29 June 1944, secretary's files, A60, D/FA, NAI.

78 [Gray] to Winant, 14 April 1944, Gray papers, File: 'Winant, John G', box 7,

FDRL.

79 Gray to Roosevelt, 14 April 1944, Gray papers, file: 'Roosevelt, F.D. & Eleanor (1942–47)', box 6, FDRL.

80 Gray to Hull, 2 June 1944, Gray papers, 'General Correspondence', box 23, folder 1, AHI.

81 Gray to Roosevelt, 24 March 1944, Roosevelt papers, president's secretary's files, diplomatic correspondence, file: 'Ireland 1944–45', box 40, FDRL.

82 'Aide-memoire handed to the Minister for External Affairs by the American Minister on the 21st September, 1944', secretary's files, P78, D/FA, NAI.

83 Walshe to de Valera, 28 September 1944, secretary's files, P78, D/FA, NAI.

84 Gray to Roosevelt, 2 October 1944, Roosevelt papers, president's secretary's files, diplomatic correspondence, file: 'Ireland: 1944–45', box 40, FDRL.

85 'Aide-memoire handed to the American Minister by the Minister for External Affairs on the 9th October, 1944', secretary's files, P78, D/FA, NAI.

86 Walshe memorandum to de Valera, 23 October 1944, secretary's files, P78, D/FA, NAI.

87 Walshe memorandum, 14 November 1944, secretary's files, P78, D/FA, NAI.

88 Walshe memorandum, 24 November 1944, War Criminals, secretary's files, P78, D/FA, NAI.

89 *Ibid.*

90 Walshe memorandum, Conversation with Mr. Gray on the 14th November, 1944, secretary's files, P78, D/FA, NAI.

91 Gray to Secretary of State, 14 December 1944, Gray papers, 'General Correspondence', box 23, folder 1, AHI.

92 Gray memorandum of conversation with Maffey, 14 December 1944, Gray papers, General Correspondence, box 23, folder 1, AHI.

CHAPTER 8

1 Memorandum of conversations between Gray and Maffey, 14 December 1944, Gray papers, File: Stettinius, Edward R, box 6, FDRL.

2 Stettinius to Gray, 6 January 1945, Gray papers, box 23, folder 1, general correspondence, FDRL.

3 Gray memorandum on conversation with Walshe, 20 January 1945, Gray papers, file: Walshe, Joseph P., box 7, FDRL.

4 Walshe to de Valera, 16 February 1945, de Valera papers, 1180, Franciscan archives, Killiney.

5 Maffey memorandum, 21 March 1945, DO 130/56, PRO.

6 Maffey to Machtig, 3 April 1945, DO 35/1229/WX130/3/40, PRO.

7 Maffey to Machtig, 2 May 1945, DO 35/1229/WX130/3/40, PRO.

8 Gray memorandum, Memorandum of Conversations with Mr. de Valera on April 30, 1945, and with Mr. J.P. Walshe on May 2, 1945, relative to obtaining possession of property belonging to former German Government in Éire including the German legation in Dublin, 2 May 1945, Gray papers, box 23, folder 1, FDRL.

9 Gray to Secretary of State, 7 May 1945, Gray papers, box 23, folder 1, FDRL.

10 Maffey memorandum on conversation with de Valera on 30 April 1945 and with Walshe on 2 May 1945, DO 35/1229/WX130/3/40, PRO.

11 Maffey to Machtig, 7 Sept 1945, FO 371/50364, PRO.

12 Boland memoirs.

13 Unsigned memorandum, Neutrality, Censorship and Democracy, S11408 A/63, DT, NAI.

14 Boland memoirs.

15 Walshe handwritten letter to de Valera, May 1945, de Valera papers, 1180, Franciscan archives, Killiney.

16 Walshe note, 1 May 1945, de Valera papers, 1180, Franciscan archives, Killiney.
17 Maffey memorandum on conversation with de Valera on 30 April 1945 and with Walshe on 2 May 1945, DO 35/1229/WX130/3/40, PRO.
18 Washington legation to Estero 4 May 1945, secretary's files, P98, D/FA, NAI. It was with some disbelief that the *Washington Post* reported: 'De Valera Extends Sympathy to Nazis'. Further cables from Washington arrived conveying the continued adverse press reports. The *Washington Post* criticised Irish 'moral myopia' saying: 'Even in death, Hitler forced a choice upon neutral Governments. By their response, they have judged themselves and that judgement in the case of Éire and Portugal is a condemnation in the eyes of all free people.' This was indicative of the wide coverage given to the event.
19 Estero to Hibernia, Berne, No. 38 dearg, 4 May 1945, secretary's files, P98, D/FA, NAI.
20 Angela Walsh to de Valera, 3 May 1945, secretary's files, P98, D/FA, NAI.
21 Keogh, D., 'Éamon de Valera and Hitler: An analysis of International Reaction to the Visit to the German Minister, May 1945', *Irish Studies in International Affairs*, Vol. 3, No. 1 (1989), pp. 69–91. In particular, Keogh makes reference to Walshe's adherence to the principle that diplomatic relations were between states and not between governments during the Spanish Civil War when Walshe's personal sympathies would not have been with the republican side.
22 Tim Pat Coogan, *De Valera: Long Fellow Long Shadow* (London, Hutchinson, 1993), p. 610.
23 Boland memoirs.
24 De Valera to Brennan, Whit Monday 1945 [c. late May or June], de Valera papers, 1304, Franciscan archives, Killiney.
25 Churchill speech, *Irish Times*, 14 May 1945, cited by Keogh, *Ireland and Europe*, p. 199.
26 Maffey to Machtig, 21 May 1945, DO 35/1229/WX110/3/40, PRO.
27 Maffey memorandum, 21 May 1945, DO 35/1229/WX110/3/40, PRO.
28 Boland was not impressed by de Valera's 'comely maidens' reply, describing it as 'awful'! He did not remember who wrote it but 'it certainly wasn't Maurice Moynihan, and it certainly wasn't External Affairs, and it certainly wasn't Dev himself. He never wrote speeches himself at that stage; he couldn't. He was blind.' Boland Memoirs.
29 It was apparent during the preparations for the American note that neither Maffey nor Gray trusted Kearney to back them up when it came to criticising Ireland. This had not changed and Gray later wrote: 'In the strictest confidence, we find the Canadian High Commissioner so disinclined to support the Allied Nations view as against Irish that we no longer take him into our confidence.' Gray to Grew, 29 June 1945, Gray papers, file: 'Grew, Joseph C', box 3, FDRL.
30 Maffey memorandum, 21 May 1945, DO 35/1229/WX110/3/40, PRO.
31 Gray to Grew, 17 May 1945, Gray papers, file: 'Grew, Joseph C', box #3, FDRL.
32 Maffey memorandum, 21 May 1945, DO 35/1229/WX110/3/40, PRO.
33 Gray to Secretary of State, Gray papers, 18 July 1945, State Department dispatches 674–1098, box 10, FDRL.
34 Acting Secretary of State, Joseph Grew to President Harry Truman, 7 May 1945, Truman papers, president's secretary's files, box 181, file: 'Ireland', Truman Library, Independence, Missouri, USA, [hereafter TL].
35 Maffey to Machtig, 2 May 1945, DO 35/1229/WX130/3/40, PRO. Since 1944 Edward Stettinius was Secretary of State and was replaced on 1 July 1945 by James Francis Byrnes. I am not sure what the reference to 'the Star business expert' means. It may be a rather snide reference to one of Harry Truman's early jobs in the mailroom of the *Kansas City Star* newspaper. Truman later opened a clothing store in Kansas city which soon failed. Gray had previously been a newspaper publisher and

may have looked down on the new President's lowly beginnings.

36 Gray to Secretary of State, 7 May 1945, Gray papers, File: 'Grew, Joseph C', box 3, FDRL.

37 Gray to Walshe, 5 May 1945, Gray papers, file: 'Grew, Joseph C', box 3, FDRL.

38 Gray to Grew, 17 May 1945, Gray papers, file: 'Grew, Joseph C', box 3, FDRL.

39 Gray memorandum, Taking possession of German legation, Gray papers, State Department dispatches 674–1098, box 10, FDRL.

40 Gray to Secretary of State, 1 June 1945, Gray papers, State Department dispatches 674–1098, box 10, FDRL.

41 There was some difference of opinion in the way in which the articles of the German legation should be disposed of. Gray had advocated no delay in auctioning the articles in Northern Ireland so as to avoid any incidents with pro-German elements in Dublin. Maffey explained that at no time was there any personal disagreement but the friction arose when the State Department had assumed responsibility for acting on behalf of the United Nations but had not clarified what procedure should be used in relation to the legation. See Gray to Maffey, 29 May 1945 and Maffey to Gray, 31 May 1945, Gray papers, State Department dispatches 674–1098, box 10, FDRL.

42 Carter, *Shamrock and the Swastika*, p. 225.

43 Germans in Éire memorandum by the Parliamentary Under-Secretary of State for Dominion Affairs annexing a copy of Maffey memorandum regarding a conversation he had with Walshe, dated 31 May 1945. CAB 78/33 gen 69 series, PRO.

44 5 June 1945 P.Q. in response to a question by C.S Taylor the Under-Secretary of State for Dominion Affairs (Mr Emrys-Evans) FO 371/50364, PRO.

45 Gray to Grew, 29 June 1945 Gray papers, file: 'Grew, Joseph C', box 3, FDRL.

46 Walshe to Maffey, secretary's files, A7, D/FA, NAI.

47 Carter, *Shamrock and the Swastika*, p. 224.

48 Fisk, *In Time of War*, p. 542.

49 Joseph Walshe memorandum, Extract from Memo for Taoiseach from Secy re conversation with British representative, 14 June 1945, secretary's files, A74, D/FA, NAI.

50 Gray to Secretary of State, 13 August 1945, Gray papers, State Department dispatches 674–1098, box 10, FDRL.

51 Resumé of conclusions, n.d., secretary's files, P100, D/FA, NAI.

52 T.J. Kiernan, 'Suggestions' [September 1945], secretary's files, P100, D/FA, NAI.

53 'Precis of some points made in course of statement by Secretary, Dept. Finance, to Heads of Missions at DEA', 12 September 1945, secretary's files, P100, D/FA, NAI.

54 T.J. Kiernan, 'Suggestions' [September 1945], secretary's files, P100, D/FA, NAI.

55 Some of the suggestions were impractical; following the establishment of an Irish shortwave transmitter, he suggested the transfer of the broadcasting service to the Department of External Affairs. Boland simply penned alongside the suggestion, 'It would be fatal'!

56 Gray to Secretary of State, 17 October 1945. Gray papers, no. 2034, State Department dispatches (2004–2096) 'Outgoing Aug 1945–Feb 46', FDRL.

57 Maffey to Machtig, 30 September 1945, DO 130/56, PRO.

58 J.E. Stephenson to Maffey, 18 Sept 1945, DO 130/56, PRO.

59 Walshe to de Valera, [September 1945], file: 'Memoranda submitted to Taoiseach 1945', Secretary's Office, EA–D, D/FA, NAI. This series of files is distinct from the secretary's files.

60 *Ibid.*

61 J.E. Stephenson to Maffey, 18 September 1945, DO 130/56, PRO.

62 Walshe to de Valera, [September 1945], file: 'Memoranda submitted to Taoiseach 1945', Secretary's Office, EA–D, D/FA, NAI.

63 Handwritten in the margin next to this comment is 'centralization via EA [External

Affairs]'.
64 Maffey to Machtig, 30 September 1945, DO 130/56, PRO.
65 Newton complained that as Walshe had come 'at such short notice and stayed with me for so long (over an hour) that there was no time to arrange other interviews'.
66 Sir Basil Newton memorandum on conversation with Walshe, 9 October 1945, FO 371/50364.
67 *Ibid.*
68 Unsigned addendum to Sir Basil Newton memorandum on conversation with Walshe, 9 October 1945, FO 371/50364, PRO.
69 Handwritten note added to Sir Basil Newton's memorandum on conversation with Walshe, 9 October 1945, FO 371/50364, PRO, dated 10 October 1945. I was unable to confirm the signed initials but they were possibly 'A.C.', conceivably referring to Alexander Cadogan, permanent under-secretary at the Foreign Office. Robert Fisk has pointed out that Cadogan had little liking for Walshe. In a previous and similar example, Herbert Shaw who, after meeting Walshe, wrote that he was 'highly intelligent'. Beside this is Cadogan's handwritten remark, 'Unfortunately small- and narrow-minded'. See Fisk, *In Time of War*, p. 425.
70 Stephenson to Newton, 10 October 1945, FO 371/50364, PRO.
71 Estero to Holy See, 7 June 1940, secretary's files, P7, D/FA, NAI.
72 Estero to Iverna [Berlin legation], 19 August 1944, no. 185, secretary's files, P12/3, D/FA, NAI.
73 Unsigned memorandum, An Outline of the Duties of the Irish Minister to the Vatican, 9 October 1941, secretary's files, P15 (ii), D/FA, NAI. The document, while unsigned, was probably penned by Walshe not least because it reflects Walshe's thinking on the matter.
74 Maffey to Machtig, 7 Sept 1945, FO 371/50364, PRO.
75 Maffey to Machtig, 17 June 1943, DO 130/33, PRO.
76 J.E. Stpehenson to Maffey, 21 March 1946, FO 371/60798, PRO.
77 Maffey's 'appreciation' of Walshe, 24 March 1946, FO 371/60798, PRO.
78 'Trimmer' meaning someone who remains neutral or who avoids taking sides or who is able to straddle both sides at the same time.
79 Maffey to Machtig, 4 November 1946, FO 371/60799, PRO.
80 David Gray memoirs, unpublished draft, contained in the David Gray papers at the American Heritage Center, Laramie, Wyoming.
81 *Ibid.*
82 Conor Cruise O'Brien, 'The Roots of my Preoccupations', *The Atlantic Monthly*, Vol. 274, No. 1 (July 1994), pp. 73–81. Also available online at: http://www.theatlantic.com/unbound/flashbks/cruise/cruis794.htm [Accessed 1 October 1997].
83 Boland memoirs.
84 It is not intended here to go into any great detail on Walshe's work at the Vatican. That would require a study of its own and it would repeat the work of others. See in particular, Keogh, D., *The Vatican, the Bishops and Irish Politics 1919–39* and most recently his *Ireland and the Vatican*, especially Chapters 5, 6 & 7, which deal extensively with Walshe's career at the Vatican. However, it is difficult to ignore the wealth of material that deals with this part of Walshe's career. When he was secretary of the Department of External Affairs he dealt with a myriad of subjects, which is reflected in the dispersed nature of his various letters and memoranda. We have already seen that Walshe was not inclined to commit matters of sensitivity to paper, and his modus operadi with de Valera was more often than not through oral communication. After 1946 the nature of the documentation changes. While Walshe was in Rome it was his duty to send home memoranda on the various issues he had to deal with. These reports were filed together and can be found in two or three files in the national archives and the de Valera papers. These documents throw light on aspects of his previous work in Dublin as he sometimes

commented directly on past concerns. This provides an interesting retrospective analysis of certain events. Other memoranda illuminate Walshe's diplomatic and administrative style as well as revealing features of this sometimes enigmatic personality. For that reason it is expedient to use certain brief extracts from this valuable documentation during an absorbing period of Walshe's career.

85 9 January 1946, extract from letter received from the ambassador to the Holy See, de Valera papers, 1529, Franciscan archives, Killiney.
86 P. Leigh Smith, British legation to the Holy See, 13 June 1946, FO 371/60799, PRO.
87 *Ibid.*
88 Walshe memorandum, Presentation of Credentials, 20 June 1946, de Valera papers, 1529, Franciscan archives, Killiney.
89 Walshe to de Valera, 21 August 1946, de Valera papers, 1529, Franciscan archives, Killiney.
90 De Valera to Walshe, 6 December 1946, de Valera papers, 1529, Franciscan archives, Killiney.
91 Walshe to de Valera, 21 August 1946, de Valera papers, 1529, Franciscan archives, Killiney.
92 De Valera to Walshe, 8 August 1946, de Valera papers, 1529, Franciscan archives, Killiney.
93 Walshe to de Valera, 21 August 1946, de Valera papers, 1529, Franciscan archives, Killiney.
94 De Valera to Walshe, 6 December 1946, de Valera papers, 1529, Franciscan archives, Killiney.
95 Walshe memorandum, The Reply to the Letter of Credence, 30 August 1946, de Valera papers, 1529, Franciscan archives, Killiney.
96 De Valera to Walshe, 6 December 1946, de Valera papers, 1529, Franciscan archives, Killiney.
97 Walshe to De Valera, 23 December 1946, de Valera papers, 1529, Franciscan archives, Killiney.
98 *Ibid.*
99 Keogh, *Ireland and the Vatican*, pp. 204–6.
100 Frederick Larkin, Chief Foreign Buildings Operations, to Gray, 21 October 1946, Gray papers, box 10, file: 'US Mission Property', FDRL.
101 Keogh, *Ireland and the Vatican*, pp. 204–5.
102 Walshe to Boland, 16 January 1947, secretary's files, P12/2(a), D/FA, NAI.
103 *Ibid.*
104 Walshe to Boland, 'The Cardinals of the Curia and Ireland', 10 July 1946, de Valera papers, 1529, Franciscan archives, Killiney.
105 Walshe to de Valera, 3 March 1947, de Valera papers, 1529, Franciscan archives, Killiney.
106 Walshe letter, 28 April [1947], secretary's files, P12/2(a), D/FA, NAI.
107 Walshe to de Valera, 3 March 1947, de Valera papers, 1529, Franciscan archives, Killiney.
108 Keogh, *Ireland and the Vatican*, pp. 207–13.
109 Walshe letter, 28 April [1947], secretary's files, P12/2(a), D/FA, NAI.
110 *Ibid.*
111 Walshe to Boland, 16 July 1947, secretary's files, P12/2(a), D/FA, NAI.
112 *Dáil debates*, 20 July 1948, Vol. 116, col. 922. Cited by Keogh, *Ireland and Europe*, p. 212.
113 Walshe to Boland, 15 October 1948, secretary's files, P12/2(a), D/FA, NAI.
114 Walshe to Boland, 22 October 1948, secretary's files, P12/2(a), D/FA, NAI.
115 Walshe to Boland, 13 November 1948, secretary's files, P12/2(a), D/FA, NAI.

116 Walshe to Secretary DEA, 20 August 1949, secretary's files, P12/2(a), D/FA, NAI.

117 Walshe to Boland, 3 February 1948, secretary's files, P12/2(a), D/FA, NAI.

118 Unsigned memorandum, An Outline of the Duties of the Irish Minister to the Vatican, 9 October 1941, secretary's files, P15(ii), D/FA, NAI.

119 Walshe to Boland, 6 May [1947], secretary's files, P12/2(a), D/FA, NAI.

120 Walshe to Secretary D/EA, 11 October 1949, secretary's files, P12/2(a), D/FA, NAI.

121 Walshe to Boland, 6 May [1947], secretary's files, P12/2(a), D/FA, NAI.

122 Walshe to Boland, 16 July 1947, secretary's files, P12/2(a), D/FA, NAI.

123 Walshe to de Valera, 17 December 1951, de Valera papers, 1529, Franciscan archives, Killiney.

124 Walshe to Boland, 16 July 1947, secretary's files, P12/2(a), D/FA, NAI.

125 Walshe to De Valera, 22 April 1952, de Valera papers, 1529, Franciscan archives, Killiney.

126 Bromage, M.C., 'Roman Love Story', *Michigan Quarterly Review*, (Winter 1963), pp. 18–21.

127 Walshe to de Valera, 10 December 1953, de Valera papers, 1529, Franciscan archives, Killiney.

128 De Valera to Walshe, 12 January 1954, de Valera papers, 1529, Franciscan archives, Killiney.

129 Walshe to de Valera, 19 January 1954, de Valera papers, 1529, Franciscan archives, Killiney.

CHAPTER 9

1   Boland memoirs.

2   Boland memoirs.

3   De Valera, it seems, may have had his own reasons for making that decision; Boland suggests that the Taoiseach did not wish for a united Ireland as it would allow too many Protestants into his electorate.

4   Boland memoirs.

5   Bromage, 'Roman Love Story', pp. 18–21. My thanks to Bernadette Chambers of the Department of Foreign Affairs for bringing my attention to this article.

6   De Valera to Walshe, 12 January 1954, DP 1529.

7   Walshe to de Valera, 19 January 1954, DP 1529.

8   Interview with Maurice Moynihan, 24 May 1996.

9   Boland memoirs.

10   Interview with Maurice Moynihan, 24 May 1996.

ACKNOWLEDGEMENTS

I WOULD LIKE to express my sincerest gratitude for the support given to me by my dad and mum, Pat and Maura Nolan. Without their love, assistance and encouragement this study would not have been possible.

My sincere thanks to Pádraic, Éithne, Aisling, Darragh, Ailbhe and Fionn Nolan, who made a second home for me during my many and lengthy stays in Dublin. Thanks also to Mary, Azad, Tara, Rena, Gerry, Jack, Mark, Liam, Barry and David.

This work was originally written as a doctoral thesis. My deepest thanks are due to my doctoral supervisor, Professor Dermot Keogh. I am grateful to him for his advice and expertise in guiding me through this work. I would also like to thank Eoin Purcell, Brian Ronan and the staff of Mercier Press for their assistance and guidance in publishing this work.

Over the years I have been greatly assisted by many friends and colleagues. In particular my thanks are due to Dr Gary Murphy, whose friendship, help and advice was invaluable. I would also like to thank Dr Michael Kennedy of the RIA and editor of the DIFP series for his generous assistance. My thanks are also due to Eunan O'Halpin, David Ryan and Maurice FitzGerald. To Esther Murnane of the *Irish Times*, thank you.

In the course of this study I have been helped by the staff of many archival institutions. They include the National Archives, Bishop Street, Dublin; Archives Department, University College, Dublin; Fr Ignatius of the de Valera Archives, Killiney, Dublin, and also Brendan Mac Goille Choille and Mark Farrell; the Boole Library, University College, Cork; the staff of the Military Archives, Cathal Brugha Barracks, Dublin; the Public Record Office, Kew, London; the Public Record Office of Northern Ireland, Balmoral Avenue, Belfast; the Franklin D. Roosevelt Library, Hyde Park, New York; the American Heritage Institute, Laramie, Wyoming; the National Archives, Washington DC; the Truman Library, Independence, Missouri; and the Library of Congress, Washington DC. My thanks to Dermot Sweeney of Stokes Kennedy Crowley and the John F. Kennedy fund, which sponsored my research in the United States.

I would also like to acknowledge the friendship and assistance of Colm O'Reilly, Deirdre Lavin, Colm Cronin, Pádraig Lankford, John O'Brien, Michael Murphy, Elaine McCarthy and Jean Wilkinson. To Aidan Murray and family for their assistance in London. To Maurice Spillane for his assistance over many years. My thanks to Liam, Dena and the McDonnell family for their support. My thanks also to Joe Ó Broin for his friendship over the years. Also, to my friends and colleagues at Intel, thank you.

My thanks and love to Joyce. Thank you for your love, support and encouragement!

To all those who helped in any way, thank you.

INDEX

CON CREMIN
IRELAND'S WARTIME DIPLOMAT
DR NIALL KEOGH

ISBN: 978 1 85635 497 4

MERCIER PRESS
WHAT YOU NEED TO READ

PARIS, 1939. A hazardous place to begin a diplomatic career, but the first in a series of vital postings for the young Con Cremin, who observed history unfolding in a continent dominated by Adolf Hitler.

After the fall of Paris (where he was one of the last of the foreign diplomats to leave as German troops marched into the French capital) Cremin went on to serve at Vichy and continued to build up a network of contacts and informants. His talent and professionalism as a diplomat for the Irish government was demonstrated by his courageous reporting of the plight of Jewish refugees during the war and he provided an eyewitness account of the fall of Hitler's Third Reich. *Con Cremin, Ireland's Wartime Diplomat* evaluates the career of one of Ireland's most influential diplomats, who proved the value of strong diplomatic reporting in shaping the foreign policy of any neutral nation.

Dr Niall Keogh was born in Dublin and grew up in Cork. A graduate of UCC, he has worked with the National Library of Ireland and the Irish Manuscripts Commission. He is currently lecturing in Moscow State University and in the state universities of St Petersburg and Voronezh.